The Promise of the East

For Balian, son of Tumult and Fantasy

In memory of Vincent Laporte

The Promise of the East

Nazi Hopes and Genocide, 1939–43

Christian Ingrao

Translated by Andrew Brown

polity

First published in French as *La Promesse de L'Est. Espérance nazie et génocide, 1939–1943* © Éditions du Seuil, 2016

This English edition © Polity Press, 2019

Maps 1-3. Drawn up by Éditions du Seuil after Karl Heinz Roth and Claus Carsten in Mechtild Rössler, Sabine Schleiermacher (ed.), *Der 'Generalplan Ost'. Hauptlinien der nationalsozialistischen Planungs- und Vernichtungspolitik*, (Berlin: Akademie Verlag, 1993) pp. 62–65.

Polity Press
65 Bridge Street
Cambridge CB2 1UR, UK

Polity Press
101 Station Landing
Suite 300
Medford, MA 02155, USA

ISBN-13: 978-1-5095-2775-5

A catalogue record for this book is available from the British Library.

Library of Congress Cataloging-in-Publication Data

Names: Ingrao, Christian, author.
Title: The promise of the East : Nazi hopes and genocide, 1939-43 / Christian Ingrao.
Other titles: Promesse de l'Est. English
Description: Medford, MA : Polity Press, [2018] | Includes bibliographical references and index.
Identifiers: LCCN 2018009174 (print) | LCCN 2018011045 (ebook) | ISBN 9781509527786 (Epub) | ISBN 9781509527755 (hardback)
Subjects: LCSH: World War, 1939-1945--Europe, Eastern. | National socialism--Europe, Eastern. | Holocaust, Jewish (1939-1945)--Europe, Eastern. | Europe, Eastern--History--1918-1945. | Genocide--Europe, Eastern--History--20th century. | Massacres--Europe, Eastern--History--20th century. | World War, 1939-1945--Atrocities. | Soviet Union--History--1917-1936. | Germany--History--1933-1945.
Classification: LCC D802.E92 (ebook) | LCC D802.E92 I5313 2018 (print) | DDC 940.53/18--dc23
LC record available at https://lccn.loc.gov/2018009174

Typeset in 10 on 11.5pt Palatino by
Servis Filmsetting Ltd, Stockport, Cheshire
Printed and bound in Great Britain by Clays Ltd, Elcograf S.p.A.

The publisher has used its best endeavours to ensure that the URLs for external websites referred to in this book are correct and active at the time of going to press. However, the publisher has no responsibility for the websites and can make no guarantee that a site will remain live or that the content is or will remain appropriate.

Every effort has been made to trace all copyright holders, but if any have been inadvertently overlooked the publisher will be pleased to include any necessary credits in any subsequent reprint or edition.

For further information on Polity, visit our website:
politybooks.com

Contents

List of maps   ix

Acknowledgements   x

Synoptic table of plans for Germanization, displacements of population,
and construction   xii

Introduction   xvii

Prologue: The moment of Utopia (September 1939–summer 1943)   1

    The mist-enshrouded time of foundations (1 September–30
       November 1939)   2

    The round of short-term plans (1 December 1939–21 June 1941)   8

    New horizons: the General Plan for the East (22 June 1941–15
       February 1943)   21

Part I The men and the institutions of Utopia

1   A nebula of institutions   29

    The diversity of the institutions of Utopia   29

      The central institutions: RKFdV, RSHA, WVHA   29

      The regional and local extensions of the SS: HSSPF and SSPF   33

      Local agencies and institutions: EWZ and UWZ   35

      Civilian administrations of incorporated and occupied territories   36

    How consensus was generated   37

    Forms and thoughts of the future in the East: the three main
       general plans   43

      The RSHA plans   43

      The WVHA memoranda   45

      Planning the RKFdV   46

2   Networks and trajectories of the men of the East   48

    'Men' of the East? A world in itself   48

    Professional networks and military networks   52

    Towards genocide? The itineraries of the experts   57

3   *Osteinsatz*: the journey to the East, a form of Nazi fervour   65
        The East, between Utopia and anxiety   66
        The myths of the Great *Trek*   72
        The racial, hygienic and educational dimensions   80

Conclusion   88

Part II Times and spaces of Utopia

4   General planning for the East   93
        The curse of Germanic insularity lifted   95
        Umvolkung: dissimilation or ethnomorphosis?   102
        The drying up of the alien ocean: mass murder and Utopia   108

5   At the School of Fine Arts   116
        Thinking about space   117
        City, *Volksgemeinschaft* and segregation   124
        Dreaming of rural space: the architect, the SS and the
            peasant   131

6   From one plan to the next? The Kammler sequence   138
        On planning *style*: the WVHA, Hans Kammler and their
            estimates   138
        Achieving Utopia? The institutionalization and failure of
            building programmes   144
        From the future back to the present: Utopia evaporates   150

Conclusion   156

Part III The case of Zamość

Introduction   161

7   The microcosms of radical policy: Zamojszczyzna   162
        The men, the space and the past of Zamojszczyzna   162
        Institutional microcosms   168
        The land of all Nazi radicalisms   173

8   The politics of the laboratory   179
        Classifying, expelling, deporting: the social engineering at
            the basis of Utopia   180
        Building: the Nazi attempt to shape the territory   186
        Building, installing, settling: at the heart of a new world 192

9   The nightmare: from the ethnic domino effect to the flames of
        despair   200
        In the full sight of all: the extermination of the Jews, prior
            to Germanization   201

A society martyred   207
Wars of the *entre-soi* ('inter-self wars'), (1943–1945)   214

Conclusion   223

Notes   229
Appendix 1: Main acronyms used in the text   274
Appendix 2: Organizational chart of the SS institutions of Utopia   276
Timeline   278
Index   307

List of Maps

Map 1   First *Generalplan Ost* (1940)   xiv
Map 2   Second *Generalplan Ost* (summer 1941)   xv
Map 3   Territories to be colonized at the height of Nazi hopes   xvi
Map 4   Warsaw, railway junction of the General Government   122
Map 5   Warsaw, railway junction allowing access to the East   122
Map 6   Plan of the conurbation of Łódź (Litzmannstadt during
        the occupation), 1942   126

Acknowledgements

It is always a little intimidating, after writing a book, to embark on the recognition of the countless debts contracted over the course of its slow gestation. But are they not a kind of bond, do they not form an inextricable network, like the cradle of this book?

This book was built a little obscurely, after a long period of wandering in the desert, a time when history could not involve the writing of a book. It started in 2002 after a summer in America when, with Christian Delage, I dreamed up a first version of this project. Life, painful and hazardous, meant that it was only eleven years later that I could pick up the traces.

Around me then gathered my attentive mentors, Stéphane Audoin-Rouzeau, Gerd Krumeich, Henry Rousso and Nicolas Werth; my fellow historians, Ludivine Bantigny, Nicolas Beaupré, Romain Bertrand, Olivier Bouquet, Bruno Cabanes, Quentin Deluermoz, Roman Huret, Anne Kerlan, Roman Krakovsky, Vincent Lemire, Benoît Majerus, Hervé Mazurel, Manon Pignot, Malika Rahal, Mathieu Rey, Anne Rolland, Jehanne Roul, Emmanuel Saint-Uscien and Giusto Traina. Some of them, such as Elisa Claverie, Catherine Hass and Véronique Nahoum-Grappe, are not historians and I am thankful to them for this – as I am to my friends of forever and never, Vincent Liaboeuf, David Ortola and Christophe Raoux.

This book also benefited from readings, encouragement, advice and information and photocopies, photos and books from Johann Chapoutot, a sure friend and a constant reader, but also from Nicolas Patin, Maciej Hamela, Élise Petit, Jean-Yves Potel, David Silberklang and Harrie Teunissen. It grew from the granitic fidelity of the Grand Elder, Olivier Buttner, the discreet and thwarted support of Sophie Hoog, a caring family and the unfailing support of parents, sisters and nieces, the Army of Those who Dream . . . and, I hope I would never forget, the sagacity of Samuel Castro, who politely but firmly told me one day in September 2012 that I should address myself to his office, which would respond to my importunity.

But let us leave such sibylline remarks there, even if they are the reality:

it remains to me to thank a poet, Michaël Batalla, who, sometimes a little silently and involuntarily, works in depth on the writing of what animates me; a journalist, Johan Hufnagel, the gruff companion of my uncertainties and my emotions; a publisher, Séverine Nikel, who found a home at Seuil for this book; and a dozen wonderful teenagers who, during Sunday rhetoric sessions, have given a new meaning to what was becoming obscure. I can assure them that the bonds between us will endure.

And Esteban, Nathan, Gaia and Balian.

At last.

Paris, 21 June 2016

Synoptic table of plans for Germanization, displacements of population, and construction

Plan	Institution of origin	Date	Territories and areas concerned
Fernplan Ost **Long-term plan for the East** (divided into *Nahpläne*)	RSHA *Amt* III B **Hans Ehlich**	End of 1939	Incorporated territories
Planungsgrundlagen der besetzten Ostgebiete, **sometimes called First** *Generalplan Ost*	RKFdV **Konrad Meyer-Heitling**	Start of 1940	Incorporated territories
Madagascar plan	RSHA *Amt* IV B 4 **Adolf Eichmann**	Summer 1940	Western Europe
Second *Generalplan Ost*	RKFdV **Konrad Meyer-Heitling**	July 1941	East Europe, including the USSR
'Provisional Peacetime Building Programme' no. 1	WVHA **Hans Kammler**	December 1941	Germany, Poland, occupied USSR
P Wannsee Conference plan	RSHA *Amt* IV B-4 **Adolf Eichmann**	January 1942	Europe
'Wetzel plan' (from the name of the advisor in the Ministry for Occupied Territories who summarized this RSHA *Generalplan Ost*)	RSHA *Amt* III B **Hans Ehlich**	November 1941– April 1942	East Europe
'Provisional Peacetime Building Programme' no. 2	WVHA **Hans Kammler**	February–March 1942	Germany, Poland, occupied USSR
Third *Generalplan Ost*	RKFdV **Konrad Meyer-Heitling**	28 May 1942	East Europe, including *Ingermanland* and Gottengau
Generalsiedlungsplan **General colonization/ settlement plan**	RKFdV **Konrad Meyer-Heitling**	28 October–23 December 1942 to early 1943	Maximum expansion: Urals, Caucasus envisaged, though not named
Beyer/Ehlich plan	RSHA *Amt* III B **Hans Ehlich, Justus Beyer**	February–March 1943	Maximum expansion: Urals, Caucasus envisaged, though not named

Jewish populations targeted	Other undesirable populations	*Volksdeutsche* migrants	Remarks
607,000	8.5 million	–	The *Nahpläne* provide for the expulsion of 600,000 Jews
560,000 expelled	3.4 million Poles	1.46 million	See map 1
4 million			
Implicit use of the figures for the Madagascar plan	–	4.55 million	See map 2
–	–	–	Quantitative plan making provision for labour force and raw materials
11.3 million–	–	European plan of deportation for extermination	
Use of the Wannsee figures, debate on the question of their prior extermination	31 million to be expelled	4.55 million	–
–	–	–	Like no. 1, the organization of building brigades
–	–	–	36 colonization bases. In a speech delivered shortly afterwards, Himmler presupposes 120 million Germans
–	36 million concerned, 5.43 million Germanizable	5.5 million migrants	Only the statistical appendices have been preserved. The extermination of Jews and the depopulation of non-natives are presupposed
–	Plans made for 70 million non-natives, 48 million undesirables, 31 million deportees	–	Death of 17 million non-natives and 11.3 million Jews

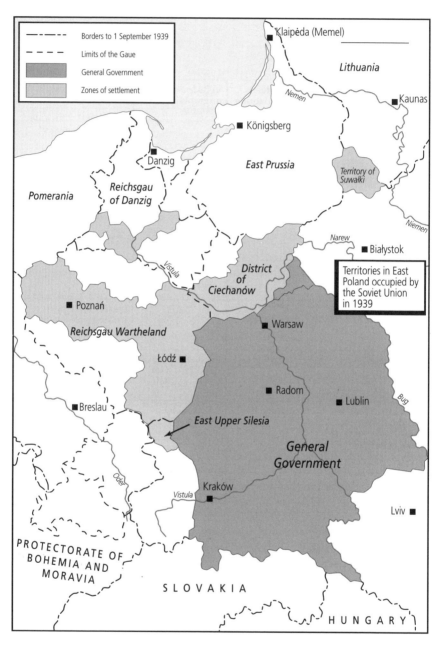

Map 1 First *Generalplan Ost* (1940)

Map 2 Second *Generalplan Ost* (summer 1941)

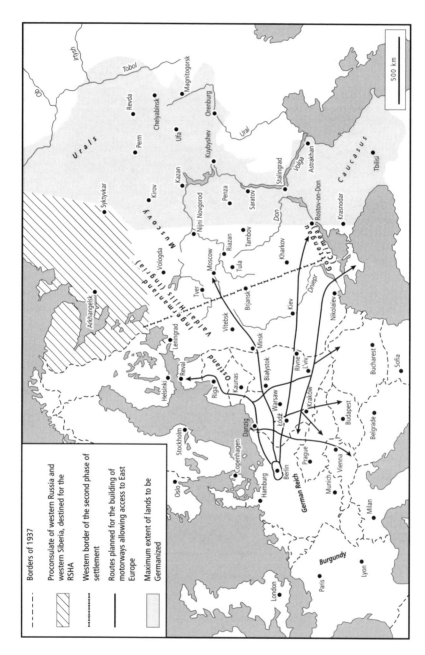

Map 3 Territories to be colonized at the height of Nazi hopes

Legend:

- ·–·–· Borders of 1937
- (hatched) Proconsulate of western Russia and western Siberia, destined for the RSHA
- ┝┥┝┥ Western border of the second phase of settlement
- —— Routes planned for the building of motorways allowing access to East Europe
- (shaded) Maximum extent of lands to be Germanized

500 km

Intysh, Tobol, Ob, Revda, Chelyabinsk, Magnitogorsk, Orenburg, Perm, Ufa, Kuybyshev, Urals, Ural, Kazan, Astrakhan, Caucasus, Tbilisi, Kirov, Stalingrad, Volga, Syktyvkar, Nijni Novgorod, Penza, Saratov, Rostov-on-Don, Krasnodar, Vologda, Muscovy, Riazan, Tambov, Don, Moscow, Tula, Kharkov, Tver, Brjansk, Kiev, Dniepr, Nikolaïev, Gotengau, Arkhangelsk, Ingermanland (Leningrad), Leningrad, Vitebsk, Minsk, Ostland, Helsinki, Reval, Riga, Kaunas, Białystok, Rivne, Lviv, Warsaw, Łódź, Kraków, Budapest, Bucharest, Sofia, Stockholm, Belgrade, Oslo, Danzig, Prague, Vienna, Copenhagen, Berlin, Hamburg, German Reich, Munich, Milan, London, Paris, Burgundy, Lyon

Introduction

On 30 March 2010, in a small two-room apartment in a home for the elderly in Stuttgart, a ninety-year-old man by the name of Martin Sandberger passed away.[1] Sandberger had been born into a middle-class family on 17 August 1911, in Swabia; he studied law, and from an early age combined this with militant Nazism. He was endowed with a powerful physique and a charismatic presence, and demonstrated both academic excellence and commitment to the Nazi cause. He enjoyed an exceptional career in the security services of the Third Reich, and was involved in the development of dogma and the in-depth realization of the regime's most murderous policies. Martin Sandberger – second from the right in the photograph below – was one of those physically attractive 'action intellectuals' who cut quite a figure in their SS uniforms designed by Hugo Boss. He was also one of those managers of genocide by firing-squad who were sentenced to death at the end of trial No. 8 held by the United States Military Tribunal at Nuremberg, though in fact the policies

dictated by the looming Cold War saved the young SS man's life and then freed him. His liberty was ensured by the particular nature of the trial, which meant that he could not be brought before a tribunal again.[2]

In a previous study, I focused in depth on Martin Sandberger and a cohort of his peers in an attempt to explain the connections that might link levels of academic achievement with ideological radicalization and the perpetration of genocidal acts.[3] However, my investigation also suggested that Nazism presented itself less as a fixed and monolithic ideology than as a flexible and complex system of beliefs structured by racial determinism. This system of beliefs, once it had been internalized by Nazi militants, provided them with a threefold certainty: a trustworthy interpretation of the past, a strong commitment to the present, and also a hope for the future. And so, in the autumn of 1939, the young twenty-eight-year-old lawyer who had hitherto been accustomed to the offices of the intelligence services and underground activism found himself on the windswept quays of a Baltic port with the evocative name of Gotenhafen (the 'harbour of the Goths', now Gdynia) to prepare for the arrival of ships carrying a German-speaking population from the Baltic States to be resettled in Polish territories newly occupied by the Wehrmacht.[4] Sandberger's operation seemed to point to the existence of a Nazi racially based humanitarian programme heralding the establishment of a German colonial system in the conquered territories. Did this mean, then, that *something* betokening the fulfilment of the promised future was now coming into being? Did it suggest that the future implicitly promised in terms of *Lebensraum* (living space) and the *Tausendjähriges Reich* (Thousand-Year Reich) was starting to become a reality?

Nazism as a *promise*: this is to be the subject of my book, as these preliminary remarks indicate. My work has not been based – far from it – on unexplored terrain: several excellent studies dealing with certain aspects of this promise have constituted a valuable source of information,[5] and the archives, mainly of Nazi institutions, that I have consulted in Berlin, Warsaw, Washington and Ludwigsburg have been complemented by life stories, memoirs and collections of documents[6] which have provided me with a wide range of valuable material ranging from institutional correspondence to exhibition catalogues, architectural plans, poems, songs and collections of diaries.

This study thus lies at the confluence of several historiographic traditions. The first of these arose in the wake of the upheaval in the human and social sciences following the resurgence of war in people's awareness, on TV screens and within European horizons of expectation – in this case, the war in the former Yugoslavia. We should be grateful to one of the most insightful of all the historians of Nazism, Götz Aly, for having grasped at that juncture that something important was at stake in the abject images reaching us, and that if we were to find a certain analytical distance to draw breath, we would need to go back to the Second World War and the population policies that sprang up during it. This would enable us to bring a fresh perspective to the columns of newsprint generated by Serbian ethnic cleansing. Published for the first time in 1995, Aly's book was the first to systematically correlate the policies of Germanization with the evolution of anti-Jewish measures, and the practices of population displacement with the slaughter of the Jews of Europe.[7]

In the introduction to his book, Götz Aly invited his readers to embark on the unpleasant experience of trying to put themselves in the place of Nazi decision-makers, assessing their room for manoeuvre, the range of their possibilities and their practices. Aly thus took a step towards the second historiographical movement, one that was also, in my view, born of the immense shock of the return of war to the European continent. Indeed, Christopher Browning, in his work *Ordinary Men* (written in that same period), had raised the question of the individual and collective attitudes of actors in the immediate experience of violence. From this book, and from the often empty polemics of Daniel Goldhagen's work, based as it was on archives identical to those of Christopher Browning, arose a new kind of research called *Täterforschung* or research into the perpetrators of crimes; this has since flourished as one of the most productive sectors in the historiography of Nazism over the last decade, the period in which the present work was conceived.[8]

Among the promising crossover approaches that draw on these two trends we find Götz Aly's work on the 'Nazi Welfare State' and studies by Michael Wildt and Frank Bajohr on the *Volksgemeinschaft*, the national ethnic group which was both a theoretical figure and a central framework for the understanding of Nazi horizons of expectation, as well as analyses of the various SS agencies.[9] And it is not the least of the merits of the work of Wildt and Bajohr that they draw our attention to the aspirations of the German peoples to form a different kind of society within the *Volksgemeinschaft*, and ponder the question of the attractions of this prospect held out by the Third Reich.[10] On the other hand, *Täterforschung* tended to focus on the personnel involved in occupation policies in the East, particularly in the occupying and Germanizing institutions, but struggled to show how the Nazi project was related to experiences on the ground.[11] So these two historiographical trends opened up paths for future study.

In the first place, by studying Nazism as a utopian promise, by following its embodiment in individuals and cohorts and not just in public policies, I hope to restore the coherence of the actors' perspectives, their horizons of expectation and their political logics.

Secondly, I will also be setting their discourses, their beliefs and their practices within a social anthropology of individual and collective emotion that alone allows one to understand the allure of the Nazi system of beliefs. The affects and emotions generated by the sense that they were working for the realization of a racial and social Utopia must be taken into account and restored in all their intensity. Nazism – this, at least, is the hypothesis that animates this book – was indeed a matter of hatred and anxiety, the main emotions that led straight to the attempt to exterminate European Jewry, but it was also a question of hope, of joy, of fervour and Utopia: it involved building a new world, an alternative future – a Nazi future.

Attempting to grasp this promise and the extent to which it was real-ized, and trying to give words to this future, also involves entering a debate with Philip K. Dick. In 2016, viewers of Amazon Instant Video were apparently able to rediscover, thanks to the television series of the same name, Dick's novel *The Man in the High Castle*, where he imagines the life of the American continent in the event of a joint victory of the Japanese and Nazi empires. 'What if . . . ?' Alternative history, which in recent times has definitely attained scholarly legitimacy,[12] has long since tackled the possibility of an Axis victory in the Second World War, as in the Film *Fatherland*, which narrates a criminal investigation in the Nazi Berlin of the 1960s led by an SS veteran who has joined the KRIPO.[13] My book, however, is concerned not with alternative history (what in French is known as *uchronie*), but with Utopia: I seek to show how the Nazis dreamed of their victory and the future that would follow it. But I needed to take as my starting point a hypothesis, one that the image of Sandberger on the quayside of Gotenhafen makes us take quite seriously: the Nazis dreamed of the fulfilment of the promise long before victory was assured. And they set out, in the middle of the war, to realize this Utopia. That is the story which my book tells.

With this in mind, it is divided into three parts.

It tries, firstly, to look at the institutions and the persons who assumed responsibility for these policies and to understand the experience of those who planned them and prepared them, and also, inexorably, tried to make them really *come about*.

Secondly, it tries to explore the content of hope, to enter into the revolu-tionary promise which was intended to give a new millennial destiny to a German nationhood that seemed doomed to disappear.

Finally, it was a certain space, on the borders of Poland and Ukraine, around the city of Zamość (pronounced 'Zamoshch') and known as Zamojszczyzna (pronounced 'Zamoitchizna') to which fell the dubious honour of being the laboratory of the advent of the Nazi Utopia that it was ultimately forced to embrace.

But before we embark on our analysis, let us first try to set it in its tem-poral framework; to put forward a narrative and a chronology.

Prologue

The moment of Utopia
(September 1939–summer 1943)

A beginning is the time for taking the most delicate care that the balances are correct. . . .[1]

When did the Nazi hierarchy believe that the *hic et nunc* had come about? When did the state and Party bigwigs, in a great movement of collective belief, decide that it was *here and now* that the German destiny sketched out by racial determinism would take a decisive turn, and that Utopia was about to be realized? To put the question this way suggests that we have here our first main theme and our first way into the subject.

If we then take this line of argument forward logically, we can also ask when this belief disappeared (the 'how?' requires another form of questioning).

In what opens up between these two questions, in the *moment* they isolate, lies our subject matter. It is difficult to define it. Let us designate it, however provisionally, as a *moment*. According to our best French dictionaries, a 'moment' refers to both 'a space of time considered in its more or less brief duration' and 'a space of time considered from the point of view of its content and the events located within it'. The notion is dynamic, and its etymology refers to the Latin *movimentum*, movement.[2]

Having summarily defined it, we now need to try and sketch out its limits. And in order to do this, we have developed one of the historian's most traditional tools: a chronologically arranged table of the events that in our view structure that moment and give it its rhythm. The interested reader will find it at the end of the volume. This timeline lists 249 facts or events between 1 September 1939 and 25 November 1944: the first date marks Germany's entry into the war and the invasion of Poland, the second the destruction of the extermination facilities at Auschwitz. The relevance of this last date will be determined later on: in any case, it does not mark the end of the moment that we want to explore. The 'end' came a long time before: indeed, of the 249 dates, only 220 really make sense for the time of Nazi hope, for the fulfilment of the promise,[3] and these 220 dates range from 1 September 1939 to 1 July 1943. These are the limits of the moment in which Nazi hopes seemed to be coming to fulfilment: the period we shall be studying lasted for 1,399 days, i.e. four years (of which one was a leap year) minus two months (of 31 days).

The great events of this period changed the moment decisively at certain specific times. So we have to follow these events step by step. The date of 22 June 1941, which marks the invasion of the USSR by the Wehrmacht, constitutes a pivotal date and closes a first period that began at the end of November 1939 when the Third Reich, equipped with institutions for thinking about the future of the occupied territories, decided to bring about Utopia. Before that, between the invasion of Poland and the end of November 1939, lay the obscure moment of the establishment of the system for managing the process of Germanization.

The mist-enshrouded time of foundations (1 September–30 November 1939)

The months of September and October 1939 were marked by intense activity on the part of the state apparatus and Nazi militant organizations.

In a thoroughly political staging of events, the Nazi hierarchy set in place a battery of public announcements and statements, mainly coming from Hitler, which symbolically opened a new phase in the exercise of power. At the same time, it produced institutions that became the main actors in the policies of Germanization. The impulse, or at any rate its formalization, came directly from the dictator. The burgeoning number of institutions reflected the balance of power between the different political actors concerned.

The invasion of Poland marked, in the eyes of the Nazis, a new phase in their history. Hitler had asserted this with great solemnity in his speech to the Reichstag, when he simultaneously announced both the invasion of Poland and the establishment of emergency measures in the event that he would no longer be able to assume his functions. Was it the state of war which had changed everything? The answer is not simple because, apart from the impact of these announcements, the transformations had started to appear long before the Gleiwitz incident organized by Heydrich's Gestapo, which had simulated an attack by Polish elements (in fact SS agents) on the radio station in the border town of Gleiwitz, giving the Wehrmacht a pretext for violating Polish borders. From 1 September 1939, Germany would – according to the dictator – be affected by upheavals both inside and outside its borders. On the same day, the Reich Chancellery retroactively authorized the use of euthanasia for incurable patients: children first, adults thereafter. On the functional level, this decree merely endorsed a de facto situation. On the symbolic and racial levels, it committed Germany to a murderous Darwinian eugenic programme central to the Nazi plan to re-establish ethnicity on sociobiological lines. The institutions promoting the Nordic racial heritage, without limits, in the German population were thus officially endowed with a tool whose radical and transgressive nature suited the upheaval represented by the return of war to the German experience. Euthanasia thus gained a rightful place in the repertoire of eugenic racial engineering. This change occurred at the very moment when the war, which gave new impetus to the selection process but also led to the weakening of the Nordic race, re-emerged as a result of a rescue of the *volksdeutsche* minorities persecuted by a Polish state which, in the view of the Nazis, was clearly bent on eradicating these minorities.

At the heart of the implementation of these plans was Hitler himself. It was he who, on 1 September, via the Leader of the Chancellery Philipp Bouhler, authorized the murder of incurable children so as to alleviate the burden on the racial heritage;[4] he who, on the same day, decided that the situation for the *Volksdeutsche* who were outside the protection of the Reich and at the mercy of the Poles was untenable and that it was necessary to act – by war; and he, finally, who, after announcing on 6 October that it was his intention to reorganize interethnic relations in Europe following the war, on 7 October named the SS as the major (but not sole) agent of this great design.

We do not have much documentation enabling us to trace the genesis of this decision to entrust the great design to the SS. However, it is probably sufficient to survey the extant documents in order to understand the very high degree of coherence and the logic of the decision. On the one hand, the SS had since the early 1930s drawn into itself the most cultivated strata and social elites who had so far not been much attracted by Nazi militancy.[5] Moreover, after the Nazis' rise to power in January 1933, in which the SS had paradoxically seemed to lose influence as powers and portfolios were shared out, it had patiently appropriated all police powers in Germany. In 1936 Himmler became the head of all the German police forces. In 1934, thanks to the 'Röhm putsch' which saw the elimination of the SA, a proletarian militia of more than one million members that threatened the stability of Germany, the SS had taken control of the concentration camps, i.e. the extrajudicial bodies of repression and imprisonment.[6] From 1936 to 1939, on the other hand, the SS had finally gained control of a far from negligible part of German clandestine diplomacy directed at the ethnic German minorities.[7] After the Nuremberg laws and the pogroms of November 1938, the SS, or rather its intelligence service, the SD, also took the initiative in terms of anti-Jewish policies. Finally, the SD emerged as the competent authority for the evaluation of public policies, in particular through a number of more or less informal agencies and discussion groups, such as Heinrich Himmler's 'Circle of Friends'. The SS thus combined all the powers necessary for Germanization, i.e. the transformation of the territories which would fall under German domination in which the Nazi future would be built.[8]

In this way, the acceleration of events on the international level coincided with the implementation of new government practices by the German authorities.

The latter had assured themselves of the cooperation of the USSR by the Non-Aggression Pact signed at the end of August 1939, as well as a secret amendment providing for the sharing of zones of influence as well as possible population exchanges between the two contracting powers. This was a way of decisively shaping the Germanization of the East and the building of the Nazi future there. The aim now, even though no territory had as yet been conquered or administered, was to 'manage' huge population displacements, organized by an intense diplomatic ballet. This was not a complete novelty. In 1923, the Treaty of Lausanne had de facto endorsed the immense population displacements between Greece and Kemalist Turkey. On 28 September, with the USSR, and then on 15 October, with Estonia, treaties were signed to ensure the repatriation of local *volksdeutsche* communities.[9] This movement had begun even before the outbreak of war. Since the spring of 1939, in fact, the German-speaking minority in South Tyrol had been the subject of discussions between Fascist Italy and the Third Reich to fix the conditions of its reception in Germany. Coincidentally, these discussions finally produced results on 21 October 1939, while a similar treaty providing for the displacement of 48,800 persons was signed between Germany and Latvia nine days later, on 30 October. A final secret agreement between Germany and the USSR, on 16 November, concerned the *Volksdeutsche* of Eastern Poland, Galicia, Volhynia and Polesia, who would now return to the territories granted to Germany by the Non-Aggression Pact.

At the beginning of the winter of 1939–40, very suddenly, 500,000 *Volksdeutsche* needed to be given a new home.[10]

Population selection, management of territories, reception of migrants and refugees: these were the main topics of those hectic weeks in September–November 1939 when the Nazis, victorious in Poland, were starting to hope that they would be able to build a new order on a renewed foundation. And if it is very difficult to disentangle the element of anticipation from that of improvisation, it is clear that the Nazis also provided themselves with a considerable number of agencies and institutions that would play a part in what they now conceived of as a magnum opus.

One of the potential aims can be seen from the fact that on 1 October there was a rejigging of the security organs, the SD and the Gestapo, a process that had been under way since the beginning of 1939 and had provoked intense debates among the elite groups in the circle of Reinhard Heydrich.[11] Though it is not possible to trace any unmistakable link between the Polish campaign and the creation of the *Reichssicherheitshauptamt* (the Reich Main Security Office or RSHA), it is clear that this was the last significant institutional development in the security apparatus of the Third Reich. In fact, if not in intention, it responded to Nazi expansion, on the Central European scale to begin with and then, from 1940–1, on the continental scale. This reorganization stemmed from a process of rationalization and mutualization on the part of the departments of administration and personnel management. It involved a new division of activities as part of a merging of institutions of very heterogeneous provenance and 'culture' within the SS. Above all, it entailed a change in the status of several departments that, moving over from the SD to the Gestapo, gained in endowment, status, emoluments and prerogatives.[12]

However, the impact of this development on Germanization policies should not be exaggerated. The institutionalization remained tentative, at least in the view of Heydrich and the RSHA: the two RSHA entities that were involved in Germanization policies were still extraordinary ad hoc groups (Special Group and Bureau) until March 1940.[13] This seems to argue for the relative disconnect between the institutionalization of investigative organs and the increasing importance of the prospects for Germanization.

This rationalization of the means of policing populations was combined, a few days later, with the creation (on Hitler's orders) of the *Reichskommissariat für die Festigung deutschen Volkstums* or RKFdV (literally, the Reich Commission for the Consolidation of German Nationhood), on 7 October 1939. The legal status of the new institution was perfectly in tune with Nazi institutional practice. This relatively lightweight body, created ad hoc and based on the person of the Commissioner, had a single task defined by certain objectives, and was entrusted with powers to coordinate – or to short-circuit – the action of existing institutions within the framework of its mission. Hitler's order laid out its mission in these terms: 'the organization of new territories of colonization by means of population displacements' and 'the elimination of the harmful influence of the categories of non-native populations representing a danger to the Reich and the *Volksgemeinschaft*'.[14] It was Himmler himself who chose the name and set out its structure.

Again, this was not a creation ex nihilo. The structures of the RKFdV and its missions came from the experiment that had begun a few months earlier with the question of the German minority of South Tyrol. As I have noted, the leaders of the Reich had engaged in discussions with Mussolini's Italy on the future of the German-speakers of this border region between Austria and Italy. A first version of the general staff of the RKFdV had been created in the summer of 1939 in the form of a body in charge of emigration and return, and was already headed by Ulrich Greifelt, the future Chief of Staff of the RKFdV.[15] However, despite the persistence of the same personnel and mission, there was a decisive change. Hitler's ordinance now gave Himmler a free hand in all population matters in Eastern and Southern Europe.

The RKFdV was intended to function by a system of delegation of powers: existing institutions would be given the powers that Hitler had vested in Himmler and that had been transmitted by him to his new general staff under Greifelt, which, in turn, would disseminate them at the local level by entrusting them to these institutions. Thus, regional and local delegates of the RKFdV came into existence as early as 1 November 1939.[16] Martin Broszat and the functionalists have powerfully suggested that the National Socialism in power had a metastatic tendency to generate institutions,[17] and the practice of Germanization was no exception. The RKFdV was representative of this Nazi propensity to create an ad hoc institution and to allow the proliferation of overlapping and competing centres of power. The fever of these weeks in the autumn of 1939, which created institutions and new fields of action for the SS hierarchs, cannot altogether be understood without taking into account the way the actors envisaged these bodies, and the context of imperial enlargement and the increasing debates on the questions of population and administration in the territories occupied by non-native peoples. It is difficult to decide how much emerged from the immediate context, how much from the structural operation of the Nazi state, and how much from the evolution of the various institutional actors. Nevertheless, these months of October and November 1939 were marked by the birth or the sudden and rapid reformation of institutions that now embarked upon the Germanization policies that would create the future of Nazi Europe.

At the local and regional level, new *Höhere SS- und Polizeiführer* (henceforth HSSPF, Supreme Heads of the Police and SS), Himmler's regional representatives, were appointed both in the *Gaue* incorporated into the Reich, i.e. Danzig, the Warthegau, Poznania and Silesia, and in the territories that, from 26 October, came under the proconsular civilian administration of the Governor-General, Hans Frank. The power of these HSSPFs and their local subordinates, the *SS- und Polizeiführer* (henceforth SSPF, Chiefs of Police and SS), were considerable, as they wielded all the authority of Himmler at the regional or local level: they ran the concentration camps, all the police forces, the SS Armed Forces and all the local or regional offices of the other SS agencies.[18] It was, quite logically, these HSSPFs and the SSPFs of the former Polish territories to which RKFdV powers were delegated on 1 November 1939.[19] On the same day, they were entrusted with the logistics of future repatriation policies. A week later, on 8 November, the HSSPFs in Poznań and Kraków, Wilhelm Koppe and Friedrich-Wilhelm Krüger respectively, met to organize the coordination of the expulsions. The next day, Odilo Globocnik, who would also be one of the key players in these policies, was named SSPF for the Lublin region, taking nominal orders from Krüger.

Two days later, on Saturday 11 November, Wilhelm Koppe set up two general staffs in Poznań, one given the task of expelling Jews and Poles to the General Government and the other responsible for settling Germans from the Baltic and Volhynia. Since 12–13 October, however, another general staff had also been made responsible for these different tasks under Martin Sandberger, and was preparing for the arrival of

Germans from the Baltic countries at the port of Gotenhafen (Gdynia), which became the gateway for their mythical return to the imperial homeland, the *Heim ins Reich*.[20] The three entities, two in Poznań and one in Gotenhafen, worked together, the latter as the reception point and the former two as the theoretical point of arrival for the Baltic Germans. Their status, however, remained somewhat imprecise: some bodies, founded by the HSSPF in Poznań, had only a regional function while it is clear, from the documentation left by the general staff in Gotenhafen, that the latter had a wider remit and reported to Himmler, Heydrich and Werner Best alone.[21] The general staff founded by Koppe and responsible for the reception and integration of migrants was then gradually merged with that of Sandberger in Gotenhafen and formed the *Einwandererzentralstelle* (Central Immigration Office or EWZ), while the second general staff, responsible for carrying out the policy of expulsion in Poznania, became in April 1940 the *Umwandererzentralstelle* (Central Emigration Office or UWZ), under Albert Rapp.[22]

The impression of a major turnaround – this is what strikes any observer of the autumn of 1939. On the one hand, the conjunction of the conquest of Poland and a number of symbolic political changes shifted the Nazi practice of power into another *temporality*, marked simultaneously by war, by what was perceived as a new radical intensity, and by the at least symbolic implementation of what was being promised by Nazi belief: the radical selection of the German racial heritage by the euthanasia of incurable persons, and the reorganization of interethnic relations in occupied Europe. This sudden change, the nature of which is difficult to grasp and whose exact genesis cannot entirely be pinned down, brought with it (or was more loosely accompanied by) sudden changes in the institutional and diplomatic landscape. It lies at the heart of our investigation.

A series of agreements, for the most part unpredictable until then – with the exception of the agreements with Italy and the USSR – led to the emergence, between 28 September and 16 November 1939, of the prospect of ethnic Germans being settled in the newly conquered territory of Poland. These agreements triggered a real institutional and logistical fever, carried out with a remarkable degree of activism and improvisation.

The resulting increase in the number of institutions led, at the central level, to the creation of the RSHA and the RKFdV. On the local level, HSSPFs and SSPFs were appointed, the civilian administration of the General Government of Poland established, and the local agencies that would implement Germanization on a day-to-day basis were set up: these were essentially the Poznań and Gotenhafen general staffs, renamed shortly afterwards the UWZ and EWZ. Add to this the foundation, on 19 October and 3 November 1939,[23] of the ad hoc financial institutions of the *Haupttreuhandstelle Ost* (HTO), a company put in charge of property confiscated in connection with the expulsions, and the *Deutsche Umsiedlungs- und Treuhand GmbH* (DUT), a financial company and trustee for resettlement, acting as a financial and management instrument for the RKFdV, we have a complete panorama of the agencies and tools created by the Nazis to fulfil their dream, providing the security and logistics, as well as laying down the raciological and financial aims of the regime. And this panorama also demonstrates the almost total domination of the SS in future policies.

Thus, as of 1 November 1939, at the end of these few weeks of fever-ish improvisation, the various newly established bodies set out to give shape and life to a post-war Nazi policy that would form the basis for the renewal of German identity and embody the future of Nazi Germany.

On 1 November 1939, there was a meeting attended by Ulrich Greifelt, the RKFdV Chief of Staff, Ernst Fähndrich, his assistant in charge of the workforce, Otto Ohlendorf, Head of the SD Inland (*Amt* III of the RSHA), his subordinate Hans Ehlich, Head of the *Sondergruppe* III ES responsible for racial questions and Germanization, and Martin Sandberger (SD), head of the EWZ Nord-Ost in Gotenhafen. This meeting took the deci-sions on which the policies of Germanization would be based.[24] At the same time, the departments of Hans Ehlich and the Planning Department of the RKFdV, led by Professor Konrad Meyer-Heitling, began to draft the first overall planning documents for these policies.[25]

On 12 November 1939, in a secret circular, HSSPF Koppe, delegate of the RKFdV for the Warthegau, set at 300,000 (200,000 Poles and 100,000 Jews) the number of people to be expelled from that area by 28 February 1940,[26] figures taken up by Bruno Streckenbach, the head of the Gestapo and the SD (*Befehlshaber der Sicherheitspolizei und des SD*, henceforth BdS) for the General Government, and by Heydrich in a circular dated 28 November 1939.[27]

No later than 28 November 1939, the *Sondergruppe* III ES submitted to Heydrich a first ten-page document outlining the long-term outlook for these policies. Planning for population displacement was therefore de facto divided in two: on the one hand, the long-term plan (*Fernplan*),[28] on the other, the short-term plan (*Nahplan*, plural *Nahpläne*). By now all the institutions were in place; the outlook was clearer; the mists of the period of foundation seemed to be dispersing. The era of Germanization was beginning.

The round of short-term plans (1 December 1939–21 June 1941)

The first *Nahplan* was an attempt on the part of the local authorities to put in place a progressive order for the pursuit of the objectives assigned by the hierarchy. On 30 October 1939, Himmler ordered that some '550,000 Jews from "Congress Poland" and an as yet undetermined number of par-ticularly hostile Poles' were to be expelled, to a total of 1 million displaced persons.[29] Koppe decided to proceed gradually and on 11 November set a first stage involving the completion of one-third of the task (300,000 persons, namely 200,000 Poles and 100,000 Jews) in the space of three months, up to the end of February 1940. On the central level, Heydrich himself introduced this new methodical spin on 28 November, and the consequence was the consensual formulation of objectives for December 1939. These objectives constituted, de facto and retrospectively, the first *Nahplan* – which would in fact be the only one fulfilled in its entirety in the view of SS leaders. Indeed, during the first half of December 1939, it projected the expulsion of 80,000 people from the Polish lands incorporated into the Reich to the General Government. The orders specified that all Jews in the old Prussian part of the Warthegau would be part of this contingent of expellees. And the concluding report of the second *Nahplan*, noting that the first *Nahplan* had resulted in the expulsion of 87,388 persons, unintentionally informs us about the 'success' of this first plan, whose objectives were even exceeded by 10 per cent.[30]

On 4 December, Wilhelm Koppe was recognized by Arthur Greiser, *Gauleiter* and *Reichsstatthalter* of the Warthegau, as the sole authority on displacements of population. He thus imposed the constraints of the new policies on the civilian administrations and the Party. This was an event of great importance, which marked the superiority of the SS in the carrying out of these policies. The two general staffs that he had formed – the EWZ and the UWZ – were now free to work out the second *Nahplan*. On 13 December, they set its start date for the following Thursday, 21 December. Originally, this second *Nahplan* logically made provision for the deportation of 220,000 people in addition to the 80,000 already affected by the first *Nahplan* and envisaged its realization in the months of January and February 1940.

It was Heydrich and Eichmann who dealt the first blow to the apparent scheduling of the different plans: on the same day of the theoretical coming into effect of the second *Nahplan*, 21 December 1939, the head of the RSHA sent a letter to all the bodies concerned in which he put Eichmann in charge of the central coordination of population displacement tasks and presented a profoundly revised version of the second *Nahplan*, which now no longer applied to only 220,000 Poles and Jews, but to 600,000 Jews.[31] Heydrich's paper referred to the *Fernplan*, and stipulated that it would be implemented by a succession of *Nahpläne*. Heydrich's sudden initiative represented a gigantic challenge for the institutions involved. And the irruption of reality into planning which remained somewhat virtual caused quite a few problems, to say the least.

On 23 December 1939, the first train bringing *volksdeutsche* migrants from Volhynia entered Łódź, even though the expulsions had just been decided on and then amended and were obviously not yet being implemented. The 128,000 migrants or so from Volhynia and Galicia who crowded into the carriages of the *Heim ins Reich* were the first in a long cohort of whom many – 101,000 – were reduced to hanging around in transit camps in Saxony and the Sudetenland.[32] The difficulties were only just beginning, in the view of the ethnic purifiers of the SS.

On 4 January 1940, Eichmann, now in charge of all logistical issues, organized a consultation meeting between the central bodies which he represented (and which had created a complete mess), the representatives of the various ministries responsible and the local officials of the Gestapo and the SD. They all agreed on the urgent need for the evacuation of Jews from the region, 'on Himmler's orders', but the figures quoted by Eichmann already reflected an attempt at correction: he mentioned 350,000 people to be expelled, which was already 250,000 fewer than on 21 December. Moreover, it was not just Jews, but also Poles. Finally, Eichmann refused to indicate a start date for the operations, merely assuring the participants that none of this could happen until 25 January. So the second *Nahplan* had already been postponed for at least a month in its implementation; and its programming and content were still not fixed even nearly a fortnight *after* the date of its commencement. A plan that was supposed to take ten or so weeks was already practically six weeks behind schedule.

It seems clear that there was a lack of coordination and agreement between Wilhelm Koppe, the HSSPF and RKFdV delegate, and the central departments of the RSHA. Heydrich and Eichmann decided to modify the key numbers decided by Koppe on the orders of Himmler. They modified them again some ten days later, and it was Koppe who reproduced these figures in a letter on the expulsion of the Jews dated 14 January, but reflecting the situation before the meeting on 4 January. In doing so, he acted on figures which Eichmann had already revised, while delaying the coming into effect of such a plan to 1 February.[33]

Undoubtedly perfectly aware that the second *Nahplan* was ineffective and that there was a lack of coordination between the HSSPF and the RSHA, Ehlich and Eichmann met on 17 January to develop an 'intermediate solution to the second *Nahplan*'. Drawing now on the census carried out between 17 December and 23 December in the incorporated territories, the two SS officers surveyed the various difficulties with which the local Germanization bodies were confronted. They started by counting the *Volksdeutsche* from the Baltic states, as well as those of Volhynia and Galicia, referred rapidly to the divergences in the assessments of the General Government, except for the BdS, and established that it would be basically necessary to settle 150,000 *Volksdeutsche*, and therefore to expel at the very least twice as many Jews and Poles; so, in this intermediate plan, they would have to 'reckon with a number of 40,000 expellees', which in their view would make room for 20,000 *Volksdeutsche*. Ehlich and Eichmann then went their separate ways, stressing the need to sort out the difficulties at the next meeting chaired by their leader, Heydrich, scheduled for 30 January 1940.[34]

On 20 January, Koppe spoke of the existence of this intermediate plan which aimed to expel 'those Jews and Poles who need to give up their homes and their jobs within the framework of the Action on Behalf of the Baltic Germans'. Only then, in his view, would the second *Nahplan* come into force, where the key figure remained that of 600,000 Jews to be expelled.[35]

On 23 January Eichmann postponed the beginning of the operations to evacuate the Poles and Jews. On 4 January he had fixed the start for the 25th of that month at the earliest, in view of the fact that a transport planning conference was to be held on the 28th in Leipzig, since the transport overload meant that operations could not commence before 5 February, and even 15 February in the case of Łódź.[36]

Also on 23 January, *Standartenführer* SS Konrad Meyer-Heitling, Chief of the Planning Department of the general staff of the RKFdV, gave Himmler a long memorandum entitled 'Planning Principles for the Building of the Eastern Territories'.[37] This was a twenty-page document in which Meyer-Heitling, a specialist in agricultural geography, detailed the organization of space and human settlements, as well as the organizational patterns of agricultural production. For the first time, the SS described the economic and social character of the area involved and sketched out a Nazi Utopia. However, Meyer-Heitling's plan still conformed to the existing consensus: he stuck to the *Fernplan* figures, followed the principle that the *Nahpläne* would be implemented and the 560,000 Jews from the territory would have 'left it in the course of the coming winter' and that 'over the next few years, the number of Germans living in this territory will have increased by 3.4 million to reach 4.5 million, while little by little 3.4 million Poles will have been expelled'.[38]

The meeting of 30 January 1940, which was supposed to give Ehlich and Eichmann a chance to smooth out all the problems generated by the lack of coordination between the different agencies and the decision-making and administrative levels, did refer to the intermediate plan and the 40,000 Jews and Poles to be expelled from the Warthegau as part of the 'Action on Behalf of the Baltic Germans', the only one mentioned by Eichmann and Ehlich on 17 January; but Heydrich added that 120,000 Poles needed to be expelled to make room for the Germans from Volhynia,[39] and especially 800,000 to 1 million Poles were to be sent as labourers to the Reich. Straight after this action, the expulsion of some 30,000 Gypsies and of all Jews in the new Eastern constituencies was to begin.[40]

The intermediate plan was clearly finally fixed both by the RSHA officials on 30 January and the Warthegau officials ten days earlier, and the logistical difficulties were temporarily and partially sorted out by the Transport Planning Conference of 26–7 January. So this plan could now be triggered. This was done on 10 February 1940. The plan was implemented over five weeks, up to 15 March, and resulted in the expulsion of 40,128 Poles from the towns and villages in the incorporated territories to the General Government. But what in the eyes of Eichmann and Ehlich was a success was actually a Pyrrhic victory: they had received approval for this plan from the agencies only insofar as it was an action for the resettlement of Baltic Germans, and any other operation with a different purpose had been formally prohibited.[41] In other words, the second *Nahplan*, whose intermediate plan was initially a mere provisional revision, was already compromised, whatever form it might take. On 29 February, in a speech to a gathering of *Gauleiter*, Himmler testified to these difficulties without mentioning any postponement.

There is one question that we have not yet raised: the destination of all those expelled, Jews or Poles, who, at this juncture, already numbered 120,000.[42] The time has come to pause and investigate this question with great care, as the destination of these people now played a role in the definition of the plans and thus in the Nazi vision of the imminent future. In the Berlin headquarters and in the local expulsion and resettlement bodies and the administrative organs of the incorporated territories of the Warthegau, Silesia and Pomerania, there reigned a soft consensus that considered the General Government as a kind of dumping ground where all those undesirable ethnics expelled to make room for the *Heim ins Reich* should finally end up. But those responsible for this border proconsulate, the collaborators of Hans Frank, imagined themselves as faced with an overwhelming and quite contradictory injunction: on the one hand, their mission was to establish a perfectly predatory economy in the exclusive service of the Reich and, on the other hand, they were supposed to house in the territory they administered populations that in their view comprised a heavy and unproductive handicap, one that would consume resources while remaining useless. By the autumn of 1939, therefore, Hans Frank's representatives had expressed their disapproval of the Germanization programmes for the occupied territories insofar as they hampered their policies of occupation. An agreement in principle was then reached between the two HSSPFs concerned, Koppe for the Warthegau and Krüger for the General Government, which provided for population movements between the two entities, but excluded the expulsion of the 300,000 Jews from the Łódź region. And yet, the same day, the immediate superior of both men, Himmler, issued an order stating the complete opposite: all these Jews were to be moved to the east of the Vistula, that is to say, directly into the General Government.[43] What had to be accepted by the two SS dignitaries, as stemming from their superior, was unbearable for Hans Frank, who was of similar rank to Himmler and in a situation of rivalry with him.

The confrontation, inevitable both symbolically and structurally, could only get worse. Those responsible for population displacements were also pondering the forms of expulsion which had a direct impact on the 'sovereignty' of Frank in his own satrapy: the question of the creation of a 'Jewish Reserve' (*Judenreservat*) in the eastern part of the General Government – the Lublin district – was, in the eyes of the SS leaders, an alternative to the dispersal of the expelled Jews throughout the General Government. On 30 January 1940, at the meeting of the RSHA officials, Heydrich had announced plans to build four concentration camps in the district to accompany the project promoted by Globocnik, the SSPF for Lublin, in which the *Judenreservat* would be transformed into a huge building site for anti-tank buildings to protect against the neighbouring USSR.[44]

This failed to foresee the protests of Frank and his team, who won the support of Goering and the economic department. In the name of the necessary stability of the territory, Goering stipulated at a summit meeting held on 12 February 1940 that uncontrolled expulsions should cease and that only the duly registered convoys were authorized to come into the General Government.[45] And even though the minutes of the meeting quoted Himmler's intervention mentioning the *Judenreservat*, a letter from Heydrich sent to Goering a week later in which the head of the RSHA spoke of the solution to the Jewish question confined itself to specifying that it was necessary to prohibit the emigration of Jews from the incorporated territories because they were scheduled to be expelled from the General Government, without mentioning the Jewish reservation.[46] Frank's offensive led, on 24 March, to the outright prohibition of evacuations into his jurisdiction.[47]

The interim plan had been implemented between 10 February and 15 March. The date of 1 April 1940 had been set as the start date for the implementation of the second *Nahplan*. The protagonists still had to agree on what this plan now involved. It had, as we have seen, been transformed from top to bottom by Heydrich and Eichmann and now made provision for the evacuation of 600,000 Jews from the Polish territories incorporated into the Reich, and had then been again reduced, on 4 January, to 350,000 expulsions (of Jews and Poles), and was intended in principle to 'resolve the Jewish question' in the occupied territories in anticipation of the settlement of Baltic and Volhynian migrants in these territories. However, by 1 April, it had become a plan that aimed at the expulsion of 'only' 130,000 Poles and 3,500 Jews in order to make a minimum amount of room for the *volksdeutsche* peasants of Volhynia and Galicia.[48] The second *Nahplan* was also given a new schedule: it would take place over practically eight months, with a deadline of 20 January 1941.[49]

Since February 1940, Eichmann and Ehlich, very conscious of the problems arising from the lack of coordination between the Poznań Germanization agencies, had been pushing for a reorganization of local departments under the aegis of their own central departments. Eichmann went to Poznań on 24 April 1940 to visit what became the Central Emigration Office (UWZ), which was now under the central administration of RSHA *Ämter* III B (directed by Ehlich) and IV D-4 (led by Eichmann), while drawing on funding from the RKFdV.[50]

In the eyes of the SS officials in charge of the displacement of populations, the situation was extremely unsatisfactory. The various displacement plans were coming up against a great number of obstacles. The transport crisis and the resistance of the civilian authorities of the General Government had reduced the room for manoeuvre of the SS officers, and the delay of almost five months that had built up between the first *Nahplan* and the beginning of the second was causing serious damage to the policies meant to welcome the *Volksdeutsche* from the Baltic, Volhynia and Galicia and, from April 1940, from the district of Lublin, Bukovina and Bessarabia. These latter were now inexorably piling up in the transit camps. The promised future of a mythical return to the Reich was ending pitifully in makeshift huts. Another symptom of the fading prospects for a general deportation of the Jews to the General Government was the fact that their ghettoization, which had come to a halt during the period when the prospect of the *Judenreservat* formed the horizon of expectations of Germanization policies, was now accelerating: on 30 April, the Łódź ghetto was definitely sealed off.[51]

The months of April and May 1940 were undoubtedly the most discouraging for the racial engineers of the RSHA and the RKFdV. The hypothesis of the 'Jewish Reserve' had failed, the economic situation of the territories concerned was worsening, and the *Volksdeutsche* who arrived had to go straight into transit camps managed by the EWZ and the VOMI. And yet, at this precise moment, though things were not yet very clear in the eyes of the SS enforcers of population displacement, a decisive shift occurred which changed the situation, and especially the question of the future of the Jews of the territories to be Germanized. Since 10 May, the Wehrmacht had overwhelmed the Allied forces during the French campaign. On 20 May, German tanks reached the sea, coming up behind the Allied troops: the British prepared to evacuate. Adapting to this major strategic and symbolic surprise, the German authorities drew up new plans. On 29 May, Himmler presented Hitler with the 'Madagascar Plan', which consisted of deporting the European Jewish communities to the great island in the Indian Ocean, and on 3 June, the head of the Jewish question in the Foreign Ministry, Franz Rademacher, openly referred to this project.[52]

The period which opened with the German victory on the Western Front represented a significant change for the men planning the Nazi future, including those who focused solely on the 'release of space' and the displacements of population. The perspective of these men had hitherto been German and then, with the conquest of Austria and Czechoslovakia, Central European. A decisive factor for our theme is the way this perspective was then broadened eastwards in September 1939. With the occupation of France, the Netherlands and Belgium, German domination assumed a decisive continental dimension. The future had changed scale.

For the racial engineers of the RSHA, with Heydrich, Ehlich and Eichmann in the forefront, the Madagascar project, which replaced the Lublin *Judenreservat* as a 'territorial solution' to the 'Jewish question', was a definite embodiment of the way their horizon of expectations, their policies and their practices were now moving up to the European level. If the reserve project in Lublin provided for the concentration of 1 million Jews (German, Austrian, Czech and West Polish), the 'insular solution' of the Jewish question (i.e. Madagscar), to quote a striking formula of Götz Aly's, anticipated nothing less than the settlement of nearly 4 million extra Jews, with all the Polish Jews together with Slovak, French, Dutch and Belgian Jews. We can see here the effectiveness of the cumulative radicalization of Nazi practice.

As a fundamental prerequisite for the advent of racial Utopia, anti-Jewish policy was inextricably linked to the implementation of the sociobiological refoundation of German identity that lay at the heart of Nazi belief. Whether coincidentally or not, the second week of May, the week of the victorious invasion of France, was marked by the adoption by Himmler and the RKFdV of an order setting out the procedures to be used by the UWZ for selecting Germanizable Poles. The aim here was to bring back the precious Nordic blood lost by crossbreeding and to restore it to the German fold. The first families destined for assimilation in the former Reich were brought by train from 17 May 1940 onwards and part of this operation was included in the second *Nahplan* that was implemented from April. Between that date and 20 January 1942, tens of thousands of people went through these selection bodies with a view to Germanization in the incorporated parts of Western Poland. A similar procedure was put in place in Lorraine and Northern Slovenia.[53] Racial engineers pursued their work on another, older dossier concerning the minority in South Tyrol. Ulrich Greifelt, the RKFdV Chief of Staff, who was here handling his first dossier on population displacement, issued a memorandum in which he envisaged the settling of these colonists in Burgundy: the occupation of France aroused territorial desires.

For an informed observer of all these policies, the summer of 1940 saw two linked developments. On the one hand, there was the increase in the flood of *Volksdeutsche* that resulted from the agreements with Romania concerning Bukovina and Transylvania, and the selection of the *Volksdeutsche* from the Lublin district; this combined with the early stages of the selection of Poles for assimilation purposes in which they would be Germanized: in the eyes of the social and racial engineers, this was one of the prerequisites for the achievement of the Nazi Millennium: the return of Nordic blood to a now extended German Reich after the invasion of the Scandinavian countries of Norway and Denmark (countries whose racial excellence was recognized) on 9 April. The heart of the Reich was strengthened, and the precious racial heritage was gradually repatriated.

In September, the directives of Himmler to the UWZ in charge of these selections revealed the prospect of winning one million racially Nordic souls by selecting eight million Poles. It was on this occasion that the racial scale was fixed in the '*Deutsche Volksliste*' (German Ethnic List or DVL): it was composed of four stages, the first one alone leading to full, rapid and complete assimilation, the others creating second-class citizenship.[54]

On the other hand, the Madagascar solution eased the now very high degree of tensions in the Nazi hierarchies in charge of both Germanization and economic plunder. This solution gave the General Government administration, which needed a break in the transport of Jews and Poles expelled from the incorporated territories, a certain respite. Hans Frank, for example, stopped the building of the Warsaw ghetto, and as early as July 1940 mentioned the prospect of deportation overseas, while he obtained Hitler's agreement in a meeting on 8 July that the transports would be suspended.

The 'Madagascar solution' was not new: it had been envisaged as early as 1937–8.[55] It was nonetheless a logistical challenge, even leaving completely aside the ultimate fate of the unfortunates who would have been sent there. And the conditions that needed to be met for its realization were so numerous that even for the most utopian SS dignitaries this prospect raised questions. One month before Eichmann submitted his Madagascar Plan to Reinhard Heydrich, the local Warthegau officials and those from the General Government, Greiser and Koppe respectively, as well as Frank, Krüger (HSSPF) and Streckenbach (BdS for the General Government in Kraków), held a consultation meeting. Streckenbach announced at this meeting that he had been told by Heydrich to assess the number of Jews under German administration – which was coherent with the plan for the 'solution of the Jewish question' being set up at the European level. But he was very sceptical about the chances of implementation of the Madagascar project.[56]

And in any case, the Madagascar Plan could only be a long-term solution. It was likely to alter the nature of the *Fernplan*, as well as the Germanization plan proposed to Himmler by Meyer-Heitling on behalf of the RKFdV, but it did not mean anything in the short term to those responsible for the settlement policies of the two occupied territories, subjected to pressures that could only get worse. The administrators of the Warthegau saw the flow of the *Volksdeutsche* being repatriated to the Reich increasing and they brought pressure to bear for them to be given room by expelling as many Jews and Poles as possible. Hans Frank and his civilian administration pointed out the explosion in the population of the General Government since the beginning of the war, with the tens of thousands of refugees who had fled first from the combat zones and then from the Soviet occupation, but also with the people expelled in accordance with the *Nahpläne*. This demographic pressure was largely caused by occupation policies. It combined in a particularly pernicious way with the economic and logistical pressures brought to bear by the Minister of Agriculture and Supply, which had considerably increased the requisitioning carried out by the Reich on the production of the General Government. In other words, the policies of Germanization, economic plunder, transport and food combined in a chain reaction that led to three phenomena: the constitution of staggering concentrations of human beings in urban areas as well as in rural areas, in the incorporated territories as well as in the General Government; a profound disorganization of the productive apparatus, which led to a collapse in the rations available to local populations which the authorities were in any case unable to cope with; and a blockage of the flows of population, whether voluntary or forced. Greiser, Frank and the SS protagonists of the policies of population and Germanization were fully aware that the conjunction of these three phenomena would irremediably lead to a catastrophic subsistence crisis for the populations concerned. Even if the Madagascar Plan were implemented, it would not solve the problem of how to get through the winter and ensure the supply of food.[57]

However, as Götz Aly has noted, the sudden emergence of the Madagascar Plan in the considerations of the SS officials and Nazi regional administrators revealed a significant change in the Nazi representations of the future and particularly the future of the non-native, those who were not called to take their place in the racial parousia. It would be illusory, in the eyes of those responsible for imagining the Madagascar Plan (i.e. the settlement of at least 4 million men, women and children, mostly from urban backgrounds, on an island that a number of studies had shown had room for only between 1,500 families and a few tens of thousands of individuals at most),[58] to ignore that this would mean sentencing them, sooner or later, to death by famine.[59] This pointed to the emergence of a murderous plan, but it was a plan that involved *leaving people to die*, not *killing* them. The blocking of Nazi prospects, however, gradually led SS leaders to skip the intervening stages on this 'twisted road'.[60]

We will have to return to this state of affairs. For the moment, let us merely keep in mind the intensity of the pressure exerted on each other by all the protagonists responsible for carrying out the population displacements meant to precede Germanization and the first phase of the advent of the Nazi Utopia. Two weeks earlier, even before Eichmann handed the RSHA's Madagascar Plan over to Heydrich, the local practitioners of the expulsions were already sceptical about its realization. A month later, on 17 September 1940, the landing in England was postponed and the Madagascar project was losing what little credibility it had ever had. The consequences were not long in coming: the pressure on Frank intensified, and came via Hitler himself. At a meeting with Frank, von Schirach and Koch, *Gauleiter* of Vienna and East Prussia, respectively, he imposed the resumption of deportations to the General Government. Three days later, on 5 October 1940, trains packed with Jewish and Polish expellees were again entering the territory of the General Government.[61]

In great secrecy, however, August 1940 had seen the emergence of initial thoughts about the desirability of a sudden invasion of the USSR. At the very moment when Nazi dignitaries were pondering the potential of the evanescent Madagascar Plan, Hitler and the military authorities were already turning to a new and even more grandiose plan. The men who practised the day-to-day administration of the occupied territories, and the social engineers of the SD and RKFdV who were planning the expulsions, did not belong to the circles in the know about these latest developments. It must be said that these first thoughts may indeed have dated back to the summer of 1940, but that the first preparatory simulations for a rapid war against the USSR occurred only in November 1940. And on 4 December 1940, in a note that he wrote for Himmler, Eichmann explained that 5.8 million Jews would have to be 'removed from the European economic area of the German People to a territory yet to be determined'.[62] Over the next two weeks, preparations for the war changed direction and accelerated with directive no. 21, which, on 18 December, set out the preparations for a rapid campaign aimed at bringing the USSR to its knees, and scheduled them for 15 May 1941.[63] There was now a clear sense of overall strategy in the eyes of the highest Nazi leaders. And it is easy to imagine that while the discussions that Himmler, Heydrich and Greifelt, Lorenz and Goering held the next day, 19 December, were ostensibly about negotiating displacements of population and a process of Germanization that were still being thought of as part of the *Nahpläne* (actually the third such, scheduled to start on 20 January 1941), they would also have referred to what must have meant a significant change in the horizons of expectations both of the SS's racial engineers and of the administrators of the occupied territories.[64]

This was the start of a period marked by three basic features. On the practical level, the third *Nahplan* in the process of negotiation and enforcement was a step forward in the increasingly gigantic nature of the quantities, projects and horizons being envisaged. Even though the second *Nahplan* had failed to realize objectives that were constantly being revised downwards – it had managed to 'evacuate' only 249,000 people of the 800,000 or so planned – the third *Nahplan* envisaged nothing less than the evacuation of 771,000 people, mainly Polish, as well as a reduced number of Jews not enclosed in ghettoes. At a meeting held on 8 January 1941, those responsible for displacement policies had spoken of 800,000 people, an approximation mentioned during the short life of the plan. The latter was becoming more complex: the figures no longer came just from the sometimes capricious calculations of the various SS agencies and administrations in charge of the occupied territories: the Wehrmacht had also started to deploy this useful means of acquiring land rights for the training of its units and demanded nothing less than the expulsion of 202,000 Poles.[65] The logics now followed by the SS did not go unquestioned.

　　Was the *Fernplan* still relevant, while a more far-reaching project, the Madagascar Plan, had been developed? The question arose but the fact that this new plan was entitled the third *Nahplan* leads the observer to deduce that the SS thought of their role as continuing what they had previously started.

　　The question, however, only made sense for a very short time: the plan was supposed to come into force on 20 January 1941 and to be completed a year later, but as Eichmann realized (having been notified by the Ministry of Transport on 15 February) the last transports left for their destinations less than eight weeks later. A month later, on 15 March 1941, the transports gave absolute priority to the conveying of men and supplies for the *Ostheer*, the army of the East, which was assembling for Operation Barbarossa. This paradoxical situation seemed to open up (at least virtually) a new horizon for short-term plans, but in fact spelled out their failure.[66]

At the same time, the template for the treatment of non-native popula-tions, which had shifted at the time of the Madagascar Plan towards an indirectly murderous plan condemning them to famine and disastrous sanitary and economic conditions, was further radicalized during the preparations for Barbarossa. Of course the players were not the same; of course those involved in planning Barbarossa had only two channels of information to circulate the local consensus on the treatment of popula-tions. Nevertheless, from the outset, the economic institutions of the Wehrmacht, the civilian supply administrations and the high command of the army took the idea of *leaving them to die* further and turned it into *killing them.* The supply plan, which consisted of not feeding the invasion units so as to encourage them to forage from the conquered territories, entailed, as its planners themselves realized, the death from starvation of 'tens of millions of people'. It was a Famine Plan in the full sense of the term.[67]

At the top of the list of targeted groups were the urban populations from the territories of the western arc of the Soviet Empire, which corre-sponded to the area of residence of the Tsarist Empire and thus included most of the Jewish populations of the USSR, now destined for slaughter without regard for sex or age.[68]

The murderous horizons of expectation described here had, however, probably not yet been integrated into the planning of the Nazi future in Poland. This planning was yet again characterized by its lack of perspec-tive. The absence of any place for the expelled Jews and Poles to go to was paralleled by the failure of the policies already being pursued. This failure was characterized both by calling a halt to the expulsions and by the fact that the number of *Volksdeutsche* to be resettled, now waiting their turn in transit camps, was growing exponentially. And it is not the least of the paradoxes of the period that it was precisely at that time that the dignitar-ies of the regime decided to start to reveal the advent of Utopia.

In January 1941, Himmler decided to organize a major exhibition enti-tled *Die Große Heimkehr* ('The Great Return'). In March 1941, the *Planung und Aufbau im Osten* ('Planning and Building in the East') exhibition, organized by Konrad Meyer-Heitling and the Planning Department of the RKFdV, opened. Both of these exhibitions were held in Berlin; they offered an extensive range of representations of the future of Nazism. One was planned and the other conceived in the winter of 1941, when the lack of prospects had seemed to provoke a feeling of crisis and discourage-ment in some of the protagonists.

Germanization was no longer thought of solely in terms of logistics. It was no longer simply a question of getting trains to depart and arrive, of expelling or resettling populations, but also of focusing on the content of these policies, in the view of at least some of those involved. Meyer-Heitling and the Planning Department of the RKFdV, as well as the EWZ and the UWZ, all vied to supply visual details of the future for these exhibitions while they were still at the planning stage. It should also be stressed that certain 'qualitative' measures were adopted by Himmler in regard to the question of the standard of living of the *Volksdeutsche*. The socio-racial parousia was being set out in greater detail at the very moment that any real prospect of achieving it was becoming uncertain.

The dream was taking shape without becoming any the more real.

There were still major changes in the plans for the coming Blitzkrieg. Frank and Hitler met two days after the halting of the third *Nahplan*. Together, they decided on a paradigm shift in terms of the General Government of Poland. While this residual Poland had, up until then, been used as a dumping ground for populations deemed undesirable by the Nazis administering the territories incorporated into the Reich, they decreed on 17 March that the General Government was a territory which had to be Germanized within 'fifteen to twenty years'. Combined with the abrupt broadening of the horizons of the practitioners of ethnic cleansing, who now saw the USSR as an immense place for shedding undesirable populations, this news triggered a kind of euphoria at the beginning of spring 1941, in very marked contrast to the winter.

In the Polish territories, however, the combination of all these factors led to the worsening of living conditions in the ghettoes and a growing tendency to reflect on the potential use of the Jewish labour force, which quite soon led to the introduction of forced labour. It was in the Lublin district, under the aegis of Odilo Globocnik, a great precursor of anti-Jewish policies and Germanization policies, that the first ideas on this score were made public. In Lublin and in the Warsaw sector, the first labour camps for Jews appeared in the spring of 1941. These measures, however, were conceived of as provisional: Operation Barbarossa opened new horizons for these policies. Admittedly, undesirables would still be piled up in the first residual spaces of the *locus* destined for the building of Utopia, but what then awaited them in the conquered Soviet immensities would combine the advantages of the Madagascar Plan and the *Judenreservat*: an unlimited (but continental) territorial solution that posed no logistical challenges but was solely dependent on a land victory and not on control of the oceans, combined with an indirect murderous plan.[69]

Himmler's observation of the last twelve months of Germanization allowed him to draw the following conclusion: the displacement of the population had not been able to follow the schedules set out in the various *Nahpläne*, and the territories concerned had been the subject of muddled and contradictory policies that had given rise to major tensions within the Nazi elites – so much so that the General Government was now being expected to follow diametrically opposed policies. Long-term plans had become obsolete: the Madagascar Plan had led to a major revision in the scale and size of the populations to be expelled. Neither the RSHA *Fernplan* nor the documents submitted by Meyer-Heitling (and drawing on the figures from the *Fernplan*) corresponded to reality, and even less to the glowing future anticipated after victory over the Soviets. Expulsion and resettlement policies had fundamentally changed their objectives and their destinations in the previous months. All this, in the eyes of the Head of the SS, made it necessary to embark on a new and clearer programme: a General Plan for the East, or *Generalplan Ost*, that Himmler put in the hands of Konrad Meyer-Heitling on 21 June 1941. On the eve of what would now be called 'the Great Racial War', what was envisaged was the pan-European extension of the Nazi Utopia.[70]

New horizons: the General Plan for the East (22 June 1941–15 February 1943)

Konrad Meyer-Heitling's teams had been at work for some time, and the command from the SS chief, while not retroactive in character, did not catch them unawares. Three weeks later, in fact, Konrad Meyer-Heitling delivered the *Generalplan Ost*. It is difficult to know the content of this document, which left no trace in the archives: the main lines can be reconstructed only from a life story handwritten by Meyer-Heitling himself.[71] It is certain, however, that it now reflected at least partially the European dimension of the Nazi future. Establishing a typology of the spaces affected by Germanization, it quantified the needs of settlers, areas to be seized and populations to be displaced. Two days later, on 16 July 1941, Rolf-Heinz Höppner, head of the UWZ in Poznań, wrote to Eichmann that the departments in the Warthegau were trying to think of some rapid means of eliminating Jews unable to work in view of the coming winter and the probable shortage of provisions.[72] This was the sign of a spreading of the imaginary of murder and its circulation among the administrative elites of the occupied territories, but it was also inexorably evidence of an ongoing shift from *leaving people to die* to actively *killing them*. On 31 July, Goering sent a letter to Heydrich ordering him to consider a final solution to the Jewish question by migration or evacuation, which implicitly confirmed the validity of the current horizon of expectation of the practitioners of Germanization, deportation and anti-Jewish policies: this envisaged mass deportation of the Jews to Siberia or, more securely, beyond the Arctic Circle. They would live in a kind of political proconsulate, with a dramatic reduction in the populations concerned, decimated by the conditions of travel, residence and labour in the polar spaces used as a world of concentration camps and forced labour.[73]

As far as we can know – and there is considerable uncertainty on the matter – the *Generalplan Ost* of Meyer-Heitling reflected the continuing expansion of the Nazi Reich, but did not mention these ideas, and did not seem to take them into account. Like the plan drawn up at the beginning of 1940, it was built on the assumption that the Jewish populations had disappeared from the territory it envisaged, without being any more precise.

This is because, at the same time, things were starting to move more quickly. On 20 July 1941, Himmler visited the Lublin district with the local SSPF, Odilo Globocnik, and announced that the territory was to be immediately Germanized – which, as will be seen, was simply an endorsement of the programmes initiated by Globocnik since his arrival in Lublin. The two men set their sights on the territory of Zamość, intending to make it an area for particularly thorough and in-depth Germanization. It was in this territory that the most complete attempts at Germanization would be carried out, and here that all the means imagined by the SS to achieve their ends would be deployed.[74]

The summer and autumn of 1941 saw a growing and unbroken crescendo of violence starting, as is well known, with the increasingly large-scale massacres perpetrated by the *Einsatzgruppen*, which, from 16 August 1941 onwards, included Jewish women and children in their killing quotas, leading to the climactic moment of the mass murder at Babi Yar and Kamenets-Podolski and the emergence of a comprehensive liquidation of Jews, executed by firing squads in occupied Serbia[75] and two specific regional extermination programmes in the Warthegau and the Lublin district.[76]

November and December 1941 were a turning point in two respects. Some writers on this period concluded that the order to carry out comprehensive extermination programmes emerged in some regions – the General Government, the Warthegau, Serbia, the USSR; later, Christian Gerlach and Florent Brayard uncovered a major paradigm shift with Hitler's fundamental decision to exterminate all the Jews of Europe, a decision he reached in December 1941.[77]

As far as the General Plan for the East was concerned, the details are unclear. As we have seen, the RKFdV document in force at that precise moment has not come down to us and it is difficult to get a clear idea of it. The situation becomes even more complicated when we learn of the existence of a second plan, this time coming from *Amt* III B of the RSHA; its existence is indirectly and belatedly certified by the criticisms directed at this plan by the *Rassenreferent* of the Ministry for Occupied Territories, Erhard Wetzel.[78] Its dating and content are impossible to establish with certainty. The most we can conclude is that the period was marked simultaneously by brutal paradigm shifts, the sudden emergence of a desire to carry out a comprehensive extermination programme, and increased institutional competition between the RKFdV and the RSHA.

If we also note one single intervention made by Himmler to the RKFdV, in which he specified a relatively minor aspect of the *Generalplan Ost* (tightening the conditions of home ownership for settlers), and the appearance of a new player in the programming and planning of the post-war era with the WVHA (the SS's Main Office for the Economy and Administration) in the person of Hans Kammler, who produced a first memorandum entitled 'Provisional Peacetime Building Programme',[79] we have a complete overview of a sequence of great complexity. It is marked by numerous events which led to Hitler's decision to exterminate the Jews of Europe, to the triggering of comprehensive killing programmes in at least some regions, to a head-on collision between at least three competing and divergent general plans for the East, and to a certain degree of cacophony. To try to go beyond this imprecise description would be too hazardous.

The historical observer of this tangled web of policies, practices and murderous impulses comes away with an impression of disorder that may be accentuated by the gaps in our source materials. The fact remains that the year 1942 does not leave the same impression as before: if the archival corpuses are tangibly more numerous and explicit, it seems that the year was also marked by attempts at harmonization and fruitful coordination in the eyes of the dignitaries of the Third Reich.

First there was the coordination of anti-Jewish policies that became overtly genocidal in intent: on 20 January 1942, the Wannsee Conference, which endorsed a pan-European deportation of Jews for slaughter, informed and coordinated the group of ministries, administrations and government departments involved in the process, all under the auspices of Heydrich and Eichmann. Second, there was the coordination of plans for population displacements: Meyer-Heitling received orders from Himmler to bring his departments into line with what was to become, on 1 February 1942, the WVHA and, with Hans Kammler, to produce estimates for the costs and finalize financing plans for the projected Nazi sociobiological refoundation in an *Ostraum* that would stretch from the Black Sea to the Arctic Circle. On 27 January and 2 February, Himmler first instructed Meyer-Heitling to estimate the costs of his plan and then confirmed that the *Gottengau* (Crimea) and the *Ingermanland* (Ingria, the region around Leningrad) would be included in the areas of colonization.[80] Meanwhile, on 31 January, he wrote to Oswald Pohl, Kammler's superior, on the very eve of the founding of the WVHA (the body that would control the entire economic dimension of the SS empire and would then be put in charge of the management of the concentration camps), asking him to provide an estimate of the expenditure referred to by Kammler in his 'Provisional Programme'.[81] On 4 February, there was a meeting of officials from RSHA *Amt* III B and those of the Ministry for Occupied Territories to discuss the problems posed by anti-Jewish policies and population displacements.[82] If the state of the sources does not give us a clear view of the balance of power existing within the small group planning for the East and the future, it is evident that the agencies were working together, that a coordinating effort was under way and that the first half of 1942 was busily occupied with preparatory work for a new version of the RKFdV's *Generalplan Ost*. At the beginning of the mass, comprehensive and Europe-wide extermination being set in motion, the planning apparatus responsible for programming Utopia was finally in place.

The end of May 1942 marked a new stage: the 'third' RKFdV *Generalplan*

Ost, the only one for which we have all the documentation,[83] was transmitted to Himmler on 28 May. The day before, 27 May, a team of Czech paratroopers in Prague carried out an attack on Heydrich. _Exactly_ a thousand days had passed since the Nazis had started to think about the East and the future of Germany. And these thoughts now reached their peak, and also their paroxysm.

The peak consisted in the fact that the orders of magnitude mentioned by all the planners were on a huge scale, and with a continental dimension. A Germanic Europe was starting to loom in the planning and – as we shall see in the third part of this book – was already coming into being in Lublin, in Zamojszczyzna;[84] Himmler mentioned it in some of his speeches as well as in his conversations with Hitler. And it is one of those conversations that shows how intolerably this peak was _entangled_[85] with paroxysm: on 22 September 1942, notes taken by Himmler in an interview with Hitler show that under the theme no. IV, 'Ethno-politics[86] and colonization', the head of the SS addressed item 1, 'Jewish emigration, how should it be pursued?' and item 2, 'Colonization Lublin (Relations General Govt. Globus)'.[87] In September 1942, the _Judenauswanderung_, the 'Jewish emigration' already announced in the protocols of the Wannsee Conference, referred to all the procedures to be used in the extermination of the Jews: forced labour, shootings in Serbia and the USSR and in certain sectors of the General Government, deportations to fixed gassing installations in the General Government and to mobile gassing installations in the Warthegau, and finally deportations to and killings in Auschwitz, the fate laid down for the greater part of the Jews from occupied West Europe.

This set of programmes for murder ran at full speed and made the year between the end of May 1942 and the end of May 1943 one of genocidal paroxysm. In May 1942, 80 per cent of the victims of the genocide were still alive. One year later, the proportion was completely _reversed_.[88] There is no better indication of the violence involved, and the way it was inextricably linked with the advent of the dream of a new Reich.

One fact, however, lay in the way of the realization of this dream, in the view of practitioners and analysts of these policies. Erhard Wetzel and Heinrich Himmler both saw a rise in the fertility of the racially desirable populations as the sine qua non for achieving their long-term plans. This was the chief criticism which the _Rassenreferent_ of the Ministry for Occupied Territories made of the RSHA's _Generalplan Ost_ in May 1942.[89] The influx of _Volksdeutsche_ into the homeland of the Reich would not suffice: the Germans of the Reich had to start producing children _in large numbers_, and over several generations. Wetzel was here hitting a raw nerve, symptomatic of a growing realization among the planners: the precious Nordic blood was missing. On the one hand, every drop needed to be removed from the non-native populations (this was an old idea of Gobocnik's that was implemented in Lublin as early as 1940, as we shall see), and on the other hand all means should be used to increase the fertility of German women.

The latest plans and estimates coming from all agencies charged with thinking out the plans for the East and its future drew a more implicit conclusion from all this. These agencies started by theorizing how, in a completely novel strategy, forces could be sprinkled across the territories to be Germanized that would now be structured by 'Points of settlement and support' (*Siedlungs- und Stützpunkte*), bases from which Nazi forces would take control of certain regions, over several generations. Despite the optimism still being voiced in most of the literature regarding the relevance of this long-term strategy, the SS planners now came out with quite different arguments without formulating them clearly, at least not in the autumn of 1942: if the German population did not increase dramatically in this competition to produce babies, a competition with the non-native Slavs with whom it would need to struggle for the lands of the German future, it would be necessary to find other variables of adjustment to ensure that fate favoured the Nordic side. And if the numbers did not increase, then, inexorably, it was the undesirable alien populations that would have to experience a demographic decline.

From the little we can deduce from documents that, yet again, are scarce, it was this new development that was reflected in the *Generalsiedlungsplan* that Meyer-Heitling was meant to present to Himmler in the winter of 1942–3, and of which he provided at least the appendices, with their tables, statistics and diagrams, on 23 December 1942.[90] At the same time, the RSHA *Amt* III B, in two unconnected but coherent events, laid bare its own view of the future of the populations involved.

On 11 December 1942, in a lecture given to the NSDStB (*National-Sozialistischer Deutscher Studentenbund* or National Socialist German Students' League), Hans Ehlich, head of the RSHA *Amt* III B and the main planner of population displacements and ethno-political policing, examined 'the treatment of foreign populations'; then, on 1–2 February 1943, a symposium of III B officials from local SD offices was held on the issue of population displacements.[91] I shall be coming back to this: the intersection of these two events also reflected how SS planners had shifted from the 'paradigm' of *Umvolkung* (transcribed by the Greek word *ethnomorphosis*, which I will here translate as *dissimilation*, a process contrary to assimilation, as will be seen in chapter 4) to the paradigms of *Entvolkung* (shift of population) and *Rückvolkung* (depopulation).[92]

This was how things stood on 15 February 1943 when Meyer-Heitling's offices sent the last letter to Himmler on the General Plan for the East, the last visible archival trace of Nazi thinking about their utopian future. Himmler never replied, and at that very moment it started to become apparent that the horizons of expectation of the SS, its leader and the planners had changed. Gradually, from this date to the summer of 1943, it emerged that the time for planning the future was now past. And it is this evaporation of the future whose history we need to trace, exploring synchronies and time gaps, and the paths that led from the Berlin offices to experiences in the field, if indeed this model is to be relevant.

In the summer of 1943, the situation seemed relatively clear. Plans for the advent of the Nazi Millennium were less important. Institutions whose sole mission was to give shape to this Utopia were being shelved, while other organizations had turned to different tasks and missions. The present was pressing, and that is what has prompted me to bring my investigation to a close at this date.

Let us pause, however, to make an inventory of the inadequacies of this first account. The narrative form has allowed us to show the development of Nazi representations and practices, and to some extent to 'unfold' the way the sequence was largely arranged; but it has de facto prohibited us from focusing, on the one hand, on the complex sets of institutions which competed, entered into alliances and collaborated on one-off projects and, on the other, to scrutinize the men who worked in them, their careers and the networks they constituted. More seriously, the narrative strategy adopted in this prologue has not allowed us to give substance and content to the dream of the East, to what Martin Broszat very rightly called the 'Nazi racial parousia',[93] the *Tausendjähriges Reich* which, at a moment I hope I have just defined precisely, these men felt they were building.

Part I

The men and the institutions of Utopia

Chapter 1
A nebula of institutions

To say that it is difficult to make an inventory of the institutions that were responsible for the Nazi future would be an understatement. And to illustrate this, we need simply review the criteria that differentiated them. The first and most important was their place in the Nazi galaxy: whether each body was a central or local organization determined in large part the content of its missions and the tasks it assumed. But this was not the only differential: some agencies specialized, while others had been assigned broader and general missions, and some were temporary or at least supposedly so while many others were permanent. We can also draw a distinction between specific or personal institutions such as the HSSPF and SSPF and organizations that branched out into local representations or offices such as the SD or the RuSHA (*Rasse- und Siedlungshauptamt*, Main Office for Race and Colonization), and between speculative organizations and operational organizations. In short: the descriptive criteria are numerous and make the picture quite complicated. Let us try to account for this diversity.

The diversity of the institutions of Utopia

The central institutions: RKFdV, RSHA, WVHA

Let us begin by trying to inventory the institutions entrusted with the central plan of thinking about the Nazi future. The only organization assigned solely to this purpose was the *Reichskommissariat für die Festigung deutschen Volkstums* (RKFdV) created, as we have seen, at the very beginning of October 1939, when Himmler received from Hitler the mission of making preparations for the Germanization of the occupied territories. The RKFdV was the archetype of Nazi institutions. It was a commissariat, that is to say an ad hoc institution, whose temporary existence was linked to the fulfilment of a specific task and whose staff was small, being taken largely from existing institutions; it could, within the framework of its missions, give them orders, directives and instructions. On 7 October

1939, Himmler was appointed Commissioner: the RKFdV was composed solely of organizations directly dependent on the previous responsibilities of the SS leader. The RKFdV comprised three groups. Group 1 included the command department, a 'Policies and Population Displacements' department, and a management and manpower department. Group 2 covered all economic, agricultural and financial departments, while Group 3 included planning, land registry and building departments.[1] As provisional bodies were now destined to last and the task was enormous, the Commissariat was transformed into a *Hauptamt* (Main Office) of the SS, and was now a permanent body on the same level as the RSHA or SSFHA (*SS-Führungshauptamt*, SS Leadership Main Office), in June 1941.[2]

The RKFdV thus grew in power in 1941 and was logically endowed with all the attributes of the powerful SS institution that Himmler wished it to be. Thus he provided it with regional and local bodies via the HSSPF and SSPF. Wilhelm Koppe, Friedrich-Wilhelm Krüger and Odilo Globocnik based a significant proportion of their security policies on the delegated power they held from the Commissariat. The decisions taken by Greifelt with regard to overall policies, by Fähndrich for the manpower issue and by Meyer-Heitling for planning were thus passed on to the most local level. All this, however, meant that the RKFdV carried out essentially speculative and strategic missions: it had virtually no operational dimension, delegating this dimension of Germanization policies to other actors, some central, others local.

At the level of the central actors, the RKFdV drew on operating institutions such as the VOMI (*Volksdeutsche Mittelstelle*, Coordination Centre for Ethnic Germans) or the RuSHA; the former was competent in providing material and ideological assistance to *Volksdeutsche*, the latter in a whole set of racial policies.

VOMI was the heir of the informal revisionist diplomacy of Weimar. It was taken over by Himmler in 1937 and it set in place a number of clandestine actions during the invasion of Poland. Beginning in the winter of 1939, it ran the network of transit and reception camps for the *Volksdeutsche* returning to the bosom of the Third Reich. It was thus one of the main beneficiaries of endowments requested by the RKFdV from the Reichsbank and the Ministry of Finance. It now underwent its biggest transformation: having been an instrument of informal and even clandestine diplomacy, the VOMI became a logistical assistance institution, managing the camps and ensuring the distribution of goods to the *Volksdeutsche*.[3]

The second operator of the RKFdV was the RuSHA. It was created in 1932 from the racial office of the SS. Originally, it was given two missions that were in Himmler's view crucial: the racial selection of candidates for entry into the SS, and the management of marriage authorizations. In other words, the RuSHA was the instrument of the eugenic ambitions of the SS. It was also responsible for colonization and settlement policies, as well as much of the SS's ideological education and training.[4]

It was based on this precise experience that the RuSHA became, under the control of the RKFdV but also with its own jurisdiction, one of the most important players in the development and building of the Nazi future. It was in charge of a far from negligible proportion of Germanization policies, sending experts in racial selection on missions to occupied territories in various institutional settings, producing racial surveys and providing assistance for settlers. The RuSHA constituted a reservoir of specialists and practitioners placed (under the control and coordination of the RKFdV) at the disposal of local actors scattered throughout Europe, from Lorraine and Alsace to Crimea, including of course the occupied territories in Poland, Belarus, the Baltic states and Ukraine.

The second central decision-making institution in the field of Germanization and development of the Nazi future was the RSHA, the Reich Main Security Office, the creation of Heydrich and his team at the time of the invasion of Poland. It was the result of intense thinking about the missions of the pre-existing security organizations, the Gestapo, the KRIPO (criminal police) and the SD, as well as a concern for streamlining and the merger of institutions that came with highly differentiated 'cultures'.[5]

The first stage of the story we are telling came at the precise moment of the internal structuring of the RSHA and its transformation. Two of its departments split off and became the main RSHA sectors for planning and Germanization.

The department involved was IV D-4 (now IV B-4) headed by Eichmann; this was a former department of the SD that specialized in intelligence and the fight against 'religious enemies' (including adherents of Judaism), now under the control of the Gestapo thanks to the creation of the RSHA. It was composed of former members of the SD, primarily SS activists who, in the Czech Republic and Austria between 1938 and 1939, had gained experience in putting forward proposals for anti-Jewish measures and logistical, administrative and financial know-how in the management of the human cohorts to be expelled or forced to leave. These men knew how to develop rational and efficient procedures, for instance by concentrating and centralizing the administrative formalities of expulsion, confiscation and withdrawal of identity documents and forging them into a single chain. A kind of administrative Taylorism, involving a kind of one-way ticket, with trains that 'they' could ensure would set out and arrive on time: this was the area of expertise of Eichmann's men who willingly grappled with the questions of Germanization and expulsion alongside the issue of the 'solution of the Jewish question'. The organic link thus created and the developing overlap between the two activities constitute one of the most interesting markers in the evolution of representations of the Nazi future.[6]

Eichmann's departments intervened in this case both in practical terms, by literally manufacturing identification, confiscation and expulsion procedures, and also by producing planning whose history is difficult to trace, as so little is documented. Here, we must note that this planning should not be confused with that of the second department of the RSHA which was involved in these policies.

While the long-term planning of 1939 and 1940–1 probably did not originate with Eichmann's departments, that relating to the Jewish question came, without any shadow of a doubt, from RSHA *Amt* IV B-4. In the summer of 1940, the Madagascar Plan was thus the first plan that can safely be attributed to Eichmann and his men. This document, like other plans originating in these departments, was based on estimates of the Jewish populations in Europe. And it is likely that the last of the plans that emerged from Eichmann's departments was that presented by Heydrich at the Wannsee Conference in January 1942, which decreed a 'final solution to the Jewish question' by direct murder on a pan-European scale.[7] The question of the status of this highly significant plan in the general policy of Nazi future-building raises the question of the link between future projects and mass murder.

On a more practical level, the RSHA *Amt* IV B-4, as we have seen, organized and implemented deportation procedures, thus disseminating a practical expertise acquired mainly during the invasion of Austria. More importantly, Eichmann was also the most central figure in charge of transport, whether this involved the expulsion of Jews and Poles or the transport of *volksdeutsche* 'returnees' to the Reich. He thus occupied a nodal position in the planning of population displacements: on the one hand, he found himself in a position where he could profoundly change – with Heydrich's approval – the numbers of Jews and Poles destined for expulsion in the second *Nahplan*;[8] on the other hand, he was the man who negotiated transport to the General Government with the military authorities, the Ministry of Transport and the Reichsbahn.[9]

The second department of the RSHA involved in these policies was the RSHA *Amt* III B, headed by Hans Ehlich. There were many differences with Eichmann's department. The two were initially departments from the SD, but Group B remained there while Eichmann's *Referat* was incorporated into the Gestapo during the merger process. And de facto, the department of Eichmann acquired an operational dimension which Group B of the SD Inland still largely lacked. Basically, we know very little about Hans Ehlich's department. The documentary evidence is extremely fragmented and incomplete. The central archives of RSHA *Amt* III B have very probably disappeared. The only coherent and noteworthy files to speak of are in Warsaw, in the archives of the Institute of National Remembrance, where are kept the minutes of the Supreme Commission of the DVL that granted nationality, and in Moscow, in the RSHA archives (as regards just the correspondence with Himmler), and in a large number of files from the EWZ, UWZ and VOMI (which provide information at the local level).[10] This shows the documentary blur which reigns over this part of RSHA activity.[11] What emerges from this documentation, however fragmented and dispersed it may be, is that Group III B of the RSHA seems to have assumed the tasks of an organization for coordination, assessment and initiative. It set up a plan for population displacements whose evolution, at least indirectly, can be reconstructed, from the *Fernplan* to the *Generalsiedlungsplan*. It provided assessment and assistance to the government in the form of memoranda, though these had little to do with the future to be planned; and, lastly, it provided monitoring, coordination and evaluation of local policies of Germanization and control of populations, particularly in racial terms.[12]

The last central institution to have played a significant role in shaping the Nazi future brought together the SS administrative and economic departments under the leadership of General SS Oswald Pohl. It was not until December 1941 that this group of SS institutions appeared to play their part in Germanization, and it was not until February 1942 that they were unified under the leadership of Pohl to form the Main Office for the Economy and Administration (WVHA). This resulted from the merger of the general administrative and economic bodies of the SS that were until April 1939 part of the SS-HA and later became the *Hauptamt Verwaltung- und Wirtschaft* with the Central Department for Budget and Building of the Ministry of the Interior, which Pohl had previously led.

It was composed of five groups: Group A was responsible for the administration of all troops and armed formations, Group B for their financial support, Group C included all questions of real estate and building, Group D encompassed the former Concentration Camp Inspection, while Group E administered SS business as a whole.[13]

Group C, led by General SS Hans Kammler, emerged in the crucial period between December 1941 and February 1942 and became increasingly important in the nebula of institutions responsible for drawing up the Nazi plans for Utopia. Kammler's departments have left hardly any documentation on this subject. Nevertheless, the key documents help us to trace Kammler's plans, as well as some aspects of his relationship with other planning institutions.

In terms of dissimilarity, the WVHA undertook planning over a much shorter period than the two previous bodies, and in a very specific way. The fact remains, however, that it was the relations between the three organizations which set the stage for the development of the main lines of the Nazi future. In terms of analogies, the WVHA shared with the RSHA and the RKFdV the fact that it could extend its power to the local echelons, with the creation of the SS Economic Officers (*SS-Wirtschafter*) on 18 June 1942 by order of Himmler.[14]

The regional and local extensions of the SS: HSSPF and SSPF

The second type of actors in these policies of elaboration of the Nazi future combined the regional and local extensions of the SS, which controlled a more or less complete set of agencies and instruments. The most important of these were the HSSPF and the SSPF, together with several regional chiefs of the Gestapo and BdS and several local Gestapo and SD commanders (*Kommandeure der Sicherheitspolizei und des SD*, henceforth KdS). The HSSPF and SSPF were the regional and local representatives of the *Reichsführung-SS*. They held authority over all SS troops on a given territory, and this enabled them to issue orders to both the KdS and local agencies of the RSHA and the local representatives of RuSHA, VOMI or WVHA, especially since in October 1939 the two main HSSPFs of the occupied territories had been appointed local representatives of the RKFdV. The HSSPF thus played a role of relaying and coordinating the policies promoted by the centres, while defending them against civilian administrations reluctant to implement Germanization plans that soon disrupted local economies already greatly affected by war and destruction, and by economic plunder.[15]

Wilhelm Koppe in the Warthegau and Friedrich-Wilhelm Krüger in the General Government were Himmler's liegemen, disseminating the radical impulses of Heydrich and Eichmann, standing up to the objections of Greiser and Frank and sometimes negotiating the numbers and criteria of expulsion. They constituted important extensions and were one of the few permanent mechanisms of coordination between agencies sorely tempted to indulge in anticipatory competition, i.e. the propensity to distinguish themselves from rival institutions by taking the initiative in carrying out what they supposed was the boss's will.

These HSSPFs and SSPFs also developed specific tools. One example was the HSSPF general staffs for settlement in the Warthegau, whose archives have preserved numerous ethnographic and planning works, notably by Alexander Dolezalek, who headed the Planning Department in Poznań. They were branches of the HSSPF under the RKFdV, and retained significant operational importance during the whole period, in terms of planning and labour policy.[16]

This type of creation was certainly not a novelty: in the Reich, the HSSPF also had the possibility of creating ad hoc institutions to carry out precise missions and the *SS-Mannschaftshäuser* were among the institutions at the disposal of the HSSPF and SSPF. Thus Odilo Globocnik created one for the Lublin district in October 1941. These arrangements, which served to federate student militancy under the auspices of the SS and the RuSHA in the Reich, were reactivated in the occupied territories to serve the same purpose by arousing the students' fervour, but also to gather and coordinate at the local level the various representatives of the central institutions, mainly RuSHA, RKFdV and VOMI.[17]

These institutions constituted an ethno-racial knowledge applied to local conditions as apprehended by experts and racial engineers. They also played an operational role in Germanization. And they acted as relays to mitigate and regulate the inevitable conflicts of interest and rivalries in the central bodies by bringing together the experts and encouraging them to work together, pooling their resources, ideas and projects.

Local agencies and institutions: EWZ and UWZ

The third type of actors in these policies included the local agencies and institutions set up in the wake of the German victory in Poland. The EWZ and the UWZ were formed in the autumn of 1939 and throughout the incorporated territories carried out all the expulsion/resettlement operations and followed up these operations. The EWZ implemented the procedures for the selection and reception of *Volksdeutsche* from Eastern Europe by subjecting them to observation, identification and evaluation procedures, and pursued this type of activity in the transit camps in close collaboration with VOMI. The EWZ created flying commissions that assessed and classified the *volksdeutsche* and Polish families in the DVL, using a set of racial, health, social and political criteria that decisively affected the fates of whole families.

The EWZ was linked to the HSSPF and its local security bodies, directly taking some of its orders from the IdS or BdS depending on the region, but centrally the EWZ was directly controlled by Group III B of the RSHA. Although this control was common to Group III B and to the *Referat* IV D-4, it still seems that it was Hans Ehlich's departments that ran things on a daily basis.[18]

Founded at the same time as its EWZ counterpart, the UWZ was under the direct nominal control of the local KdS and the HSSPF and remained organically linked to Adolf Eichmann's RSHA *Amt* IV B-4, before being transformed from 1942 onwards into a coordination HQ for the 'final solution of the Jewish question'. These missions – in short, the expulsion of undesirables and their 'management' – emerged clearly from the 'negative dimension' of the displacements of population that was inevitable in the eyes of the Nazis. For evidence, one needs merely to look through an activity report listing the actions of the Litzmannstadt office for the month of July 1942. The date was not innocent. This was the beginning of a year of extraordinary intensification in the murder of the Jews. They are not indeed mentioned in the activity report: their expulsion and their concentration in the ghettoes, missions which in 1940–1 were the responsibility of the UWZ, were now complete, and they now lay outside its scope of activity.[19] The UWZ now operated in two areas. The traditional functions of the *Volkstumskampf*, the ethno-identity struggle against the Poles, involved 'pressurizing' (*Zusammendrängen*) the Poles by expelling them to make room for the *volksdeutsche* settlers. This was a strictly repressive and predatory mission: it consisted literally in driving the Poles away from their villages and places of residence, in confiscating as many provisions from them as possible, and in confining them to what the report itself calls the *Polenreservat* (the 'reserve' for Poles). Obviously, the paradigm of the anti-Jewish policy of 1939–40 had been transferred to the Poles. Though this was not a harbinger of the way things would eventually work out, it showed how the practices of occupation had become radicalized.

Beyond this radicalization, new tasks had been devolved to the UWZ. Instead of deportations to the General Government, it was now sending labour convoys to the Reich and carrying out major selections to fill them only with people able to work.[20] Although it was a key player in policies of occupation that were becoming ever more predatory and violent, the UWZ was only ever a marginal institution of Nazi plans: its action intervened at an earlier stage, and played a part in this 'necessary and prior evil' which was the sine qua non of Utopia.

The tableau of these institutions might seem complete, and it would be possible to conclude our account here, emphasizing the diversity of these institutions, their proliferation and the dividing lines between them, differentiating between central and local institutions, concentrated and branching institutions, planning institutions and operational institutions. It should also be noted that, in their great diversity, most of them were essentially militant Party institutions, all or almost all under the control of the SS and its principal dignitaries, Himmler, Heydrich, Pohl and Greifelt. This observation, though not inaccurate, would, however, be incomplete; and in order to render the details of the narrative plot as accurately as possible, we must take into account one last category of actors that, as we have seen, intervened indirectly: the civilian administrations of the occupied and incorporated territories.[21]

Civilian administrations of incorporated and occupied territories

These civilian administrations are now relatively well known thanks to recent work on their role in anti-Jewish policies.[22] They were of two types, depending on whether they were set up in incorporated territories and thus built on the model of the civilian administrations of the Reich, or, like the General Government of Poland or the *Reichskommissariats*, they were entities created ex nihilo to administer Congress Poland and the Soviet territories from 1941 onwards.

In the Warthegau, civilian institutions were spread over a very dense administrative network, from large urban centres to small rural towns and villages. Undoubtedly the greater part of this mesh had only a distant relation with the building of the Nazi future, but the great spatial cohesion was echoed by a great thematic coherence: probably nowhere else in the East did civilian institutions concentrate so many means into the administration of occupied territories. Among the institutions most involved in the development of the Nazi future were the general departments of civil administration, the 'Health and Population' department and the 'Economy and Labour' department.[23] However, they were in the forefront only when it came to the day-to-day management of populations and therefore had only an operational capacity at a later stage of the implementation of these policies, which reduced their importance. The East, as we shall see, was indeed the space of the Nazi future, but the civilian administrations thought of it in the present, as a place for action.

The situation differed in the unincorporated territories with civilian administrations of occupation: they were chronically under-administered and sometimes suffered from a drastic lack of personnel. Also, the 'colonial' or frontier dimension of the occupation was felt to be more important: in the General Government, a significant part of the German civilian administration personnel were freebooters who had had run-ins with the law. The mix of people in these administrations is rather difficult to characterize: they were neither the administrative elite nor the 'dustbin' of German administrations, but a heterogeneous gathering resulting from a negative selection which meant that these entities had little to do with the traditional Prussian administration.[24]

On the quantitative level, 1,218 civilian servants administered the central organs of the General Government in 1940 and practically 2,000 in 1944. The number remained relatively stable throughout the period, and one has to realize that most of these officials had nothing to do with the Germanization policies which the General Government was supposed to implement.[25]

Nevertheless, these civilian administrations formed the last category of institutional actors involved in shaping the policies of Germanization and the destinies of the occupied territories. They did not, of course, have the central importance that certain agencies of the SS assumed; their role was, of course, contingent or even marginal; but their presence did play a significant role in the evolution of the practices we are observing.

It was the interaction between the various elements of this institutional nebula which imprinted on the plans for Utopia the form and the evolution which they assumed in the general context of the war years thanks to the establishment of successive consensuses between these different actors.

How consensus was generated

Between November 1939 and the summer of 1941, the institutions preparing for the future of Germany built a consensus, the heart of which was that this future would involve significant spatial expansion to the East, via the integration of ever more territories resulting from the conquest of Poland first, and the Baltic states and the USSR afterwards. This expansion of space created the framework in which policies of Germanization – i.e. appropriation – were to be implemented, consisting on the one hand of 'promoting' the presence of racially desired populations and, on the other, of getting rid (in various different ways) of 'unwanted' populations. Expressed in this way, the Nazi dream acquired contours and objectives which, in the view of the officials and activists responsible for it, needed to be given substance, a content, and clearly defined stages.

This was precisely what the RSHA attempted to do in November 1939 with the *Fernplan Ost*. This document, just a few pages long, sets out the 'long-term' objectives of population displacement policies in incorporated Poland. This text is difficult to date precisely, but it is certain that it was contemporary with a telegram sent by Heydrich to the HSSPFs of the Warthegau and the General Government on 28 November 1939 in which he announced that the deportation projects discussed before were now to be synthesized and coordinated in a plan in two parts: a long-term plan and a short-term plan.[26] The RSHA intervened as a coordinator of the expulsions implemented by its local relays, the KdS, the IdS and the specialized agencies, but it also assumed a role of investigation in racial policy and population control. As such, it was empowered to provide population numbers. The *Fernplan Ost* took particular care to reinforce this legitimacy by indicating that reliable figures were not yet available and mentioned the census to be carried out by the institutions at the end of December 1939. From the materials available, however, the plan says that it was possible to acquire a tentative picture of what might be called the 'ethnic situation', and the census should not fundamentally affect these first impressions.[27]

The RSHA experts then continued by assigning to the occupation policy the objective of 'de-colonizing and de-judaizing' the new territories in several stages in order to avoid adverse consequences for the local economy. And the plan defined a six-step process for the Germanization of incorporated territories. It was very clearly conceived as a guideline which must then be worked out in the *Nahpläne*, which involved assigning numerical data and time limits. If the *Fernplan* remained vague, the *Nahpläne* reflected a sudden acceleration. It should be remembered that the first *Nahplan* provided for the expulsion of some 80,000 Jews and that the first version of the second *Nahplan* totalled 220,000 deportations, which was suddenly increased by Heydrich and Eichmann to 600,000. This could perhaps be seen as a dysfunction, of a type familiar to functionalists, between two offices of the same state entity locked in a struggle for the acquisition of new prerogatives.[28] However, in the longer term, the evolution of the figures reflects a 'negotiation' between the entities concerned, and the plan drawn up by the RKFdV in January 1940 – less than two months later – seems emblematic of this state of affairs: in the *Fernplan*, the *Zwischenplan* and the second *Nahplan*, and in Meyer-Heitling's 'Principles of Planning for the Building of the Eastern Territories', the key figure for the evacuation of Jews was almost the same: 560,000 Jews were to be evacuated 'this winter' according to the RKFdV.[29] Beyond questions of rivalry and institutional competition, numerical data and other information about populations were indeed circulating from one agency to another and a first consensus between the actors elaborating these policies was emerging, a consensus expressed by *Fernplan Ost* in the process of Germanization it depicts.

Meyer-Heitling's plan came at a time when clarification of the strategic objectives that the practitioners had set themselves became a necessity, pursued by the central echelons – Heydrich and Eichmann in the first place – and the regional echelons: on 20 January 1940, Wilhelm Koppe published an order redefining all the quantitative objectives and ordering the different protagonists to prepare to resume evacuations of the Jews in the General Government.[30]

This is only one emblematic example of the vagueness and chaos that historians of the population displacements and the Nazi state have rightly noted. The fact remains that in the somewhat longer term (it is out of the question to speak of long-term policies when their implementation would be confined to less then a decade) these were what Götz Aly has called 'minimal consensuses',[31] imposed successively on every sudden transformation in the horizons of expectation of the social engineers responsible for developing the Nazi dream.

Beyond these temporary consensuses, however, there was one that had assumed more permanent form since the *Fernplan Ost* in 1939 and constituted such an unquestioned foundation that it became the unconscious basis of all the policies of Germanization and plans for the Nazi future. And it is well worth quoting from it at some length:

(1) First, Jews and Poles appearing as politically dominant must be expelled to the General Government (obligatory service for 18–60-year-olds).
(2) Poles living in the occupied territories must be subject to racial investigation.
(3) The Reich's labour needs must serve to weaken Polishness by depriving it of racially valuable Poles who can serve in the Reich over time. This selection must also take place in the General Government.
(4) A skilled labour force, from trained workers to craftsmen, postal workers, building workers, etc., when they are of good racial quality and well-assimilated, must be gradually replaced by labour coming from the Reich.
(5) To a certain extent, the Eastern provinces may retain a Polish labouring stratum for subordinate service in the agricultural and industrial sectors.
(6) Poles of no use to the Reich and the Eastern provinces are to be expelled to the General Government.[32]

These were the guiding principles of all the social and racial engineering agencies. They included the displacement of the population as a tool for the control of the German racial heritage, as a tool for the plunder of territories and the productive apparatuses, and as a prerequisite for the building of the harmonious society latent inside the utopian realm. They also involved the neutralization or even the elimination of the cultivated classes of the non-native populations as a prerequisite for their supervision, which would precede their 'dissimilation'.

Here, then, there was a set of structures that were the basis of a con-sensus between all agencies and were no longer up for discussion. The *Nahpläne*, for their part, consisted of a tool for sequencing the process and setting out the requisite stages – a tool which mirrored (or refracted) negotiations between the protagonists, social engineers, practitioners of *Umsiedlung* (displacement of populations, both expulsion and settlement), civilian administrations of departure and destination, and central agen-cies. An intermediate stratum finally existed, as expressed in point (6) of the text just quoted: the question of the basic geographical framework for planning was changing in such clear and important ways that it led to revision of this prerequisite for the Nazi future. And this framework was less immobile and structural than the consensus that took ethnic cleans-ing as an indisputable given, though it was much more reliable than the endless round of figures and quantities that became ever more radical.

The structure of the Nazi consensus was thus constructed somewhat like Braudel's temporality. Deep down, as a basis, there was a fundamen-tal agreement between all the actors which made plunder, the violent neutralization of the alien cultured elites, as well as the displacement of racially *differentiated* populations[33] and ethnic cleansing, an almost unquestionable set of methods for appropriating a space perceived as the framework for the fulfilment of the Nazi Utopia. An intermediary 'layer' – a stratum, perhaps? – embraced the exact spatial framework of this future and underwent modifications that were few in number (three, four at the most) but decisive in changing the dimension of the plans. And finally, on the surface, there was the merry-go-round of plans and statistics or, perhaps, of practically continuous renegotiations: the impression of sta-bility or final a posteriori definition gelled only at the very beginning of 1943, i.e. at the very moment when these futures lost their sharpness in the eyes of Nazi dreamers.

Thus the different states of Nazi planning were structured: the 'meth-odological' basis of Germanization, made up of expulsions, ethnic cleansing and the repression of elites, was never discussed between the SS agencies in charge of this file. The different transformations in the geographical framework of this planning resulted from decisions taken at the very top of the hierarchy, from meetings between such men as Hitler, Himmler, Heydrich and his subordinates, Greifelt, HSSPFs and the most eminent regional officials: Hans Frank, the proconsul of the General Government, the *Reichskommissaren* Kube and Koch for Ostland and Ukraine, the *Gauleiter* Greiser, von Schirach and – again – Koch for the incorporated Polish or Austrian territories. An initial decision by Hitler triggered the process of Germanization of the Polish territories – having initially been envisaged at the European level; it was formalized in a speech in the Reichstag on 6 October 1939.[34] A second decision, circulated on 21 June 1941 in a directive from Himmler to Meyer-Heitling, made the General Government an immediately Germanizable territory and a land of the Nazi future.[35] It was made official two days after a meeting between Hitler and Frank which had seen the latter entrusted with the task of ridding the territory of its Jews;[36] it resulted in the drafting of the second *Generalplan Ost* of the RKFdV. A third decision, which took place on 2 February 1942, thirteen days after the Wannsee interminister-ial conference – in which Eichmann participated, as did Hofmann, head of the RuSHA[37] – endorsed the extension of the plan to the regions of Leningrad, Crimea and Ukraine.[38] Finally, what appears to have been a final decision to bring the plan to its pinnacle seems to have been a broadcast by Himmler on 16 September 1942 which looked forward to fruition within twenty years and imagined broad horizons for a Nazi future in the Urals and the Caucasus.[39] As can be seen, these announcements reflected structural decisions which always involved the highest authorities in the Berlin centre and the most powerful regional authorities, and were promoted by the upper levels of the SS, ostentatiously supported by the Führer. The centre imposed its will, invariably. In rare cases, it pushed things forward with great suddenness; more often, it endorsed the plans; and sometimes, it settled ongoing debates.

But the centre was not just Nazi policy and decision. It was also assessment; the development and circulation of consensuses between the various agencies, between rivalry and collaborative work, in the service of planning.

No fewer than eleven plans for long-term Germanization succeeded each other between the end of 1939 and the beginning of 1943; eleven plans coming from three administrations – the RSHA, the RKFdV and the WVHA – whose frequent contacts are at least partially documented.[40] These plans are difficult to compare because they reflect the geographi-cal extension of Poland incorporated into Eastern Europe as a whole and because these agencies did not share unified criteria: the figures given in the documents vary widely, often due to differences in approach or cat-egorization. Only two categories of figures can be (in part) studied. First, the figures of the Jewish populations present in the territories concerned, which can be traced from the *Fernplan* included in the RSHA plan, com-mented on by Erhard Wetzel in April 1942, via the first two *Generalpläne Ost* of the RKFdV, show that the RKFdV was drawing on the numbers indicated by the RSHA, even though the last two plans implied only the figures mentioned by Eichmann in the Madagascar Plan and then at the Wannsee Conference.

The second set of figures involves the number of migrants, which remained highly stable throughout the planning period, with less than 20 per cent of variation in the numbers projected between July 1941 and the beginning of 1943. The plans thus reckoned on 4.55 million migrants at the disposal of the installation operations, which became 4.84 million in the General Plan of the RKFdV of spring 1942 and 5.5 in the *Generalsiedlungsplan* of early 1943.

What can we learn from these two series of figures and their evolution?

The manufacture of statistical knowledge is, as we know, one of the keys to state power, and more so in Germany than elsewhere in Europe. The demographic data for Jews were aggregated by Eichmann's men and formed the basis of the work of the SS agencies until 1943, when Richard Korherr was given the task of compiling aggregate figures for Jewish population numbers.[41] No doubt this first point needs to be qualified: the plans of the RKFdV and the WVHA do not mention the Jews, their 'evacuation' being invariably a prerequisite for planning. While it can be said here that the RSHA had the initiative, it was very limited. The same applies to the number of migrants: the RSHA relied on the statistics of the EWZ and the RSHA *Amt* III B, but the fixed figures, far from reflecting the initiative of the repressive organizations, probably illustrate more clearly how the available migrant numbers were initially extremely low. The figures did not change because nothing happened that could modify them, and not because the agency that produced them remained the most dynamic.

It is this fact that encourages us to remain cautious in the examination of consensuses and to discern a hierarchy between the agencies. Some actors doubtless did just this as these plans were circulating, such as Erhard Wetzel, the *Rassenreferent* of the Ministry for Occupied Territories, who pointed out in several documents that he considered the RSHA – and in particular *Referat* III B headed by Hans Ehlich – to be the initiating and dominant institution of the *Generalpläne Ost*.[42] Wetzel was an observer of note: he was a high-ranking official in the ministerial hierarchies and had direct responsibilities with all the parties involved from 1939 onwards.[43]

In support of Wetzel's diagnosis, therefore, the fact that Meyer-Heitling and the RKFdV drew on the figures of the *Fernplan Ost* of the RSHA in the plan of the first half of 1940 – called the 'First *Generalplan Ost*' – and that the key numbers of migrants and Jewish populations were also drawn from the departments of Eichmann or Ehlich suggests there was a certain preponderance of the RSHA at least for the period up to the summer of 1942. This first statement must, however, be qualified because the planning of the WVHA in December 1941 and March 1942 had absolutely nothing to do with the RSHA; and, in the second place, Eichmann's office was almost completely indifferent to questions of Germanization, dealing only with the plans for the deportation of Jews from January 1942.[44] In other words, if the RSHA was ever dominant at the central level, this applied between the autumn of 1939 and the end of 1941 or the beginning of 1942, and was confined to a stand-off between the RSHA and the RKFdV.

The fact remains, however, that a certain number of consensuses were actually established between these different institutions and that the succession of plans was *also* a succession of more or less formulated agreements: the key population figures were established, rather, by the RSHA, and used by Meyer-Heitling and the RKFdV, which, from the end of January 1942 onwards, endeavoured to synchronize its work with the nascent WVHA under the impetus of Himmler, who was particularly active in drawing up plans for the East at the beginning of 1942.

Immediately noticeable is the very close synchronization between the 'final solution of the Jewish question' by direct extermination which had been fully set in motion with the Wannsee Conference of 20 January 1942,[45] the quantifying effort resulting from the requirement of the *Reichsführer* having created the WVHA on 1 February 1942,[46] and a new utopian impulse represented by the instructions given by Himmler the next day to Meyer-Heitling, ordering him to extend the *Generalplan Ost* geographically.[47]

One could practically conclude that there was *systemic interference* generated by the three institutions here. As in quantum physics, three systems theoretically independent in their behaviour – the RSHA and its policing, logistical and genocidal activities, the RKFdV and Germanization, and the WVHA and building – exhibited evolutionary congruences and interdependencies of such a kind as to form in reality one single system comprising these three objects: this 'third system' – with 'system' also being understood in the quantum sense – was that of the Nazi advent, definitively institutionalized in three complementary dimensions that never merged but refracted each other in three very different plans.

Forms and thoughts of the future in the East: the three main general plans

Three radically different thoughts, three 'institutional cultures', are expressed in three large documentary ensembles that allow the historian of the Nazi imaginary to explore the paths followed by the SS's fervent dreams for the future.

The RSHA plans

The first of the plans was the one drawn up by the RSHA. It is also the one whose documentary posterity and nomenclature are the most difficult to determine. The *Fernplan Ost* was found by Götz Aly and Karl Heinz Roth only in the early 1990s and published in 1997. In addition, we only have partial *Nahpläne*. Next came a *Generalplan Ost* of the RSHA probably dating from the end of 1941 or the beginning of 1942, of which we have only an indirect version in the memorandum already quoted where the *Rassenreferent* of the Ministry for Occupied Territories, Erhard Wetzel, voiced his thoughts on the content of this planning; then a *Gesamtplan Ost* of the RSHA of which only one mention in a letter has come to our knowledge.[48] Finally, we have taken the initiative to consider as a final version of the RSHA's plans a set of documents dating from December 1942 to February 1943, and composed of a lecture by Hans Ehlich, the leader of Group III B of the RSHA, delivered on 11 December 1942 in Salzburg,[49] and notes by Hermann Krumey, head of the Łódź UWZ, at a conference of this same Group III B for its regional leaders on 1–2 February 1943.[50] In other words, if the archival basis on which we work is both limited and difficult to interpret, it does give us an indirect view of the full extent of the activity.

It can be combined with the second plan developed by the RSHA, which concerned the Jewish population alone – as in the Madagascar Plan and the statistics from the Wannsee Conference – and we then have a much richer range of documents, while still maintaining a marked thematic unity, as one might hope for given the intricacy involved.

These plans are not very long: the one that Erhard Wetzel had access to is no more than twelve pages long, the *Fernplan* has nine pages. Hans Ehlich's presentation to the National Socialist students and the notes taken by Hermann Krumey in Bernau at the symposium of the heads of *Amt* III B of the local SD offices total about twenty sheets.

It is necessary to realize that the succinct character of the documentation is a trademark of the RSHA and in particular of *Amt* III B. The Madagascar Plan barely goes beyond fifteen pages,[51] just like the Protocol of the Wannsee Conference, also fifteen pages long, two of them devoted to the discussions which followed Heydrich's speech.[52]

So it is therefore a relatively small volume of documentation that was produced by the security organs of the Third Reich. Its essential purpose was racial and demographic. It includes key selection statistics and assessments of the capacity for Germanization or assimilation/dissimilation, and essentially involves aggregates of statistic data. There is nothing very surprising about this: the inquisitorial and security logics that were deployed by the SD and the Gestapo undoubtedly conditioned the form of the documents presented here. The RSHA relied on what it practised and knew best throughout the period in which it produced these plans: population control. The *Fernplan* was written a few days before the carrying out of a major census of the population of the occupied territories. Eichmann, acting with the Zentralstelle für Judische Auswanderung (Central Office for Jewish Emigration), had in 1938 inaugurated the registration of Jewish populations and then, at the end of 1939, practices for racial evaluation and census. It was the techniques of population governance that made up the basis of RSHA planning. Beyond descriptions of the practices and methods of Germanization (assimilation, dissimilation, displacement, deportation and physical elimination) which sometimes appear explicitly in the documentation, one could hardly ask this group for more details on Nazi representations of the future. Of course, other documentary collections may prove useful in examining the contents of these representations – memoranda, correspondence, messages, preparations for exhibitions(s), press kits and so on – but they do not constitute the main active contribution made by the RSHA to the Nazi preparation for the future.

What *can* be asked of this documentation, on the other hand, is to give us very precise information on two points: first, on the status and scope of these 'solutions to the Jewish question', which seem to be (aside from the diversity of their content and sequencing) the prerequisite for any Germanization; and, second, on the scales on which policies of ethnic cleansing would have to be carried out in order to achieve a second prerequisite for the Nazi future, i.e. demographic domination over a territory whose expansion was also evident from September 1939 to 1942.

The WVHA memoranda

The second type of planning consists of the two memoranda produced by Hans Kammler. These documents are still very short, less than half a dozen pages each. They are difficult to compare with those of the RSHA because their views are essentially quantitative and attempt to plan the financial and human needs of the various post-war SS building programmes.[53]

This planning took place at the crucial moment between December 1941 and 10 February 1942 when a 'final solution of the Jewish question' in Europe by direct extermination and a definitive enlargement of the Germanization zones was probably formulated, changing the scale of the Nazi future by giving it a literally European framework. However, few details of these developments can be found in the two WVHA memoranda, which are symptomatic rather than indicative. They are not very eloquent, as they were written by engineers and technocrats accustomed to figures, accounting and engineering techniques. In short, their version of the Nazi dream was a matter of presenting a quote.

This explains why we cannot ask them for any vivid or precise images. These were essentially plans that followed a spatial and institutional logic – a map is attached to the plan – and this organization somewhat obscures the purpose: this merely quantified vision of what each institution (*Waffen-SS*, police and 'special missions') was planning for the area concerned was highly abstract. True, this was only part of the planned projects, as 'the enormous projects that we [the *SS-Führung*] have devised for the *Waffen-SS*, the general SS and the police have not yet been quantified', as Himmler wrote in his reply of 31 January 1942.[54]

This indicates both the fairly mediocre quality of this first document and its inadequacy when it comes to our quest for the Nazi future. Nevertheless, it is an indication that a rational, quantified and all-embracing approach to Utopia as dictated by accountancy criteria was then implemented by the SS and the WVHA. On 10 February 1942 Hans Kammler addressed a second memorandum to Himmler, which broadened the temporal horizons and sought to define the institutional frameworks in which these huge projects would take place, taking up the existing frameworks – the building battalions (*Baubataillonen*) – and integrating them into SS building brigades (*SS-Baubrigaden*) that were to be the units for the implementation of the planned projects. Finally, this second memorandum tackled head-on the issue of manpower and stipulated that its inadequacy made any realization problematic.[55] Finally, there was a final document, a letter dated July 1943, sent by Hans Kammler to the Unruh general staff, mentioning the post-war building programme in connection with the labour census and mobilization issues, in the total war effort now being carried out by the WVHA in the present, an effort that (as it were) replaced thinking about the future at some date between January and July 1943.

As can be seen, the two WVHA memoranda constitute a technocratic, quantitative and purely financial version of Utopia, and allow us to imagine it very vividly, while giving a valuable overview of the issues raised both by the prospect of its implementation, and by the disappearance of this prospect and the evaporation of the forms of representation of the Nazi Utopia.

Planning the RKFdV

Finally, the planning implemented by the RKFdV must be tackled. It was the most important, numerically, with four plans listed. These plans are distinguished from the other two piles of documents by their magnitude: what is called '*Generalplan Ost* no. 1', i.e. the 'Planning Principles for the Building of the Eastern Territories' produced at the beginning of 1940 by the departments of Konrad Meyer-Heitling, is about twenty sheets long, and is the smallest document delivered by the agricultural geographer and his subordinates.[56] The second *Generalplan Ost*, dated July 1941, is only indirectly known to us through the autobiography of Meyer-Heitling, and it is very difficult to know what material form it took.[57] The third *Generalplan Ost* has survived in its entirety and has seventy-one pages combining text and summary tables of the means and resources to be implemented. As regards the *Generalsiedlungsplan*, dating back to the end of 1942,[58] our documentation is again incomplete. We have fragments of the plan, as well as a draft table of contents without pagination and about twenty pages of statistics.[59]

The great care taken in drafting and the detail of the subjects tackled, ranging from agricultural and urban surface areas to anticipating the numbers of migrants via questions of workforce, give us a much clearer outline of the Nazi future as the experts of the RKFdV conceived it. On the one hand this is because the plans were much more detailed than those of the competing agencies and on the other hand because the RKFdV was the SS institution which had been entrusted with an overall approach to the problems of colonization and development. As an aggregate of specialists from a variety of institutional backgrounds all gathered into one of those ad hoc institutions that the Nazis liked, the RKFdV was the only institution that thought of the East, Germanization and the Nazi utopian future in and for themselves. Its archives are rich in documents enabling us both to trace the evolutions of the Nazi dream and to gain an overview of the experience of those who were led to work there. The archives of the

RKFdV – so long as we do not neglect those of the VOMI or the EWZ – are likely to help us understand the springs of the fervour generated by the Nazi feeling that Utopia was nigh.[60] Maps, graphic representations, works by architects, town planners and rural geographers, reports by SS raciologists and demographers give form and content to the advent of the *Tausendjähriges Reich* announced by the plans, an advent whose first fruits the actors strongly felt they were experiencing between the autumn of 1939 and the first half of 1943.

The institutional constellation that determined the evolution of the Nazi future has thus appeared to us in all its profusion: central institutions and local actors and practitioners interacted to create a complex object resulting from the interaction of three dynamics. Utopian tension was combined with the inquisitorial logic of control and the shaping of populations and with a quantitative managerial effort to produce a set of roundabout, sometimes contradictory plans and policies structured in three strata. First, there was a remarkably stable basis, crystallizing a consensus among all the actors designating the control, selection and displacement of populations as the main tool and sine qua non of Germanization, the heart of the Nazi utopian project. Constructed on this substrate, a second dimension, which developed in a more uneven way, assigned to Germanization increasingly gigantic areas that, in 1943, extended practically from the North Sea to the Caucasus and the Urals and from the Arctic Polar Circle to the Meuse or the Adriatic, endowing it (though this is still a hypothesis) with a powerful magnetism in the eyes of the actors in charge of it. It was within this two-dimensional framework that the game of polycracy and cumulative radicalization between the different institutions took place, in a mixture of rivalry and overbidding, but also of collaboration and the circulation of information, particularly statistical information. While it is possible to conclude that the RSHA dominated the other actors during the few months of the winter of 1941 and the spring of 1942, this predominance remained limited: on the documentary level, the RKFdV was the only institution for which the thought of the realization of the Nazi future constituted an object in itself, an object which went beyond statistics and which embraced the social frameworks and the space and time of this society of the *Tausendjähriges Reich* which constituted the promise of the National Socialists' reign.

Chapter 2

Networks and trajectories of the men of the East

In institutions, men find their niches. Men – that is, individuals, social groups and networks. However, this misleading cliché must be treated with suspicion right from the start, even in its most cautious form, which emphasizes the individuals, the groups which form them and the bonds which unite them. First of all, were the 'men of the East' really in their vast majority men? Other examples, in particular those of the *Einsatzgruppen* of the *Sicherheitspolizei* sent out during the invasion of Barbarossa, suggest that we need to be cautious: the presence of female secretaries and technicians was, if not a majority, at least relatively huge.[1]

Thus, we must first try to make an overall assessment of this 'world in itself', the cohort of Germans both female and male sent to the East to work for the future that seemed to be dawning there.

'Men' of the East? A world in itself

Attempting to measure the commitment or involvement of individuals and social groups in Nazi utopian dreams and action is not as simple as one might think. Nazi Germany, a bureaucratic state accustomed to counting its numbers and managing them in a 'modern' way, still did not always leave rigorous records of all the agencies and institutions involved. Nothing stops us undertaking the process while being aware that this will only lead to the establishment of orders of magnitude, and that it is advisable to move from the certain to the less certain.

What is certain concerns the central authorities of Berlin, whose records are often better preserved. It is known that in December 1939 the staff of the RKFdV comprised no more than twenty-nine people.[2] Their job was to take charge of all Germanization and population displacement policies, to coordinate them at European level and to draw strategic guidelines for them. Of course, these numbers are those of the misty time of its foundation. The RKFdV, at the time when Nazi hopes were at a high, was a flourishing institution with more than a hundred collaborators,[3] and

Isabel Heinemann estimates that 500 experts were involved in population displacement and racial assessment policies applied by the RKFdV, the RuSHA and the various central or local agencies in the incorporated territories.[4] As well as these racial experts there were, on the one hand, town planners, agrarians and agronomists, architects and resettlement specialists, and, on the other, logisticians and members of the police responsible for missions of protection and constraint that inexorably accompanied the programmes in question. Without counting the possible regiments or battalions of police officers, we will limit ourselves to estimating some hundred or so additional persons.[5]

Then we have to take into account the actors of the other institutions. As far as the RSHA is concerned, this is relatively easy: the organizational charts and various directories make it possible to draw a relatively clear picture of the offices involved in Germanization. About 40 employees of the RSHA *Amt* IV B-4, in addition to the 15 employees of the RSHA *Amt* III B6,[6] formed an initial group of 55 officials. The local *Judenreferents* and the local leaders of Group III B need to be added: if we count one official from each of the two groups for the 11 internal constituencies in the Reich, plus the 48 regional or local offices of the SD,[7] we have a minimum of 120 people.

There remains a fringe element, difficult to assess: this comprises the civil administrations of the occupied and incorporated territories, which were probably rather large at local level.[8] The civil administrations of the Warthegau, the Gau of Danzig, Upper Silesia and East Prussia, as well as that of the General Government, were involved in the policies of bringing about the advent of racial Utopia, but we do not have reliable and specific estimates for the number of departments that may have participated. Let's say that 1 per cent of the civil servants – one can hardly imagine fewer – were actors of these policies, so at least 60 people need to be added.

Finally, if we include the 56 SS officers and the 210 NCOs of Hans Kammler's 'Central Department for Budget and Building' at the WVHA,[9] we will have a clear, if not accurate, view of the men involved in the institutions responsible for planning the Nazi future. In all, around one thousand SS officers and NCOs, civil servants of a median or superior rank, were involved in the planning and practices of Germanization.[10]

To conclude from this state of affairs that Germanization and the Nazi future remained to the very end the prerogative of a dreamy elite concentrated in the very Nordic SS and some minority and marginalized offices of the Third Reich is a little premature. First, the relatively massive presence of the RSHA and the WVHA illustrates the fact that these policies were one of the cornerstones of SS activity, even if the RKFdV and RuSHA were disregarded;[11] on the other hand, it was certainly an active and decisive cornerstone, but there were other institutions, other actors who sent personnel on a much bigger scale than the SS or civil administrations that were chronically understaffed; and these institutions provided the first inklings that the embryonic Nazi plans for Utopia could be realized, thus constituting (this is one hypothesis) a vector for the spreading of the fervour which this state of affairs generated in the experiences of the actors.

Elizabeth Harvey, in her fine study of women as actors and witnesses of Nazi Germanization policies, has shown that the engagement of large contingents of women was rooted in an earlier cultural and political militancy that predated the seizure of power. According to her, the *Bund Deutscher Mädel* (BDM or League of German Girls) set up a programme for sending out activists in the summer of 1940, involving almost 3,500 people in 1941 alone. In 1943, 1,027 young women were sent to the East for long periods while 2,683 short stays were also organized. Even though rural service never became a mass movement, no fewer than 13,000 women from the Labour Service came to perform part of their service in the occupied territories.[12]

Add to this that the *NS-Studentenführung* also set up a 'student action' which resulted in the sending of several hundred students, male and female, to the occupied territories between 1940 and 1944, with for example 2,000 students in the Warthegau in 1940, 1,200 in 1941 and 2,500 in 1942.[13] Again this figure concerns the Warthegau alone and leaves out Silesia, Danzig, Eastern and West Prussia, as well as the unincorporated occupied territories, the General Government and Galicia, even though there were many camps of *Volksdeutsche*. Again, the estimate of 6,000 students involved does not appear unreasonable.

Thus, in all, we can say there were at least 27,400 people[14] who, mainly in the Eastern occupied territories, actively sought to bring about the Nazi dream, and whose activities gave it some shape between 1939 and 1944–5. By way of illustration, 100,000 individuals are generally considered to have participated in the criminal policies of the Third Reich.[15] The numbers meant to bring about the advent of Utopia certainly fell far below those who carried out the killings; the fact remains that they are not negligible. They constitute an indication of the efforts made by the Third Reich, and doubtless by German society too, to build what they considered to be the future of Germany. Does the very high degree of diversity of situations and backgrounds of these people make this group a world in itself?

From the generational point of view, it is possible to outline the group, paradoxically, by denying its specificity: the age classes represented are those of the original groups and if the *Kriegsjugendgeneration*, the generation of the children of the Great War, is clearly dominant in the positions of responsibility of the various agencies (and in particular in the SS agencies) the youngest cohorts are the most numerous, if only because of the weight of actions performed by students and young people, who made a big contribution to the workforce. The compulsory nature of a number of practices linked to the *Osteinsatz* also reduced the major social characteristics that could affect the group. While some form of conscription led to the departure of most of the protagonists on the *Osteinsatz*, and even if one is aware of the fact that there were ways of wriggling out, we cannot fail to see this as a sample of German society, excluding children and old men.

The group of theoreticians and practitioners of population displacements was overwhelmingly composed of members of the repressive apparatus of the Third Reich and of SS officers or NCOs. As such, they were members of militant organizations. While their transfer to the East did not generally take place on a voluntary basis, it cannot be regarded as a form of coercion exerted on them. The journey to the East took on characteristics similar to those of a civil servant's or soldier's mission, and was, as we shall see later, a form of militancy. In terms of social characteristics, there was an excessive number of young graduates socialized in universities undergoing Nazification between the wars and trained in human and social sciences, law or medicine in this particular framework, thus combining the internalization of Nazi belief and careful academic training.[16] The presence of all the major institutions of the 'Black Corps' explains why this group's profile is in line with the sociology of the SS,[17] though we cannot characterize its members more precisely: there were many engineers in the WVHA, EWZ, RKFdV and VOMI, many lawyers in the Gestapo and specialists in the humanities and social sciences in the RKFdV and RSHA. Altogether, virtually all academic backgrounds were represented, with the exception of the basic and applied experimental sciences.

This elite and militant dimension was reinforced by the presence of some 6,000 students of the *NS-Studentenführung*. It may have led to a relative under-representation of rural and low-skilled populations. But this proposal must be taken with caution: almost half of the individuals involved in this *Osteinsatz* (13,000 out of 27,400) were women sent under the *Arbeitsdienst*, a form of labour conscription, an additional argument in favour of the group's relative social indeterminacy and its representativeness of the whole social spectrum of German society.

This was, in sum, a cohort whose mixed nature cannot be doubted (it probably achieved parity), and whose social composition makes it representative of the society of the Third Reich: it also makes sense given its functions. This set of actors was composed of officers and officials whose job was to administer, expel, welcome, assess and repress; of students and young activists who were to teach, run camps, nurseries and organized holidays, and be responsible for short assessment reports and brief internships; and of women who worked in the household, child care and social work. Indeed, it was a group of actors whose heterogeneity made it a world in itself.

It is this heterogeneity that we must finally investigate. In my view, it stems from the fact that the *Osteinsatz* assembled, if not massive contingents of the German population, at least a representative sample of its social spectrum.

In the second place, this heterogeneity, which emerges in the enumeration of the actors and practices of Germanization and in the improbable connection between what some actors themselves called a 'positive side' and a 'negative side' of the Nazi Utopia, also says something about the *Osteinsatz*, as we shall see later on.[18]

Professional networks and military networks

The human nebula that appears here is structured by networks of three kinds: academic, professional and militant.

Numerous studies have highlighted the existence of a few key university centres which played a fundamental role in guiding young elites towards the institutions of Utopia.[19] The approach, here, is regressive: it is by taking an interest in the paths that led these men to the EWZ, the UWZ or the RKFdV that these centres are identified and the contours of these networks drawn. It is often difficult to go beyond this simple mapping. It is rare for actors to have left more convincing traces that would help to describe the connections that structure these networks. But this rebuilding, however rudimentary, contributes to displaying the structures that presided over the paths of these men towards, and within, the institutions of the Nazi past, and to characterize the steps that led them to it.

When we survey the biographies of those responsible for Germanization in the SD, we are struck by the way a number of university centres were shared by large contingents of actors.

The University of Tübingen was attended by many young officers of the SD who then became the practitioners of the policies of Germanization. Albert Rapp, head of the SD in Poznań, Martin Sandberger, head of the EWZ, Gustav Adolf Scheel, *Reichsstudentenführer* and responsible for the *Osteinsatz* of students of the NSDStB,[20] Erich Ehrlinger, future Weißrußland BdS, and Ernst Weinmann, future head of population displacements in Serbia, all attended this prestigious Swabian University between 1931 and 1935 before entering the SD in Stuttgart and joining the Berlin HQ and then embarking on ground-level work during the war.[21] Their activism was embodied in the corporatist student organizations, in the NSDStB and in the SA, in what Michael Wildt calls 'revolutionary militancy'.[22]

Nothing here suggests that these men had developed specific skills which prepared them for the tasks they assumed in these policies. Their academic backgrounds and their training were very disparate. And while Ehrlinger and Sandberger definitely knew each other,[23] Weinmann was trained in odontology and probably had contact with the others only through the *Studentenschaft*. There were many lawyers: Ehrlinger, Rapp and Sandberger all came from a background in law.

The second university that played an important role in the structuring of the group we are studying was Leipzig. This was a frontier university, like Bonn and Königsberg. A semi-clandestine activism, at the very least, developed there in which many future SS officers assigned to Germanization policies distinguished themselves. While Hans Ehlich came from Leipzig, there is no trace of his having participated in this dimension of Nazi student militancy. He was a medical student, particularly interested in the issue of racial hygiene and eugenics. He became head of the forerunner of the RSHA *Amt* III B after working in the institutions controlling health policy after the Nazis took power, becoming medical expert for the Ministry of the Interior of Saxony in 1936.[24] His subordinate, Heinz Hummitzsch, also came from the University of Leipzig and mentions in his short official biography his involvement in border activism. Rolf-Heinz Höppner, the head of the UWZ in Poznań, also went on to study in Leipzig and joined the SD.[25] Other future SS officers such as Heinz Gräfe – responsible for the Zeppelin operations of RSHA *Amt* VI[26] – and Wilhelm Spengler – later head of the SD Inland culture department – engaged in this type of activity but did not always immediately join the Saxon NSDStB; nor did they always later have anything to do with Germanization policies. The two latter men, however, were at that time very close to Erhard Mäding, with whom they formed a kind of clandestine student fraternity; in 1941–2, he became one of the editors of the *Generalsiedlungsplan* RKFdV.[27]

Other universities played a less marked but still real role in the education of these networks of men: Bonn, with the presence of structures that emerged from resistance movements against the French invasion of 1924; and Königsberg, with the presence of academic militant networks like those of Franz Six, future head of the ideological documentation of the RSHA, and the academic historian (and future president of the Scientific Committee of the *Institut für Zeitgeschichte*) Hans Rothfels, was attended by men such as Friedrich Buchardt, a Baltic German who worked successively at the EWZ with Martin Sandberger and Hans Ehlich at the RSHA *Amt* III B-2,[28] dealing with population displacements, and Hans Joachim Beyer, who worked successively for the same departments and for the 'Reinhard Heydrich Foundation' in Prague.[29] Bonn, Leipzig, Königsberg and probably, in a more minor way, Tübingen: all these universities were close to borders. Students were confronted with the proximity of a national and ethnic other, and this experience, most of the time marked by the potential of conflict, was one of the specific features that influenced the paths of young activists towards the institutions of Germanism and Utopia.

These academic hubs may seem to have structured genuine networks of acquaintance, but are undoubtedly difficult to summarize in terms of academic institution. In Tübingen, student organizations seemed to constitute the heart of social life, but in Königsberg the strong influence of Hans Rothfels, Franz Six and revisionist historians played a decisive role in the formation of groups of young people, the bodies of socialization that shaped the student experience.

Let us return to the case of Tübingen. The university and student associations contributed decisively to the structuring of the pathways leading to
the Nazi institutions of Utopia. However, they are far from being enough
to explain the high concentration of young officers from Tübingen, especially in the EWZ and UWZ. In order to gain a better understanding of the
social dynamics at work in these officers' itineraries, we need to broaden
the focus and try to grasp the socio-politico-professional environments
in which they operated during their years of study. In Tübingen, the
university was part of an institutional ecosystem marked by the presence
of Gustav Adolph Scheel, both *Reichsstudentenführer*, head of the regional
office of the SD and a major recruiter of the student *Osteinsatz*, and also by
the Deutsches Auslandsinstitut, an organization at the interface between
research in humanities and social sciences and revisionist activism on
behalf of German minorities. What emerged in the case of Tübingen
was a network born of the student organizations and the academic
framework which emanated from the university but was not reducible
to it: the organic link established after the seizure of power between the
Studentenführung, the main office of the Gestapo (supervised by Franz
Walter Stahlecker, future commander of *Einsatzgruppe* A) and the regional
office of the SD (headed by Scheel with, less evidently and less significantly from our perspective, the municipal institutions of Tübingen,
headed by Ernst Weinmann who became mayor of the city) makes this
institutional constellation a vast regional professional network, able to
employ young activist students trained in Tübingen.[30]

Professional networks were those with the most immediate structuring
effect on the institutions preparing for the Nazi future. Why? Because
professional logics predominated; because the officers involved in those
institutions tended to attract their former comrades and/or subordinates
to follow them; and because the professional habitus and the know-how
accumulated in the days of militancy (and even more in the period of their
first professional experiences) had a decisive weight in the mechanics of
recruitment in the Nazi institutions of Utopia.

Thus a considerable number of specialists who flocked to the RKFdV
were experts who proved themselves in the RuSHA before 1939; and
almost all of the men incorporated by Ulrich Greifelt into the special
general staff in charge of population displacements in the South Tyrol,
organized in 1938–9 between Fascist Italy and Germany, moved to the
RKFdV during its formation in 1939.[31] For RSHA *Amt* III B, the Saxon
network seems to have constituted a strong framework, though it is not
really possible to separate the academic logic from that of professional
networks. Hans Ehlich, for example, re-encountered Heinz Hummitzsch,
a major planner of population displacement, Rudolf Oebsger-Röder,
a secret service agent and clandestine action leader in Poland, Bruno
Müller, the police chief in Kraków, who would lead an *Einsatzkommando*
killing women and children in Tighina in Soviet Moldavia, and Herbert
Strickner, head of the SD in Poznań. Thus, the Leipzig network of officers

is relatively over-represented in these RSHA and EWZ groups responsible for one of the cornerstones of planning, probably because of the particular border identity shared by all the components of the Saxon institutional ecosystem, whether academic or professional.[32]

What was true of professional structuring in the RSHA and in the local institutions of Germanization was doubtless even more so in the institutions promoting the concrete and technical dimension of Germanization. The case of the WVHA, with its engineers, is a good example of this state of affairs. The WVHA Building Department, which, as has been said, had 56 officers and 210 NCOs in 1940, had seen an increase in personnel from 1941: at least 70 officers, 123 NCOs and troops as well as 125 employees assigned to building, and to planning building, in the occupied territories. Hans Kammler was the architect of this department. A trained engineer and an early Nazi militant, Kammler conformed to these elite SS models, combining proven ideological radical worth and reliability with a technical excellence enabling him to pursue a prestigious academic path.[33] Having worked for the Ministry of Supply and the Ministry of the Air from 1933 to 1940, he took many of his collaborators in these two departments with him when he founded the department on 1 June 1941.[34]

At the interface between professional networks and sociability was also the large cohort of women recruited by the Nazi women's organizations for service in the East. This service was somewhat occasional in nature, as is evidenced by the 'Christmas actions' carried out by the BDM in 1940 and 1941, with a total of 450 and 3,500 young women respectively taking part. The same applied to the *NS-Frauenschaft* (League of National Socialist Women), which sent several hundred aid workers to the settlers in the occupied territories. In these two specific cases, institutional and professional logics were closely combined with membership of political supervisory bodies. The women and girls who met in the *Osteinsatz* were all volunteers, but had also came to practise their craft.[35]

In the same vein, although there is no evidence of volunteerism, EWZ doctors arrived there through a network of professional practice and institutional logic: most of them were doctors from the Waffen-SS.[36] Their leader, *SS-Sturmbannführer* Hanns Meixner, shows, however, that the mere analysis of professional and institutional networks does not exhaust the question of recruitment mechanics. Meixner, in fact, had arrived at the EWZ only after an already significant career. Born in 1906, he combined his student curriculum with a militant itinerary that made him an 'old fighter', part of the *völkisch* movement since at least 1928 and a member of the SS from 1930. Becoming a doctor in Dachau at the heart of the concentration camp system, Meixner also continued his training in racial hygiene and hereditary biology at the Kaiser Wilhelm Society for the Advancement of Science.[37] He devoted his doctoral thesis to a question of racial micro-demography before joining the RuSHA, an institution he never left until he finally joined the RSHA in 1943, even though he had become head of the Medical Service of the EWZ as soon as this was set up in October 1939.

The example of Meixner shows how the different types of networks that we have tried to differentiate between were in fact interwoven: he was certainly a doctor, but the medicine he studied was in no way a mere professional practice; similarly, the networks of sociability that structured his curriculum were not in any way social groupings; they were those of a convinced Nazi who found in his activism resources that opened the doors of prestigious research institutions and those of elite SS organizations in which he successfully pursued his career.[38]

In sum, therefore, the question of the differentiation between types of networks in line with the categories chosen here seems to be irrelevant: few networks were purely professional or purely academic; all seemed to mix professional habitus and geographical or institutional origins by supplementing them with an almost invariably militant dimension.

It is not at all surprising to see militancy arise here and occupy a kind of omnipresence and pre-eminence in the way that a route to the *Osteinsatz* was laid out. Indeed, this militancy of cultural and political action in the territories of Eastern Europe and towards minorities left outside the borders of the German-speaking states by the Treaty of Versailles in 1919 had appeared long before the Nazi seizure of power. And the question of the German nationhood of the frontiers and of the foreign other had made its appearance at the behest of the German authorities in the Great War, and then took a semi-private, practically clandestine and militant turn during the interwar period.[39] The historian Elizabeth Harvey rightly points out that this militancy was not the prerogative of male actors and emphasizes the role of women in ethno-identity border activism in the immediate aftermath of the Great War.[40]

The coming to power of National Socialism and its imperial expansion from 1939 onwards broadened existing movements, controlled them and strengthened them, but did not fundamentally change their nature. Networks, whether professional or academic, were made part of the Nazi framework, state actors became more and more inextricably linked to militant bodies and worked together to structure the nebula of institutions which, from 1939 onwards, imagined the advent of the Nazi Utopia.[41]

The institutions of youth supervision were militant. This was again the case of Swabia, which best illustrates the entanglement of these institutions. Gustav Adolf Scheel was at the same time *Reichsstudentenführer*, i.e. head of the NSDStB for the Reich, local head of the NSDStB for the University of Tübingen and head of the SD regional bureau for Stuttgart, which also became the flagship of border ethno-identity activism with the *Deutsches Auslandinstitut* (Institute of Germans Abroad, henceforth DAI). Students from the *Studentenschaft* in Tübingen, lawyers such as Ehrlinger and Sandberger or Rapp, joined local law enforcement bodies and, from

1939 onwards, worked in the bodies for Germanization and repression in occupied Poland.[42]

In the case of all these men, their academic, professional and social group paths brought them to militant bodies, and this seems to be the least imperfect way of representing the logics of their assignment to occupied Poland, the land of the realization of the Nazi Utopia, from 1939.

Towards genocide? The itineraries of the experts

We have highlighted the diversity of the profiles of the actors mobilized in the work of the Nazi future, brought out the networks structuring the worlds of the Germanizing *Osteinsatz*, and stressed the importance of the militant dimension, at least for actors not drafted for Labour Service.

To finish this overview of the individuals and groups seeking to bring about the Nazi Utopia, we need to ask ourselves about the significance and the importance, in their itineraries, of this journey to the East, which we can now sense was marked by militancy and the longing for Utopia. This question was not formulated by the actors themselves. Or rather, we are formulating it as observers introducing a regressive approach: by examining the evolution of the career of many actors of Germanization, we can see their involvement in most of the predatory and murderous policies put in place by the Third Reich from the invasion of the USSR onwards.

It is very difficult to provide any general information about this involvement, including by focusing on SS officers and leaving aside students, girls and women giving Nazi assistance in the *volksdeutsche* camps. Even if we focus on these few hundred people, we do not have enough precise data to support an assured approach.

However, it is clear that a large number of SS officers – probably several dozen – were involved in the most deadly and transgressive dimensions of the Third Reich after endorsing the Germanizing trend of the Nazi imperial policies, especially in Poland.

For this, no doubt, there is one first explanation: the *Osteinsatz*, the journey to the East, the action in the East, covers in its meanings all the dimensions of Nazi imperial policies, from support for kindergartens available to migrants in the Warthegau to murder pure and simple in Belarus or Ukraine. There immediately arises a second question on the connection between these two dimensions of the *Osteinsatz*, a question we saw making a discreet appearance in the prologue of this work, when, from the first half of 1942, the intensification of the planning of Germanization policies appeared to go very closely with the general genocidal impulse extending to the whole of occupied Europe. We will revisit here, looking at specific individuals and itineraries.

Curt von Gottberg seems to be an interesting case. This SS General was an extremely early Nazi militant who assumed very important functions in the institutions responsible for the racial future of the SS and Germany. Born in 1896 to a noble Pomeranian family, a veteran of the Great War and trained in agriculture and agronomy, he was appointed head of the *Siedlungsamt* (settlement department) of the RuSHA in 1937 and then of the land registry services of Prague, where he set up an ambitious policy of land predation directed primarily against the Jews of Bohemia, but later intended to constitute the first step towards a Germanization policy in Bohemia, with the acres of arable land and forests that were confiscated being entrusted to pro-German settlers, SS militants or *Volksdeutsche*.[43]

He was subsequently assigned to the *SS-Hauptamt*, where he took charge of the service for the integration and release of NCOs, before being appointed SSPF Weißrußland in the summer of 1942.[44] It was at this post that Curt von Gottberg attracted the most intense attention from historians, taking over in the summer of 1942 all of what might be called Nazi security policies in Belarus, notably with the creation of the eponymous Combat Group.

Belarus in the summer of 1942 was the epicentre of the struggle against a rapidly growing partisan movement.[45] This policy was based on large sweeping operations in rural areas aimed at catching and destroying partisan units, but more fundamentally on depriving them of any supply base by destroying villages and their agricultural production in very large rural corridors. This unfathomably violent policy was carried out with an iron fist by von Gottberg, an officer marked by the Great War and by his training as a combatant officer. Remember, however, that this policy was one of combat in name only. One example is enough to show this: during Operation Nuremberg, Gottberg and his units reported: '799 bandits, 300 accomplices and 1,800 Jews' killed. 'Losses on our side: 2 dead, 10 wounded.' In the same report, von Gottberg referred to the fact that heavy weapons had done wonders, putting to flight those 'bastards, even when, from place to place, they regularly allowed themselves to be killed or burnt on the spot'. And he concluded: 'The weather was good: sunny and icy. Just the right weather for a hunt.'[46] An examination of the content of von Gottberg's activity will be complete if we add that these great operations, already murderous, were on his own orders systematically concluded by the massacre of the last large Jewish communities in the last ghettoes from November 1942 onwards.[47]

Did von Gottberg still have functions in connection with the policies of population displacement and Germanization? Apparently yes: members of his general staff contributed in the spring of 1944 to the establishment of a new strategy against the partisans, which closely interwove security policy and settlement policy, even though the populations concerned were not *Volksdeutsche*. It was a matter of establishing populations loyal to Germany in the *Wehrdörfer* (armed villages), so that they could then fight the Soviet partisans for control of the land.[48] Von Gottberg seems to have been joined by an expert on settlement issues known to him at the time of his activity in Prague, evidence that in this new practice there was some circulation of information about, and experience of, Germanization.[49] Does this mean, however, that von Gottberg acted as a conscious actor pursuing the Germanization of the lands concerned, and as a specialist in Germanization continuing by radical means the policies of land predation he had set up during his stay in Prague?

Perhaps not. On the one hand, the *Wehrdörfer* project appeared in Belarus, when it was almost a year before that the SS institutions had allowed the representations of the Nazi future to evaporate: for any clear-eyed observers of contemporary events, now was not the right time for Utopia and the future, it was the present and the struggle that mattered. Even if the current circumstances were ignored, RSHA and RKFdV planning provided for the total Germanization and resettlement of colonists in the vast territories of Belarus, but critical commentators on the *Generalpläne Ost* such as Erhard Wetzel pointed out in 1942 the unrealistic nature of this project in the near future.[50]

One final fact needs to be emphasized. Curt von Gottberg's itinerary was not the success story of a practitioner of Germanization moving from one accomplished mission to another, even more ambitious and more delicate. His career was actually paved with humiliating failures that led to his being sacked from the *Siedlungshauptamt* of the RuSHA in 1938 for administrative incompetence, and then from the land registry department of Prague for various financial and administrative errors. He had even been the subject of SS judicial inquiries to determine whether these errors were in fact embezzlements.[51] As far as Himmler was concerned, he was not being transferred to Belarus so as to be entrusted with an even more ambitious Germanization, but rather to finally find a job for a rather coarse soldier, ill at ease in the administrative and bureaucratic assignments – a job that would suit his aptitudes, now essentially linked to the hunting and slaughtering of tragically large contingents of human beings.[52]

Von Gottberg's journey, at bottom, was that of a man lurching from failure to failure, just like the Nazi policies for building Utopia. In both cases the outcome was an increasingly radical and increasingly unfathomable violence. His itinerary is of little use for anyone trying to understand the connection between the utopian components and the purely murderous components of Nazi practice: von Gottberg could not adduce the one as a basis for the other, the contexts were too different, and he lacked legitimacy. We must therefore look elsewhere.

Might the case of Martin Sandberger be more enlightening?[53] He was a Swabian, socialized in Tübingen in the wake of the NSDStB and Gustav Adolf Scheel, and we have seen him becoming involved in Nazi revolutionary militancy after the Nazis' seizure of power, and joining the training services of the SA in 1934.[54] Having qualified as a lawyer, he took his state examinations and then his doctorate in 1934 and entered the administration of the *Land* of Württemberg.[55] He simultaneously joined the VDA (*Verein für das Deutschtum im Ausland*, Association of Overseas Germans) and also indulged, within the NSDStB, in clandestine activism aimed at *volksdeutsche* students during the annexation of the Sudetenland, as is indicated by the record of the presentation of the commemoration medal of 1 October 1938.[56] He finally joined the local Southwestern office of the SD led by Gustav Adolf Scheel in 1939.[57]

It was most likely around 10 October 1939 that Sandberger was appointed 'Commissioner of State for the Baltic Germans', whose job was to prepare for their settlement in the occupied territories of Poland with a small general staff in Gotenhafen (present-day Gdynia).[58] He then set up what would become the EWZ, which he headed until January 1941. In this role he thus participated in all resettlement campaigns of the *Volksdeutsche*. He led this waltz of *Nah- and Fernpläne*, and his departure corresponded to the implementation of the third *Nahplan*, which was supposed to definitively establish the quotas of colonists to be resettled up to the end of January 1942.[59]

Martin Sandberger thus conformed to the ideal of the SS officer who combined excellence in training and ideological radicalism. He could claim to have assembled experience in three areas. First, he was a revolutionary militant trained in organization and militant and physical skills. Second, he had developed the versatile skills of a lawyer capable of organizing and running an administration and had accumulated a relatively brief but important experience of intelligence work within the SD. Third, it was surreptitiously understood that he had also indulged in clandestine work under cover of the DAI, the *Studentenführung* and the VDA. It is here, too, that he was introduced to the problematic of ethno-activism, and it is this set of experiences which tends to explain his appointment as an expert in the resettlement of *Volksdeutsche* in October 1939.

He was appointed to the Personnel Training Department of the RSHA in March 1941, and then, in May 1941, he became head of *Sonderkommando* 1a of *Einsatzgruppe* A, with which he entered the Baltic countries on 22 June 1941.[60] In Estonia, where he settled in July 1941, he took over the struggle against partisan networks, but also, from September, the extermination of the Jewish community.

This is a good example of an itinerary leading a Nazi activist and SS officer of Germanization policies in occupied Poland towards the most transgressive practices of violence, including the genocide of the Jews. Unlike von Gottberg's, the linearity of the course is not deceptive: there was no hierarchical intervention to pluck him from failure, no judicial procedure, no punishment. Sandberger was considered the archetype of the effective SS officer, his advancement was exceptionally fast and his appointment as leader of *Sonderkommando* 1a and then as KdS (leader of the Gestapo and SD) in Reval was obviously not a punishment, especially since the posts he occupied on his return in 1943 were senior posts, first as head of the police and SD in Italy,[61] and later as head of department in the external SD.[62]

In the spring of 1941 Hans Ehlich felt there was a clear coherence between his experience as an expert in Germanization and the resettlement of colonists on the one hand, and the tasks that *Einsatzgruppe* A was supposed to assume on the other: would not the *Sonderkommando* 1b also assume tasks of colonization?[63] Written in November 1941, the messages from RSHA Group III B mentioning this role came at the very moment when an order for the total extermination of the Jews of the USSR had probably been circulated among the *Einsatzgruppen*.[64] The link between the missions of Germanization and eradication was thus being forged in fact, if not in intention, even if it were surprising that Ehlich had not been kept informed of the evolutions of the murderous practice of the groups in the USSR: he was one of the recipients of the *Ereignismeldungen UdSSR*, those round-ups issued by the groups every day that reflected the now genocidal dimension of the practice of group killing.[65]

Neither Sandberger nor the men he led were murderers before entering Russia, however.[66] No doubt he had indeed been transferred there because of his experience of the *Osteinsatz*, and no doubt too this experience was still marked by Germanization and Utopia. It remains for us, however, to try to understand how the connection between these two dimensions of the *Osteinsatz* was enacted on the ground.

In order to do this, we have to go through the very valuable sources comprised by the testimonies and statements left by the witnesses and defendants in the investigations carried out by the German justice system after the war. In 1968, the authorities focused on the activities of *Sonderkommando* 1a. Not to try to incriminate Martin Sandberger, who had been condemned to death in Nuremberg in the trial of the *Einsatzgruppen* then amnestied, but rather some of his former subordinates. It is in this context that a former member of the commando, Erich R., a jeweller by trade, laid down detailed information on the complex of facts concerned. Having few concrete elements to divulge, he was questioned about the framework of the orders under which the commando had acted. It is worth quoting at length:

> The basic order, according to which all Jews, Gypsies, etc., had to be wiped out for political reasons and with a view to establishing lasting security in the Eastern regions, is known to me. [. . .] These orders, however, were not announced in front of a gathering of the troop [for this purpose]. I remember that we [the anti-partisan commando of which he was a member] had gathered at the beginning of August 1941 around Kostyi, at the Jam railway station. It was about thirty kilometres from Narva. This is where Dr Sandberger visited us. He was celebrated by the whole Wehrmacht as 'the hero of the Battle on the Ice', because he had come on across the lake by patrol boat, while the lake was still controlled by the Russian gunboats. That evening [. . .] we had a party, with alcohol. Sandberger, during the evening, removed his jacket. By taking it off like that, he became an ordinary soldier like us. That's how we saw it. Then we started to say things you don't dare

say in other cases, namely the truth. I suppose it was that evening that Sandberger or the head of our commando, Feder, revealed to us, in small committees, these orders and the objectives of German policy in the East.

These objectives were rather loosely stated: we wanted to colonize the Eastern spaces. This is why the local intelligentsia was to be exterminated [ausrotten]. It was better to shoot one Russian too many than not enough. It was better to place an Estonian officer – though to some extent he was part of our unit – in a position where it was certain he'd be killed than not to place one there at all. It would make it all the easier to colonize the region and put it to economic use.[67]

This is valuable testimony for us: it shows us a young SS officer behaving very freely with his men and suiting his behaviour to a fighting fraternity. But more importantly, the order to exterminate the Jews and, more generally, the attacks on the local civilian populations are here legitimized by the Nazi utopian project. Mass murder was the sine qua non of the *Tausendjähriges Reich* and the tone of Erich R.'s testimony describes precisely the fervour felt by the guests at this dinner, held with divulging this aim in mind: the sense of a unique moment, the intimacy between fellow soldiers, the expression of fraternity and union, the euphoria blending this sense of union with a certain victorious intoxication, all of which were given their setting by plenty of alcohol and the festive atmosphere. One could indeed still argue that this was a one-off practice, but the rest of Erich R.'s testimony shows things even more sharply:

I want to add something else: KdS Sandberger was a man of great intelligence. I belonged to his close guard during the invasion and we travelled together in a car for hours. Sandberger explained to us the political objectives of the Reich government for the Eastern regions. The content was always the same: the colonization of Eastern spaces. Push the borders as far as Leningrad, where a border commissariat was to be set up under the responsibility of the police. Elimination of the Russian intelligentsia. We knew that it involved shooting [these people]. That way, we would control the territory better and faster. This was always the tendency of conversations with Sandberger, a conversation which he conceived as a form of political education. I am quite sure that every member of the KdS present at Reval must have known this type of conversation and the remarks made by Sandberger.[68]

Sandberger thus behaved in the genocide as a pedagogue of Utopia, attentively taking advantage of every moment so as to found the legitimacy of the murderous present and give it meaning through the utopian prospect of the future. Note the acuteness and freshness of the information distilled by the KdS. To some extent, including the RSA proconsulate, what is described here corresponds to the state of the Germanization plans as they were elaborated in the documents produced by the RKFdV and the

RSHA in the summer and the autumn of 1941. And Erich R. was not the only member of the commando to emphasize the exceptional presence and intelligence of Sandberger and the SS officer's mentioning of utopian projects.[69]

Martin Sandberger, while exceptional in many respects, is not an isolated case. In all the mobile groups set up by the RSHA, the number of SS officers who had taken part in the Germanization operations in the occupied territories of Poland, or who had participated in their planning in the Berlin HQs, was remarkably high. Undoubtedly the force of certain networks had prevailed over any explicit criteria demanding experience in bringing about Utopia. Nevertheless, many former members of the EWZ or the UWZ, or former ordinary officers of Group III B of the RSHA, helped to fill the commandos who were to take over the genocide of the Jews and the struggle against partisans in the USSR.

In *Einsatzgruppe* A, in addition to Martin Sandberger, there was Hanns Meixner, head of EWZ racial experts, and Sandberger's deputy in the EWZ and former RuSHA officer, Karl Tschierschky. In *Einsatzgruppe* B, there was Albert Rapp, the former head of the UWZ of Poznań, then leader of *Sonderkommando* 7b. We can also mention Friedrich Buchardt, a Baltic German author of a thesis on the right of the German minority in Latvia and a former collaborator of Sandberger in Gotenhafen in the EWZ, who became head of *Einsatzkommando* 9 after being head of the SD at KdS Lublin and Head of Office III B-2 under Hans Ehlich in Berlin.[70] In *Einsatzgruppe* C, Hans Joachim Beyer, a former colleague of Hans Ehlich, a professor at the universities of Poznań and Prague and a specialist in the processes of dissimilation, served as a collaborator of the Head of the Otto Rasch group. There was also Erhard Kröger, former collaborator of the VOMI and head of *Einsatzkommando* 6;[71] in *Einsatzgruppe* D, the historian Fritz Valjavec[72] and Bruno Müller, former KdS in Kraków, and in particular a former close collaborator of Hans Ehlich.[73]

Again we have concentrated on the cutting edge of Nazi aggression. Had the focus been extended to the occupying and security institutions throughout Eastern Europe, the number of men involved would have been even greater. Thus Erich von dem Bach-Zelewski, HSSPF (*Höhere SS- und Polizeiführer*, Supreme Head of the Police and the SS) for Upper Silesia and at the forefront of Germanization policies in his area,[74] became HSSPF in Central Russia and responsible in the whole of Europe for the struggle against the partisans. In a different vein, Hermann Behrends, the VOMI Chief of Staff, was involved in anti-partisan politics in the 13th SS Handschar Division, using his experience of the *Volkstumskampf* (ethnocultural confrontations in time of peace), and finally became HSSPF for Serbia and Sandjak, playing a key role in the bitter civil war instigated by the Nazis in Yugoslavia.[75] This significant presence of men who participated intensively in Germanization policies in the institutions most involved in the Nazis' murderous practices underscores the inextricability of these two facets of Nazi activity.

Surprisingly, weighing up this world in itself, which brought together the actors of the future Utopia, the *Tausendjähriges Reich*, has provided us with a more profuse and more diverse image than one would have supposed at first glance. In the first place, it is a massively mixed world: half of the people concerned were women, even though their functions were confined to practical and subordinate roles – child care workers, health and home economics advisors. These functions, moreover, will have to be carefully investigated, and it should be emphasized that this study of personnel has also led us to providing some inkling of what the *Osteinsatz* was.

This group, despite the presence of women and men of the *Arbeitsdienst*, was basically composed of volunteers for service in the East. NSDStB students (male and female), BDM or *NS-Frauenschaft* activists, SS officers involved in the central or local Germanization administrations, SA executives employed in the local administrations of the General Government or the *Reichskommissariat* formed a large majority of Nazi activists, although the type of their Nazism can be given an extremely nuanced assessment. Of course, not all the 27,000 people who are concerned here and who conceived or implemented the policies of the Nazi advent were Nordic theorists, members of the Black Corps; of course, the actors mentioned here were not all involved in the same way in utopian policies and especially not in murderous policies, the case of Martin Sandberger being as exceptional as it is revealing. Nevertheless, this state of affairs calls for the precise study of an *Osteinsatz* which now appeared to be marked both by a paroxysm of killing and by fervent hopes for the advent of Utopia.

Chapter 3

Osteinsatz: the journey to the East, a form of Nazi fervour

Attempting to write the history of the Nazi representation of the journey to the East, and above all trying to adopt an approach that will grasp the emotions that this journey could generate, is a challenge. On the one hand, the history of the emotions may have developed significantly over the past decade,[1] but it barely exists in the historiography of Nazism, marked as it is by a neo-positivism that takes little account of emotions.[2] On the other hand, the epistemological presuppositions of such an approach make it tricky. Attempting to restore the emotions generated by a representation requires the use of particular sources, leaving their authors with the discursive and social spaces necessary for the expression of their emotions. But here we find ourselves faced with a paradox: the sources that describe the *Osteinsatz* are for the most part institutional sources and they do not give much room to writers, who also move in a professional framework not very favourable to introspection.

Among the other difficulties to be solved is the fact that the representation of the journey to the East is closely linked to the representation of those spaces and the populations in them, and this was not something that had emerged fully armed at the time of our investigation. Hence the necessity for us to carry out a regressive approach and to study these representations at least during the time when the participants in the *Osteinsatz* were socialized; and at least throughout the period from the end of the Great War to the time occupying us in this work. There is one last major difficulty: we must try to embrace the experience of very diverse categories of protagonists. Some of them left many archival traces, others were less forthcoming. We will need, as far as possible, to try to account for all the experiences encountered in this moment of Utopia.

For all these reasons, we will have to use a very diverse and disparate documentation, composed of reports, statistics, publications, lectures, but also diaries, poems and songs. Let us begin by outlining this space and the populations that inhabited it in order to understand how the actors represented the East, before turning to the two major forms of representation of the *Osteinsatz*: the mission of resettlement/repatriation, commonly depicted in the form of the *Trek*, and the mission of assistance to migrants, the prerogative of the students and the various female actors in this sequence.

The East, between Utopia and anxiety

The institutions which thought out the Nazi future and tried to bring it about in the territories occupied by the Third Reich were the depositaries of a system of representations of these territories which developed at the beginning of what is now known as the interwar period. When studying the networks of the actors of these policies, historians of the ethno-cultural policies pursued by the German state almost all insist that there was indeed a major break in 1933, marked by the Nazification of institutions and the emergence of new actors; but they also point out that there was a remarkable continuity in the representations distilled by this set of institutions, mostly created in the nineteenth century or immediately after the First World War.

The institutions dealing with the Eastern question, the fate of the *Volksdeutsche* and border problems were extremely numerous and remarkably durable throughout the interwar period.[3] The German Protection League (*Deutscher Schutzbund*), the VDA, the DAI, the *Deutsche Stiftung*, the *Publikationsstelle* of Dalhem and innumerable associations dealing with cross-border labour were active throughout the period. All constituted an important framework of socialization, in which many future cadres in SS agencies gained experience.

These institutions were very often semi-public and worked closely with university professors. Their activity was at the interface between ethno-identity activism of a more or less clandestine kind and traditional academic work. This was an extremely diffuse nebula: the VDA had 27 regional directorates, 300 local groups and 5,500 school associations. Similarly, no fewer than 120 associations were members of the *Schutzbund* in the mid-1920s.[4] This cloud of associations, organizations and coordinating bodies left important documentation which, although disparate, gives us a precise sense of the ideas that were developed at the colloquiums, meetings and various information and consciousness-raising sessions they set up, in the Reich as well as in the communities concerned.

Of course, these institutions were brought under control after the Nazi conquest of power. The National Socialists began by trying to centralize their actions and coordinating them more effectively. They set up a *Volksdeutsch* Council under the leadership of a number of activists combining traditional commitment and a profile compatible with Nazi power. The Council, which was under the direct supervision of the Chancellery, of Hess and of Bormann, had no organic connection with the SS, which nevertheless concentrated all police powers in its own hands and had also taken partial control of clandestine diplomacy via-à-vis the *Volksdeutsche* and the VOMI. Inevitably, this Council attracted the resolute hostility of Himmler and his offices. The latter then embarked on a strategy of taking control of the inner workings of institutions, trying to place their own men in their governing bodies. Thus the VDA leader Hans Steinacher was finally dismissed in 1938 at the instigation of Hermann Behrends, and Theodor Oberländer had to relinquish his position as director of the *Bund deutscher Osten* (German Eastern Society) to the same Behrends, who was also Chief of Staff of the VOMI.[5]

Nevertheless, the activist landscape had not fundamentally changed in 1939. None of the significant institutions had been dissolved. Their leaders had often been replaced by younger individuals who were closer to Nazi activist bodies. They were now more closely coordinated by the Ministries of Foreign Affairs and the Interior, and especially by the SS, through VOMI, RuSHA and RSHA, but not even this had really altered the situation; it had simply led to an increased Nazification of the social sciences, which were, however, already being defined as 'combatant sciences'.[6]

It was in this milieu that many actors of Germanization policies were socialized throughout the 1920s and above all the 1930s. One of the most important institutions in this sequence was the 'ethno-scientific' studies group or *Volkswissenschaftlicher Arbeitskreis* of the VDA.[7] The attendance lists at the colloquiums it organized point to the regular participation of several historians from the RSHA and RKFdV, including Alexander Dolezalek, future head of planning for the local resettlement headquarters in Poznań, and Hans Joachim Beyer, one of Hans Ehlich's collaborators in Group III B of the RSHA.[8] It should be noted that part of Alexander Dolezalek's work in Poznań in the first phase of Germanization policies was the subject of a parallel 'scientific' formulation in these working groups. In October 1939, Dolezalek, assigned to the Poznań *Ansiedlungsstab*, still participated in the sessions of the *Volkswissenschaftlicher Arbeitskreis* and reported the results to Poznań.[9]

In 1939, in the documents drawn up by practitioners and planners, it was indeed two decades of thinking about the East that emerged and fed into Germanization plans and practices. This seems to justify taking a close look at the whole of this documentation describing German nationhood from the outside and from the frontiers, although it is not always possible to link it with the agencies or practitioners of the Germanization policies put in place between 1939 and 1943. Two main themes emerge: the East crystallized, at least from 1918 onwards, a set of menacing representations in which it appeared as a land of dangers; very paradoxically, however, the East was also a *terra nullius* whose occupation and exploitation were not only legitimate but necessary for its development.

Thus, in the course of a great number of scientific studies, memorandums and research reports, the 'combatant sciences' which, after 1918, became the human and social sciences of the East constructed an alarmist image of the territories of the former Russian and Austro-Hungarian Empires. German nationhood was presented as being in existential danger in those areas. While this image was nuanced and varied from region to region, it was constant and concerned all German communities. I have decided to capture these diverse representations by examining an illustrated book that enjoyed a wide circulation; the banality of its expression was matched only by its exhaustive nature. Entitled *Was weißt du vom deutschen Osten?* ('What do you know about the German East?'), this book continually harped on the essence of what in the eyes of the Nazis it was necessary to know about the countries that were now to be colonized and made use of.[10] Over 196 pages, the authors focused on origins, on the East as an original place of settlement and as a space for the migration of 'Indogermans', then described the Hanseatic and Teutonic immigrations and the Tatar, Hussite and Turkish dangers. Then came the Thirty Years War, the vicissitudes of the frontier territories of the East and the South, and then what the authors called 'the inexorable decomposition of Poland'. The eighteenth and nineteenth centuries were then described, including the policies of Napoleon and Bismarck, the departure of the latter marking the beginning of the fateful drift to world war. This war was represented in the most commonplace terms, as a 'war of encirclement' led by a world of enemies. After the peace of Versailles, Germany found the strength to rise again and to face the 'will to annihilate' of the enemy powers, thanks to Adolf Hitler and the Nazi movement.

In this grand narrative, the German settlements in Poland, Russia and the Balkans were treated in such a way as to highlight their antiquity, to describe the mechanisms which presided over their establishment and to demonstrate their leading role in the economic development of these territories, from the Adriatic to the Urals through the Baltic and Transylvanian regions. But attention was also drawn to the extreme danger in which the 'chauvinism' of the countries that emerged from the Treaty of Versailles placed those communities which a fateful destiny had left outside the protective borders of the Reich. Oppression was multifaceted: political, economic and cultural. It was imposed, of course, by the new states, but they operated only with the complicity of the victors of the first global conflict and the two great internal allies of these states: Bolshevism and Judaism.

The East was therefore the site of the *Volkstumskampf*, the clash over ethnic identities that, since 1918, had become an unequal struggle in that the ethno-racial enemies of German nationhood now relied both on sovereign states and on a mortifying ideology whose sole aim was to oppress or even annihilate (the term 'will to annihilate' was used) the German-speaking communities of this German East.

This type of representation was very commonplace and was widespread throughout the German social fabric. The SS agencies produced an equally racialized scholarly description and published a large body of work seeking to prove this picture and put it on a secure statistical and historical basis. Some of the students sent from 1939 to the East undertook historical and ethnographic studies that were in every respect in keeping with this discourse.

As in *Was weißt du vom deutschen Osten?*, the student memoranda insisted on the danger threatening the German communities outside the borders of the Reich, and the feeling of danger was even greater in the works dating back to the pre-war period – the soteriological dimension of the advent of National Socialism and of the entry into the war was undeniable.

And, with regard to the case of Poland, it was probably the Polish international law specialist Gustav Adolf Walz who most clearly summarized the situation as it prevailed in the eyes of the Nazis. It is worth quoting it at some length here:

> In Poland, population growth is so rapid that the question of minorities is first and foremost the question of property. From the racial [*blutmäßig*] point of view, 'Polishness' believes that it can submerge and neutralize [*ausschalten*] minorities very quickly by breeding in great numbers. This is why the struggle is taking shape so decisively around economic positions . . . And onto this is grafted the fight against German education and language . . .
>
> Germany has more to lose here than does Poland; Poland can accept the loss of 10,000 Poles in Upper Silesia if in exchange it can liquidate the much larger and culturally and economically more important group of Germans in Poland. It is this calculation which seems to lie behind the Polish policy described here.[11]

This dread of being swamped, based on the belief in the overpopulation of Polish spaces, is very prominent in the writings of the 'thinkers of annihilation'.[12] Gustav Adolf Walz was also considered to be an expert in these matters: he had founded an Institute for East European Studies at the University of Breslau, which, in the eyes of the Nazis, was a frontier university, whose situation was referred to in the lecture as a sort of laboratory of ethnic identity clashes between the German communities and the Poles, whose tendency to be aggressive about their ethnic identity was emphasized in all the studies.[13] These remarks were made at a session of the Akademie für deutsches Recht attended by many leaders of the institutions of border activism already mentioned and chaired by Hermann Behrends, SS General, head of the VOMI general staff and responsible for much of the more or less clandestine cultural diplomacy that constituted the *Volkstumskampf*.

It was an *imaginaire* of danger in the shape of demographic swamping that characterized those Eastern spaces. At this stage, however, we need to make a basic qualification: if the texts mentioned here all share the same representation of the East as a place of every danger and likely to be swamped by the Slavs, the texts dating from the interwar years, especially those produced during the period of Nazification of the main policy bases for giving support to minorities, differ fundamentally from the line set out in *Was weißt du vom deutschen Osten?* Published in 1942, this book did describe the East as a territory of danger for outnumbered Germans, but it also revealed the reversal of perspective and the triumph of German nationhood in the victorious assault on Poland and the USSR. The *Osteinsatz* was thus viewed as an unexpected rescue operation and a reversal in the destiny of Germany. If the utopian dimension did not appear as such, the *Heim ins Reich*, the return of the *volksdeutsche* communities to the motherland, was highlighted, and gave a perspective and a hope which had remained largely outside the purview of documents from before September 1939.

The East was a land of anxiety, but this anxiety was controlled and mastered, at least partially, after the autumn of 1939. And more profoundly, the dominant impression in the period after the conquest of Poland was that the East had become a space of Nazi possibilities for Germany.

In the first place it was a space freed from any rational occupation. Even if different ethnocratic studies showed that the Germans had settled there centuries before and that non-natives had imposed their presence, the latter had not left any lasting imprint on these spaces. Here, one of the hymns of the *Reichsfrauenführung*, an institution for the supervision of women which became numerically important in the practices of the *Osteinsatz*, can serve as an example:

> To the East is our tomorrow, is the coming year for Germany;
> There is a people's care, there await danger and victory.
> There brothers were faithful, and never lowered their flags,
> Five hundred years of fidelity: they kept watch and were given no thanks.
> There are neither farms nor hearths, there the earth cries out for the
>   plough.
> There we must conquer foreign lands that once belonged to the Germans.
> There a new start can take place, so take up your weapons, Germans, and
>   listen![14]

The East is the future of Germany. And in accordance with the structures of Nazi belief, the song becomes a discourse within history, taking up the great narrative of the East but insisting, despite this historical discourse, on the fact that the East is still a *tabula rasa*. 'The earth cries out for the plough', says the song. The *Volksdeutsche* – the 'brothers' – are here a vanguard who watched over a land awaiting real development, real fertilization. Here we are faced with a very classical formulation of *Blut und Boden*, the 'blood and soil' ideology as promoted by Richard Walther Darré, first head of the RuSHA, and within the various Nazi neo-agrarian institutions.[15] But here the formulation takes a specific shape in that it is assigned to those spaces of the East which give it a powerfully utopian dimension. A whole literature made up of press articles, journals, memorandums on agronomy and the landscape disseminated this representation of an East that was pure of all representation, constraint or inertia; a virgin land that would welcome Nazis possibilities.

The East is also the land of Nazi freedom. This is what another poem, written by a woman student during her *Osteinsatz*, asserts:

> *Ostland*, far-reaching *Ostland*,
> Here, freedom has taken up its rights without hindrance;
> Free is the spirit, free the belief,
> Ever a lord and never a serf,
> The bonds of those years have finally been withdrawn from you
> And in your space man never feels constrained
> And I have recognized you,
> *Ostland*, my new homeland.[16]

The great poverty of expression in this poem by an anonymous young woman must not make us lose sight of the emotional dimension of the poem: it celebrates the spaces of the East which are places of freedom. This is, of course, only one stanza. The others are different: they evoke the East as a place of battle and as a land of agricultural fecundity, illustrating perfectly, in all their literary lameness, the Nazi representations of the East.

This kind of discourse was internalized by the young women, students and activists whom the various Germanization agencies enlisted to preach the Nazi 'gospel' to the *volksdeutsche* communities, though in the winter of 1940 they often languished in transit camps deprived of any prospects. A virgin land, a land of liberty, the East was the space in which would be written the destiny of Germany – a destiny which, in the eyes of these militants, had been given a decisive new turn by the Nazi conquests.

It was this fervour that added its lustre to the *Osteinsatz*. It attracted a large number of young students staying in the occupied territories and in those virgin lands territories that, after 22 June 1941, were comprised of the Reich *Kommisariate* in Ostland and Ukraine. Was it really this ebullient utopian fervour that generated such fascination among the students? It is very difficult to give a simple answer to what is a simple question. What can be safely said is that the protagonists of this programme were the Nazi militants who joined the founding networks of former NSDStB student activists who, in 1939, became the IdS in Stuttgart and head of the EWZ in Poznań; and that in October 1939 they organized the initial forms of Student Service in the East. Scheel and Sandberger, both Nazi militants from a very early stage,[17] were actors in the institutional and emotional quickening marked by the prospect of the advent of the Nazi Utopia. Student Service was immediately successful: 3,000 students travelled to the East in 1940.[18] Excluding cultural action in transit camps and settlement villages, some 730 posts were set aside for students in the administration of the incorporated territories in 1941.[19] In total, their numbers were assessed at 1,200 in 1942 and 2,500 in 1943[20] for incorporated territories alone. And it is likely that no fewer than 6,000 of them made the journey Eastward between the conquest and the liberation of these territories, and probably over 2,000 went to the territories of the expanding empire, including the *Reichskommissariat* of the occupied USSR. In total, from 1936, no fewer than 50,000 students had responded to the summons to the *Osteinsatz* issued by the NSDStB.[21]

These students have left many traces, journals, annotations and other personal writings that evoke the utopian dimension and fervour that presided over this journey. The functionalist observer will probably object that a large part of this documentation has come to us via copies, made by the institutions, of these specific forms of documentation. Nevertheless, the fact remains that their utterances, however mobilized and exploited, had not been actively solicited. It would therefore be beside the point to reject as a whole the spontaneous character of these expressions of fervour. Nor should we deny the emotional dimension of the *Osteinsatz* of these students. The number of utterances, their status, the periods for which students and women stayed in the East, all suggest the power of that region's call. It was a place of combat from 1936 to 1939 and a place for building Utopia from 1939 onwards, and even beyond the year 1942, which undoubtedly saw the culmination of Nazi millennial hopes.

A second point to be made is the very great diversity of people's experiences on the *Osteinsatz*, which in practice, for the men of the *Einsatzgruppen* in the Soviet Union, involved killing one person per day for six months,[22] while a nurse or young woman student will relate that she met only *volksdeutsche* families and newborns. In order to account for this diversity, we can point to particularly gendered experiences of the *Osteinsatz*. On the one hand, as mainly experienced by men, SS officers and members of the Germanization agencies, their experiences revolved around the figure of the great redemptive *Trek* and the *Heim ins Reich*. On the other hand, there was Nazi 'care', symbolized by the action of the raciologist doctor, the nurse who imposed sanitary order, and the female student educator who taught German nationhood to the *Volksdeutsche*. These were the two axes of *Osteinsatz* fervour to which we must now turn our attention.

The myths of the Great *Trek*

From treatises anticipating the return of ethnic Germans to the motherland on the one hand to the logistical practices set up to repatriate these communities to the Reich on the other, there are many sources that describe the soteriological dimension of this SS practice. The achievement of Utopia, from the autumn of 1939 onwards, first meant, in the eyes of SS ethnocrats, assembling the Germans into immense so-called caravans to reach the territory of the extended Reich, but it also meant bringing back into cultivation the Eastern territories which until now had been unworked by the German plough.

To try to get to the heart of this representation, the way it was organized and expressed itself among those who operated it, let us look at the case of Lieutenant SS Wallrabe, who has left us a detailed report on his experience. Typewritten on five pages, this document is already well known.[23] Wallrabe was one of those young *Akademiker* recruited into Nazi agencies because of their scientific skills *and* their undeniable militant commitment.

On 14 April 1942, on his return from the mission, Lieutenant SS Wallrabe completed a report narrating his mission within the VOMI *Sonderkommando* R, which had appointed him to send a resettlement team to the Leningrad region.[24] He begins his narration in these terms:

> On 10 January 1942, therefore, I was at my request incorporated for the second time into the *Volksdeutsche Mittelstelle*. [It was only when I arrived in Karlsbad] that I was informed that I was assigned to the Petersburg commando as part of the *Sonderkommando* R. To my surprise and delight I recognized the head of the commando as Lieutenant Preusse, one of the teachers of the school where I myself had had to train. While initially scheduled to be the deputy leader of the Petersburg commando, on my arrival in Karlsbad I was appointed head of the Kauen [Kaunas] commando [that had become vacant] after the defection of Lieutenant Hans Freytag. The mission of this commando was to receive into Lithuania the *Volksdeutsche* who had been directed there and registered by the Petersburg commando, to settle them in camps and to instruct them ideologically. It turned out the same day that the Petersburg commando could not be committed to this task as planned. The Wehrmacht informed us that the *Volksdeutsche* of the Leningrad crescent would not be delayed, that the commando would arrive too late and that the *Volksdeutsche* had been told to set off for Tilsit. Fortunately we were able to dissuade the Wehrmacht from sending the *Volksdeutsche* back into the Reich and to at least preserve for our commando the mission of hosting the *Volksdeutsche* in Lithuania. The commando, consisting of two detachments, was immediately reorganized into a commando of 32 men who took charge of the mission initially devolved to the Kauen commando. Thus I became the deputy and aide-de-camp of the commando leader.[25]

From the very first paragraphs, we can see the fairly clear mixture of improvisation, lack of strategic perspective and institutional friction, opportunism, adaptability and cumulative radicalization that characterized the Nazis' policies on population displacement and occupation. One aspect, however, had changed profoundly since the first *Umsiedlungen* of 1939. The latter had led the *Volksdeutsche* of the Baltic states into the occupied and incorporated territories, whereas now there was no longer any question of sending them to the Reich. They were to be hosted in transit camps in the Baltic states and were probably destined to ensure the Germanization of the Soviet territories. It is here that we can see, very concretely, the contradictory nature of these policies: some *Volksdeutsche* evacuated in 1939 were now to be resettled, paradoxically, on the very territories they had left.[26]

But this impression is very far from being the only one created, even involuntarily, by the young lieutenant, who continues thus:

> From the moment when, on 12 January, our car left Berlin, until 9 April, the day of my return from operations, I remained constantly with the head of the commando. His experience was my experience, I shared his joys and sorrows with him and I hope I was a good comrade and a faithful companion. Our driver, Martin Vosen, was practically included in this camaraderie. It is a real stroke of luck to have a good driver, who is distinguished by his tact and delicacy.[27]

From the beginning of his narrative, Wallrabe evoked a fellowship expressed in the same way as those fighting comradeships born in the Great War. It was not confined to the circle of officers alone: the *Kampfgenossenschaft* dear to the Nazis was a fusion of combatants, without regard to their rank or distinction.[28] We need just recall the memory evoked by Erich R. when, in *exactly* the same region, probably almost at the same time and under similar circumstances, he had swopped impressions with Martin Sandberger, the head of his *Kommando*:[29] the importance placed by the narrator, an ordinary soldier, on the fact that uniform jackets had been removed and the insignia of rank had disappeared is reminiscent of the account given by Lieutenant Wallrabe, who, despite this National Socialist egalitarianism, aspires nevertheless to have a driver distinguished by his tact and his decency. The *Osteinsatz*, in its guise as *Umsiedlung* (the displacement of people, whether expelled or resettled), was thus experienced in a combatant mode by its protagonists, if we are to believe this report.

However, there can be no combatant or quasi-combatant experience unless there is a danger. It is therefore quite logically that Wallrabe stated immediately after this passage that the mission was not without risk – which was a way of giving it added allure:

> In the event that something happens to the head of the commando – the mission takes place near the front, in territories infested with partisans, dangers to which is added the risk of accident and the possibility of diseases [due to exposure] – I would obviously have taken over the commando. This was conditioned by the fact that I was associated with every affair concerning the commando, and that I was involved in the planning and arrangement of the mission, giving my advice and proposals.[30]

Beyond this functional consideration, however, it is not wrong to see this as expressing a desire for war, or at least a curiosity that exceeded the framework here set out.

The journey by car will remain unforgettable for someone like me who did not yet have close experience of war. I was astonished by the railway lines perfectly maintained by the columns clearing and polishing the tracks. I had a sense of the violence and the power of the German attack when I contemplated the countless wrecked Soviet tanks strewn along the roadsides; I was deeply impressed by the towns, which increasingly looked like the Army's entrenched camps, as we approached the front. We also saw, along the roads, witnesses of the great famine migration, Russians armed with handcarts retreating towards the rear, where they hoped to find bread and lodging. But our job here was not to allow our compatriots to become entangled in this disorderly and savage stream, but to get them out in rail convoys that would take them out of the theatre of operation to the Reich.[31]

Wallrabe's description combines curiosity about the war with a vision of the East as a country of hunger and dread; this vision was common among the young practitioners of Germanization. It echoes the sense of dread that imbued the prejudices of the soldiers of Barbarossa, who imagined Russia as the place of all fears and cruelties.[32] He says the same thing a little further on, in some very vivid lines that read like the account of a racialized journey:

I have always wanted to know Narva. In the Hermannfeste[33] and in Ivangorod, the German-Western and Asian-Russian worlds face each other, threatening each other as they do nowhere else. It was a stroke of luck that many comrades managed to soak this image in![34]

Wallrabe's description is extremely banal and his lack of experience added to the lyricism of his pen. Nevertheless, he does emphasize two central dimensions of the Nazi experience of the *Osteinsatz*: on the one hand, it was a kind of combat; on the other, it occurred in the very heart of savagery. It is in this context that the second fundamental feature of this precise form of the *Osteinsatz* was the *Umsiedlung*. If Wallrabe was a novice in war, he was far from a newcomer to operations of displacements of population. He participated in the population exchanges of 1939 and this experience had a profound impact.

Unfortunately, I had to drive to Reval with the head of the commando on the day after we arrived in Krasnogvardeisk. So I didn't hear a single shot and could not even gaze from afar at the huge danse macabre that was being played out in the big city. But orders are orders and a stay in Reval meant for me a return to a beloved city. While, the year before, I had only been allowed to cross the city under the escort of a Soviet Jew, in 1928 I'd enjoyed a few memorable days there during a trip to the Baltic.[35]

He describes his mission and the installation of his commando in these terms:

It was then that we embarked on the second mission of our operation, still unclear when we got into our cars in Berlin: transporting the Germans from Tschudowo, Novgorod and St Petersburg who were evacuated to Taps and Aegviidu (Charlottenhof) after their quarantine period. So we had to quarter in Reval. Thanks to the talents of the commando leader, we were soon settled with our comrades from the Kauen detachment in the house of the Jewish doctor Epstein.[36]

Finally, we have the description of the content of the mission, with its barely concealed sense of adventure:

In the succeeding part [of the operation], we occasionally had to work with Estonian institutions, when *volksdeutsche* refugees came from the Gdow camp over the ice of Lake Peipus under the leadership of the Estonian self-defence militia in concert with the Estonians and Finns, and were to be taken to the Aegviidu camp which we had taken over. If I were to regret anything about this mission, it would be that I hadn't been able to take part in one of these adventurous sleigh journeys, I would have happily endured the cold which we had already got accustomed to.

Be that as it may, this was the occasion for frequent trips by car and train. In particular, I will remember the journeys to Aegviidu with the rumbling mail train, partly because of the frequent delays, sometimes several hours long, but also because of the excitement/fever of travel/euphoria [*Stimmungsreiz*] that accompanied it. In a rapid sleigh ride through magnificent snow-filled wintry woods worthy of fairy tales, we made for the buildings of the commando in charge of the transit camp. This was when there was immediate contact with the *Volksdeutsche*, a contact I had enjoyed every day as an OB in Lithuania, a contact I had intensely missed during the operation. What animated, and indeed disorderly movement there was on the platform when the first train left on 20 February! Conversely, barracks accommodation greatly affected our mood. It is difficult to imagine a stronger contrast between the almost idyllic accommodation of Aegviidu and the Taps barracks. The migrants did not perceive much of this. In both places they were happy and grateful for having been freed from Bolshevism. I did not find that they were deeply infected by this plague, even if twenty-five years of Soviet domination cannot fail to leave some traces. Certainly, pro-Bolshevik positions can be detected in those who had been taken directly from the Leningrad sector to the Konitz camp, but education, in so far as it is addressed to Germans, will change all this to the very foundation. We were not spoiled by Lithuania, as regards the value of the migrants.[37]

The *Osteinsatz* is described in adventure mode: the sledges and the snow give a magical dimension to what was a mission in time of war, and Wallrabe never forgets it. It is described by a Nazi militant whose racial categories are deeply internalized, and the biologized representation of Bolshevism as a microbial infection or plague is not the only occurrence of the biological imagination that lay at the foundation of the Nazi faith. In his eyes, after all, the theatre of operations was *'infested* with partisans'.[38] The mission of the *Osteinsatz* was twofold. On the one hand, it was a matter of saving the *Volksdeutsche* by organizing their evacuation from the war zone and territories in immediate danger. On the other hand, it was a question of re-educating people who had faced Bolshevik contamination for twenty-five years. The *Osteinsatz* had a therapeutic and redemptive dimension.

> When we received precise news of the last *Volksdeutsche* in the Luga sector, we were able to leave a small contingent behind us in Aegviidu and, after a pleasant last evening saying goodbye to some of the gentlemen of the General Commissariat, we left on 29 March via Riga and Kauen, where some individual cases of migrants needed to be settled, and made for Konitz. It was there that some 3,500 migrants virtually without identity documents were registered, more or less efficiently. With the exception of five comrades who are to lead the remaining transport to Neustadt in East Prussia at the end of April, the Petersburg commando is assembled in Konitz and looks forward impatiently to further action. Many men had held out higher hopes for their first mission. But anyone who had already participated in an operation of population displacement thought with a degree of melancholy of these times, both hard and beautiful, where we were measuring ourselves against the Soviet opponent. The commandos of the *Umsiedlung* at that time constituted sworn communities, while now some were having to learn to behave and fit in for the first time. You must have a passion for *Umsiedlung*. No matter where you come from. What is important is to be caught up in the passion of the mission, to repatriate [*heimzuführen*] Germans back into the Reich.[39]

Herbert Wallrabe is describing the mission of state-imposed socio-racial engineering which consists in registering migrants who will be re-educated in camps before being eventually relocated to territories to be Germanized. More profoundly, Lieutenant SS Wallrabe insists on the passionate nature of the action, on the emotion that arises in him at the prospect of repatriating *Volksdeutsche*. Before being expressed so clearly in conclusion, this passion had already imbued the whole of the text: the fascination with war, the passionately racial reading of space, men and history, the hatred of Communism viewed as a microbial contagion – the whole formulation sprang from the political passion of Nazi belief, from the redemptive and euphoric dimension of the return home. This seems to have been the overall experience of this particular *Osteinsatz*, less marked by murderous paroxysm than the genocidal *Osteinsatz* of the men of the *Sicherheitspolizei* and the SD within the *Einsatzgruppen*, or of those in the ORPO (*Ordnungspolizei*, the police charged with maintaining order) in the police battalions and the SSPF and HSSPF staff troops.[40]

The critical reader may object that my approach should not have been dictated by one exceptional document, namely the report by Herbert Wallrabe, but I can say straightaway that many other sources also bring out this emotional tonality, sometimes finding it in different contexts than the *Osteinsatz*.

A similar study could thus be made of the figure of the Great Return. '*Die große Heimkehr*' is a dominant figure in the discourse on repatriation. It is evident, passionately expressed, in the last sentences of Herbert Wallrabe's account, but the expression enjoyed a much wider circulation. It was to be found in a series of exhibitions organized by the central and local administrations in various parts of the Reich and the occupied territories. It could also be met with in the fiction produced in the years 1939–41.

It is no coincidence that the spread of the myth of the Great Return was the subject of heightened institutional activity in the years 1939–43. The *Heim ins Reich* was a convenient theme. It meant one could both stigmatize the world of enemies who encircled the Reich and legitimize the restorative war waged by Germany between 1939 and 1941, and subsequently the Great Racial War against the Judaeo-Bolshevik enemy. It also saw the Nazi Reich as able to accomplish the pan-German dream and the advent of the *Volksgemeinschaft* in this area of Nazi conquest, now extended to the European borders. The myth of the *Trek*, the *Heimkehr*, was a particularly productive theme rich in emotional representations. This is evidenced, for example, by an exhibition by the Department of Propaganda of the General Government on the evacuation of the Germans of Galicia.[41] Held between 2 and 12 February 1940 at the Stephansplatz Art Museum in Kraków and inaugurated by the district governor, this was a carefully prepared event. The exhibition was based on the paintings of Otto Engelhardt-Kyffthaüser, a figurative artist whose austere and pseudo-realistic paintings and political views met with Nazi approval: he became one of the most exhibited painters of the Third Reich.[42] Engelhardt-Kyffthaüser is described in the catalogue as 'the painter of the experience of lived war'.[43] According to the exhibition curators, his legitimacy was based on his status as a Great War fighter who had been able to transmit his own lived experience, and a concern for documentary detail that made him a cricual witness of this Great Return, this *Trek* of the *Volksdeutsche* of Galicia.

Room 1 presents the main factual data which, in the eyes of the exhibitors, were necessary for a proper understanding of the exhibition. They aimed at internalizing the providential dimension of the sequence: 30 January 1933 is described as 'the day on which the Führer grasped the means of imposing the realization of the programme of the movement for German renewal'.[44] This was followed by the various stages in which this aim was realized: referendum on the Saar (13 January 1935), the evacuation of South Tyrol (February 1940), the *Anschluss* and the annexation of the Sudetenland. All Nazi foreign policy is re-read as the succession of so many steps in the application of a soteriological programme. On the walls numbered 2, 3 and 4, the exhibitors included drawings and paintings by Engelhardt-Kyffthaüser showing the means of transport used for the evacuation, immediately establishing the image of the *Trek*. Several thousand carts, sledges and carriages were used to this end, and three depictions of the *Trek* (the head of a column and various views of a convoy) were hung next to seven portraits of migrants.[45] No further details of this exhibition are necessary: once the items have been put in place, the language used, embellished with many portraits, evokes the conditions of travel and the polar climate which presided over it, and it describes ideal families – we will come back to this – both phenotypically and demographically. It shows the gendered distribution of Nazism, celebrating northern motherhood and childhood. Providentialism, historical discourse and racial determinism are all embodied in the portrait: the rhetoric of *Umsiedlung* is as complete in this type of document as it was in Herbert Wallrabe's report. It might be objected that the emotional dimension in the SS officer's report is not to be found here. The exhibition catalogues are accompanied by texts by the painter talking to the *Volksdeutsche* or describing their attitude, and these texts abound in intense emotional reactions: tears of joy, expressions of gratitude and relief, political fervour for the Führer.[46]

A work of fiction such as *Die Große Heimkehr*, written by Karl Götz, a successful Nazi author, a specialist in frontier and foreign German nationhood and a VOMI officer too, enjoyed a 1943 circulation of 30,000 copies; it depicted exactly the same sentimental world, projecting it onto the *Volksdeutsche*, the heroes of this novel, as incarnated by the young Michael and a head smith of a German village in Volhynia.[47] The emotional universe of the *Volksdeutsche* that was evoked here was no less rich than that depicted for the SS officers involved in *Umsiedlung*, making of the latter (and of the *Osteinsatz* in general) a main site of Nazi fervour. This is basically not surprising: the men describing it are the same, and here there are no migrants to tell us what they *actually* felt, but trained and educated SS officers in charge of logistics operations, racial and social engineering and media processing. The *Trek*, the *Heimkehr*, the *Umsiedlung*, the *Osteinsatz* in general, were the site of a purely political and militant emotion. It was closely related to the feeling of being involved in the ongoing process of realizing the utopian project of a sociobiological renewal via the fusion and reunification of northern blood within a territorial entity, the vital space of the Reich, swollen by war and conquest. The *Osteinsatz* of SS officers/social engineers was imbued with fervour because it was the realization of what Alphonse Dupront called, in another context, the 'promise of a reign':[48] the advent of the Thousand-Year Reich.

As we move on from this study of the ways in which service in the East was metaphorized, we should probably qualify the subject somewhat, and recall the gendered dimension of this experience and the emotion it generated among those taking part. It was an essentially masculine experience, an essentially male emotional system linked to service in a commando and the question of resettlement; it involved almost solely Nazi militants with a very clearly formulated faith. It cannot be generalized except to the SS officers involved in Nazi Germanization policies. Other formulations, rawer, less diffuse, closer to the violent and/or combative dimension of the reality of ethnic cleansing, undoubtedly co-existed with what we have just described. Practitioners of the expulsion of non-natives, such as Albert Rapp and Rolf-Heinz Höppner, probably imagined things with emotions more akin to hatred, which, as we have seen, was not absent from the discourse of the engineers of resettlement. Nevertheless, the few testimonies of the practitioners of expulsion at our disposal also express the fervour for the realization of Utopia. The nuance lies in the expression, not in the structure of the emotional universe of the *Osteinsatz*.

The latter, however, was also couched in other terms that were produced by other categories of Germanizers.

The racial, hygienic and educational dimensions

To attempt to define the second experiment of the *Osteinsatz*, organized as a Nazi form of care, we must pause for a moment to look more closely at the frames into which it was inserted.[49] How, indeed, were the practices deployed by these rather large groups of people who were neither combatants nor specialists in the displacement of populations?[50]

If we take the case of EWZ doctors, the type of activities they assumed responsibility for is well documented. During settlement and naturalization procedures, they were called upon to examine candidates for return and citizenship during highly supervised procedures that nonetheless continued to be the subject of debates that continued long after the Nazi dream had evaporated under the impact of war. They were placed in health stations (*Gesundheitsstellen*), themselves incorporated into triage commissions for the *Volksdeutsche*. In these health stations, health and racial examinations lasted between one hour and one and a half hours out of a total of three hours allocated to the 'assessment' of a family.

The work was divided into six stages: the taking down of identities and the drawing up of a file destined for the register of migrant health; a history of hereditary biology and a biographical survey conducted by an employee; a medical visit by an SS doctor; racial assessment by the RuSHA expert; a second medical examination of fitness for resettlement, also conducted by an SS doctor; and finally a terminal examination concerning the entire family. Depending on the cases and the periods, this six-stage course was supplemented by an X-ray (which was not, however, systematically performed).[51]

It is very difficult to see in this racialized version of social engineering (that is also to be found in the repertoires of modern states) any practice that might have inspired fervour in those who implemented it. But the institution itself, in describing the stakes it assigned to this practice, expressed the emotion that was invested in it. On 14 December 1939, the head of the RuSHA, Günther Pancke, wrote a letter to the staff at the health station of the Poznań resettlement headquarters in which he quoted *Mein Kampf*:

> If the fecundity of the healthy portion of the nation should be made a practical matter in a conscientious and methodical way, we should have at least the beginnings of a race from which all those germs would be eliminated which are to-day the cause of our moral and physical decadence. If a people and a State take this course to develop that nucleus of the nation which is most valuable from the racial standpoint and thus increase its fecundity, the people as a whole will subsequently enjoy that most precious of gifts which consists in a racial quality fashioned on truly noble lines.
>
> To achieve this the State should first of all not leave the colonization of newly acquired territory to a haphazard policy but should have it carried out under the guidance of definite principles. Specially competent committees ought to issue certificates to individuals entitling them to engage in colonization work, and these certificates should guarantee the racial purity of the individuals in question. In this way frontier colonies could gradually be founded whose inhabitants would be of the purest racial stock, and hence would possess the best qualities of the race. Such colonies would be a valuable asset to the whole nation. Their development would be a source of joy and confidence and pride to each citizen of the nation, because they would contain the pure germ which would ultimately bring about a great development of the nation and indeed of mankind itself.[52]

The issues at stake in this apparently unalluring exercise of racial engineering could hardly have been more intensely radicalized. On the one hand, quoting Hitler, Pancke placed this practice under the symbolic patronage of the supreme authority of the Third Reich; but by also quoting a text that was intended to be prophetic, General SS Pancke turned doctors and racial experts into the instruments of the realization of this prophecy. What in 1924 had been Utopia and prophecy became, thanks to the practice of these doctors, a reality in 1939. In order to drive home his millenarian message, Hitler prophesied that it was the whole destiny of German nationhood and thus of mankind as a whole that would be influenced by this racial selection. It was the very actions of the doctors themselves that would bring about Utopia.

This dimension of the *Osteinsatz* was thus imbued with an atmosphere of hierarchical euphoria, tangible but difficult to measure because of the lack of sources. Indeed, very paradoxically, while doctors comprised one of the main militant bodies in the Third Reich, and RuSHA doctors constituted the most ideological sector of the most ideological organ of the most successful Nazi elite, we do not at present have access to sources that would inform us about their experience of the *Osteinsatz*. This prevents us from assessing the frequency of the forms of expression which we have seen in the case of Wallrabe, and the spread of this particular state of mind. The documentary situation does not allow us to go any further.

However, as in the case of Wallrabe and the specialists in *Umsiedlung*, and also of a large majority of the Germans sent on the *Osteinsatz*,[53] the SS doctors saw it as a confrontation with an East European exoticism that the great majority of the groups concerned could not have experienced during the Great War, and relatively few during the Weimar Republic, for generational reasons. It should be remembered that most of the 27,000 Germans sent on the *Osteinsatz* were young, even very young, and many of them were students; they were therefore socialized under the Third Reich and were unlikely to have visited the East before the war. Like their counterparts in VOMI and RKFdV, the EWZ and RuSHA doctors conceived their task and mission as a key element in the realization of the *Tausendjähriges Reich*, which was, after the victory over Poland, a distinct possibility. Hitler's language and the language deployed by their hierarchy also placed the elitist and militant SS nucleus at the heart of the racial apparatus for bringing about Utopia.

The *Osteinsatz* as an experience of assistance to the *Volksdeutsche* was first and foremost the imposition, in the strong sense of the term, of a racial order by Nazi militants convinced they were changing history. This Nazi form of the welfare state, of the 'society-as-garden', as Zygmunt Bauman put it,[54] also imposed other norms, and sent other men and women to the East to implement them. Thus, after passing before the SS's socio-racial assessment committees, migrants, most of them in transit camps and some of them on confiscated farms, were then confronted with activists from the NSV, the *NS-Frauenschaft* and the NSDStB, who were all trying to get over to them their hygienic and educational message.

As regards in particular the practices of running houses, making homes and training bodies to stay clean, this norm was imposed by women on women. The centrality of gender, central but tacit in other facets of the *Osteinsatz* experience, was here brutally explicit. We have already seen how the representation of the East as *terra nullius* had been prevalent in the irredentist and Nazi imagination. In the domestic sphere, the responsibility of the Polish women for poor housekeeping and lack of upkeep of gardens became a common feature of the reports of Nazi activists sent out to incorporated territories. The *Osteinsatz*, for them, was first of all the discovery of a land which had worn down the human beings who worked it, and subdued Polish men and women; it was a vast immensity, almost empty of people, with evanescent and filthy houses, without curtains at the windows, without a vegetable garden worthy of the name, with no flowers lining the window sills.

An organizer of student sojourns, Hertha Midzinski, told the NSDStB's *Osteinsatz* newspaper:

> We experienced the necessity of a great German settlement on this land, whose immensity we started to love thanks to our Sunday walks. Large proportions of this fertile land still bore traces of the time when Poles lived there; this land demanded the hand of a master – and the significance of the immense territories of East Germany became evident to all of us, for we all came from territories of dense settlement, where people are always bumping into one another, while here there is land and more land, for hours on end neither village nor farmyard; and where we did come across the latter, they created the impression of an unimaginable misery, which contrasted fundamentally with the lush fertility of the land. We will never forget those villages, more frequent concentrations of clay huts which never had any right angles, or trees or proper streets or gardens or flowers.[55]

Conversely, the clichés found in these testimonies depict the arrival of the *Volksdeustche* as the starting point for the transformation of houses, gardens and landscapes, a transformation so radical and visible that it took place in a few hours.

> At first glance, we see that German settlers have here restored order over the last few weeks. What a contrast to the half-ruined, run-down Polish huts which, until the last few days, reminded us of the Polish pseudo-state.[56]

Here we see the ductility of the categorization of the *Volksdeutsche* and the Poles: racial determinism plays a fundamental role in giving coherence to this system of representations and to its building of *differance*, characterized by its immediacy and its ubiquity, and the combination of the two can be explained only by racial determinism. Landscapes and houses change immediately because the *differance* between Poles and *Volksdeutsche* is biological. It transpires everywhere and always, quite apart from any agronomic or hygienic education. This immediacy is the innate racial factor as internalized by the militants and incarnated in landscapes, houses and forms of behaviour.

The fact remains that if racial excellence was decisive and innate in the eyes of Nazi militants, the greater part of the *Volksdeutsche* lived in contact with non-natives and this prolonged stay left traces on their mentalities and their behaviour. This is why the action of the Nazi women students and activists was fully legitimized, as one of them explained:

> We must of course be clear that all those who until now have lived only among Russians and Poles do not know the full extent of the German rhythm of work, or of German order and cleanliness. There remains an immense work of education which we women students need to tackle.[57]

This was a work of re-education and civilization which also had a racially performative character: this discourse *also* outlined and actualized the racial hierarchy, placing the *Reichsdeutsche* at the top of the scale, their racial excellence embodied by their commitment to Nazi values; then came the *Volksdeutsche* who had passed through racial selection, but who needed to be re-educated before they could join the *Volksgemeinschaft* and its socio-hygienic order, all of them definitely separated from the non-natives – here, Polish men and women – whose inability to assume control of these territories was proof of the legitimacy of their expulsion.

The Nazi women and female students involved in these programmes were thus, given the nature of their *Osteinsatz*, at the very heart of the consequences of the practices of ethnic combat which constituted the heart of Germanization, even in their most brutal consequences. An annual report presumably written by SS officials of the UWZ of the Vistula described it in these terms:

> It should be noted here that there was intense collaboration in the resettlement operations of the permanent camp of the Marysin Girls' Labour Service and the Rzadka Wola intervention camp. Thanks to the marked interest in the activity of the SS working staff shown by the two female chiefs of these camps, their girls became practically full-time colleagues on resettlement days. Because of the lack of manpower, the assistance of young girls was particularly valuable in the eyes of the general staff. The young girls began to work with discipline, as well as with exemplary enthusiasm and creative joy. On these days, they ensured that the expelled Poles did not take everything, but left the necessary equipment for the new arrivals. They cleaned the farms and the houses of the dirt that often reigned there, decorated the tables with flowers for the migrants so that the latter would feel good when they arrived. And in view of the hovels, this warm welcome proved invaluable in maintaining the morale of the new [*volksdeutsche*] arrivals.[58]

Let us take a look at this text, which sheds interesting light on the feminine *Osteinsatz*. It adds something quite new to our argument in that it primarily concerns women who are not, at first sight, volunteers: the young women of the *Arbeitsdienst* are conscripted, but the zeal described in the report has no reason to be feigned by them or enhanced by it: it is not a propaganda report. Here, the categories of analysis sometimes used in history, insisting as they do on conviction or constraint, show their limits:[59] these women have no choice in their activities, but they carry out their work with a zeal and fervour underlined by the SS.

Second, the feminine *Osteinsatz* that emerges here does not exclude the most 'negative' aspects (to use the Nazi term), the most brutal of Nazi practices: they are present alongside the police and security forces as the expulsions happen.

In the third place, it is easy to see how they constitute a group of actors who, from the outset, are endeavouring to impose a hygienic and aesthetic order on the *Volksdeutsche*, an order that is the foundation of the Nazi project. To put it another way: Utopia, as far as the Nazis are concerned, needs the broom and the towel of women's work.

One of the common characteristics of the student *Osteinsatz*, both male and female, went beyond the diversity of its content and involved its 'educational' dimension: it was a matter of transmitting, inculcating and educating. And if the racial and hygienic order placed the adults in the front line, a significant part of what the Nazis imagined to be this educational work was directed towards the children, of which there were many in these villages and transit camps. And de facto, a whole swathe of the contents of the Nazi Utopia is revealed also through the action of those who took care of children.

One of the innumerable reports on student experiences kept in the archives of the RKFdV can here serve as a source to help us understand its dynamics. The student, who remains anonymous in the archive, is keen to relate her *Osteinsatz* in one of these resettlement villages.

When we come to the village, we meet a lot of children and peasants who obviously want to attend our 'school festival'. Upon our arrival, the crowd of children arriving at the school door stands there in uneven lines and, partly curious and perky, partly timid or even frightened, stares at us. Until now, the children have known only their 'mamoiselle' [*Frollein* (sic!) in the original German text], as they generally call the female students who work in their village. But we came from the surrounding villages on this Sunday to help our comrade Annelies organize her 'school festival'. An ordinary mortal has no idea what it's like to organize an afternoon of painting with migrant children in which we are not the painters as it is the children who are the artists.

In the classroom, parents and brothers and sisters had already assembled and waited in something of a huddle to see what would happen. Annelies gave a small welcome speech and presented the programme. First of all, children's songs and then short dramatic sketches. The little assembly was somewhat intimidated, but after the first enthusiastic applause, all trace of timidity disappeared. [. . .]

The old fable of the housekeeper who waits for a prince and marries a swineherd so moved the little actors that they had red cheeks and wide-open eyes. The time passed too quickly!! Then we took a break; and next up was the sack race and the apple and spoon race. [. . .] Then came the return to the classroom which in the meantime had become a stage scene. It was the highlight of the party, the children performed 'Hansel and Gretel'. There was certainly not much left of Grimm, but the old gentleman will doubtless not be too cross with us. The children performed with such naturalness and enthusiasm that they were a pleasure to watch. The main actors were particularly delighted to nibble at the little house in real chocolate and real cake, which the 'mamoiselles' had brought for the occasion.

With this tale, the school festival had reached its climax and its conclusion. One more song and we went home. The mothers were proud of their little actors and there was a lot of talk about how little Aline or the boy had performed 'terribly well' [*arg gut*].[60]

What first draws our attention is the way the student action is essentially cultural. Getting children to learn traditional folk songs; Grimm as an archetype of German children's culture – these were all part of the cultural Germanization programme, which was addressed here to the *Volksdeutsche* who had already passed through the narrow straits of racial examination, examination for aptitude, and hygienic re-education. Culture was the last stage of Germanization, and here it involved the children as vectors of the Nazi future.

Beyond this first observation, the feeling of superiority of the young Nazi *Reichsdeutsche* woman, who contemplates the children and their parents from the height of her cultural superiority, mocking their uncertain German accent, is here perfectly representative of the Nazi hierarchy of races, classes and cultures. She is a student, conscious of her social, cultural and racial background, who is carrying out a process of education in German nationhood. She does so in all 'benevolence', with the prejudices of a Nazi activist. Her conviction is that she is thus building up a *Volksgemeinschaft* based on benevolence, and on this sense of fellowship, which means that the 'mamoiselles' she mentions support each other and come to help each other from village to village at the time of the school festival. Fellowship, the central figure of Nazi militancy, is thus itself one of the narrative resources used to convey the feeling of plenitude expressed by the young woman in her narrative.

Racial, hygienic, educational: such was indeed the content of the new order which Germanization was meant to transmit to these newcomers (or returnees), the *Volksdeutsche*; such was the content that the students were to transmit during their *Osteinsatz*.

And the *Osteinsatz* was truly a militant act, an act of belief: this is what ultimately characterized the journey to the East. Its content varied greatly between individuals and groups, depending on the periods and areas in question. Sometimes it involved a form of Nazi care where, although violence was not absent from the field of experience, it still did not play a foundational role; sometimes it involved missions which, as we shall see in the case of the Zamojszczyzna, combined the struggle against partisans and the predation and expulsion of communities – missions that were at the interface between the experience of fighting or massacre and the experience of Germanization.

Undoubtedly the journey to the East cannot easily be grasped in all its diversity and complexity. Undoubtedly it also varied over the period in terms of intensity and content. Undoubtedly the experiences of boredom, disappointment, fear, insecurity, hatred, hostility from local populations and of course also from *Volksdeutsche* are needed to complete this picture of the experience of the *Osteinsatz*.[61]

Nevertheless, the *Osteinsatz*, as depicted in the writings of its essentially militant protagonists, strikes us as an experience of alterity marked by the peculiar seal of the fervent hope for the realization of Utopia. And one of these female activists puts it very clearly. Attempting to legitimize her BDM action in East Prussia during her Labour Service, Melita Maschmann wrote: 'The fact that I [there] experienced *Volksgemeinschaft* with such intense feelings of happiness generated in me an optimism which held me in its thrall up until 1945.'[62] It is indeed because the *Osteinsatz* was the framework for the advent of this *Volksgemeinschaft*, the social locus imagined for the realization of the prophecy that German nationhood could be re-inaugurated, that these tens of thousands of men and women devoted themselves to it with such fervour.

Conclusion

At the end of this first part of my survey, in which I have attempted to grasp and delimit my subject by studying its protagonists, three series of conclusions seem to stand out.

In the first place, by studying the institutions of the Nazi dream and their interaction, I have been able to specify the modalities of its emergence in the autumn of 1939. It was generated by the tension between an imperial hope (one of the foundations of Nazi belief) and military success. Institutions were then created and took over its formulation and implementation. The complex interaction of these institutions gave substance to a project which presented itself as the realization of utopian prophecy, a realization seen as a three-dimensional object based on a consensus across the entire Nazi institutional landscape. Utopia involved ethnic cleansing, and the spatial, racial and social homogenization of living space through expulsions and resettlement. This first invariant dimension became ever more gigantic in scale as the imperial military expansion of the Third Reich progressed between 1939 and 1942, conferring on it an unprecedented scope for the ethnocrats themselves. The incredible nature of what was then in progress, in their eyes, most likely explains some of the magnetism and fervour that emerged in this planning, carried out as it was by these central institutions.

In these institutions, men found their niches; or rather, as we have seen from the outset, men *and* women who, through the widespread use of conscription within the Labour Service, came from all the social and cultural strata of German society. Although, on the political level, Germanization was largely a matter of Nazi militants, it was the business of German society as a whole as far as service in the East was concerned, since the *Osteinsatz* was its accomplishment and the many different practices associated with the latter have appeared to us in all their detail. To administer, expel, welcome, evaluate, repress, educate, store, wash, sweep, scrub, organize, hunt and denounce; to take charge of children and theatre plays: these were the main dimensions of the practice of tens of thousands of militants who experienced the journey to the East; such were the outlines of this journey, experienced with all the fervour of the fulfilment of the promise of the Thousand-Year Reich and the advent of the harmonious *Volksgemeinschaft* which, in 1942, was to embrace Europe from the Rhine to the Black Sea. The *Osteinsatz* was a sequence of struggle, work and joy of such intensity that actors sought – often in vain – narrative spaces to express it. The monotonous obligation to give a written account of their action undermined any real opportunity for hinting at the feeling they were writing history, overthrowing a curse they believed to be a thousand years old, building a new society. They constantly ran the risk of going off-topic or, somewhat like Lieutenant Wallrabe, giving into a certain silliness or sentimentalism which verges on the ridiculous. Modesty, vanity, the fear of mockery, the difficulty even for a cultivated officer to find the appropriate words to describe his feelings, make the expression of these very rare, unless we seize on a few exceptional sources and archives of self-presentation such as diaries and interviews.

And yet the *Osteinsatz* may well be a key element for understanding the dynamics of Nazi society, right up to its end: the ex post facto testimony of Melita Maschmann cited above, which makes this fervour for a realized *Volksgemeinschaft* the main factor in its constancy until the collapse of 1945, may well give us the key to a *possible* understanding of the incredible resistance of the society of despair which was Nazi Germany in its death throes in the first half of 1945.[1] If the Germans resisted for so long, was this not partly because it was impossible for them to *abandon their dream*?

Part II

Times and spaces of Utopia

Having completed the first part of our survey of the Thousand-Year Reich, we have learned a great deal about the constitution, the diffusion and the imposition of this Utopia as well as the institutional, social and individual actors who promoted it. We know, to be sure, that it could not happen, in the eyes of those who dreamed it, without displacements of population as massive and forced as they were brutal; we also know that it fitted into and was embodied in the reality of the Eastern experiences of the tens of thousands of people sent to the occupied territories; we know, finally, that it was the advent of a racial, hygienic and social order that the actors were trying to impose on the ground and inculcate in the *Volksdeutsche*, but this first description needs to be filled out.

The rest of our investigation will attempt to clarify its content, but also to account for what happened when, in the summer of 1943, it was suddenly no longer an urgent matter, in the eyes of Nazi dignitaries, to kindle people's hopes.

Chapter 4

General planning for the East

In order to give substance to the Nazi Utopia as it needs to be seen and was, in the eyes of those who formulated it, to come into being in the expanding territory of the Third Reich, we must go back to the invasion of Poland – to understand under what auspices this sequence began, and how the Nazi hierarchies apprehended it. On 1 September 1939, the Wehrmacht, on the pretext of a completely fabricated pseudo-incident at Gleiwitz on the border, invaded Polish territory,[1] an event which Hitler announced to the Reichstag solemnly assembled for the occasion. It is worth quoting here at length:

Deputies, men of the German Reichstag!
For months we have suffered under the torture of a problem created by the *Diktat* of Versailles, a problem that has degenerated to the point where we can no longer tolerate it. Danzig was and remains a German city. The corridor was and remains German. These two territories owe their development only to the German people. Danzig was separated from us by the corridor, annexed by the Poles. As in all German communities in the East, all the minorities living there have been mistreated in the most shocking way.
    As always, I have attempted, by peaceably proposing revisions in a peaceful way, to change this intolerable situation. The outside world lies when it claims that we have undertaken our revisions only through pressure. Eighteen years before National Socialism came to power, there was an opportunity to carry out these revisions through peaceful agreements and negotiation. [. . .] For your part, you know the incessant attempts I made for the purpose of a clarification and an understanding in the case of Austria, and later with regard to the Sudetenland, Bohemia and Moravia. And all this in vain.
    I tried in the same way to solve the problem of Danzig by proposing peaceful discussions [. . .] and they [the Poles] not only responded by mobilization, but they accentuated the terror and the pressure against our German compatriots, and [resorted to] a slow strangulation of the Free City

of Danzig by economic and political means and, in recent weeks, by logistical and military means. [. . .]

I am determined (1) to resolve the Danzig question, (2) to resolve the issue of the corridor, (3) to see whether there is any development in German—Polish relations that could ensure peaceful coexistence. [. . .]

Last night, for the first time, Polish regular soldiers fired on our territory. Since 05:45, we have been firing back and now bombs will be met with bombs. Anyone who fights with poison gas will be fought with poison gas. [. . .] I will continue this fight, against no matter who, until the borders of the Reich and its rights are assured. For six years already, I have been working to rebuild the German defence system. It is now equipped to the best of its ability and goes beyond any comparison with what it was in 1914. . . . If something were to happen to me, then my first successor would be Comrade Goering. [. . .] As a National Socialist and as a soldier, I enter this fight with a valiant heart. My life has been nothing but a long struggle for my people, its restoration, and Germany. [. . .] I would like to assure the world, for all these reasons, that a November 1918 will never be repeated in Germany. [. . .] It is relatively insignificant that we ourselves live, but it is essential that our people live, that Germany live. The sacrifice that is asked of us is no greater than that which many generations have made. If we form a community closely united by oaths, ready to do everything, resolved never to capitulate, then our will can master all the difficulties. If our wills are so strong that no difficulty or suffering can make them bend, then German nationhood will conquer.[2]

Two things must be taken into account here. On the one hand, even beyond the obvious Machiavellianism that had presided over the Nazi attack on Poland, the dictator and, consequently, his subordinates conceived the invasion as a rescue operation for German communities suffering the blows of Polish oppression. On the other hand, in Hitler's speech we can see an obsession with 1914 and especially 1918, and this brought out one thing very powerfully: the Nazi dignitaries grasped what was then being triggered by resorting to very specific mental tools that led them to apprehend the war against Poland as a war of memory. The campaign and its consequences – the Germanization which was soon to take place – were part of an eventual concatenation that made Nazism an eminently memorable system of beliefs endowed with its own historicity and temporalities.

Let us now explore the contents of Utopia; we are particularly interested in the tool that allows us to see the overall vision of the Nazi future: the General Plan for the East.

The curse of Germanic insularity lifted

In the speech quoted above, the dictator was hardly making any rhetorical innovations. The 'pressure' on the communities of *Volksdeutsche* and the 'slow strangulation' of the city of Danzig by 'economic and political means and [. . .] logistical and military' means did indeed constitute a rhetorical figure, almost a commonplace but also a discourse of commemoration that was widely disseminated and shared in German society. This figure was part of the representation of a pathological evolution among the German communities from at least the end of the war – the 'apparent silence of arms', as one SD historian put it[3] – and the signing of the Treaties of Versailles, Saint-Germain and the Trianon, leaving large German minorities outside the borders of the Reich and Austria.

In the documentation produced by the institutions responsible for thinking of the East, the question of the endangerment of these German communities cut off from the Reich was one of the focal points of reflections both before and after 1939. The whole question of German nationhood abroad is imbued with this theme.[4]

The 'German nationhood of frontiers and of foreign countries' had, after 1918, become at once an object of study for these new committed 'social sciences', the *Volkstumswissenschaften* (social sciences of ethnicity), for the future ethnocrats of the SD and the RKFdV, and a hotbed of irredentist demands. For example, when in December 1938 the SD produced a voluminous report describing Polish policy in the Baltic, it certainly described the diplomatic dimension of Polish action in the three Baltic countries, but what it was trying to demonstrate first and foremost was the shared Germanophobia of the Slavic, Jewish and Baltic populations, circulating via Marxism or nationalism, and thus the re-forming of the 'world of enemies'[5] leagued against the Germans left struggling behind thanks to the Versailles and other treaties. The syllogical demonstration of the *volksdeutsch* isolation contained in this report was part of a history that deserves a little attention. The merger of the German Baltic community with the Latvian population had a biologically limited character and remained elite and urban. Indeed, the SD saw it in a positive way, as a Germanization of the Latvian elites. But it was interrupted from the middle of the nineteenth century onwards by the Russification policy of the Tsar's governments. This resulted in an 'alienation' (*Verfremdung*) of the two communities, while the rise of revolutionary Marxist ideology further reinforced Germanophobia.

Surrounded by a Russian-speaking administration, Germanophobe revolutionary currents and Baltic nationalisms, the German Baltic community was progressively isolated in 1850, encircled by Baltic communities who joined forces solely out of Germanophobia.[6]

Another example: the ideal type of this alien pressure was also embodied in the representation of the 're-Polonization' (*Wiederverpolung*) of the Warthegau Germans, as described in a brief report by the RKFdV office of the Warthegau. The report, dated 1942, insists on the change in the evolution of ethnic relations in the Warthegau, which, characterized before 1900 by 'slow Germanization', was transformed into a rapid 'Polonization'. The author, Dr Luise Dolezalek (wife of the *Hauptsturmführer* SS of the RKFdV whom we have already met several times, and who was responsible for the *Osteinsatz* of the students), then attempts to discern the Germanic presence in the occupation of the land.[7] In a series of seven maps she gives a Nazi view of the evolution of German–Polish relations between the fifteenth century and the 1930s. If, until the eighteenth century, this analysis merged with a history of German settlements, the situation changed in the twentieth century. After the Great War, the German communities suffered their biggest decline, due, of course, to the loss of Posnania, which now came under the Polish state that emerged from the peace treaties, and which in her view was leading to a 'policy of cultural oppression'. In addition to quoting word for word Hitler's rhetoric of 1939, Luise Dolezalek restates a vision commonly accepted before the war in the institutions responsible for *Auslandsdeutschtum* (German nationhood abroad): a vision of German isolates, gradually being assimilated as a result of the loss of their language,[8] by crossbreeding, by a Polish immigration depicted by the Nazis as significant, and by the loss of their land after 1918.[9]

However, to judge from other works, German minorities did not allow themselves to be swamped without reacting: the Institut für Staatsforschung, a branch of the University of Berlin directed by Reinhard Höhn,[10] produced a memorandum on the struggles of the German of Poznań. The latter, between 1887 and 1907, asked to retain a German clergy so that the German-speaking Catholics would not be subjected to Polonization. Taking the *Kulturkampf* waged against the Catholic Church by the Wilhelminian administration completely out of context, Höhn's men turned what appeared to have been a local variant of this political episode into an interethnic confrontation, depicting the German Catholic elites as seasoned in *Volkstumskampf*, in the struggle for ethnic identity.[11] However, in the eyes of Luise Dolezalek, these struggles on the part of the Bishop of Poznań had not prevented the Polish advance. At the time of the invasion of Poland, the Polish people, 'particularly fit for *völkisch*' fighting, according to the SD and RKFdV cadres, were thus in the process of undermining that German nationhood cut off from the soil still under German rule.[12]

We can thus see how Nazism constituted a racial determinism inserted within a specific space and historical sense, a historical sense that *guided* the destiny of German nationhood. Until the invasion of Poland, this Germanic insularity in a Slavic ocean was an extremely distressing state of affairs, which everything seemed to render inescapable. It was in this context that the invasion of Poland took place; its soteriological dimension, as underlined by Hitler, was perceived by all the SS protagonists.

And so, after this lightning victory, there began what they saw as a new era, that of imperial hope and the realization of Utopia assuming the character of a providential inflection of destiny, a lifting of the curse.

It is in this light that we must now examine the shape taken by the policies of Germanizing territory as reflected in the planning activities of the agencies responsible for realizing the dream of the East. Within this time frame, these agencies – mainly the RSHA Group III B and the planning department of the RKFdV headquarters led by Konrad Meyer-Heitling – produced what would become the General Plan for the East.

Early in 1940, RKFd's planning services produced a document entitled 'Planning Principles for the Building of the Eastern Territories'.[13] This document, the first to claim to embrace all the policies for Germanizing the territories conquered since September 1939, laid down broad guidelines for the measures which, in the view of the Nazi lecturer in agricultural geography Meyer-Heitling, would need to be implemented in order to make those lands German. His document is worth quoting at some length:

> In what follows, we assume that the entire Jewish population of this territory, approximately 560,000 persons, will have been evacuated and will leave the territory in the course of this winter.
>
> In the former Prussian provinces of Danzig and West Prussia, at the start of the war, the German population stood at about 50 per cent, i.e. it was in equilibrium with the Polish population.
>
> The first of the objectives, one that can be attained over the next few years, will at least restore the situation as it was in 1914. When this objective has been attained, an ever-widening process of Germanization will be achieved thanks to the participation of biological and economic forces from the colonies and the new territories. The restoration of the situation in 1914 would mean, first of all, the addition of 1.1 million German inhabitants to this territory of more than 3.4 million, bringing the total number to 4.5 million, and the gradual expulsion of 3.4 million Poles. In the former provinces of Poznań and West Prussia, the Poles who settled after 1918 must leave the territory.[14]

The first observation to be made here is that the precondition of Utopia was the restoration of the old order, the situation prior to defeat and the Treaty of Versailles. In this sense, Nazism presented itself yet again as a discourse on and in history, a discourse set in a specific historicity. The time of Utopia involved first and foremost a restoration of the previous order, to stop the fateful destiny that had been unfolding since at least 1918 and make possible an alternative future to that entailed by the curse of a German nationhood that found itself isolated in those territories.

The text could stop here, if it were simply a matter of avoiding that menacing future. However, its real aim was to propose another future, which Meyer-Heitling sets out as follows:

To delimit the territories to be recolonized urgently, the following strategic considerations are definitively to be taken into account:

(1) First of all, it is necessary to build a German ethnic wall along the border with the General Government, in the form of a broad cordon of *Germanic farms* [italics in the original]. This frontier wall immediately and definitively separates the Polish element left in the Reich from its hinterland.

(2) There is an urgent need to populate the basins of the biggest cities with German peasants.

(3) It is also necessary to found a large German ethnic bridge, to some extent as an East–West axis, connecting the frontier wall to the Reich. Finally, a narrower wall needs to be constructed through the old corridor through the districts of Zempelburg, Bromberg, Kulm and Graudenz. These ethnic bridges separate the remains of the Polish communities still there and form Polish islands.

In order to trigger the process of settlement, the more or less extensive ethnic German islands constitute the points of crystallization from which the East–West connection and the border belt must begin. Along the boundary of the [General] Government, the islands of German nationhood west of Petrikau, the areas occupied by the Vistula Germans and the Narew Germans farther north and east must be connected to each other. A wider East–West link begins at the Germanic centres around Birnbaum and Neutomischel and runs along the Warthe through Poznań, Schrimm, Wreschen, Konin, Kolo and the industrial basin of Łódź.[15]

For Meyer-Heitling and his colleagues, German nationhood was insular, and its 'emergence' from this status requires, as the text explicitly says, the insularization of 'Polishness'. Population damming, rural cordons, ethnic walls and human bridges are the racial instruments needed to transform the Polish population of the incorporated territories, literally cutting it off from its ethnic hinterland, 'polderizing' it, transforming it into a succession of small and easily swamped ethnic isolates. In this sense, Germanization begins by lifting the curse on the *Volksdeutsche*, but, on the other hand, it turns the curse against those who, in the eyes of social and racial SS engineers, had placed it on them.

The agricultural geographers of the RKFdV set up a careful spatial system designed to allow the archipelagos of German nationhood to expand and merge to become a continent, which would eventually coalesce with the Reich, thus forging a spatio-ethnic link by means of Germanization.

This spatialized *imaginaire* can be found, as far as we can determine given the lack of documentation, in the following versions of the *Generalplan Ost* of the RKFdV, with simple changes in the names of the different zones and a change of scale due to the invasion of the USSR. The spatial provisions of the second known version of this *Generalplan Ost*, delivered on 15 July 1941 by Konrad Meyer-Heitling, has reached us only indirectly, via the latter's post-war memories. Nevertheless, if we are to trust these memories, the difference lies neither in logic nor in categorization. These ethnic bridges and this belt along the border of the General Government, which turned the alien insular continent into an island and extended the archipelagos of German nationhood, remained the Western basis of the new plan, which added a new border belt to what would become the *Reichskommissariat* of Ukraine and Ostland, stretching from Lemberg to Kaunas and creating a new ethnic bridge from Warthegau and Poznań to the region of Białystok.[16] This was still a spatial and hydraulic *imaginaire* which aimed at rescuing German nationhood from out of the alien ocean.

Thus, when the Great Racial War was unleashed, the agricultural geographers seemed not to have abandoned the mental and memorial frameworks that were theirs some eighteen months earlier when they formulated the 'Planning Principles' for the occupied Eastern territories. This was not so surprising. Of course, the invasion of the USSR had fundamentally changed the symbolic and imaginary situation: having initially been a matter of memory and vengeance, the Nazi war had become racial, fundamental and decisive. The army of revenge, which had successively defeated Poland, France and Yugoslavia, was henceforth an army of Crusade.[17] But this change did not seem to have affected the planning bodies for the displacement of the population. There was undoubtedly a lukewarm attitude to spreading representations of the future. But on a deeper level, the spatial *imaginaire* that emerged in these plans seemed to survive in the even more gigantic planning envisaged in the third *Generalplan Ost*, which Meyer-Heitling sent to Himmler on 28 May 1942:[18]

Part C. Delimitation of colonization areas in the occupied territories and principles of organization.

The penetration of the great open spaces of the East by German life imposes on the Reich the imperative need to find new forms of occupation which will adapt the numbers of available German men to the areas available.

In the *Generalplan Ost* of 15 July 1941, zones of colonization were set out for a period of thirty years. On the basis of new instructions from the *Reichsführer* SS, the following colonization zones will be used as a basis:

1. *Ingermanland* [Ingria] (territory of St Petersburg)
2. *Gottengau* (Crimea and territory of Kherson, formerly Taurida)
Other proposals include:
3. The territory of Memel-Narew (district of Białystok and Western Lithuania)

This territory belongs in the background with the territories incorporated in the Reich, and constitutes the point of separation of the two axes of colonization [*Siedlungsrichtungen*]. The Germanization of Western Lithuania is under way, with the return of the *Volksdeutsche*. It seems necessary to place these three territories, the marches of colonization, under a particular legal status, for they are in the front line of the Germanic area and therefore have a special imperial mission.

To link these border marches closely to the territory of the Reich, and to secure transport and communication routes, 36 colonization bases [*Siedlungsstützpunkte*] (14 of which are in the General Government) are proposed along the motorways and main rail lines. These bases of colonization are in line with the existing central points and also coincide with the major significant police and SS bases. The distance between these bases is approximately one hundred kilometres. The total area of these bases is about 2,000 square km, and roughly corresponds to that of two rural districts of the former Reich [Germany in 1937]. The bases towards *Ingermanland* have been planned to extend in two directions, considering the special importance of the Baltic area for the Germanic peoples.[19]

This was a visualization of the gigantic plan for the Germanization of Europe, from the Black Sea to the Arctic Circle. Apart from the immensity of this plan, what strikes us is the surprising fixity of the spatial principles of organization: penetrating cordons connect the zones of colonization to the old Reich. Ethnic bridges have become the axes of settlement bases, but the areas of settlement to be Germanized continue to be represented by what geographers call 'surface figures'. The *imaginaire* at work is always, to coin a phrase, intent on 'polderizing' the alien ocean by making ever more vast Germanized colonization territories emerge and linking them to Germany by means of penetrating axes. Admittedly, the vocabulary of hydraulic engineering and the ocean is no longer used in this new document, which differs from previous ones in its concern for quantification and the forecasting of costs and resources. Nevertheless, the mental tools for conceptualizing the spaces to be won over to German nationhood have hardly changed. Except on one point: the bases of colonization are now thought of in terms of discontinuity, as the penetrating axes are no longer continuous. Over the hundreds of kilometres which separate one base from another, the aliens are at least numerically dominant, in the absence of any Germanic presence. The bases are artificial ethnic islands along the axes. The impact is not inconsiderable. The developers are here admitting that they now have to organize the *sprinkling* of their demographic reserves, which are too limited for the immensity of the Eastern spaces. This third version of the *Generalplan Ost* tacitly assumes German insularity by integrating it as a given of the real situation, and it sets out to *organize* it so as to conquer and Germanize more effectively.

It is hardly possible to go further in this study of the *imaginaire* coiled within the heart of the Nazis' Germanization planning. I will conclude by emphasizing the quite stupefying breadth of what the agricultural geographers of the SS and the RKFdV were here planning, and the vastness of the promised reign. A few weeks after the delivery of the plan, in Hegewald, the centre of SS Germanization, Himmler addressed the main dignitaries of the police and the SS and expressed the situation in these terms:

In the next twenty years after signing the peace, we, the present generation, and especially we in the SS, must set ourselves the following objectives:

(1) We have as our first fundamental objective, in this territory, to do everything possible to attach the Germanic peoples to ourselves, both externally and internally. We must win the Germanic peoples not only externally but internally so that the 83 million conscious Germans can become 120 million.

(2) In the most important issue for a people, that is to say, in the issue of blood transmission, we must dare to make the decisive breakthrough, to give our own men a sense of morality, so that it becomes 'natural [*selbstverständlich*]' – I mean without discussion, without debate, without problem – that no family will be extinguished, that there will be children there.

(3) The problem: territory and land for men! In the next twenty years, we have to populate and colonize the present German provinces of the East, from East Prussia to Upper Silesia, and the General Government as a whole; we need to Germanize and colonize Belarus, Estonia, Lithuania, Ingermanland and Crimea. In the other territories, along the penetration routes on which lie our roads, railways and aerodromes, protected by our garrisons, there will be founded small towns of 15–20,000 inhabitants and, in a 10 km radius around, German villages so that they can always be integrated into the German life and the urban cultural centre. These colonies are like rows of pearls that we will extend to the Don and the Volga, and hopefully to the Urals; one day, with the passing years, they will create, in the course of a generation, thanks to the actions of our eternally young successors, new strata in Germanic blood.

This Germanic East stretching as far as the Urals must – and this is what, as SS, we are working on – be the nursery of German blood. It must be this in our thoughts, in our lives, in our education, following the example of our comrades fighting for it and suffering a premature death, so that in 400–500 years, if the destiny of Europe leaves us this time until the moment for intercontinental confrontation comes, there will no longer be 120 million but 600 million Germans there.[20]

Himmler was literally describing Meyer-Heitling's *Generalplan Ost*, extending the temporal horizon far beyond what the RKFdV ethnocrat had in mind. The Nazi project, embracing virtually all of Poland, as well as the bulk of the Baltic countries, Crimea and Novgorodian Russia around St Petersburg, provided for the establishment of structured German communities along a network (mainly of roads), which in some sketches extended from the radials of Berlin to the Caspian Sea.

In the summer of 1942, practically at the peak of Nazi hope, the new Germanic Reich of which they dreamed, based on the old Reich, was to stretch from the Black Sea to the Arctic Circle and the Urals. A generation later, it was to have included the 'Germanic peoples' (Scandinavians and Batavians essentially) and to have embarked on a battle for babies and the space to house them, extending to the Urals. The aim was to reach, over the generations, a German nationhood dilated in space to include more than half a billion people.

Beyond this expression of Utopia, beyond the fervour expressed by Himmler through the use of the semantic fields of 'eternity' and 'blood', there was, however, one tacit point shared by the *Generalplan Ost* and the language of the head of the SS: they pretended to set out quite naturally from the fact that these spaces were empty, even though their authors knew perfectly well that this was not the case. The reality repressed here was the presence of aliens and the question of *Umvolkung*.

Umvolkung: dissimilation or ethnomorphosis?

It would be somewhat premature to conclude that aliens were absent from the General Plan for the East on the basis solely of the RKFdV documents and the Nazi hopes that were expressed in 1942. A quick examination of the 'Planning Principles' – the first *Generalplan Ost* – will be enough to qualify or even to invalidate this thesis. However, we need to try and understand the status of such aliens, and one concept that arises as soon as the question of ethnic differentiation emerges is that of *Umvolkung*. The reader will have noticed a paradox: I have left this term in German in the body of the text, while the title of this section of the chapter offers a potential translation.

This paradox, in essence, simply points to the fact that we must first explore this notion before hoping to understand the place of the Other (in the sense of *fremd*) in the General Plan for the East. I will begin by trying to give a definition of it before considering the real evolution of the ethnic groups represented by the SS ethnocrats and the 'processes of *Umvolkung*', and then defining the place of aliens in the programmes for the Nazi future.

Anyone who wishes to attempt to define the notion of *Umvolkung* must go back to the interwar period and to those circles that promoted a 'legitimating history' and a 'combatant Nazi science' which dealt with the German nationhood of the frontiers and the foreign territories even before the Nazi imperial hope arose.

If we look for a first definition of *Umvolkung* in the textbooks on Nazi vocabulary, we get what is initially a rather reassuring answer: the *Vokabular des Nationalsozialismus* by Cornelia Schmitz-Berning gives two definitions, one that makes it a synonym for assimilation and the second, from 1940 onwards, the equivalent of 'Germanization' (*Eindeutschung*).[21] The problem with these two definitions is that they are too partial and that no other author reaches this conclusion. While Schmitz-Berning cites sources related to the *Generalplan Ost*, her use of them is somewhat summary. We need to try and investigate the etymology of the notion before proceeding.

It was Karl von Loesch, a geographer at the interface between academic networks, militant geography and diplomatic advice to the governments of the Weimar Republic, who seems to have used the term for the first time in the 1920s.[22] He saw it as the equivalent of *'Entdeutschung'*, 'de-Germanization', and conceived a model extending over four generations describing the loss of national characteristics of individuals and social groups, describing the situation of German migrants in the United States as a completed *Umvolkung*, once the children of third-generation migrants had received their education there. Other specialists in sociology and social psychology introduced the concept in the study of frontier dynamics and it was in this context that Max Hildebert Boehm, the central figure in pre-Nazi *Ostforschung*, took up the term, linking it to a rise in individualism, the loss of the link between communities, and the denationalization (in the sense of loss of national characteristics) of social groups. Gunther Ipsen, who replaced Hans Rothfels at the University of Königsberg, the stronghold of the *Volkstumswissenschaften*, used the term *Umvolkung*, on the one hand, to describe the processes under which German communities abroad were subjected to pressure from the Treaty of Versailles and, on the other hand, to account for the processes of the loss of the national characteristics of the Slavic peoples who arrived in German territories during industrialization.[23]

These theorists lead us very quickly back to the heart of the milieu which was conceptualizing the East even before the emergence of Nazi hopes; so the concept of *Umvolkung* was inextricably linked to what culminated in the General Plan for the East. Without altogether dropping the German phrase, let us try to define more precisely what *Umvolkung* involved, together with a possible translation of the term.

The term *'Umvolkung'* resurfaced between 2012 and 2015 in Germany, under the influence of a wave of xenophobic nationalism, in which, contrary to the racist French belief of the 'big replacement', the neo-*völkisch* Germans claimed to be concerned about the changes that could affect German 'ethnic substance'. This was how they designated any transformation affecting it in their eyes, and they suggested as a translation a neologism based on the Greek root suggesting 'change', without it being connoted in terms of loss or gain, without a negative or positive dimension. The equivalent *ethnomorphosis* thus emerged in this particular public debate and, ignoring the odious dimension of the circumstances of its elaboration, I will from time to time resort to this neologism capable of describing the transitive dimensions of *Umvolkung*.

Nevertheless, this transitive dimension of the notion is very unusual: in practically all the theoreticians who use the concept, it refers to processes that are the prerequisite for the integration, within a people, of different ethnic or national groups. *Umvolkung*, however, does not appear to be synonymous with 'assimilation' because the term refers to a process that seems to take place before integration. For *völkisch* and Nazi theorists, assimilation can only take place between groups with similar racial characteristics. *Umvolkung*, it seems, is the loss, prior to assimilation, of original linguistic and ethnic cultural characteristics. In this sense, the term cannot be equivalent to *Eindeutschung* (Germanization) or assimilation. Conceived as a primary process of stripping off certain traits prior to acquiring new social, ethnic and cultural characteristics, its most faithful translation seems to be a neologism associating a privative prefix or expressing at least a centrifugal character (the prefix *dis-*, as in dispersion, disappearance) and the root (*similation*). It is in this sense that the term 'dissimilation' struck me as the most faithful.[24] And the fact that some specialists in the German social sciences use this term is an additional legitimating argument.[25]

How do the ethnocrats of the SS imagine *Umvolkung*, how do they describe dissimilation? The simplest way of illustrating it is undoubtedly to take an example from those specialists in the *Volkstumswissenschaften* and SS officers who treat it in the most detailed way. The case of the Baltic has the advantage of having been examined by a large number of institutions responsible for thinking the East and its General Plan, as well as the fate of the populations, whether Nordic or not, which were found there.

I have already quoted the SD report from 1938 dealing with Polish policy in the Baltic. The main point of the demonstration was to describe this Baltic German nationhood which had initially assimilated the Baltic elites, a prey to adversity as a result of the alliance between Polish politics, the Russification of institutions and the rise of revolutionary Bolshevism. Given the world of enemies who agreed on nothing except their intense hatred of Germans, Baltic German nationhood was not defenceless in the eyes of Nazi experts: in 1940, another report by the *Amt Raumplanung* of the RKFdV described it as numerically weak – notably, its birth rate was lower than the Lithuanian average – but economically stable. In short, according to the author of the report,[26] a racially 'healthy and vigorous' population, but in a state of cultural suffocation, to such a point that its situation is described as 'hopeless [for lack of] schools, a sufficient number of teachers, [for lack] of written material'.[27] One of the recurring *topoi* of any evocation of German nationhood abroad, beyond the nuances sometimes expressed by the various agencies responsible for ethnicity and the Nazi future, is to show that this German nationhood was exposed to constant pressure from aliens.

It is the same type of description that was given during the winter of 1941 in the Leningrad region by the Petersburg *Sonderkommando* of the VOMI, which included the same Herbert Wallrabe whom we have already studied. Instructed to carry out an assessment of the situation of the *volksdeutsche* communities, its leader, *Standartenführer* (Colonel) von Hehn, conducted a careful village-by-village survey, a real racial X-ray of the German communities around Leningrad. This series of reports thus provides us with an extremely interesting illustration of dissimilation as a *process*.

The author always proceeds in the same way, beginning by dating the settlement of the *Volksdeutsche* and then evaluating their condition. He thus gives us indices for the level of preservation or disintegration of German nationhood, as internalized by the SS *Volkstumswissenschaftler*: one village (Duga) retains religious festivals in the German style; another sees the individuals of the community maintaining relations with one another (the colony of Strelna, a district of Leningrad). The report on the city of Kiopen is a typical example: according to local memory, this was a colony founded around 1610 by migrants from Darmstadt. It was no longer *reindeutsch* (purely German) because of frequent 'mixed marriages' and no longer had a German school, even if the inhabitants still spoke a German sprinkled with a few words of Russian. German nationhood is described as weakened because of the absence of a German school and because of a Russian desire to 'repress' (*unterdrücken*) Germanic culture.[28]

This German isolate in Slavonic (here, Baltic) lands, in the process of being culturally stifled, was thus threatened by intermingling and indeed the dilution of its very substance. Dissimilation – social or cultural – starts by accentuating the insular character of the community, as villages lose contact with each other: the isolate, having become an increasingly sporadic archipelago, then sees its external character traits disappearing: associations, schools, newspapers, but also religious festivals. Finally, the colony loses its character of 'racial purity', either by continuing to cross-breed or by the settlement of aliens. Swamping by dissimilation is then completed.

Clearly, as in many other areas of the Nazi imagination, mental tools were forged in the analysis of German destiny. Werner Best, Heydrich's deputy and Gestapo theorist, *völkisch* student activist in the 1920s, for the first time expressed the exterminating impulse in the form of an eschatological anguish projected onto the invasion of the Ruhr;[29] likewise, the SS reflected on the dissimilation that affected their own community before projecting it onto this alien world that would have to be mastered and subjected in order to bring about the imperial Nazi dream. However, very soon, the *Umvolkung* seems to have been reflected in the General Plan for the East. The reader will have noticed that the hydraulic metaphor was perfectly capable of rendering the dynamics of dissimilation, and perhaps the priorities formulated by Meyer-Heitling as early as 1940 in his 'Planning Principles' already to some extent constituted in his view a process of dissimilation of the Polish populations.

What, finally, is the message of the different *Generalpläne Ost* of this *Umvolkung* of aliens? I have already suggested one answer for the RKFdV: the 'Planning Principles for the Building of the Eastern Territories' of 1940 were an attempt to reverse the curse of German insularity. By announcing the 'polderization' of the Polish ocean, by embarking on its spatial and cultural stifling, they were organizing an *Umvolkung* even if this was not stated as such and remained implicit. On the other hand, these references seem to disappear in what is known of the plan of 15 July 1941, and no mention of aliens was made in the *Generalplan Ost* of 28 May 1942. It must be said that the content of these documents was more economic (in terms of finances and land tenure), agronomic and geographical, and did not really focus on defining the social, cultural and security conditions that should prevail in the territories.

So if we wish to go further, we need to complement this plan with that of the RSHA, as the WVHA plan alone, focused essentially on forecasting the quantities of raw materials and manpower, is too rudimentary to provide any information on this subject.

Hans Ehlich's departments drew up two plans that provide information on the treatment of aliens: the *Fernplan Ost* of 1939 and the *Generalplan Ost* reported in early 1942 by Erhard Wetzel, Racial Affairs Officer of the Ministry for Occupied Territories. We can probably add the intense activity that led to the memoranda produced by the RSHA and the SD in those years, as well as a number of speeches delivered by their senior figures during this period. Let us first recall what the *Fernplan Ost* envisaged for the Poles and Jews of the territories incorporated into the Reich in November 1939:

(1) First, Jews and Poles appearing as politically dominant must be expelled to the General Government (obligatory service for 18–60-year-olds).
(2) Poles living in the occupied territories must be subject to racial investigation.
(3) The Reich's labour needs must serve to weaken Polishness by depriving it of racially valuable Poles who can serve in the Reich over time. This selection must also take place in the General Government.
(4) A skilled labour force, from trained workers to craftsmen, postal workers, building workers, etc., when they are of good racial quality and well-assimilated, must be gradually replaced by labour coming from the Reich.
(5) To a certain extent, the Eastern provinces may retain a Polish labouring stratum for subordinate service in the agricultural and industrial sectors.
(6) Poles of no use to the Reich and the Eastern provinces are to be expelled to the General Government.[30]

The system which emerges here is strictly speaking a device for dissimilating the Polish populations of the incorporated provinces, but also, to a certain extent, those of the General Government. In the occupied territories, the Polish population must first be deprived of its elites, and then, after a racial evaluation procedure similar to that we observed in the previous chapter, submitted to a compulsory labour service. The most racially valuable individuals and groups and those who might comprise an elite are to be sent to the Reich in order to cut them off from the population, while they must be replaced on the spot by individuals from the Reich. The rest of the Polish population must be able to remain on the spot as a subordinate labour stratum.

This is therefore a first definition of the process of dissimilation that the Polish population must undergo in the incorporated territories. It is perfectly in line with the principles of colonization which Reinhardt Heydrich referred to in his famous speech in Prague on 2 October 1941:

> It is these spaces that we must now control and preserve in the East, spaces in which a German elite [*Oberschicht* = upper stratum] must, in accordance with military evolution, be engaged in a form of clear domination far inside Russia, as far as the Urals, as a deposit of raw material, [and its population] as workers, as helots, if I have to be explicit.[31]

The head of the RSHA and *Reichsprotektor* of Bohemia and Moravia, two years after the *Fernplan Ost* of 1939, expressed the same ideas. The rigidity of the description of the policy applied to aliens, a policy of domination seeking explicitly to deprive the relevant populations of their elites, their education systems and their learned culture, and to transform them into a labour force that could be allowed to exist only as a labour force, did indeed constitute a policy of dissimilation. Along with population displacements, it lay at the heart of the consensus which, over and above the various options and strategies for positioning the various SS institutions within the state polycratic apparatus, united them in fostering the Nazi Utopia.

Umvolkung, the loss of the characteristics of a population or an ethnic group, was not, however, thought of solely in terms of dissimilation; it was also an ethnomorphosis prior to Germanization. This is how Erhard Wetzel presented it in reference to the Ruthenian populations of Belarus:

> There is no doubt that in Rutheniandom [*Weißruthenentum*, sic!] there is a strong Eastern Baltic racial contribution, and thus Belarus, Lithuania and Western Russia are perhaps the territory of the greatest presence of the Eastern Baltic Race. Nevertheless, one cannot ignore the fact that practically pure northern types have also been preserved among the white Ruthenians. I myself have seen Belarussians whom one might have imaged to originate in the regions of Lower Saxony or SchleswigHolstein if they had been German. We should dissimilate and Germanize these racially precious Ruthenian *Sippen* [lineages] before a Belarusian ethnic identity and consciousness appear, making dissimilation more difficult.[32]

In Wetzel, the use of the term *Umvolkung* corresponded closely to the privative acceptation of ethnomorphosis (i.e. dissimilation), and indeed constituted a prerequisite for Germanization. But the difference between the treatment of the Poles dissimilated by the RSHA in 1939–40 and what was visibly envisaged for the Belorussians of northern race was immense. It illustrates how complex and ambiguous the concept of *Umvolkung* in Nazi planning was.

Erhard Wetzel was not one of the men who drew up these plans. Given the sometimes incomplete documentation on the planning activities of the RSHA, he remains one of our most valuable informants. He is a critical commentator, not because of any moral condemnation of a plan whose absolute violence is becoming evident, but because he is a convinced Nordicist, keen to participate in the discussion of these documents, to make their grandiose objectives achievable. Critical he may be, but only in the service of the realization of Utopia. And de facto, it seems that we must go back to his careful examination of the RSHA's *Generalplan Ost* to understand what is very rarely expressed directly in any documents planning for Utopia: its fundamentally homicidal dimension.

The drying up of the alien ocean: mass murder and Utopia

For this privileged observer of SS planning, Erhard Wetzel, the success of any colonization project was not related to the extent of the spaces to be occupied nor to the extent of population displacements. Here is how he sets out his thoughts:

> As early as November 1941, I was informed that the RSHA was working on a General Plan for the East. The competent expert for this work, *Standartenführer* Ehlich, mentioned the figure, contained in the plan, of 31 million aliens to be expelled. In this business, of all the agencies of the SS *Reichsführer*, the RSHA is the one that has the strongest position today. Here, the RSHA, according to the theories defended by the agencies of the RFSS (*Reichsführer SS*), also acts as a delegate of the RKFdV.
> [. . .]
>   As regards colonization territories, it appears that the territories of *Ingermanland* and the Dnieper, Taurida and Crimea loop have been removed from the plan. This is obviously due to the fact that, in the meantime, new colonization projects have emerged which we will have to discuss in conclusion. Moreover, it seems that today, the eastern frontier of colonization is being described as a much more offset line to the East, from Lake Ladoga to the hills of Valdai and Brjansk. I cannot conclude that this is a change of plan on the part of the SS. In any case, this will probably result in an increase in the number of people involved in expulsions.
>   A reading of the plan shows that it is not for immediate effect, but rather that the colonization of space by Germans must take place over thirty years. It is apparent from the plan that fourteen million aliens [*Fremdvölkische*] can remain in this space. It seems more than doubtful that they can be dissimilated and Germanized in the period of thirty years under consideration, not least because the number of German settlers is not especially high. According to the plan, obviously, the tendency developed by the RKFdV to send Germanizable aliens to the former Reich has been abandoned. It is explicitly stated on page 3 of the plan that the aliens who are not expelled will remain in the Eastern spaces as a population.

The nodal question of the whole question of colonization in the East is whether we will succeed in arousing once more the colonizing impulse [*Siedlunsgtrieb*] of the German people. The fact that it is partially present cannot, in my opinion, be doubted. But we must not lose sight of the fact that another major section of the population, particularly in Western Germany, decisively and trenchantly refuses to be settled in the East, including even the Warthegau, Danzig or West Prussia, simply because it views the Eastern territories as too monotonous or depressing, or too cold and primitive. All these tendencies, which act against the desire for colonization in the East, must be monitored and propagandistically countered by the competent authorities, in particular by the Ministry for Occupied Territories.

Besides the question of the will to colonize, and equally decisive, is the question of the desire for children which it is necessary to awaken on a quite different scale than hitherto in the German people and especially among Eastern settlers. We should not be blind to the fact that the current increase in the number of births since 1933 is pleasing in itself, but it is by no means sufficient for the numbers of the German population, especially if one takes into account the immense colonizing missions in the East and the monstrous biological force of demographic growth among the neighbouring peoples. [There follows a long paragraph calculating the populations available for a resettlement in the East, resulting in a total of some 4.45 million individuals, then 8 million.][33]

In the eyes of the racial expert from the Ministry for Occupied Territories, therefore, the question of the growth of fertility and the awakening of a pioneering spirit among the Germans is the key to colonization. Of course, the measures taken by the Nazis when they came to power – interest-free credit for young couples, facilities for settlement, compensation for women who left their jobs, reduction of credit interest for each child born[34] – led to a slight rebound in the birth rate in a country which, after having experienced a very large demographic increase in the nineteenth century, then moved towards Malthusian post-transitional behaviour. But in the eyes of the racial expert, this slight recovery is very, very far from being enough, especially as the demographic haemorrhage of the Great War and the conflict now affecting the Reich are very large, and in the view of the Nazis have an impact on the most valuable part of the northern racial heritage. The Nazi hierarchy had a particularly acute awareness of this state of affairs. It was precisely this which had legitimized in their eyes the post-mortem legalization of the marriage between soldiers and their pregnant and widowed fiancées.[35] Here, this anguish mingled with an older anxiety, widely projected onto the territories of the East: an anxiety about being swamped. The 'monstrous biological force of demographic growth among the neighbouring peoples' meant that 8 million Germans in the *Generalplan Ost* of Ehlich and Group III B of the RSHA would eventually have to face 45 million aliens. And Wetzel, in the following paragraphs, invalidated the calculations of the RSHA experts:

in a few well-weighed words, he corrected the inaccuracies which, in his view, peppered the plan – notably the fact that the latter did not take account the fertility of aliens – and provided an estimate of 51 million aliens.[36]

The second limitation that at least partially undermined the feasibility of the RSHA plan was the 'pioneering drive' of the German population, obviously rather fragile according to the author. The Third Reich was faced with a double dilemma. On the one hand, it could not resolve to introduce forced population displacements for its own citizens, but considered this measure for aliens, thus depriving itself of a valuable means of making the plans feasible. On the other hand, the various plans envisaged a predominantly agricultural colonization, but they were destined for a predominantly urban German population.

Anxiety over demographic swamping, refusal of any authoritarian planning of Nordic migration, a paradox of structural reform which went against the industrialization of German territory: these were the main challenges at least partly underlined by Erhard Wetzel as he sought to produce constructive criticism of the plan for the SS.

It was by operating within this set of paradoxes, and endeavouring to give them an answer, that the Nazi plans integrated the various paradigm shifts that affected the treatment of non-Nordic peoples between 1939 and 1943.

In my history of the successive plans for Germanization over the 1,399 days which this survey embraces, I briefly noted how these plans had their own special statuses. They represented successive consensuses between institutions; they also integrated – often with a time lag difficult to evaluate – the new developments and the often abrupt changes and shifts in Nazi occupation policies. In short, they refracted the conceptual ecosystem generated by the institutions in charge of the policies shaping the Nazi future. And this ecosystem became tragically radicalized during these 1,399 days, giving to the General Plan for the East at the beginning of 1943 a stake and consequences that it did not have in the mists of the foundational period in the autumn of 1939. Three types of experience of occupation thus found their place in the prerequisites of these plans; indeed, they constituted implicit but necessary conditions.

The first of the 'innovations' reflected in the RSHA plans was the idea of eliminating specifically the elites of the populations encountered in the course of the conquest. Thus, between November 1939 and the spring of 1940, the local security authorities of the General Government launched two operations whose unprecedented character was evident. The first such action was the Special Action in Kraków, where on 6 November 1939 the forces of the *Sicherheitspolizei* imprisoned 144 professors, members of the Jagiellonian, the University of Kraków, assembled on the pretext of a lecture delivered by Bruno Müller, KdS of the city and international lawyer. The aim was to eliminate part of the Polish intelligentsia even though the victims were sent to concentration camps and not executed.[37] Bruno Müller was one of those SD intellectuals who later became involved in the genocide of Soviet Jews, but he was mainly, in our view, principally one of the main deputies of Ehlich in Group III B-4 of the RSHA, the one who specialized in population displacement issues, a position he held until May 1941, when he joined *Einsatzgruppe* D,[38] a mobile security unit which then took over the genocide of the Jews in southern Ukraine and Crimea. Müller was thus the man who could circulate what current management theorists call 'good practice' from one domain to another: in this case, aggression against elites was shifted from security policies towards ethnomorphic policies.

A second example: on 22 April 1940, Bruno Streckenbach, the BdS for the General Government, asserted during a session of the government that his services had identified some 2,500 people acting under pseudonyms on behalf of the Polish resistance and announced the unleashing of an 'extraordinary action of pacification' which would target Polish elites. It consisted of a coordinated wave of arrests, with many people being sent to concentration camps or executed by shooting, after summary conviction if need be. This action, carried out under cover of the invasion of the West in May 1940, was certainly not conceived in the name of Germanization, as the General Government was not yet one of the places set aside for the Nazi future, but marked the radicalization of a policy that after 'Action Kraków' and the *Fernplan Ost* was specifically aimed at alien cultural elites. In May 1940, physically destroying the elites of a population seemed to have become one of the possible elements of a policy of dissimilation.

In any case, when in June 1941 the *Einsatzgruppen* set out in the wake of the Army of the East to take control of the invaded Soviet territory, aggression against the political and cultural elites was already firmly rooted in people's minds and the only specific orders given to these groups mentioned the functional and political elites as targets for immediate execution. But the entry into the war against the USSR marked the generalization of other practices which were later to find their place in the conceptual background of the General Plan for the East. Preparations for the invasion had, as the reader will recall, led the economic and logistical institutions of the Wehrmacht to decide not to supply the troops, which meant condemning 'tens of millions of people' to starvation, first and foremost the inhabitants of the great urban centres.[39] This could be seen as the permanent implementation of an *imaginaire* of extinction, of letting people die, whose first stages could be observed in the creation of the Madagascar Plan, which foresaw the deportation of all European Jewry to an island incapable of ensuring their survival. And this *imaginaire*, which circulated in decision-making spheres to which the social and racial engineers of the RKFdV and the RSHA were close, did not fail to permeate the General Plan for the East. Did Erhard Wetzel, who criticized the RSHA plan, not suspect that the difference in figures between the calculations of

Ehlich's services and his own was probably due to the fact that tens of millions of famine deaths were taken into account, deaths that the RSHA had approved in the negotiations with the Wehrmacht? It is very difficult to take this speculation any further given the documentation at our disposal. In any case, the RKFdV and RSHA plans reflected all these developments in their figures: the remarkable fixity of the numbers of 'migrant reserves', with their precious Nordic blood, led observers to seek other methods to overcome the imbalance in the stand-off between German colonists and the swarm of aliens. Again, it was really a matter of fighting German insularity in the vast expanses of the East.

As we have seen, Erhard Wetzel was a remarkably well-informed commentator on all the policies of occupation in East Europe. A racial expert in the Ministry for Occupied Territories, he had participated in the meetings following the Wannsee Conference,[40] and was therefore informed of the option of exhaustive homicide, with direct genocide by deportation and execution of the unfit for work as described by Heydrich at the meeting. That is why, in his criticism of the figures mentioned in their plan by Hans Ehlich's department, he questions whether 'Jews were eliminated before evacuation' or not.[41] In so doing, he implicitly admits that he knows that the Jews will be exterminated *in the USSR*. Nothing here suggests that it is Soviet Jews who are being mentioned: the *Einsatzgruppen* had already killed nearly 700,000 people by March 1942, and since November 1941 they had been engaged in a phase of total and exhaustive liquidation of the Soviet Jewish communities, probably to make room for the deported Jews from Western Europe and particularly from the Reich.[42]

The direct homicide of massive population contingents and indirect homicide – by famine and probably labour – together with the elimination of elites were thus added to the range of tools used by social and racial engineers to plan Utopia. *Umvolkung*, both as a concept and as a policy, already possessed immense potential for repression and violence, and was thus added to the murderous tools of which the Nazis were now making ample use in the year 1942, which marked the peak of their hopes. The security policies inaugurated precisely in the regions embraced by plans for Germanization included such elements as 'hunting down partisans', economic rationalization, predation and the undifferentiated massacre of Slavic rural populations: in other words, all the means available to SS experts appeared complete. Christian Gerlach has written a remarkable history of these policies in the case of Belarus, the origin of the great operations for mopping up partisan units which were the pretext for the massacre of populations incapable of work and the deportation of those who could work and had survived the predation of all agricultural production.[43] They now had a directory of practices at their disposal that really made them 'designers of annihilation'.[44]

In actual fact, at the beginning of 1942, and in the words of Wetzel, while the most radical tools had appeared in the planners' arsenal, the exhaustive and direct murderous *imaginaire* was directed exclusively against the Jewish populations. Wetzel referred to the thoughts of a former assistant to Eugen Fischer (raciologist doctor-in-chief of the Kaiser-Wilhelm-Institut (KWI) and a great friend of Heidegger), namely Wolfgang Abel, who had undertaken a survey of physical anthropology on behalf of the Wehrmacht in the winter of 1941, and in a talk at a symposium (probably organized by the KWI) referred to 'the extirpation of the Russian people'.[45] But these were just vague evocations. More significantly, Wetzel and the RKFdV and RSHA experts had gone from an ethnomorphic *imaginaire* to policies aimed at curbing the population growth of aliens. Confronted with an inadequate supply of precious Nordic blood, they had to succeed in limiting the alien ocean so as to control swamping. In any case, this is what transpired in the 'Wetzel Plan'. Still speaking of the Russian question, he said:

> In the territories concerned, we must carry out a consciously negative demographic policy. We must take propaganda measures, using the press, radio, cinema, leaflets, small brochures, educational conferences and the like, by which the [Russian] people must be convinced of the mischief of producing many children. We have to talk about the costs, as well as everything you have to install and acquire. We can also address the dangers that women face during childbirth. In addition to this propaganda, there must be ambitious propaganda in favour of the means of contraception. We must develop an industry for such means. The commercialization and spread of contraception must be legalized, as must abortion. The establishment of abortion centres should be promoted. One could, for example, train midwives and female medical auxiliaries [*Feldseherinnen*] to carry out abortions. The longer abortion is practised, the more we will gain the confidence of the population. Doctors themselves must be trained in this practice, without it being seen as a contravention of medical ethics. Similarly, voluntary sterilization should be promoted. We must not fight child mortality. Similarly, the training of mothers in neonatal and perinatal care as well as in treating infantile diseases should not be undertaken. In these areas, the training of Russian doctors should be limited to the lowest possible level. In addition to these negative health policy measures, it is necessary to avoid making marital separation difficult. No specific measures should be taken for illegitimate children. Child care facilities, tax reductions for births and generally all measures to promote the birth rate should be avoided.[46]

Wetzel here presented an intermediate state of Nazi thinking about the East and the subsequent treatment of aliens. In the face of the scarcity of northern blood, the mental means of mass murder emerged. The actors, observers of the predatory and murderous policies of occupation and genocide that had emerged since December 1941, had an advanced awareness of these means, but their use was not yet envisaged. What Wetzel aimed at in his long text was a biopolitics of ethnomorphosis marked by the struggle against the allegedly rampant fertility of aliens. A reduction in the birth rate as a paradigm of *Umvolkung*, in short. Nevertheless, the General Plan for the East had become considerably radicalized and this process was now largely under way.

In order to understand the demographic stakes of the General Plan for the East, we must refer to the last plans of the two great institutions responsible for thinking the East and the aftermath of Germany. The RKFdV plan, dated 23 December 1942, signed by Meyer-Heitling,[47] now based on a sharp decline in the numbers of alien populations, took into account both the latest state of the policy of exterminating Jews in the East, the food supply policy of the Wehrmacht and the Ministry of Agriculture, and the concept of 'extermination by work' developed by the WVHA.[48] It was this mechanism, called 'depopulation' (*Rückvolkung*) by the RKFdV and the RSHA, that was reflected in the figures of the SS plan.[49] Herbert Backe, Minister of Supply and Agriculture, had, together with the Wehrmacht, invented the 'Famine Plan', sealing the destiny of 'tens of millions of individuals'.[50] And it was not surprising to see Konrad Meyer-Heitling appointed, at the instigation of Himmler, as responsible for the planning, alongside Backe.[51] The policy of saving Germans from the alien ocean had thus given way to planned depopulation, the only way of ensuring, along with expulsions, the 'ethno-cultural survival' of the Germanic communities among the Slavs. Germanization effectively took into account the genocidal policies and the decimation of the Slavs, and without scheduling it in detail, SS experts foresaw its application over thirty years. But it is the *Generalsiedlungsplan* of the RSHA which, in the last instance, gives us the full measure of the consequences of this 'depopulation'. As we have said, we do not have this plan but a combination of two documents allows us to access its encrypted data.

At a symposium of the RSHA *Amt* III B held in Bernau, on the northern outskirts of Berlin, on 1–2 February 1943 under the direction of Otto Ohlendorf, Hans Ehlich and Justus Beyer,[52] the last of these presented, in an introductory lecture, the latest version of the General Plan for the Germanization of Occupied Territories, the *Generalsiedlungsplan* of the RSHA, to the racial affairs officers of all the local offices of the SD, and mentioned the numbers of aliens to be expelled.[53] A few weeks earlier, on 11 December 1942, Hans Ehlich, the head of the RSHA Group III B and principal author of the *Generalsiedlungsplan*, had delivered a lecture to the leaders of the NSDStB on the 'treatment of foreign peoples'.[54] He envisaged four methods for dealing with the 70 (68.6 in fact) million people who, for him, peopled the territories that needed to be Germanized: 'life in community with racially related peoples, dissimilation within the German nationhood, spatial repression and physical extermination [...] of undesirables'. According to Ehlich, 'life in common' concerned only the mainly Nordic peoples, who did not exist in the East. The dissimilation was in his view conditioned by a selection within the peoples, a selection that would make it possible to tap northern blood and to expel those who were considered unfit. Less than a fortnight later, Ehlich, Ohlendorf, the head of the SD, and Justus Beyer produced, at the conference of the *Referenten* III B of local offices of the SD,[55] percentages of expulsions broken down by peoples.[56]

By combining the numbers given by Ehlich in his lecture with the percentages of 'persons to be displaced' given by Beyer, we can finally gain a clear idea of the fate of these aliens. Ehlich mentions 22.5 million Poles, in Beyer's view 85 per cent (19.125 million) of them expellable, 7 million Czechs with 50 per cent (3.5 million) expellable, 4.1 million Baltics also with 50 per cent (2.05 million) expellable, 5 million White Russians with 75 per cent (3.75 million) expellable, and 30 million Ukrainians – the rate only concerns the Ukrainians of Galicia, more 'naturalised' than the others in the eyes of racial experts, so that the figure represents a *minimum* – with 65 per cent (19.5 million) expellable. This results in a total of 47,925,000 undesirable people.

Wetzel's *Generalplan Ost*, however, foresaw the expulsion – the 'spatial repression', as Hans Ehlich put it – of 'only' 31 million people:[57] thus, there remained almost 16,925,000 'undesirables' who could not be dissimilated, and whose deportation was not foreseen. Only then was the fourth solution envisaged by Ehlich: physical elimination. Again this figure did not take into account the Jews, whose number was estimated in January 1942 in Eastern Europe at 8,391,200 individuals (about 11.3 million in the whole of Europe), all now destined for extermination; their number, according to the report of the Inspector General of Statistics SS Richard Korherr, had already been halved.[58] The plan thus seemed to be based on the expulsion of 31 million people and the violent death of 25,316,200 individuals,[59] starved to death, exterminated by labour, or killed by anti-partisan units and in extermination camps. The practice of genocide, which had been on the march since the autumn of 1941, was not merely integrated into the plan, but had become a condition of Germanization, the final aim of the Nazi Utopia.

At the beginning of 1943, overcoming German insularity meant that the RKFdV and RSHA experts had to dry up the alien ocean. The plan described in its figures both their hopes for the lifting of a curse on Germanic destiny, and mass murder as a means of attaining it. The advent of the Thousand-Year Reich and the hopes of the Nordic *Volksgemeinschaft* were to be realized at the cost of more than 25 million 'non-native' lives.

Chapter 5
At the School of Fine Arts

The Nazi Utopia was a socio-racial project anchored in a certain space. Thus, at all levels, both locally and in Berlin, this sequence of actions leading to Utopia was also marked by intense design and foresight, preparatory studies to visualize the future once victory had been achieved. In order to understand and probe this last facet of the Nazi Utopia in the making, we need to look more carefully at some of the documentary sources that we have already fugitively discussed, and in particular at two exhibitions that were scheduled to be held: one, eventually aborted, at the Princesses' Palace on Unter den Linden, the other, which took place, at the Hochschule der Bildenden Kunst (School of Fine Arts) on Hardenbergstrasse next to the Zoological Gardens railway station. The SS asked the architects to set out a design for the future of the peasants and workers in the Great East once it had been conquered and redeveloped. The documentation was carefully presented and there are many indications that the Nazi hierarchy took a close interest. Himmler showed the exhibition twice to other dignitaries, and on 20 March 1941, Daluege, Bracht, Hess, Bormann, Bouhler, Behrends, Todt and Jüttner were given a guided tour by Meyer-Heitling,[1] who wrote the introductory text to the 'Planning and Building in the East' exhibition catalogue. On the basis of this document and the plans for urban and regional renewal, we can start to understand how the Nazi project first presented itself as a general redevelopment project, encompassing at the very least the Eastern territories and proposing ways for them to be joined to the West by granting a central and structuring place to the old Reich. Second, this documentation also allows us to understand how the cities of the incorporated territories were to be reorganized, and how the *Volksgemeinschaft* would be shaped. Finally, the Nazis dreamed of new rural spaces, which assumed shape, if not reality, in the competitions of architects and landscapers exhibiting at the School of Fine Arts.

Thinking about space

In his introduction to the catalogue, Meyer-Heitling begins by recalling the specificity of the period that had emerged since 1939:

> Every great era shapes new forms and generates new wills. This is especially true for colonization policies.
> We are now definitively confronted with the great cause of colonization, with the rebuilding of this recovered East and the expansion of the Reich.
> By the will of the Führer, this cause is now placed under the aegis of a strengthening of German nationhood.
> The policies of settlement and colonization had never before been placed under the auspices of this theory. Between urban–rural antagonism and the lack of an overall theory, they transformed the territories into urban and rural areas that were increasingly distant from each other and prey to differences of opinion and interests among the various parties and factions. This is also the explanation for the ideological vagueness and the multiplicity of conceptions and motives that are so often seen at work in the issues raised by colonization.[2]

The important thing to remember here is that the question which arises, between the lines, is that of the *Volksgemeinschaft*, in the sense that practices of colonization had hitherto reflected the multiple conflicts which ran through the very social body implementing these practices. According to the SS agricultural geographer, National Socialism, strong in its victory and its colonizing mission, should reflect the new harmony of the Nazi refoundation: free from internal conflicts and antagonisms, the new society must find forms of spatial settlement that would be unified and harmonious. After this introduction, which remarkably sets out the utopian context in which the planning is taking place, according to the SS officer, he continues by focusing on the stakes of this programme:

> Planning for the organization of the East must face up to the shortages to come and the obstacles that await us. With the colonization of the East, it is not only a matter of refounding a new German peasantry, or of building social housing, small estates, or property, but rather of *the Germanization of new territories, the arrangement, the ordering and the differentiation of spaces and landscapes as the future fatherland of Germans* [italics in the original]. It will therefore be necessary to build new villages with common facilities, to build new towns or to completely reshape others, to give back to neglected [*verwahrlosten*] landscapes a rational figure and, finally, to reconnect the city and the countryside in an orderly fashion, economically, politically and culturally.[3]

In the eyes of this academic, the issues at stake in planning are not technical, but political and racial. Spatial rearrangement and the rationalization of land and cities have but one aim: to serve the political and racial project. It is a matter of reinventing a new society through redevelopment. And he continues:

> In view of this higher objective, the different aspects of colonization are only means to an end; the different aspects and actors of colonization must act in a concerted and collective way. It is only via such collective work [. . .] that we will obtain the guarantee that of all these plans will give birth to a rational General Plan [*Gesamtplan*]. The Master is recognized not in the plans and projects generated by synergy, but in their structuring [*gestalterische*] insertion into the Whole and the idea of the overall plan.[4]

The hierarchical nature of all this is clear, at least once we can shake off the lyrical jargon of the SS academic: the approach is scalar, and it is taken from racial discourse. The idea is to think of the new society on a continental scale and in its entirety, and then to descend to the smallest scales, into the detail of socio-spatial modelling. Once these details have been presented in the introduction, the catalogue of the exhibition abandons the lyrical tone, but conforms rather strictly to the scalar approach here outlined by Meyer-Heitling.

Logically enough, the first part of the presentation, signed by Udo von Schauroth, a close collaborator of Meyer-Heitling in the second *Generalplan Ost*, is devoted to the structuring of space in the incorporated territories. The territory embraced by the exhibition is in keeping with the context: in March 1941, in spite of the secret preparations for Barbarossa, the territories destined for Germanization were those of the first *Generalpläne Ost*, namely the territories incorporated into the Reich, while the General Government was excluded from the projects.

In this framework, the first question is the calibration of clearly hierarchical networks. Based on the principle of a population density of nearly ninety inhabitants per square km, SS planning is apparently to be implemented using a strictly functionalist approach, differentiating between local functions, central functions and special functions. According to von Schauroth, the size of the population that performs local functions is determined by the distribution of agricultural facilities, land structure (size of farms) and the 'necessary agricultural and mechanical facilities'. The proportion of population determined by the central functions is deduced from 'the operation of storage and transport enterprises and from the processing of the market produce of the regions concerned'. The economic and cultural needs of enterprises and institutions as well as the needs of administration and governance must be met. Finally, special productions are 'units of production whose zone of activity and sale lies outside the territories incorporated into the Reich, being directed towards populations outside these territories (soldiers, the retired, tourists) and cultural and administrative institutions at national level'.[5]

The elements of typology are then detailed in this introductory text, which specifies that the structure of population settlement must be determined according to 'human creations worth preserving' and on the basis of the state of communication with the Reich and Europe, in purely rural areas, in purely industrial settlement basins and in territories that must coordinate industry and agricultural activities.[6]

Once the orders of magnitude and importance of the different settlement units have been defined (three hierarchical levels: villages, main villages, small towns), von Schauroth sets out the functions that must be assigned to each level.

The first sketches that are reproduced in the catalogue logically conform to this discourse, which rather strictly follows the precepts of Walter Christaller. Christaller, a geographer, spelled out the theory of central places in his thesis on the city networks of South Germany, published in Jena in 1935; it led to a model for structuring space as an expansive field of influence, defining more or less circular zones. Not surprisingly: Christaller was hired by Meyer-Heitling in the summer of 1940 and appointed to the Institute of Agronomy in Berlin; he was a member of the *Nationalsozialistische Deutsche Arbeiterpartei* (NSDAP or National Socialist Workers' Party); and participated – though we do not know to what extent – in the development of successive versions of the *Generalplan Ost*.[7]

And this is how the maps hierarchize the central spaces: the example of the Kutno district in Wartheland, fifty kilometers north of Łódź, serves as an illustration of von Schauroth's remarks and of the application of Christaller's model. Only the town and two main villages are mentioned in a district which was meant to have eleven. Von Schauroth explains this by stating that deciding on the concrete and precise situation of the central villages is left to the local rural planners. A brief glance at the contemporary situation shows a relatively macrocephalic district composed of a town centre of 47,000 inhabitants, two medium-sized towns with 9,000 and 12,000 inhabitants respectively, and villages forming a loose and not very hierarchical network.[8] Even apart from von Schauroth's description of population sizes that are a tenth as big, the planning of the network of human occupation already seems problematic: nine main villages of similar rank to the two already existing are supposed to emerge. The East, thus, is indeed a spatial *tabula rasa* where everything is possible.

However, the SS engineer (and the second *Generalplan Ost* as a whole) could fill in the *tabula rasa* in some places more than in others: von Schauroth states that the examples developed up to this point had emerged from the 'new building zones' (*Neubauzonen*) which constituted the true pioneering front of Germanization, where it was more a question of creating something from what was considered as underexploited and underdeveloped, as opposed to the 'transformation zones' (*Umbauzonen*) in which, in the words of the engineer, 'restoration of order will consist in a more or less profound correction of what already exists'.[9]

The town of Bromberg and its district fell into this category. Bromberg, as we know, had been predominantly German until 1919, when it was ceded to Poland, and in 1939 was still 10 per cent German and 90 per cent Polish, of all religions.[10] According to the principles of colonization of the East put forward by Meyer-Heitling in early 1940, Bromberg and its district were part of the German ethnic bridge crossing the corridor and intended to separate out and force back the alien ocean.[11] In 1941, the city still had 144,000 inhabitants and benefited from transport infrastructure and Wilhelminian town planning. It was this state of affairs that legitimized Bromberg's classification as a 'transformation zone', as it was a question of rebuilding it on the basis of the imperial legacy. Without referring to any causal link, von Schauroth mentioned the fact that the Bromberg district had pre-existing industrial functions with genuine development capacities. Future settlement structures in his view essentially depended on the expansion of urban rights of way, communication channels (the Vistula, canals and land networks), as well as the development of local industrial sectors. The engineer noted that some of the central rural areas had pre-urban characteristics and in other cases the central functions had been taken over by neighbouring urban units, but thought that this would not prevent the creation of the network of major villages, especially since these were often already present.[12] All the same, the map and its legend tell us a little more about Bromberg, its region and the measures that the SS were planning.

Two main surface figures appear on the map: on the one hand, the rural rights of way, and on the other hand, the surfaces marked down for urban buildings. When von Schauroth's scheme is crossreferenced with the topographical maps of the period,[13] it can be seen that developers strictly respected the rural rights of way and therefore had no intention of promoting any significant expansion of the peasantry in the district of Bromberg. In addition, urban expansion seemed to require the coalescence of Bromberg with the village of Fordon, to the east, slightly north of the town, with a large freight station located between the two agglomerations. The desire to develop two administrative sites (*Amtsitz*), apart from Bromberg and Fordon, is clearly announced by the legend and by the presence of pre-emptive rights of way that do not correspond to the buildings of the two villages found on the topographic map. Promotion to the rank of administrative centre is thus clearly accompanied by an effort to acquire land tenure probably anticipating urban growth. The map then lists seven major villages, the location of which was clearly chosen, unlike Kutno, but it is not possible to determine, from the documentation, the criteria by which choices were made between the main villages, in a network where the habitat was divided into relatively well-balanced villages, with street-villages of colonization intercalated between villages formed by spontaneous agglutination.

Then come four villages designated as future major villages. Situated at the extreme south, northeast and west of the district, they show by their location a desire to balance the network of rural villages. For those that can be compared on the topographic map, however, they appear to exist in extremely heterogeneous situations, which explains why von Schauroth wrote that certain villages – as can be seen from the case of Naekel (west of Bromberg) on the topographic map – were urban in character, as they already had the main features of a town, while for others the central functions had been taken over by neighbouring urban facilities. Von Schauroth does not deny this heterogeneity, but it is not in his view an obstacle compromising the search for balance in the network.

On the whole, in terms of local and regional network planning, the Nazis thought they were acting in a differentiated way: when it was a matter of creating ex nihilo – and of course destroying if necessary – in new building zones, they tried, as far as possible, to respect existing facilities in transformation zones and to discriminate between building units to create hierarchized but balanced networks.

The last, but not least, dimension of thinking of space in terms of networks involved the articulation of communication networks on the scale of Germany and Europe. The planners do not refer to this in the catalogue for *Planung und Aufbau im Osten*. It is known, however, that this was an important concern for the ethnocrats of the RKFdV, and the abundance of experts and of projects, some of which were put into practice, is a clue. Its absence in the catalogue of the exhibition forces us to look for other sources. One of the documents that allows us to understand how the developers planned how to connect the conquered East to the rest of Europe is a work written by Friedrich Gollert, head of the urban planning office of the governor of the district of Warsaw, Ludwig Fischer. Written in 1942, this work begins by retracing the history of the 'German presence' in Warsaw, before setting the city, the district and, more generally, the General Government in the geographical context of Europe as a whole. Warsaw thus becomes the gate to the East, and the expert demonstrates this with the help of a great number of maps.[14] The first maps he adds to the dossier concern railway communications. The first is careful to present the railway network of the General Government as always having Warsaw as its centre of gravity – while the administrative centre is Kraków, the residence of the Governor General and his institutions – and shows what is very clearly a network with two foci. This first contradiction, however, demonstrates the way the space of the General Government was thought out, with the territorial entity relying on these two foci to anchor the north of the territory to the historical Reich in the direction of Danzig and Berlin via Poznań, while the network passing through Kraków firmly anchored the General Government to the southern fringe of the empire, via Breslau, Prague (not mentioned by name) and Vienna.

A second map then presents Warsaw as the gateway of Europe to the East. Partly due to graphic artifices of which contemporary advertising agencies and promotional cartographers would be proud, the city finds itself at the centre of a radial network, with railway tracks from

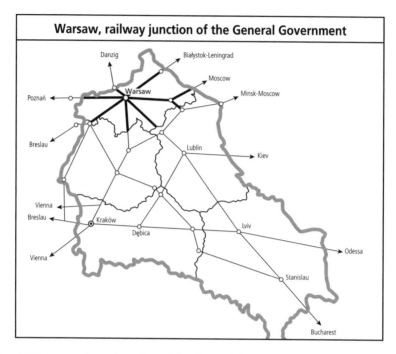

Map 4 Warsaw, railway junction of the General Government

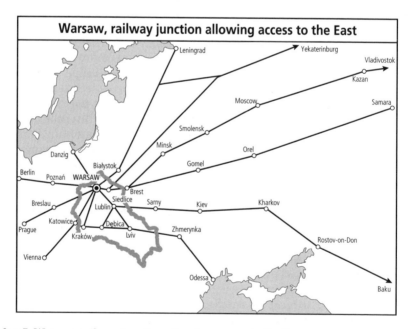

Map 5 Warsaw, railway junction allowing access to the East

Bucharest, Odessa, Kiev/Kharkov/Rostov-on-Don and Baku in the south to Minsk, Moscow, Königsberg and St Petersburg to the east and north. This is where the network is at its widest. We have just seen how it extends to the Caucasus, the Caspian and Azerbaijan by way of Baku, with lines stretching from Brest to Gomel in the Pripet Marshes, Orel and Samara, then from Minsk to Moscow via Smolensk then Kazan (and on to Vladivostok, as the map stipulates, as it acknowledges the Trans-Siberian) and an intermediate route between Moscow and St Petersburg, towards Yekaterinburg, possibly via Nizhny Novgorod and Perm. The desire to link European Russia as far as the southern sectors of the Urals to the Nazi Empire is evident and requires great lines of penetration whose radial centre is Warsaw, according to Fischer's planning department, with Kraków confining itself to radiating out to the south and Crimea.

The rest of the cartographic documentation stems from the same process. On the one hand, it is a matter of anchoring the territory of Warsaw in the Reich and of making it a native German territory, situated in the territorial and networked continuity of the empire. On the other hand, it is to be turned into a gateway for expansion to the East, attaching the East to this interface territory.

One final word: between the documents presented by Konrad Meyer-Heitling and Udo von Schauroth at the School of Fine Arts and those produced by Friedrich Gollert in Warsaw, only twelve months have passed, yet the two ways of thinking about space, while showing remarkable constants in terms of reflection about the networks – the importance of using Christaller's theory of central places to structure the area, the desire to anchor these places in the Reich, and the emphasis on the centrality of the Polish provinces – are now quite different in their overall aims. What Meyer-Heitling presented in March 1941, clearly based on the second *Generalplan Ost*, was already a utopian project in the process of being realized, but deeply regional in nature, even though it was conceived by the institution that thought of space and the Nazi Utopia as a whole. The Gollert project, issued by a local planning agency, was, however, immediately thought out on a continental scale at the beginning of 1942. This means that, within a year, the Nazi representation of the future as the advent of empire had been circulating from top to bottom of the planning organizations.

However, the ambiguity of all this must not be obscured: the documentation insists on the place and importance of Warsaw in the networks and shows a willingness to promote it, but Friedrich Gollert had been instructed to reduce its significance as much as possible and to reduce its population in the most drastic way, in particular by deindustrializing it: this shows what we are obliged to call a *hatred* for this particular city, a hatred which also imbued other sections of the documentation,[15] and became tragically evident when, on 1 August 1944, it rose up and Himmler, for at least four days, issued orders for the total and absolute destruction of the city, *population included.*[16]

City, *Volksgemeinschaft* and segregation

As we can see from the example of Warsaw, the Nazi developers had an ambivalent attitude towards the cities of the conquered territories. No doubt Warsaw was a specific case. Nevertheless, urban planning is perhaps the activity that most clearly embodies in spatial form what the *Volksgemeinschaft* was to have been, as well as pointing to its hidden aspects. This suggests a new question: perhaps the Nazi developers knowingly decided not to dedicate any place in the exhibition mounted by the RKFdV to urban planning? Of course, Meyer-Heitling's agrarian tendencies undoubtedly played a considerable part in this situation; of course the issue of urban planning was also decided on the local and regional level, from which the RKFdV was largely excluded. However, of the seventy pages of the exhibition catalogue, eight are devoted to network studies, sixty or so to multiscale studies of rural rights of way, and only half a page refers to 'rural forms and urban forms'.[17] This underlines the absence of cities from the School of Fine Arts.

It is possible to explore the Nazi projects for the reorganization of urban rights of way and their representation, even though they were not shown to the Berlin public. A remarkable amount of work was devoted to the planning of the two main urban centres of the incorporated territories, Posen/Poznań and Litzmannstadt/Łódź, and many plans, maps and models provided a relatively precise idea of what the future urban centres of the conquered East would look like.

A functional study of the two city centres makes it possible to specify the functions put forward by planners. In the centre of Poznań, the plan was to renovate the station area and turn it into the city's (and probably the province's) main administrative area.[18] The idea, developed by the Berlin architect Walther Bangert between the summer of 1940 and the first quarter of 1941, consisted in relocating a large number of command authorities to a new district situated to the immediate south of the castle, seat of the *Gau- und Reichsstatthaltung* (and therefore of all the provincial administrations of the state and the Party), where they would be near the railway station. Here, government and police functions would be concentrated, as well as a large concert hall and a theatre. Opposite the castle, the military command and the regional management of the *Reichsbahn*, both of which existed already but were to be visibly enlarged and monumentalized, were to complete the command structures.[19] Even more significantly, Bangert had designed a forum space with two monumental squares, dominated by the administrative building of the *Arbeitsfront*, opposite the station itself. The symbolic aim was very clear: to place at the heart of the city, and thus of the *Volksgemeinschaft*, the institutions that organized labour relations and the social world. In the eyes of the Nazis and architects who were to reshape the urban fabric, the harmony of labour relations was as central in theory as the political command functions of the Party.

Speer, Hitler's favourite architect and by now responsible for munitions, industrial production and urban planning, was, however, contemplating no more than a complement to the installations of this district and rejected any major building plans. As a result, in March 1941, at the very moment when the *Planung und Aufbau im Osten* exhibition opened, Bangert ceased work on the plans for the city.[20]

Litzmannstadt/Łódź was probably a more significant case, as it was more specific. While Poznań was considered to be a German city, Łódź was part of the Russian Empire in 1914. It was in consequence a *tabula rasa* to a much greater degree than Poznań, where there was of course an infrastructure dating back to William II.

To gain an overview of the whole Nazi plan for the 'renovation' and reorganization of the city, we must examine its different scales and focus first on the city centre project in its greatest detail. Here too the plan came from architect Walther Bangert. The architects finalized their drafts between the winter of 1939–40 and the beginning of 1941. By that time the plans were completed in overall shape, and all the parties had agreed on a redesign of the city centre. Walter Bangert's idea, put forward in the summer of 1940, was to 'renounce' (*aufgeben*) the existing city centre[21] so as to establish a new one, west of the *Volkspark*; urban activities and functions were to be more strictly zoned. The aim was the Germanization of the city centre. In 1939, Łódź had 378,000 Poles, 158,000 Jews and 113,000 Germans, as well as nearly 4,000 people of other origins.[22]

The new heart of the city was to be situated to the west of the great *Volkspark*, beyond the railway lines and the present central station, all situated a little to the south. To the east of this new Western German city, the second half of the city centre was occupied by monumental and cultural activities. Cinemas, theatres, museum, town hall, concert hall and Government House all comprised a monumental scheme structured around a Great Hall of the People (*Volkshalle*), a place for meetings and events opening onto a monumental square for parades and political gatherings. The heart of the city was here 'liturgical' in character, meant for assemblies; a zone combining the cultural and service activities of government and command surrounded this first heart, constituting a pole to the east of the central station. To the west, the new German city was to rise, consisting of two 'cells' composed of large housing complexes of nearly 25,000 dwellings, accompanied by collective facilities. Connecting the two poles, a monumental axis completed by an amphitheatre-shaped stadium presumably created the majestic perspective which the planners were aiming at.

What is striking about this whole arrangement is the place and importance accorded to militant institutions and collective political organizations. Each of the city's settlement cells was thus equipped with a *Hitlerjugend* centre, a collective house for collective events on the scale of

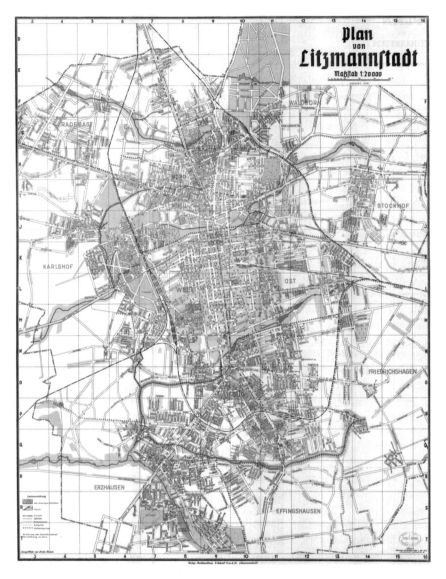

Map 6 Plan of the conurbation of Łódź (Litzmannstadt during the occupation),
1942. *Source*: Library of Congress. Thanks to Harrie Teunissen for the digitization.

the cell, or bringing together several blocks of buildings and schools. Here
we see the care taken over 'collective life', social control, and the political
mobilization of young people.[23]

   In Łódź, plans for the city seem to be at least partly a vision of the
Volksgemeinschaft: a frame for the management of populations and the

staging of power, buildings and monuments dedicated to cultural and sports activities of all kinds, dwellings and social relations marked by control and mobilization: all this foreshadowed the new society for which the planners were endeavouring to create the basis.

If we try to work out the common aspects shared by Poznań and Łódź, it seems that the developers, who were working here – as in the case of the *Planung und Aufbau im Osten* exhibition – in close consultation with Germanization agencies and politicians, were developing a relatively homogeneous representation of the *Volksgemeinschaft*. In both projects, the city centres favoured the institutions that promoted a Nazi view of the social bond – a social bond marked by work, by political and cultural mobilization, and by the structures governing young people. Institutions meant to build up the community (such as the common houses) and social concord (such as the corporate houses) were placed at the most central points and surrounded by great monumental ensembles. It may be objected that this was the aim of all urban planning at the time, and that apart from the racialization of denominations, this was basically merely a conventional functionalization of urban planning. But this would be to forget that these city areas were saturated with references to the Third Reich and its elite, with Adolf Hitler Streets and Hermann Goering or Rudolf Hess Squares in every urban project. The aim was indeed the building of sociability, but it was a specifically Nazi sociability, based on a very specific conception of what a community could be.

What we observe here as an empirical planning practice, however, was to become the norm and the model for all the urban planning of the conquered territories. While Walter Bangert was clearly setting out a model of planning that favoured the institutions of the social bond and militant mobilization, the fact that he had worked on the two main towns in the Warthegau did not mean that this all formed a system. In January 1942, however, a general ordinance issued by Himmler, reprinted by the Ministry of Labour in its official bulletin for 9 March of the same year, laid down the basic norms of 'urban planning and arrangement for the incorporated territories':

The basic unit for the organization of the settlements is constituted by a sector of the general size of a local Party group [*Ortsgruppe*], that is to say 4,000 to 5,000 inhabitants. It is an order of magnitude that is still capable of being grasped; on the other hand, this unit can be endowed with all the facilities for community and consumption/provisions that are desired and necessary in everyday life. Local Party groups thus play a fundamental role in that they are in charge of the NSDAP common houses, which serve political, social and cultural purposes and constitute the culmination of the framework in the NSDAP local group. In large cities, according to the organization and delimitations of the *Volksgemeinschaft*, several local groups will have to be assembled into larger dwelling units, which will have to be coordinated with those of higher-level organizations and facilities.[24]

The guidelines faithfully reflected the general principles that had governed urban reshaping in Poznań and Łódź as regards their city centres, a strategic location for residence and community life. The importance given to human-sized living spaces, and to the neighbourhood organization of cultural, social and Party institutions, by the planners in Łódź and Poznań thus explicitly became the norm, and formed the structuring principle behind the future *Volksgemeinschaft*.[25]

A somewhat critical observer, however, will note that, unlike in Poznań, the institutions of the social labour relationship were not present in Łódź. In order to understand this absence, we need to think about the planning of productive spaces in the two cities. This is no easy task: the information available to us is not homogeneous and an exhaustive study of the Nazi plans is unfortunately not possible due to the lack of documentation available. This heterogeneity can also be explained by the major differences between the two cities: Poznań was an average city of 274,000 inhabitants, with only about 6,000 Germans in 1939 and probably 3,000 Jews,[26] whereas in comparison Łódź was a metropolis of more than 650,000 inhabitants, of whom, as we have said, 378,000 were Poles, 158,000 Jews and 113,000 Germans. So these were not plans of the same scale, nor did they concern cities of comparable status. Indeed Poznań was an integral part of the Reich until the uprising of 1919, while Łódź, an incomparably more working-class and industrialized city, was nicknamed the 'Polish Manchester' and was one of the industrial flagships of the Tsarist Empire until the First World War. The workers' movement here was one of the most significant in the Russian Empire, especially during the great revolts of 1905.[27]

Poznań, thus, was a city of reconquest; Łódź was the city of non-native inhabitants and class struggle, a true *hostile* urban pioneer front. This is doubtless what we must bear in mind when we consider the plans for the development of peripheral areas devoted to residential needs and industrial production.

The study of the maps at our disposal is somewhat arduous: they are not very easy to read, the memoranda are relatively vague and information is particularly fragmentary. Thus, for Poznań, we have an Urban Development Planning Memorandum dated 1942 and embellished with maps and sketches that give an image of the desired future of the city's administration. The memorandum describes the ideal situation of a city, a nodal crossroads on road, rail and inland waterways, although navigability was one of the projects mentioned as needed to improve the situation. Poznań was, in the eyes of the engineer running the city's urban planning offices, the capital of a surplus agricultural region, well equipped for the agricultural processing industries, chemical industries and the manufacture of machine tools and agricultural equipment.[28] The maps and memorandum highlight a broad swathe of commercial and industrial settlement extending from the southwest through the east to the north of the city, leaving the western, central-western and northwestern parts available for residential areas.[29]

A town planner will easily detect the internal contradictions of city planning here. The net separation between industrial and manufacturing production and residential areas generates unwanted and massive pendulum movements. Moreover, the residential areas of the city are obviously designed for workers working in the city centre, that is to say, they are mainly involved in the service sector and in political functions. It is therefore foreseeable that there will be built areas close to the industrial sectors – sectors which are no longer supposed to exist in the context of a 'subdivision policy oriented towards the reconquest of the *Volksgemeinschaft*'.[30] Further on, the engineer ends up explaining somewhat casually why this type of organization no longer has its place in the *Volksgemeinschaft*: 'For the evolution of Poznań, this unilateral localization of industry and manufactures represents a danger to which practically all the metropolises built under William II succumbed: the constitution of a west that was well-off, not to say plutocratic, and of a southeast/east for the "have-nots", predestined for industry.'[31] Class struggle embodied in space: such was the danger of the spatial organization of the political capital of the Warthegau, a fundamental danger for a plan which aimed at creating a harmonious *Volksgemeinschaft* entirely rid of the toxic atmosphere created by class struggle – a solution that, in the view of the developers of Poznań, could be found only in the city centre.

All in all, this documentation poses more problems than it solves: it does not allow us to understand how Poznań's industry was meant to fit into the Nazi plans. The experts' conclusions called for the decentralization of industrial plants and their distribution out to the peripheries, at the four cardinal points, in order to avoid spatial as well as social imbalances. On the other hand, the memorandum, while espousing the Nazi phraseology and the representations of the *Volksgemeinschaft*, maintained a complete, and deafening, silence on a central element: the racial question. It has been said that Poznań had only 6,000 Germans and no fewer than 268,000 Poles, including 3,000 Jews residing in the city at the time of its invasion. No mention was made of their fate, their habitat or their employment, even though the question of reconquest was at the heart of Nazi concerns; nowhere was the question of the migrants who were to lead the reconquest approached by the engineers. There is no shortage of reasons for this: it was a town plan, not a settlement plan, and the issue of settlement was not the responsibility of the municipal engineer or his collaborators. Nevertheless, our quest for the contours of the *Volksgemeinschaft* is disappointing: at best, we have discovered that the *Volksgemeinschaft* designed by the planners was the opposite of the 'liberal' city, whose spatial segregation was a foil as it reintroduced class struggle into space. And this is all the more unsatisfactory as the racial question, which is at the foundation of any Nazi representation, is literally foreclosed.

Let us turn now to the representations of Litzmannstadt/Łódź, in an attempt to get beyond this impression. As we have said, the city was not a city of reconquest, but rather the place in which, as far as the planners were concerned, the worst and most menacing aspects of Poznań seemed to be concentrated: Łódź was the city of the class struggle, but it was also, even more clearly, the city of the struggle between the races. It had a large Polish majority (378,000) and an extremely large minority of Jews (158,000), who faced a large and stable German community (113,000). The planners were perfectly well aware of all of this: one of the planning documents stated that 'Łódź will never become a German city if the pre-conditions are not fulfilled [. . .] if the Asian genetic component has not been totally extirpated [*Stumpf und Stil*: root and branch, says the text] and their gametes, that is to say the habitat of the town, have not been made healthy.'[32] The planners therefore worked with eloquent demographic assumptions: the city had to be reduced to 500,000 inhabitants, all Jews had to be expelled as well as more than 50,000 Poles, while 300,000 of them were, according to other documents, to remain to constitute the labour force necessary for an industry vital to the war effort.[33]

As in Poznań, and in the case of the two city centres, it was Walter Bangert and his office who were given the task of implementing the plans by the RKFdV. And the plans they provided constituted a coherent representation of what, in the eyes of SS sponsors, would be a city suitable for the *Volksgemeinschaft*. Without dwelling any further on the city centre, which had already been noted as being in conformity with the institutions of the Nazified social and cultural bond, we can observe how Walter Bangert organized hemispherical zones, excluding the west from the forum devoted solely to new settlements destined for Germans. These zones were distributed to the north, east and south around the city centre, consisting first of mixed zones of residential and commercial areas, then of industrial zones developed at the periphery, at the intersections of major roads and railways. Located outside the Ring,[34] these industrial zones were surrounded by areas intended for Polish residents and each flanked by a German settlement area.

What was taking shape here was a reflection of the *Volksgemeinschaft*, as the Nazis imagined it. To the west and south, as far as the Ring, protected from industrial effluents and nuisances (like the bourgeois districts of the Wilhelminian industrial cities), huddled around the forum, the new railway station and the city centre, lay the 50,000 new homes for the Germans who were the only real beneficiaries of the new harmonious layout of the city. Around this first zone that benefited from the services and the renewed architecture of the city centre lay a mixed intermediate zone; on the outskirts, the *Volksgemeinschaft* was strictly segregated, assigning the less well-served and more isolated residential areas to the industrial zones whose labour force they were meant to constitute. If we add the police establishment that was missing from the Poznań projects, located just above the city centre to the north, near the roads to the various outskirts of the city, we can surmise that the possibility of a revolt of the labouring classes had been foreseen by the planners, although this was not clearly stipulated.

All in all, the city presented itself clearly as a prefiguration of the *Volksgemeinschaft*. In general, such cities, with their industrial and service functions, were an anchor for political and cultural mobilization, but also for the neighbourhood structuring of the social and political bond for racially desirable populations. The cities were thus transformed into strict instruments for segregation and exploitation, relegating alien populations to the periphery in isolated facilities and within range of large police contingents.

Dreaming of rural space: the architect, the SS and the peasant

The study of the urban maps of the Nazi Utopia has led us to take a long detour away from the School of Fine Arts and its exhibition of the Nazi Utopia. This was due to the lack of attention paid to the urban dimension of this Utopia in the exhibition. Konrad Meyer-Heitling, an agricultural geographer above all, had little taste for urban planning and so had neglected it in preparing the exhibition. He had concentrated on the rural areas, the true centres of German renewal in his eyes. And it is this dream of rural space that we must study in order to finish our survey of the future that was planned for Germany.

The exhibition was largely the result of a desire to display to the public the work of the winners of an architectural competition entitled 'New Villages in the East', which brought together research departments based in Berlin and Danzig, but also work produced by the planning and land activities department of the RKFdV, as well as studies produced by other research offices for the occupied territories (but not only these).

The catalogue, which presents thirty-three projects, therefore reflects both a concerted desire to create a wide audience for these representations and an intense set of activities that were not related to the exhibition.[35] In practice, the catalogue is divided into four parts, the first one dealing with final studies of cities in the occupied territories over eleven projects, while the second puts forward nineteen models of farms and buildings, the third reveals the interior of houses (three projects) and the fourth focuses on the profiling of village centres in the occupied territories. The competition, therefore, holds an important place in the first and last parts of the catalogue, while not exhaustively detailing the representation of the future of rural spaces.

The award-winning architects came mostly from Berlin (nineteen projects), followed by those from Dresden (only four projects), and the other cities were credited with two projects or even just one: Hanover, Danzig, Poznań, Breslau, Düsseldorf, Stuttgart were the last cities mentioned. It is hardly possible to discern what could be called a border sensibility: these were towns situated more in the eastern part of Nazi imperial territory (with the exception of Düsseldorf and Stuttgart, located in the south and the west) and on the margins of this territory (with the huge exception of Hanover and Berlin). Berlin's macrocephalic shape, atypical of German territory, reflected the importance of the political bodies and the role of the RKFdV planning and land activities department, which was both the prime contractor of the architects' competition and the planner of many projects.

What emerges here, supplemented by the first ten pages on the reticular development of the occupied territories, is a coherent image of rural planning, and the observer is struck by how complete it is. The development of villages and buildings shows the social, economic and political order of the *Volksgemeinschaft*, while the houses and their interiors reveal a domestic, even intimate order. Let us try to sketch out how it all worked.

The exhibition carries out the work of representation on three axes, which reflect the three dimensions of this rural social order of the Nazi future. In the first place, the exhibition focuses on the material organization of villages. The forms of the villages promoted by the winners of the 'New Villages to the East' competition were inspired by most of the three types of settlements observed in the then dominant agrarian geography in Germany: *Straßendorf* (street-village), *Waldhufendorf* (forest village) and *Angerdorf* (street-village with central square).[36]

The main common characteristic of these three forms of villages was their planned genesis ex nihilo in medieval and modern Prussian agrarian history, but also the fact that these villages involved a landscape of open fields in strips of land and, in the contemporary period, a three-year rotation with strong collective constraints. This resulted in an important collective village life and we may decide – without too much evidence, let's face it – that it was this state of affairs that attracted the attention of developers and politicians thinking about the Nazi future.

Nevertheless, Nazi projects did not merely repeat previous methods of settlement without amending them. The street-villages that the developers sketched out were no longer confined to a main street, but stretched along a crossroads on either side of the intersection on both roads, becoming more complex.[37] Other villages combined forms. One of them combined the shape of street-villages with isolated buildings in hamlets, planned some distance from the River Warta, all adjacent to a main road. Linked to it by the main street of the village, the farming area was also traversed by a clear neighbourhood network which structured access to an open-field landscape, here too in strips, ending on the banks of the river. The project won the favour of the jury and was awarded first prize for its organization and the classicism of its design.[38]

Many such examples could be given. The street-villages were thoroughly studied by German geographers[39] and then in a more visibly ethnicized way in the *Volkstumswissenschaften* (ethnic sciences) of Adolf Helbok, and these are only some of many reference points.[40] Some villages broke away from this heritage without difficulty, and the fact that they were awarded the prize shows that this was not a major transgression. The Nazi rural architectural future was not a simple reaction, an attempt to reproduce the glorious example of the ancient Prussians. One village will bring together two or three hamlets organized as street-villages,[41] another will be a compromise between a structure of hamlets and the shape of those spontaneous mediaeval villages called *Haufendörfer* (heap-villages).[42]

Beyond this morphological diversity, one main issue seems to emerge from the presentation of each plan by the catalogue: the importance of collective facilities. This is not surprising. On the one hand, the regions concerned are open-field regions with strong collective constraints and, on the other, it is on collective facilities that the peasant identities of these new villages in the East must be based. Not all projects detail them; eight out of ten projects presented, however, mention them and specify their location. It should be remembered that the planners sought to prioritize the village networks into main villages and secondary villages in the Warthegau. And the catalogue presents the plan for a main village which is particularly detailed on the issue of the facilities for the village centre.[43] This was an *Angersdorf*, a street-village with a square in its centre. The authors emphasize the quality of the development, the addition of groves and meadows, with plenty of trees to bring harmony to the appearance of a village whose profusion of equipment they highlight. Mention is made of collective economic service facilities, workshops, a hotel, small industry, individual detached residences, but also a militantly excessive number of facilities, something which a historian is bound to find significant.

In the heart of this village, there is a square which, while accommodating the sole hotel, the school, a small belfry and the town hall, is a parade place (*Aufmarschplatz*) surrounded by institutions of militant supervision. We here find the Party, the NSV (*Nationalsozialistische Volkswohlfahrt*), a Nazi charity,[44] the *Hitlerjugend* and a work camp for young girls. The Nazi institutions represented here are those of an attentive and caring *Volksgemeinschaft*, with supervisory but also charitable/assistance institutions and a remarkable lack of the police supervision that, at this level of the reticular hierarchy, we should expect to find at least somewhere in the landscape.

This is the figurative quintessence of the agrarian dream of Meyer-Heitling, of the RKFdV and probably of the SS: a *Volksgemeinschaft* freed from the dross of the conflicts caused by class struggle. After the time of conquest and struggle came the time of colonization, the time of the elimination of internal conflict and the rise of a society that was non-confrontational because it was racially pure.

This *Volksgemeinschaft* is not only presented in the form of plans or rather lofty and superficial prospects; it is also a plan for life, production and residence, and the planners have projected these elements into the study of the habitat and the building environment. This aspect occupies a significant volume: the catalogue devoted only six double pages to the plans of the villages, but it dedicates fourteen to the buildings. Nine plans and models of farms and eight plans and models of services and support facilities for agriculture (seventeen pages) – workshops, small industries, services – draw the outline of a specific productive world.

The nine farm buildings are of a uniform area and are designed to work 25 hectares of land. Most of them have buildings designed for livestock-based agriculture – although the case of cereal farming is also considered, on a lesser scale – and therefore involve very large stables.[45] In the vast majority of plans, the key word is that of a 'clear separation' of spaces.[46] The thinking behind this is very clearly segregationist, though it cannot be clearly discerned as anything other than functionalist. Separation of functions, habitat, breeding, garden cultivation, farmyard, storage: these are the first separations created. They shape the outline of an agriculture that is at least partially commercial, leaving a large proportion to the domestic economy, as evidenced by the farmyard and the vegetable garden which are practically enough to ensure self-sufficiency in food.[47]

This seems to be a rational and modest, even frugal agriculture; the buildings and the surrounding space are worked in the most intensive manner possible, with a vegetable garden of appreciable size, doubtless largely intended for the cultivation of potatoes, the basis of human and animal food[48] as indicated by the mention of a large potato patch on one of the farms,[49] with the presence of fruit trees enhancing the diet and probably providing it with an appreciable intake of carbohydrates.

On another one of these plans, horses, cows and pigs are located next to a poultry yard. The limited space given to them suggests that this is an adjunct farm on a smallholder's land.[50] In this example, it is a two-storey farm for the residential part, while the remaining ceiling height is used for storage facilities.

The agriculture planned here is therefore rather parsimonious. It is certainly commercial, but it still seems conditioned by the ideal of 'living of your own land' dear to the peasants of the *Ancien Régime*. It may be a Nazified ideal, however, of the agrarian dream of *Blut und Boden*, something which could be discerned more clearly by looking at the village plans. The fact remains, however, that it would be a mistake to identify it with a dream of reaction, a desire for archaism: on all the plans, what we see here is another mode of mechanical use; on all plans, the sites of the agricultural machines are laid out and rural exploitation is thus largely mechanized, providing up to three machines for each farm of 25 hectares, even if it is not specified what kinds of machines they would be. The ethnocrats of the RKFdV do not want a return of the plough and the oxen or horses. They are determined to combine technical modernity with a return to the land, and agrarian colonization with modern productivity.

The countryside outlined by the plans is populated not only by farms: they are partly autonomous production areas, with farm workers' houses that fulfil a labour function and evince an agriculture dominated by farmers but also occupying non-landowners – probably racially fit, as their habitat is planned without their being segregated from the rural population.[51] There is also a petrol station, proof of the mechanization of production but also of the penetration of the individual car into the Nazi future: in addition to refuelling, a maintenance and repair workshop lies next to a residence space for the owner and his family.

Rural craft is the final point of this part of the exhibition. A dairy and a distillery constitute collective installations illustrating the two scenarios clearly envisaged (breeding or cereal farming) and complete the at least partially commercial character of the agriculture dreamed of by the developers. Rural crafts also mean the presence of collective services such as a bakery or a butchery, and a forge, which constitute the social and commercial heart of the villages, together with administrative and political functions.

This provides an extremely detailed and coherent vision of the rural life imagined by the RKFdV and the various architects commissioned and rewarded with prizes during the competition. This coherence went beyond the development of villages and the shaping of rural economic and social life. At the School of Fine Arts, the developers finally entered the interiors of peasants' dwellings and imbued them with their ideals, their demographic and aesthetic ideals in particular.

It must be acknowledged that, on the documentary level, our argument is less well founded: only three plots are represented.[52] The little that can be said must also be based on the examination of the plans of farms, which also give a certain idea of the domestic order promoted in the exhibition.

The first trait of this domestic order is omnipresent and shows an obsession that will come as no surprise to the reader: the demographic obsession. All the plans of farms sketch houses with more than three children's rooms, the double house for agricultural workers offering up to four. The benches in the dining room whose interior is displayed allow up to eleven people to co-exist in the room, and at least five (and thus three children, as far as the developers are concerned) are explicitly planned for. In the living room, five people must to be able to press themselves around the ceramic stove, giving an ideal of *Gemütlichkeit* (an untranslatable term, denoting the feeling of the emotional and physical comfort and welcoming familiarity of the home).[53] The third interior shows us an adult room with a double bed and a cradle, opportunely recalling that the alcove is perhaps the place of conjugal pleasure, but that such pleasure is intended for procreation.[54]

'The land will be enlarged by your grandchildren', say the family booklets distributed to newlyweds in Poznań during the elaborate Nazi and neo-pagan wedding rituals reminding spouses of their duties towards the Nordic Race, their lineage and their ancestors, as well as towards those still to be born.[55] This is the unconditional and obsessive norm that emerges from the representation of the domestic order. The other representations which may sometimes be tentatively described do not have the imperative character of this first prescription. They simply express the austere dimension of the decoration, the scarcity of images, paintings and illustrations in interiors, the rustic furniture meant mainly for collective family life, the absence of individual spaces, the presence of a new level of comfort and hygiene in the eyes of the developers, with toilets and bathrooms being discreetly presented. However, we cannot go any further in our analysis of the domestic order as it appeared in April 1941 in the School of Fine Arts in Berlin, as transformed into an exhibition hall for the Nazi dream.

This long detour through the *Planung und Aufbau im Osten* exhibition has finally allowed us to discover the essence of the Nazi future. It has allowed us to emphasize its internal coherence and its great significance. It has also allowed us to enter its meanderings, as they were displayed to the visitors to an exhibition conceived at a time when the rulers could feel secure. In April 1941 the Third Reich was in the midst of secret preparations for the invasion of the USSR and was preparing to enter the Balkans unexpectedly, but neither the exhibition visitors nor, most probably, the RKFdV were informed of this. To their minds, the *hic et nunc* was the Germanization of the occupied territories at the end of a war which would not last long. It was this illusory conviction that undoubtedly allowed Meyer-Heitling and his services to present this exhibition of the Nazi future.

The latter appeared as a projected socio-racial rebuilding, it embraced embedded and annexed territories, and it claimed not to be conditioned by technical considerations: what counted was the setting up of spaces for living in, spaces for a future German nationhood. Planning was not a technical and architectural task, but an existential and political mission.

To plan and build in the East was to implement an ambitious transformation of the networks of settlement and circulation in Europe as a whole. By incorporating the territories of Warta and Danzig, by making the General Government a proconsulate whose urban network was attached to the communication structures of the Reich, the developers were by April 1941 drawing up a developing European network whose full extent was found in the *Generalpläne Ost* of 1942.

Through urban planning, Nazi developers designed forms of urban facilities that made the Nazi city a spatially and functionally coherent set of cells, connected and shaped around a city centre, and structured by the authorities of political mobilization but also by Nazi assistance and charity bodies. A society of social control but also of solidarity, the

Volksgemeinschaft operated in a very coherent environment, marked by monumentality. In cities, the monuments and the facilities suggested the grandiose, gigantic and benevolent dimension of the Nazi future as imagined by the ethnocrats; a strictly segregationist future incarnated even in the city plans, marked at their periphery by the establishment of housing estates for racially undesirable populations but kept for productive purposes under constant police or SS supervision.

However, in the eyes of Meyer-Heitling and the architects and urban planners to whom he had entrusted the *Volksgemeinschaft*, it ultimately seemed to remain a rural entity: the village plans and the structuring of the countryside constituted the heart of the exhibition. The village gave an important place to collective life, either in the exchange of goods and services – forge, service station, bakery – or in a sociability no longer marked by the church but by the presence of the *Hitlerjugend*, the Women's Labour Service and the NSV charity. Here again, it was a *Volksgemeinschaft* full of solicitude for a racially selected population that was being set up, displaying a 'strictly positive' Nazi Utopia in the eyes of the SS. This Utopia was not an archaism, it was not conceived as a return to the mythical past. It dreamed of a society that harmoniously combined the frugality, modesty and domestic economic autonomy of the peasant past with the mechanization and commercial modernization of the agricultural sector. This Utopia penetrated into conjugality and family life, celebrating *Gemütlichkeit* and austerity, but also fertility, as both a condition and a result of the advent of the Nazi parousia.

Chapter 6

From one plan to the next?
The Kammler sequence

Observers of Nazism and its institutional development agree that, from 1942 onwards, SS influence expanded across practically all areas of state activity.[1] Attempting to determine the importance of this movement in the imagination and representation of the Nazi future would clearly not be very meaningful: the SS was the main – but not the only – actor in the crystallization of this moment of Utopia which we are focusing on.

The fact remains, however, that from the beginning of 1942, at a time when institutions were beginning to coordinate their activities in many areas, the SS was becoming an increasingly omnipresent actor. We must avoid teleology here: on 1 January 1942, no one knew how the plans for the Germanization of Europe would work out; no one knew what would happen to the Nazi utopian hope in the last eighteen months of its existence; and, finally, no one knew how the first signs of this Utopia were to be brought to completion.

One thing is certain: a new central SS institution was created and started to play a part in the planning which was then coming to a peak of activity, and gave it a new spin. Also, at the regional and local levels, new actors were expected to play a role in the implementation of the building programmes for realizing Utopia. But then, twelve months later, hope seemed to vanish into thin air.

On planning *style*: the WVHA, Hans Kammler and their estimates

Before attempting to understand how the WVHA (Main Office for the Economy and Administration) was given a central place in the planning arrangements that structured Nazi discourse on the future, we must return to the genesis of this institution and seek to grasp how its leaders pioneered the institutional jungle that the SS was inexorably becoming.

The WVHA or the agencies that prefigured it in matters of Germanization and land confiscation began to play a significant role with the conquest of Czechoslovakia, even before the question of realizing the Nazi Utopia had arisen. The SS dispatched Curt von Gottberg, in charge of agrarian colonization and settlement affairs at the RuSHA, to the Prague land registry department to set up an ambitious land confiscation policy, notably through the German Settlement Society (DAG), of which he became president. The affair turned into a fiasco, von Gottberg was dismissed and subjected to an investigation, and the job was given back to Oswald Pohl, head of SS administration, in January 1940.[2]

In this way, Pohl was introduced to the world of Germanization, reacting to the administrative negligence of von Gottberg by emphasizing his own assessment and that of his departments. Management orthodoxy, administrative know-how and organizational expertise: this was the triptych on which the SS administration office constantly relied to legitimize its growing influence, its gradual takeover of entire sections of the SS world, which itself was continually expanding.

From January 1940 onwards, the SS's economic and administrative departments patiently set their sights on a range of activities that made them an inescapable presence. The Prague affair was a decisive event: Pohl and his departments had proved their efficiency, and Pohl had even managed to impose his solutions on the RSHA of Heydrich and the RuSHA of Hildebrandt. In the settlement of this case he had shown an imperialist attitude that led him to absorb businesses, real estate and an entire foundation, and obtained from Himmler a promise that the RuSHA could no longer engage in any economic activity. The absorptions we are talking about were not of any real significance in the eyes of Pohl and the managers of the SS's administration departments. But symbolically, they had two advantages: on the one hand, they helped to make Pohl's SS administration look like a significant industrial group; on the other, they constituted a Trojan horse legitimating further involvement in Germanization.[3]

At the same time that Pohl was succeeding von Gottberg as head of the Prague Land Affairs Department, Meyer-Heitling gave the first presentation of his 'Planning Principles for the Building of the Eastern Territories' in which he stated that 'the production of bricks in the Eastern Territories and the General Government should be sufficient to cover the needs [of planning] provided that current production is increased three- or fourfold'.[4] The production of bricks in the occupied territories had been entrusted to the SS group run by Pohl, which gave it a significant role in any building programme in the occupied territories.

While the contribution of SS institutions remained modest in this first phase of planning for the colonization in the East, things were different once the invasion of the USSR had begun.[5] After this time, it was the Building and Works Department, the second pillar of the SS economic administration, under Hans Kammler, that was to be involved in the decision-making institutional complex through the intermediary of the industrial and economic power of the SS.

In order to understand the mechanism of this involvement, we must try to understand how Pohl made his departments an essential intermediary in the eyes of Himmler. And for this, we have a precious tool for the period we are interested in – roughly the year 1941 – namely the desk diary of the *Reichsführer*, which lists all his appointments together with their aims. Magnificently edited by a team of the best German historians, it makes possible a quite analytical approach to the relationship between Himmler and the person in charge of economic and administrative matters.[6]

During the period from January 1941 to 1 February 1942, when the rising influence of the administrative and economic departments became manifest, with the merger of departments within the WVHA, Himmler and Pohl met twenty-three times; the frequency of these meetings tripled in the second half of the year.[7] The questions tackled by the two men illustrate the extent of the competence of Pohl and his departments: matters of stewardship, building, financing of operations of the *Ahnenerbe* (an esoteric foundation preoccupied with the 'heritage of our ancestors' and focusing on medical experiments and expeditions to Tibet), the *Lebensborn* ('source of life': a kind of stud farm for humans) and the HSSPF. The extreme diversity of the activities covered is striking.

Three main areas, however, seem to emerge: the question of concentration camps; equipment and stewardship, including its financial side; and industry and building. It was via these issues that Pohl's administrative and economic departments gradually took root in Germanization and planning affairs, as two examples will show. On 10 January 1941, Himmler received Pohl together with Ulrich Greifelt, Heinrich Müller, Gestapo chief and Eichmann's direct superior, and Werner Lorenz, the head of VOMI, to discuss the situation of the *Volksdeutsche* who were languishing in the VOMI camps. Pohl was present at this meeting because he provided the cement and the bricks, and more generally the building materials for the camps. So it was matters of logistics, supply and building that allowed Pohl's departments to enter the charmed circle of the Utopia makers.[8] Nine months later, on 10 September 1941, Himmler received Pohl and Kammler together at Hegewald to discuss building plans for Auschwitz. In terms of building plans, it was a matter of approving the building of model farms on the site of the concentration camp.[9] The question here was not really that of building, but of land use. The slippage towards a grabbing of operational functions was overt.

And this example shows that this was indeed the goal pursued by Pohl and Kammler. The outcome of this development was evident in the crucial weeks of December and January. On 9 December 1941, Oswald Pohl lunched with Himmler and handed him the 'Provisional Peacetime Building Programme', the first draft of the plans for the future WVHA. In so doing, Pohl's ambition was to control all the building programmes carried out by the central departments of the SS, but also by the HSSPF. This demand was clearly accepted by Himmler.[10] On 14 and 15 January 1942, Himmler organized a meeting of all heads of central SS departments. And while the raison d'être of this meeting is not known with any certainty, it was most likely a matter of redefining and coordinating the prerogatives of each man with a view to the future unification of the administrative and economic departments.[11] It was Himmler who, in a meeting with Greifelt and Meyer-Heitling on 27 January 1942, ordered them to work with Pohl's departments to estimate the costs of their programmes.[12] On 28 and 31 January Himmler responded to the 'Provisional Programme' drafted by Kammler and asked for it to be extended into a more detailed version, while enjoining Pohl to coordinate both with Goering's economic departments and those of the RKFdV.[13] On 1 February, an ordinance by Himmler officially created the *Wirtschafts- und Verwaltungshauptamt* (WVHA), a major player in the building, finance, planning and administrative policies of the SS.

We can see here the arrival of a new actor, whose profile and style differed visibly from those of previous protagonists. No doubt, as we have said, the WVHA shared sociological and political characteristics with the other central departments of the SS, in terms of generation, social extraction, and the internalization of Nazi belief combined with technical expertise. But its men seem to have been distinguished by a technocratic dimension underlined by all historians who have studied their case. This can be seen from an examination of the planning documentation.[14]

The provisional peacetime building programme consists of a simple list with a chart that allows the quantitative data mentioned by Hans Kammler to be visualized. A typed sheet with a handwritten map and legend is the only planning record of the WVHA for the whole of Europe. Accompanied by a letter from Pohl to Himmler, these three pages summarize the WVHA's style of planning: strictly quantitative, lapidary and aimed at efficiency. It is a plan couched in terms of financial estimates.

The letter of presentation written by Pohl is the only place where room is made for any kind of argument, and it is worth citing:

> *Reichsführer!*
> The current situation of the labour market and raw materials and the preparations being made for peace by the various competent authorities of the Reich have led me, in consultation with the chief of staff of the Führungshauptamt and the Head of the Main Office of the Police, to draw up a provisional building programme for the *Waffen-SS* and the police. It provides for special missions of the building and maintenance departments, as well as the economic and administrative departments.
> [Two paragraphs provide a brief reminder of the figures mentioned.]
> Please note how important it is for the *SS Reichsführung*, on the outbreak of war, to be given independence in terms of building and the main role among the recipients of resources for building purposes.[15]

We are far from the lyrical flights of Konrad Meyer-Heitling! The planning presented here has a primarily institutional role. Its first aim is internal – to legitimize the administrative departments vis-à-vis the other central SS departments. Externally, in the eyes of Pohl, it is crucial to draw on this programme to ensure, among the various actors of the economic policies of the Third Reich, priority in the allocation of raw materials: this will ensure the programme's feasibility.

The plan provided for thirteen billion Reichsmarks invested over five years after the conclusion of the peace, of which six billion were for the Eastern territories, three billion for the Reich and 2.5 billion for specific projects such as hospitals, schools, special equipment for furnishing, supply or clothing for the police, the *Waffen-SS* and the general SS.

The document did not give any more details of the projects covered by these figures; nor did the chart and the covering letter. More worrying, no doubt, to the *Reichsführer's* own eyes was the fact that the plan was obsolete from the beginning, and incomplete. On 31 January 1942, the eve of the official founding of the WVHA, Himmler replied to Pohl's letter and to the sending of the plan:

> Dear Pohl,
> I have read your letter concerning the provisional programme for the creation of the Building and Maintenance Department. According to this document, official building alone, that is to say SS and police buildings, comes to thirteen billion RM. I do not think that provision has been made for the vast projects we want to start for the general SS, the *Waffen-SS* and the police.
>
> We have already discussed orally the question of the allocation of raw material resources [. . .].
>
> I would like to share with you my position on another subject. Until the end of the war, I expect that we will have an internal war debt of some 100 billion RM. For each measure, therefore, we must take into consideration the fact that the State will have to take over, in peacetime, large-scale social and cultural building programmes and that in every budget, every measure and every necessity we must act with the greatest Prussian sense of thrift.
>
> It is for this reason that I ask you today to ensure that, during each action, specialized manual workers in detention will be incorporated [. . .]. The costs of building of all our public or private projects for the SS and the police will have to be kept to the minimum of what we cannot produce ourselves: electric cables, wire, tenders, locomotives (we produce the piping), refrigerators, all other machines . . .
>
> We must produce and build 80 per cent of our homes and public buildings from our own resources and with our own workforce.[16]

This was a language and a semantics that differed from those used up until then in the planning of Utopia. This was the language of accountability and efficiency, a sign that, in the eyes of those responsible, it was now time for these projects to be implemented – something that had been true since at least December 1941, the date at which Kammler had drawn up his report.

Nevertheless, the impact of these few sheets seems to have remained limited; it is not enough to assess the role played by the WVHA in Germanization and the creation of Utopia. An investigation of its influence, its involvement in RKFdV planning, and its capacity to modify the *Generalpläne Ost* will provide us with a more accurate view of this rising influence, here considered indirectly.

It was Himmler, as we have said, who on 27 January 1942 ordered Meyer-Heitling to take account of the economic dimension of Germanization, a dimension which required cooperation between the WVHA and the RKFdV. The traces of this cooperation, though not numerous, are clear, and the tone used in the correspondence between Meyer-Heitling and Kammler seems to indicate a cordial relationship. Meyer-Heitling, moreover, mentions a phone conversation between them; and on 18 April 1942 he sent Kammler a letter with an estimate of the building volumes for the settlement territories covering the ten years after the end of the war.[17] This suggests that we should view the connections between the two plans rather differently: Meyer-Heitling sent his estimates to Kammler for information, presumably so that the latter would integrate them into his own work: this in turn leads one to think that there was a document which supplemented Kammler's 'Provisional Peacetime Building Programme' dating from 4 December 1941, and that the 67 billion RM for work over ten years announced by Meyer-Heitling were perhaps at least in part the 'immense labours' that had not been accounted for mentioned by Himmler in his letter to Pohl at the end of January. The influence, here, was transitive: Meyer-Heitling was *informing* Kammler. But we can also see that, following Himmler's order, and in contact with the WVHA, this new *Generalplan Ost* was very different from the other documents hitherto produced by Meyer-Heitling's departments.

This can be shown by a few rapid calculations. On the one hand, the strictly quantitative approach occupies more than a third of the plan in its number of pages. In the second place, no fewer than fourteen tables, histograms and graphs represent the projections made by Meyer-Heitling, following the example set by the WVHA.[18] At the peak of its ambition, the utopian plan for Germanization had thus become a compromise between the fervent enthusiasm of the RKFdV agricultural geographer and the meticulousness in terms of accountancy and technocracy of the WVHA engineer.

The figures quoted by Meyer-Heitling were identical to those indicated to Kammler in the letter of 18 April.[19] The geographer also used the same calculation keys (notably in terms of the amount of capital allocated per square kilometre and population density), and these figures gave this plan a very different appearance: much more voluminous than anything that had previously been produced by Meyer-Heitling and his departments, the document was also much less subject to lyrical flights of fancy and more inclined to a programmatic statement of the measures that needed to be accomplished.

This was undoubtedly a decisive point: in comparison with its predecessors, the plan of June 1942 quantified raw materials, labour and the financial resources to be invested. It also gave precise details of the origin of the funds that would be used, carefully differentiating the non-redeemable capital of the funds that would be committed with no expectation of return on investment. Finally, it made careful plans for the twenty-five years after the conclusion of the peace, ensuring that a gradual effort would be made by the Reich in terms of equipment.

We can see the influence of the style of the WVHA, the *economicization* of hope, the irruption into Utopia of a managerial dimension.

But, in addition to these questions, we can also ask whether this development did not *also* reflect an aspect of the zeitgeist, the imperial hope: did the protagonists not have the impression that the time for the realization of Utopia was approaching and that it was now necessary to prepare for its accomplishment? At this juncture, it is a legitimate question.

Achieving Utopia? The institutionalization and failure of building programmes

As we have seen, the question of building was considered relatively early as one of the main issues in the Germanization of space. It was necessary to populate the space conquered, of course, but if it was truly to be a space for living in, it was still necessary to equip it. The SS and its administration had not waited for the invasion of the USSR to think about this, and the men of the Building Department had anticipated the invasion and reorganized accordingly. In January 1941, discussions between the SS and the Ministry of Finance had made it possible to expand considerably the staff of the Department of Building, and to consider placing at its head a general officer with the rank of *SS-Oberführer*. And so it was that Kammler was appointed head of the department on 1 June 1941. Three weeks later he reorganized it. Its new organizational chart already reflected the idea of a central control over all questions of building: a Central Inspection was created in which the work was distributed geographically. This new structuring, however, did not really take shape locally until November 1941, with an order from Pohl announcing the creation of regional inspections for the HSSPFs, central building directorates for the SSPFs, and finally, on the local level, managing bodies for building.[20]

It is very difficult to understand the reasons for this delay. The principles had been formulated in June and endorsed by Himmler and Pohl, and the question of building and its planning was very much on the agenda. More incomprehensible still: on 17 July 1941, Himmler had appointed Odilo Globocnik, the SSPF of Lublin, to manage the building of the 'Points of settlement and support for the police and the SS' for all territories in the East. This meant – as we shall see in the following chapters – endorsing the initiatives taken by one of the most active and

brutal of Nazi dignitaries, and attempting to spread them to the very territories that the Wehrmacht was in the process of conquering. It was also
a matter of extending the SS empire by taking advantage of the vacuum
left by the other pillars of the regime, less reactive to the events that had
been accelerating since the beginning of Barbarossa. The SS was becoming
the only organization to have a complete administration for the occupied
territories.[21]

   All of this, however, faces an observer with certain questions. The
incoherence threatening the institutional edifice lay mainly in the relations between the apparatus built up by Globocnik to cope with this
new task and the departments created by Kammler. Globocnik, in fact,
created an administration responsible for taking over, on the instructions
of Himmler, the building of all the 'Points of settlement and support for
the police and the SS'.[22] The order was given to Globocnik by Himmler in
person, in Lublin, during an interview which we will discuss in detail in
the third part of our inquiry – in the presence of Oswald Pohl and Hans
Kammler![23] The only possible explanation for such a paradox seems to
be the following: Himmler felt that what had been the experience in the
Lublin district with regard to building needed, albeit amended by the
orders he gave the same day, to be extended to the whole Eastern space
of the imperial conquest by those who had previously been responsible
for it at the local level. This generalization, however, was to be carried
out under the control of the Central Department for Budget and Building.
In a way, the administration set up by Globocnik was a prefiguration
of the one that Kammler, still a new appointee, was supposed to set up.
The fact that three days earlier, on 17 July, Himmler had indicated that
'the collaboration with General Pohl [Central Department for Budget
and Building] is settled' seems to confirm this hypothesis. On 21 July, he
stated in another document: 'the organization of the building offices for
Department 2 (Inspection of Building, Central Building Directorate) is
approved by the RFSS – as are the measures prepared and already under
way'.[24] In people's minds if not in actual fact, the administrative and
operational structure had been fixed. The same document stipulates in
particularly high-flown language that Globocnik, designated as delegate
for the *Reichsführer*, had until the autumn to execute, in the first place, the
'measures ordered [sic!]'.[25]

   From this tangled skein of events, one can draw but one conclusion: the
power that Himmler agreed to delegate to Globocnik had undoubtedly
been imposed by force on Pohl and Kammler. The texts that organized it
did so by placing Globocnik under the tutelage of the two SS specialists
in building and administration. Perhaps there was a division of tasks
between Kammler and Globocnik, one responsible for the building of
the Lublin concentration camp (the future camp of Majdanek) and the
other for the task of colonization, with the building of the 'Points of settlement and support'.[26] But the authority of Pohl and Kammler over the
whole chain of command was reasserted by Himmler, and no room for

manoeuvre was left to Globocnik's initiative: the memorandum stated that, in the first place, it was a matter of executing the measures *already ordered*, all under the aegis of the Central Department for Budget and Building.

This muddled activism is not surprising: the war had started three weeks ago, and levels of uncertainty were high. According to Christopher Browning, this was a time of euphoria, and there had been many new initiatives. The agreement of July 1941 was followed by the establishment of these regional and local institutions.[27] Following Himmler's order on 20 July 1941, Odilo Globocnik set himself the task of building an organization to oversee the erection of the 'Point of settlement and support for the police and the SS', while Kammler set up a parallel organization which was supposed to take over the rest of the building in the occupied territories. This was yet another example of the institutional Darwinism typical of the Third Reich, and this competitive situation quickly came to a conclusion with the clear victory of the central institution over the local institution.

Hans Kammler began by creating the Central Inspectorate of Building in Lublin to 'support' Globocnik's projects. This was a Trojan horse introduced into the very heart of the organization created by Globocnik. Kammler took care to appoint to it one of his followers, Wilhelm Lenzer, who came to the SS in his wake in 1940. The man and the institution quickly made themselves indispensable to Globocnik, while clearly taking their orders from the Berlin head office.[28] Attempts to neutralize Lenzer and his office remained fruitless, however, and the conflict ended up going back to Himmler, who again tried to settle the problem with Pohl.

Himmler therefore reiterated the division of tasks, but visibly without success. These conflicts, however, remained limited to the local level, as the relationship between Pohl, Kammler and Globocnik was unaffected by these tensions.

Under the leadership of Globocnik, however, results were a long time in coming and, at the end of autumn 1941, though Himmler had imposed a 17 July deadline, the Lublin SSPF had still not built a single 'Point of settlement and support' in the territories of the occupied Soviet Union. While some factories and workshops had been requisitioned, it was difficult to discern the advent of an economic empire, or a *limes* of small forts to safeguard settlement. Kammler and Pohl took advantage of this unacknowledged failure to set up their own administration and push forward their own advantage.

Building on the need to construct a support and logistics network for the SS and the police in the occupied territories of the USSR, on 18 August 1941 Pohl created an Economic Inspection for the three HSSPFs for the USSR which were competent for the territories under civil administration. Although these inspections were largely unknown to the other occupying institutions, at the beginning of 1942 they received orders from Pohl to erect 'shelter camps for future Support points for the SS and the police'.[29] Five weeks later, Odilo Globocnik was relieved of his functions as delegate to the building of 'Points of settlement and support' by Himmler, who named Pohl as his successor.

On 15 May 1942, a new order from Himmler was published in the collection of WVHA orders and circulars, determining the hierarchical way in which the 'Points of support' were decided and approved before building. On 10 June, a Department of Building was added to the RKFdV general staff, again by order of Himmler. It was exclusively meant for officers of the WVHA.[30] In addition to the way the whole formal managerial and economic apparatus of the WVHA had been added to the third version of the *Generalplan Ost* submitted to Himmler on 28 May 1942, as we have seen, this integration of staff said a great deal about the importance of Pohl's department, while a thousand days had passed since the beginning of the age of Utopia.

This third version of the *Generalplan Ost* provided for the building of thirty-six 'Points of settlement and support' for the police and the SS, which were to correspond to those initially mentioned by Globocnik and taken over by Kammler and his administration. The integration of the SS administrations was thus completed by the hybridization of the projects. All central administrations now seemed to be working in a coordinated manner, with a clear sharing out of tasks.

Finally, at the local level, Kammler had reacted in February to an order from Himmler demanding the establishment of brigades of building that would take charge of the project management of building plans. He had been careful to send back, not a document similar to that of December 1941, but a memorandum of about ten typed pages in which he discussed in detail the way the WVHA viewed the situation, before detailing its conception of the policy to be followed in building. After insisting on the fact that the SS could not carry out a policy of public bodies alone, but that it should also draw on private companies, the document summed up the current needs and the production of raw materials, as well as an inventory of the labour available to set up, on the one hand, the building policy and, on the other, the operational apparatus for its implementation.

In the view of Kammler and the engineers of the WVHA, the SS building corps would be composed of specialized regiments and battalions. One brigade consisted of two regiments, themselves composed of three specialized battalions, and each subdivided further into four companies: one battalion was responsible for deep infrastructure (the foundations), a second for building, a third for equipment.

A building regiment was mobile and mechanized and its accommodation was based on a mobile camp system of tents. The first battalion was composed of four companies: the first for digging and drilling, the second for services, the third specialized in road works, and the last was responsible for the building of quays, crossings (bridges) and the installation of water points and pipelines. The second battalion consisted of a masonry company, another for welding, a third for framework, and a fourth specializing in insulation, plumbing, roofing and carpentry. The last battalion, responsible for interior equipment, was composed of one company of cleaners, plasterers and painters, another of electricians and installers of strong and weak currents, a third of civil engineers, responsible for drainage and water piping, heating and ventilation, and a last company for general brigade support. In this way, all public bodies were supposed to be represented in these brigades, supervised by thirty SS officers, and a surveillance body whose numbers, curiously enough, were nowhere specified. The twelve companies were served by 180 detainee workers and by twenty men for service, including drivers and coachmen.[31] There were 2,400 men per regiment, 4,800 per brigade, essentially from the worlds of the concentration camps and the prisons: all in all, with regard to the occupied territories in the USSR, three building brigades – a total of 14,400 men – were established.

The question that arose was obviously that of manpower: the figures mentioned by Kammler and transmitted to Himmler did not go uninterrogated. According to the document, 8,800 detainees, of whom 2,037 were specially trained and 6,763 were unskilled workers, were available for these brigades, albeit scattered across the site of twelve concentration camps.[32] In the eyes of the WVHA engineers, these numbers comprised a labour force that was half the number of free German workers. And the manpower numbers necessary for the implementation of the plans far exceeded those mentioned in Kammler's memorandum in relation to the brigades, which stipulated that no fewer than 175,000 prisoners would be required.

Kammler's distribution plan involved a massive increase in the prison population while at the same time already implying that the building brigade system was inadequate: they could employ only 14,400 detainees while more than four times as many needed to be mobilized for the USSR alone.[33] Kammler and Himmler had started from the idea that an exponential extension of the system of concentration camps in the occupied territories would be necessary. Two remarks could be made here: on the one hand, Nazi Germany, as Kammler and Himmler were exchanging views on manpower, literally *exterminated* between 2 million and 3.3 million Soviet prisoners of war that had fallen into its hands since June 1941; and the problem of manpower figured by Himmler and created by the expansion of the concentration camp system was therefore a problem artificially created by the Nazi impulse to extirpate whole populations.[34] It was because the Third Reich combined an absence of looking forward in the definition of its policies with an almost atavistic propensity to kill *more* rather than less that it was confronted with problems of labour quotas. In the second place, a transformation in the Nazi paradigm was occurring: the anticipation of the Nazi future now involved mass slave labour, that is, implicitly but *imperatively*, the use of barbed wire and watchtowers.

This set of transformations was reflected in the summer of 1942 in the third *Generalplan Ost* sent by Meyer-Heitling to Himmler, on 28 May, the day after the attack on Heydrich that, as Florent Brayard has shown, led Himmler to order a genocide to be committed within one year.[35] The terrible paradox is all too apparent: the SS had been diagnosing for at least six months a shortage of the manpower necessary to carry out the labour that would make the Germanic Utopia possible, but the Nazis were initially unable to halt their murderous instincts, and left 2 million Soviet prisoners of war to die even though they would have constituted a valuable labour force. Then, in order to find a *via media* between the imperative of extermination and the need for manpower, the SS came up with a paradigm, formulated between the Wannsee Protocol of January 1942 and the Pohl report of 30 April 1942, defining a form of extermination through labour.[36] This paradigm, which consisted in establishing 'working columns' of Jewish slave labour destined to die from exhaustion, had emerged and was thus encapsulated in the third *Generalplan Ost*, just one week before Himmler gave a general order to accelerate as much as possible the process of mass murder: yet again proving an inability to defer the drive to genocide, even in view of the material building of Utopia.

It would be an exaggeration to see this mechanism as the main reason for the failure of the SS building plans in the East. Nonetheless, this inbuilt incoherence in Nazi policies became blatantly obvious in the summer of 1942. However, for anyone who is trying to sketch an assessment of the WVHA's operational activity, i.e. to take stock of what amounted to constructing Utopia *in concrete terms*, the results are meager. Building Utopia first of all involved providing oneself with the means to do so by drawing on the productive apparatus, and the quantitative indicators unambiguously point to the WVHA's failure: only a few hundred businesses and workshops were led by the WVHA and mobilized for the great task of Germanization. Only three districts in occupied Eastern Europe saw genuine central offices of building led by the WVHA, delegated by the RKFdV, and only one of these – the one in Zamość, which we will be examining in the last part of this study – had an existence that was more than merely symbolic. In the area of the HSSPF for Southern Russia, the RKFdV and the WVHA controlled 50 farms, 12 refuelling facilities and 220 trustee companies. This was very little for a territory which, according to the third *Generalplan Ost*, was meant to cut a great transversal road structured by 'Points of settlement and support' linking the Reich to a large territory of colonization in Crimea and southern Ukraine. The vision of Utopia was certainly there, palpable and almost institutionalized. But the policies implemented by the SS were all simultaneously incoherent in their murderous management of slave labour and muddled or even powerless in their productive and operational dimensions.[37] The failure was already clear, in this summer of 1942 when Utopia reached its paroxysm and its peak.

From the future back to the present: Utopia evaporates

In the summer of 1942, however, the SS dignitaries were far from drawing the conclusion that their enterprise had failed, as our discussion might have suggested. Quite the contrary: it was a time of renewed and powerful euphoria. On 16 July 1942, Himmler gave Hitler a long account of the latest developments in the ongoing third *Generalplan Ost*, and he recounted that the dictator, flushed by the initial successes of the great summer offensive towards the Caucasus, again believed in victory. Indeed, during the interview, Hitler had shown himself to be more than just interested in Himmler's account. Himmler described the encounter to his confidant and masseur, Kersten:

> The Führer not only listened to me, he even refrained from constant interruptions, as is his usual habit . . . today he went so far as to approve of my proposals, asking questions and drawing my attention to important details. [. . .] This is the happiest day of my life! [. . .] Everything I have been considering and planning on a small scale can now be realized. I shall set to at once on a large scale.[38]

Throughout the second half of the year, the SS institutions involved in the formulation of Utopia continued to work for Himmler, having the impression that they were acting in order to bring about Utopia. From the summer of 1942 onwards, however, some had the the growing impression that their time was being taken up by other sectors of activity which gradually and increasingly visibly took over from the beginning of 1943.

Ever since its foundation, the WVHA had been oscillating between four main missions. In the first place, ever since the sacking of von Gottberg from the land registry department in Prague and his replacement by Pohl as the trustee of all the companies confiscated, the WVHA had taken as one of its main aims the concentration of industrial firms which were supposed to make the SS a major group with a significant place in the German war effort. Second, the WVHA, taking over the workforce of slaves and concentration camp inmates, became one of the main leaders in the management of the immense contingents of workers with diverse status whose sweat had been nourishing the Nazi war efforts, whose importance had increased since the failure of the Blitzkrieg in December 1941. Third, the WVHA was at last managing a vast network of concentration camps, broken up into a multitude of sites. Lastly, the WVHA retained control over the implementation of operational policies for realizing the utopian plans made by the bodies responsible for Germanization.

In the summer of 1942, a decisive turn was taken; it has been vividly described by the British historian Adam Tooze. On the economic level, it was marked by three developments. First of all, a condominium was set up within the Nazi hierarchies, bringing together Himmler, Backe, the Minister for Agriculture and Supplies, and Goering's organization, to help to run the food industry. Hitler then gave the signal for an immense hunt for labour power when he appointed Fritz Sauckel as general pleni-potentiary for the mobilization of labour (*Arbeitseinsatz*).[39] Finally, the appointment of Albert Speer as Fritz Todt's successor gave a decisive impetus to the full mobilization of the war industries.[40] In all three cases, the WVHA was involved to the highest degree.

The establishment of the implicit alliance between Backe, Himmler and Goering had had repercussions for the Nazi future. On 29 May, Himmler, Backe and Greifelt organized the new alliance, renewed on 22 June.[41] Meyer-Heitling was appointed Head of Planning at the Ministry of Supplies in July 1942, although this alliance did not really affect the planning of Utopia, but was meant to address the rationing of populations and an increased pressure on the occupied territories, in particular those of the General Government.

As early as August 1942, the discussions between Backe and Himmler took a new turn, and the topics of discussion became inexorably tied to current events. Recent research has shown how the acceleration in the murder of Jews – especially in the General Government – which rose to a paroxysm of intensity in the summer of 1942 was also triggered by considerations of logistics and food supply. While the Nazis were deeply imbued with a sense of the fulfilment of the new realm, current considerations were increasingly pressing.[42] And this mechanism, which gradually made considerations of the *hic and nunc* more urgent than those of the utopian future, also imprinted its marks on the other dimensions of the WVHA's activity.

The same was true of the production of the SS group and its grip on businesses, farms and workshops in the occupied USSR. In May 1943, for example, in the HSSPF Rußland Süd, Hans Kammler was still ordering the inspection of buildings for the erection of a 'Point of settlement and support' in Dubno.[43] On paper, the balance sheet seemed quite good: no fewer than 420 workshops or companies were being managed by the SS in the HSSPF Rußland Süd.[44] On closer inspection, however, these were small production units, mainly artisanal in nature. The SS economic authorities had not succeeded in imposing the building of the facilities of the future Nazi colonizers as one of the priorities of the occupying bodies: the local Wehrmacht economic administrations were the dominant actor here and the position of the SS was weak if it came to a confrontation. But there was more to it than that: at a time when only production of strategic importance in the war effort was seen as of value, the economic bodies of the SS had failed to get their hands on a single armaments or munitions factory. The SS industries were capable of honouring nothing more than orders for basins, bowls and glasses.[45]

We need to dwell on this last mechanism because, in the last instance, it probably marked the final stage in the disappearance of Nazi hope. The significant change in the activity of the WVHA's regional offices, which consisted of a slippage in priorities between activities of building or preparation for the facilities of Germanization, and those of mobilization with a view to the total war effort, implied a change in their horizons of expectation. The advent of Utopia and its projection into the future gradually but inevitably gave way to a new temporality of perspective among the actors, a perspective now firmly rooted in the present of total war.

And what was discernible in the production policies of the WVHA in the occupied territories was even more evident in the third area of SS specialization: the question of the concentration camp labour force. We have seen that Meyer-Heitling's projections had been issued in consultation with Hans Kammler's offices, and the figures quoted by the racial engineer of the RKFdV were unambiguous: hundreds of thousands of detainees, probably over 800,000, were necessary for the fulfilment of *Generalplan Ost* in its third version. But the times had already changed: the great operation for exploiting the European workforce reached its peak with the appointment of Fritz Sauckel as General Plenipotentiary for the mobilization of labour in the summer of 1942, and the labour force now came from all over Europe, and was of all conditions. As long as Sauckel and his administration were able to provide private industry with 'free' labour in the guise of compulsory labour, the SS could only play a marginal role in the war effort in Germany, especially since the situation created by Speer was not compatible, in the eyes of Pohl, with his own plan to create a significant armaments industry within the WVHA.[46] Beginning in September 1942, representatives of the industrialists and Speer had ensured that the SS remained limited to the allocation of labour on Hitler's orders. This decision reflected both the failure to set up an SS group for arms production and the limiting of the WVHA to labour issues.[47] All of this interacted in the practice of manpower allocation from the concentration camps to the German war effort. On a deeper level, however, the situation, which seemed to bring together two programmes for exploiting men in the service of two fundamentally different, or even antagonistic, objectives (economic mobilization of total warfare versus the building of the postwar Reich), was a clear expression of these developments. Utopia was vanishing into the distance; the future was fading. The present concerns of the war and the gigantic effort to win victory had invaded the horizon of expectation and brought it back to more immediate concerns.

This phenomenon of a 'return to the present' which affected the horizon of expectations of the actors and their repertoires of action must in no case be apprehended as a linear process. It would of course be too hasty to attempt to grasp this development all at once, especially since the actors did not all have the same temporalities: but one conclusion we might draw is that the institutions that were focused on those sectors that were most deeply affected by the war situation, in terms of economics and management, were undergoing a process marked by the rise of Utopia with a constant sense of being tugged back to the present – witness one first stage of this in December 1941, when an attempt was made to foster a greater degree of mobilization among the actors (Central Department for Budget and Building, Economic and Administrative Department and Inspection of Concentration Camps) within the German war effort, while assigning to the first two at least a more significant role in the formulation of the Nazi Utopia in view of its implementation.

After a new surge of utopian imperial hope during the summer of 1942, however, the WVHA, which now brought all of these actors under its own aegis, was increasingly focused on issues of resource mobilization and allocation of manpower. It had to some degree come under the war effort, now dominated by the Speer and Sauckel administrations, which were to become preponderant especially after January 1943, when it became clear that the changing expectations of the actors were making them turn their attention more to the here and now and less to the utopian future.

In the winter of 1942–3, at the very moment when the great summer offensive was stalling and turning into a desperate battle of encirclement in Stalingrad, the WVHA had clearly moved on from the implementation of utopian plans. Gradually, all the institutions had adapted to the new reality and this return to the present. Nine months later, the *SS-Wirtschafter* of Ukraine set up a new plan, to be implemented in case the Soviets invaded in return – a clear expression of how times had changed.[48]

The other protagonists in the creation of the new Nazi order underwent a similar evolution and adapted to this new set of circumstances by focusing on areas and prerogatives likely to give them an existence in what would prove to be the beginning of a desperate fight for the survival of the Third Reich. Only one institution lacked such room for manoeuvre: the RKFdV, alone of all those bodies to have been expressly born of utopian imperial expectations, and the organization whose sole raison d'être was the formulation and preparation of the racial parousia.

At the moment when Himmler was, according to Kersten, wallowing in the euphoria of utopian communion with Hitler, the departments of Greifelt and Meyer-Heitling were deploying a great deal of energy to produce the third *Generalplan Ost*. The autumn of 1942 was then spent in managing the communication of the plan through the upper echelons of the SS hierarchy. We need merely remember at this juncture that Himmler commissioned Meyer-Heitling's departments to produce a final version of this plan, called the *Generalsiedlungsplan* (General Settlement Plan), of which Meyer-Heitling sent a first incomplete version, reduced to its archival annexes, to Himmler on 23 December 1942.[49]

The month of January 1943 was apparently marked by work on composing the *Generalsiedlungsplan*, meant to support the statistics already received by Himmler. On 31 January, however, the capitulation of the 6th Army at Stalingrad confirmed a major geopolitical change: Germany had lost its strategic initiative on all fronts, the horizon of expectation was changing inexorably, and most of the actors were now aware of this. *All* of them, indeed – except perhaps the RKFdV, whose sole raison d'être was the utopian future.

Virtually as if nothing had happened, on 15 February 1943, Konrad Meyer-Heitling addressed a letter to the *Reichsführer* to ask for further information as to the modifications of the *Generalsiedlungsplan* he had requested in a letter of 12 February.[50]

On 23 March, the Director of the Secretariat of the general staff of the RKFdV received a letter explaining that the written documents on the *Generalplan Ost* and its state of preparation were 'so incomplete that [it is] preferable to send a generic documentation [*Zusammenstellung*] to *Obersturmbannführer* SS Dr Brandt [Himmler's personal advisor]'. The letter went on to note that the latest entries in the file dated from 12 November 1942 and that the SS captain supposed to follow up on the file considered it useless to bother Himmler over such a question.[51]

There followed two months of letters exchanged at a very slow rate so as to try and reduce the bureaucratic jungle that had by now entangled all matters of Germanization, and to unify the three files on the *Generalplan Ost* for the personal general staff of the *Reichsführer*, while searching for the missing pieces. It was clear that a halt was being called to the process: this was a problem of bureaucratic macrocephaly and of the actors' torpid reluctance to have to tackle a file that had become gigantic in volume; but it *also* marked a flagrant lack of interest on the part of Himmler's general staff: neither the SS captain acting as secretary, nor Brandt, the personal advisor to the head of the SS, made the least effort to try to make any progress on a file whose outdatedness was now clear to everyone. A note sent to Brandt by the records management office of the secretariat of the general staff on 15 May 1943 summarized the situation thus:

> I need to talk to you about the *Generalplan Ost*. The parts missing from this procedure – letter from *SS-Oberführer* Meyer-Heitling of 15 February 43 concerning the modified plan – have not yet returned to the records management office. Nor are they with the officer dealing with the matter in Berlin. Since you do not have them, there is only one possibility: the fact that they are still in the hands of the *Reichsführer*.
>
> I think it would be wise to speak to the *SS-Reichsführer*. From the letter sent in copy on 15 February 1943 by the *SS-Hauptsturmführer* Hefermehl, it can be deduced that the *SS-Oberführer* Meyer-Heitling can continue to work only after the *Reichsführer* has taken a decision.[52]

There could be no better illustration of the unusual carelessness of Himmler: he had negligently failed to return the letter addressed to him by Meyer-Heitling, had made no decision regarding it and had not dealt with it in the usual way, and was obstructing the work of one of his most important agencies. 'The most important', really? What was true between 1 September 1939 and the autumn of 1942 was in fact no longer valid in the spring of 1943. And this note to Rudolf Brandt announcing that this insignificant matter of a lost file was going to be brought to the knowledge of Himmler did not change anything: on 10 June, a new note examined the problem and remarked on the lack of progress, and Meyer-Heitling even said that Himmler had replied in the following words, when he inquired about the progress of the process: 'Yes, I remember, it's on my desk. I'm still thinking it over.'[53] Nothing, however, changed: letters of 10 September and then a new note of 13 September 1943, all addressed to Brandt, show that Himmler never again took any interest in the *Generalplan Ost* file, and it was only on 6 January 1944 that an SS NCO forwarded a short and modestly triumphant note to indicate that the missing documents from the *Generalplan* file had been found, in the middle of a dossier on structures and property in Ukraine and the occupied territories.[54] The following document freed the last planners from their activity and told them to take up arms and fight in this army of despair, which, in this terrible final year of the war, attempted to lessen the inevitable pain of defeat.

Slowness, negligence, the subordinate status of those now in charge of the *Generalplan Ost* all highlight the new reality. The future and the Utopia it had promised were no longer relevant, and had no part in a Reich now fully mobilized in the intense effort to mobilize men and resources and attempt simply to survive, which would require victory in battle.

Let me be clear: the Third Reich was not dead, nor was Nazi belief. The faith remained alive, in all its diverse forms. But hope was fading, the horizon of expectation had changed and the advent of the new Reich had vanished, to be replaced by a less multidimensional horizon of expectation, more focused on the present with its combat.

The Nazi Utopia was no more.

Conclusion

In the light of a varied but sometimes impressionistic or fragmentary documentation, this study has brought us to the heart of the planned socio-biological refoundation that underlay Nazi hope. And at the end of this singular journey, it seems to me that a number of facts must be emphasized.

In the first place, it is the magnitude of the Nazi project that strikes the observer. From 1939 to 1943, it was shaped by the idea of a gigantic expansion of the Reich, and, in the midst of the SS euphoria, it was indeed a Germanic empire from the Seine to the Urals, from the Arctic Circle to the Black Sea, which over the centuries would have seen a population of 600 million Nordic people swell its confines, which constituted the horizon of the SS dignitaries. From the Baltic *Ingermanland* to the *Gottengau* of the Black Sea, from the Sea of Azov to the Poznań countryside, the Nazi planners dreamt of an immense Europe.

This Europe was also to be carefully and spatially reconfigured. The creation of cities, the redevelopment of urban centres, urban architecture and planning with open squares and many facilities, the rebuilding of village networks and land structures – all this formed a coherent and profound whole, covering every scale of reality, even in the bedrooms of married couples and their children, sketching a social, racial, economic and emotional order that filled the contours of this *Volksgemeinschaft* that was so celebrated by propagandists.

The precision of this figuration of social hope was one of the greatest strengths of SS planning, and the dignitaries of the order did not hesitate to give it concrete shape so as to allow representations of this utopian hope to spread, especially since the actors felt they were working for its realization.

We must then emphasize the very great plasticity of this artefact, its propensity to present itself under so many facets that it could exert a powerful attractiveness on practically all the social categories of the population to which it was exhibited. Anyone who successfully passed through the ordeal of the SS's socio-racial examination was offered a place in this Utopia.

The corollary of this last statement is that, quite obviously, the vast majority of Europeans had no place and destiny other than in the form of social and racial dissimilation and ethnomorphosis for the few individuals who were the closest in phenotypical terms to Nordic canons. Otherwsie their destiny was to be slaves or helots at the mercy of policies of segregation and, at worst, outright extermination, whether *directly*, with regard to the whole of the Jewish population, doomed to this fate from December 1941, or in part *indirectly*, as in the case of those 17 million Slavs whose existence was no longer permitted by the immense operation of predation and murderous social engineering that was to precede Germanization.

Such was the foundation of Nazi hope, that hope that ethnocrats figured in a multitude of plans, maps, sketches of houses and memorandums, and that they continued to refine for as long as their military success seemed to them secure. Indeed, from the beginning of 1942, the Nazis thought themselves sufficiently advanced to be able to move from the planning phase to programming and implementation, and this resulted in the arrival on the scene not just of dreamers and practitioners of the ethnic cleansing of the RKFdV or the RSHA, but of the empire-building engineers and managers assembled in the WVHA. The latter formulated the financial estimates of Utopia and set off in search of the productive apparatus capable of bringing it about and of the various labour forces that could be exploited in the service of this dream.

These engineers, however, were quickly confronted by a competition between two horizons of temporality which they could not reconcile: on the one hand the horizon of expectation of a future marked by the racial parousia, on the other the ever more imperious injunctions of the here and now of total war and total mobilization. After January 1943, this last imperative completely occupied the Nazi consciences, and gradually but definitively marked the end of the configuration of the *Tausendjähriges Reich*. Hope did not die. But it did become subordinated to the present and its struggles.

Part III

The case of Zamość

Introduction

There is a land, on the borders of Poland and Ukraine, a fertile and densely populated land, on which fell the dubious honour of becoming the site of all the Nazis' attempts at social and racial engineering in this sequence. Our investigation requires us to look more closely at it.

This land, the Zamojszczyzna, was a *topos* for all the dreams of the SS. It has been the subject of intense research work, both German and Polish,[1] and a careful selection of the many documents that have been preserved was published in the 1980s, before the opening of the archives, by the man who was at that time the best Polish historian of the Second World War, and also a specialist in the *Generalplan Ost*, Czesław Madajczyk.[2] Finally, Zygmunt Klukowski, a doctor in Szczebrzeszyn, a town in the Zamość area, kept a remarkable diary that reports on the martyrdom of the region and the society that gave life to it: it is a remarkably rich source, and a valuable aid to understanding how the Nazi promise became a nightmare for all the populations that were confronted by it.[3]

The geographical situation and strategic *imaginaire*, as well as the exceptional documentary and archival status of this area, will enable us in the last part of this book to present a description embodied in the local detail of Nazi practice, not only from the point of view of the actors, discourses, *imaginaires* and practices of planning, but also based on concrete experiences and practices.

In other words, we will be seeing Utopia in the act; Nazi building as embodied in a particular region, a microcosm whose features we must first try to describe before focusing on the policies produced and, finally, trying to measure the impact these violent and highly specific policies had on the different populations of this land.

Chapter 7

The microcosms of radical policy: Zamojszczyzna

In the 1990s, an anthropologist and a historian, Édouard Conte and Cornelia Essner, decided, for different reasons, to conduct a joint field survey in southeastern Poland, which had recently emerged from Communism. Édouard Conte was a specialist in the peasant worlds beyond the Berlin Wall. His wife, Cornelia Essner, devoted her work to the anti-Semitic policies of the Third Reich. By conducting oral surveys with peasants in the Zamość country, they observed the persistence of the figure of a sort of symbolic Nazi ogre, Odilo Globocnik, and decided to devote time and energy to the history of this region under German occupation.[1] Thus was born the first great anthropology of Nazism, an exemplary model, twenty years later, for the present work. If our approaches differ somewhat, so that I take a broader interest in all the practices designed to foster the advent of Utopia in the region, this study has many topics in common with *La Quête de la race* by Édouard Conte and Cornelia Essner, and the same spatial framework. As we come to the end of this study of Nazi representations of the utopian future, it is therefore on Zamość that we must dwell in our turn.

We need therefore to understand the specificities of Zamojszczyzna, and grasp what led SS dignitaries to make it the place for all their ethnic, economic and infrastructural experiments. Zamojszczyzna was specific in its situation, its settlement, its spatio-economic organization and past, but also in the way an occupying apparatus was set up there that made of it a particular microcosm. This set of factors conditioned the emergence of a radicalism that was probably unique when seen in the context of the Nazi imperium in Europe.

The men, the space and the past of Zamojszczyzna

The sources agree that the region of Zamojszczyzna was first mentioned in 1580, the date of the foundation of the city by the hetman Jan Sariusz Zamojski, who soon granted it privileges intended for Catholics and

Armenians first, and then for Sephardic Jews, as he expected that their set-tlement would bring about the extension of trade networks from Southern Europe to the confines of Eastern Europe. Jan Sariusz Zamojski was one of the leading dignitaries of the Kingdom of Greater Poland, including Poland and the Grand Duchy of Lithuania, and a regular visitor to diplo-matic missions in the West. So he went on an embassy to France in 1573, when the crown of Poland was offered to the future Henry III of France.[2] The foundation of the city seems to have been based on calculations both political (enabling it to assert its domination over its lands) and economic (the desire to polarize trade in the region).

We learn from the *Encyclopedia of Jews in Eastern Europe* published by the YIVO Institute that this foundation was successful, and Sephardic Jewish families from Lemberg/Lviv/Lvov settled in Zamość between the end of the sixteenth and the beginning of the seventeenth centuries: this urban centre became an important trade hub between the Slavic and Muslim worlds, and some of the families who settled there came from Constantinople.[3] At the interface of the world of the steppes (as we shall see) and that of fields and forests, between the Ottoman Orient and the edges of Eastern Europe, Zamość seems to have been able to build up an economic function quickly enough to ensure rapid growth, a strong identity and an urban character.

From the time when he founded the city, Zamojski had taken care to attract Italian architects who drew up the city plan from scratch and gave it the architectural characteristics of an Italian Baroque city, in stark con-trast to the urban centres around. In 1657, the city had 222 houses, making it an appreciable market town, with a population approaching 4,000 souls and one of the largest textile industries in Ruthenia.

In the multiple partitions that saw the Kingdom of Poland disappear in the eighteenth century, Zamość initially fell under the control of Austria, then, following the Napoleonic wars and the Congress of Vienna, under the Kingdom of Poland (Kongreßpolen, the Congress Poland mentioned by the Nazi documentation), a title and domain of the tsars of Russia. The town was bought in 1821 by the government and ceased to be a city of private law.

The long nineteenth century, as far as can be judged, seems to have been that of a quiet frugality in an economic environment quite different from the Northeast and Łódź, which were in the midst of an industrial revolution. This rather poor, provincial, small town in Poland did indeed experience something of a boom, with an apparent tripling of its population over the century, but this was all in a clearly traditional and pre-industrial way. Its population of just over 5,600 in 1827 had risen to almost 20,000 in 1921.[4]

It was caught up in the specific turmoil of the Great War in the East. Zamość was located in a border position between the Tsarist Kingdom of Poland and Austrian Galicia. When the war broke out in August 1914, the plans of the General Staff provided for a large Austro-German movement in the East to counter the great Russian offensive. It was between Zamość and Hrubieszów that the stabilization of the Polish southern front was decided; the Austrians won a clear victory, halting the advance of the Russian Fifth Army in a series of defensive battles. The two armies were of equal size, each consisting of 200,000 men, but the Russian army had already suffered a first setback a few days earlier and was unable to oppose the Austrians. From 26 to 29 August 1914, the Austrians led a flanking attack which succeeded in encircling a large section of the Russian army, which had to withdraw to avoid annihilation near Zamość and Hrubieszów.[5]

The war rather moved away from the city in the ensuing period, but Zamość, like the rest of the region, was affected by the associated conflicts over a long period of time: this began in 1914 and did not stop in 1918, but was prolonged between 1919 and 1921 by the Soviet–Polish war. Once again, the immediate vicinity of the city was the scene of a pitched battle between the Soviet cavalry led by Boudienny and the formations of the Polish state under Piłsudski.[6]

The city suffered little damage in comparison with neighbouring Galicia, and especially with Soviet Ukraine, which remained a prey to a devastating civil war.[7] In the interwar years, the city was part of the COP (Central Industrial District) organized in 1938 to plan the country's economic and industrial development, and was thus identified as belonging to a sort of sub-industrialized inner periphery, wedged between the West, dominated by Kraków and Łódź, and the East, with Warsaw and Białystok, both of which were seen as industrially dominant.[8] It still enjoyed good apparent growth between 1921 and 1939, and had about 25,000 inhabitants when the war between Poland and Germany broke out. On 17 September 1939, the Wehrmacht entered the city.

The Germans thus found a region – not only the Zamojszczyzna, but the entire district of Lublin – which had always been a land of edges and borders, a margin between several worlds; its toponymy was there to remind any observers of this fact. On leaving Lublin, a small village called Tatarski Majdan (the Tatars' Camp) reminded people that the area had once been steppe and constituted the territory of migrations of populations of nomadic Tatar breeders until at least the thirteenth century and the Mongol invasion. So Zamość lay at the interface between the world of the steppes, the world of forests and the world of agriculture, to which it undoubtedly belonged from the start of the modern era.

In terms of ecosystem and climatic-geographic conditions, the continental region comes with harsh winters and hot, dry and stormy summers, with a wet season in the spring and another, snowy, in autumn, as in a large part of Ukraine and southern Poland, little affected by Nordic and maritime influences from the Baltic Sea. A rigorous and constrictive climate, though not deleterious, did not in any way prevent people from cultivating the soil, even if they did so in a less intensive way.

The soils of Zamojszczyzna are exceptionally good because they have a composition similar to that of chernozem, the thick, loamy and loessy black soil of Ukraine, which promises profuse cereal harvests and high levels of legume production. Even today, the documentation produced in the wake of the Sixth Framework Programme for Research and Technological Development of the European Union highlights the remarkable quality of this land and the agrarian misuse of it by the local peasants,[9] similar here to the Polish elites of the 1930s, the Nazi agronomists (especially from the RuSHA and RKFdV) and the future local administrators sent by Hans Frank.

The reason for this astonishing consistency in the judgements of outside actors is undoubtedly an extremely tenacious prejudice against the local peasantry, which added to Nazi racism; but all investigators have based their conclusions on a shared observation, astonishing in its persistence: it is the land structures here that are largely responsible for the agronomic indigence of the region. And one need simply look at the satellite photos of the region or even more simply use Google Earth, that wonderful visualization tool, which shows Zamojszczyzna covered with a beautiful open-field system set up in the nineteenth century, one which survived both the war and the horrendous Nazi occupation, as well as the forty-five years of Communist government, which in theory was eager to collectivize the land and consolidate the open fields. These myriad open micro-fields, the result of the practice of an egalitarian sharing out of land, were a very striking feature of the Zamojszczyzna landscape when the German invaders set their eyes and then their boots in it in 1939.[10] Even today, it is an area intensively farmed for crops, and only 25 per cent of the land was then forested.[11] Édouard Conte summarizes the plot and property situation at the outset of the war in an illuminating way, although his statement concerns neighbouring Galicia as much as the region of Zamość:

> A crazy counterpoint of tiny plots of land. Often, just one peasant can hold sixty strips of land two metres wide, separated by several kilometres. [. . .] They spend hours going from one strip to another; the use of agricultural machinery is absolutely impossible; a considerable amount of time and money is wasted on trials relating to demarcation.[12]

In Zamojszczyzna, almost 413,000 people lived on these micro-plots,[13] engaged largely in subsistence farming, with little monetarization of their produce, in an endemic situation of land famine that struck all observers. On these 'microfundia', whose maximum surface area was, in 89 per cent of cases, 15 hectares, while almost half of them were of less than 5 hectares,[14] the peasants practised an ingenious form of mixed agriculture with mainly cereals, wheat, rye, barley and oats, in combination with herbaceous plants such as turnips. Then as now, the sources also mention a notable production of tobacco and potatoes, probably partly developed in the fields or vegetable gardens of villages, themselves consisting of wooden houses grouped along various routes, but rather recalling the planned street-villages and the more spontaneously formed heap-villages defined by the agro-geographers of Germany between the wars.[15] If we add that pig and cattle breeding had apparently been reduced to the level of domestic economy, we can start to grasp the image of an open-field country, a landscape both open and kaleidoscopic, bristling with more than 380 windmills and water mills, populated by a peasantry largely restricted to the food economy,[16] evolving within an egalitarian transmission system that pushed the land into a state of extreme fragmentation and led these families (of which there were many, since this was a time of significant population growth) to a situation of precariousness that remained a constant factor from the 1930s to the 2010s.[17]

In 1939, Zamojszczyzna had some 517,000 inhabitants, of which probably about 20 per cent were urban and 80 per cent rural. As a borderland in the area of residence of the Russian Empire, in the Kingdom of Poland and on the borders of Ruthenia and Galicia, its cultural background was almost as fragmented as its land.

Three religions competed for the souls of these populations, and three languages for their speakers – if we adopt the simplistic view that each person spoke only one language, which would have been quite impossible. And there were three 'nationalities' within the Polish citizenship that prevailed in 1939 in Zamość. It is again Édouard Conte who gives the most subtle account of this state of affairs and describes the situation clearly, showing how, at the end of the twentieth century, the people he interrogated carefully differentiated between language, nationality and sovereignty in these borderlands. In Zamość, the same was true in 1939, and any sense of belonging, which would very soon be simplified to the extreme given the fateful issues at stake, remained complex.

The Jews, with an overwhelming Ashkenazi majority after an initial influx of Sephardim in the sixteenth century, accounted for 10 per cent of the population. They had predominantly settled in urban areas: nearly 12,000 lived in Zamość itself, where they constituted almost half of the population, while 11,000 Jews lived in Hrubieszów, the second largest settlement in the region, and 4,600 in Biłgoraj.[18] As a matter of fact, the urban population was composed of nearly 50 per cent Jews throughout the region, with the Jews being present in large numbers or even constituting the majority group in all the important boroughs. In Józefów, a district of Biłgoraj, Jews constituted the majority, with a population of 2,000.[19]

Ukrainian-speaking Uniate and Orthodox Christians constituted the second, rather rural swathe of population. They represented a quarter of the population and were distributed fairly uniformly across the territory of Zamojszczyzna, more densely in the east and with a tendency to gather in villages.

Polish Catholics were the most numerous, comprising two-thirds of the population. They lived both in town and in the countryside and were no different from the Ukrainians in socio-economic terms. These two groups *together* constituted a small local peasantry restricted to growing food and tobacco, potatoes and cereal crops – a socio-economic identity that could have unified these two groups, which their language and/or religion separated.

No studies have shown how ethno-national polarization came about at the local level in Zamość. It can be assumed that the long war, begun in 1914 and completed around 1921, with its attendant destruction, rigorous occupation policies and besieged cities, played more than its share in this process. Nevertheless, the policies carried out in these regions by the political authorities in the 1930s accelerated the rise in national and cultural antagonisms as well as incubating their transformation into ethnic splits.[20]

In 1921, Poland had some 4 million landless peasants, a logical situation in a system of equal transmission, where 65 per cent of these landowners held less than 5 hectares, a limit commonly accepted at that time as enough to support a family. Land reform, involving land consolidation, was a logical solution and was voted in on 15 July 1920. It organized the transfer of property and in theory limited the maximum landholdings held by landowners (*zemlianstvi*), those 19,000 latifundians who alone held 43 per cent of the land. Between 1919 and 1937, 2.5 million hectares changed hands and another 5 million were allocated to land consolidation: in all, almost 30 per cent of Poland's arable land was affected. Despite its magnitude, this reform did not solve the agrarian crisis: it reduced non-viable micro-farms of less than 2 hectares by one-third, but on sensitive sectors of farms of 2 to 5 hectares it had no effect, as land was not distributed to these owners. This is not surprising, in the local context of these borderlands, and in particular in Galicia, adjacent to Zamojszczyzna: agrarian reform was not designed to upset land structures but at most to strengthen the middling peasants, considered as a bulwark against Bolshevism. Here we see ideological considerations coupled with an ethno-national logic: indeed, the 70,000 Polish peasants in the Galician lands to the south and east of Zamość (the latter mostly Ukrainian) were the main beneficiaries of agrarian reform to the detriment of the Ukrainian majority. The phenomenon would not show up in the statistics if religious identity was not mentioned in the 1931 census. The times, already difficult because of the circumstances, became even more so because of the global crisis, and agrarian reform threw oil onto an ever-menacing ethnic fire, and the so-called 'national-radical' programme of 1937 also reaffirmed the objective of cultural Polonization: it was a matter of gaining the 'Slav minorities by assimilating the masses and fighting against hostile elements'.[21] Ukrainians responded in Galicia by giving mass support to cooperation, but a politicized minority chose to plunge into armed struggle, and by the summer of 1930 a genuine climate of guerrilla warfare had taken hold of the countryside. There were no fewer than 2,000 acts of sabotage, aimed at practically all the middling peasants and the Polish latifundians. In retaliation, 800 Ukrainian villages were subjected to dragonnades imposed by a Polish army incapable of resisting ethnic polarization. Therefore, the Fascist Organization of Ukrainian Nationalists, the OUN, opted for a strategy of assassinations and targeted attacks in Galicia, resulting in a reaction from the Polish central government which restricted the political rights of the minority. Between 1932 and 1938, however, the Polish confines constituted a haven of calm in comparison with neighbouring Soviet Ukraine: the immense famine, conceived by the Soviets both as a famine to extirpate Ukrainian peasant nationalism and as a form of agrarian predation pursuing the primitive accumulation of the capital of the 'black lands', brought about millions of deaths. Echoes reached the Ukrainian and Polish peasants, even though the Polish governments agreed, following the non-aggression pact with the USSR signed in 1932, to carry out joint policies against Ukrainian nationalism.[22]

Galicia and Zamojszczyzna had until then shared the same fate, even though their configurations remained different. They were both empire lands (Austro-Hungarian and Russian) that had become Polish in 1921; both consisted of open fields, and a complex ethnic chequerboard. One, Zamojszczyzna, was largely Polish with few latifundia, while the other, Galicia, was mostly Ukrainian with a massive Polish latifundian presence. Beyond this difference in structure, they were both subject to the same policies, a façade of agrarian reform and policies of forced assimilation to Polish culture.

The year 1939 and the subsequent invasion by Nazi Germany and the Stalinist USSR drove a wedge between the destinies of the frontier regions for at least twenty-one months. While Zamojszczyzna came under the Germanic yoke of the General Government and the RKFdV, Galicia was to undergo one of the most brutal campaigns of collectivization and Sovietization orchestrated by Stalin and his deputies.[23] This is another story, true, but can we not already see how this borderland constituted, from at least 1930, a laboratory for the great radical policies of the twentieth century?[24]

Between 14 and 17 September 1939, then, it was this small territory, 85 kilometres from east to west and 45 kilometres from north to south (equivalent in area to Tarn-et-Garonne or Vaucluse, the smallest French provincial departments), a region where many ethnic tensions were already brewing, a prey to the hunger for land of the microfundia, into which the German institutions of occupation moved.

Institutional microcosms

The Nazis set up a series of abundant and diverse administrations, with great rapidity, in the district of Lublin, of which the district of Zamość was a part. These administrations were partly civilian and partly directly derived from the SS empire. They made the district of Zamość and its three cantons (Zamość, Biłgoraj and Hrubieszów) a special case, on account of both their density and their specific qualities.

Local civil administrations were indicative of the character of the German occupation, which was from the start arbitrary and repressive. Their development was paradoxical. Inadequately staffed, they could not cope with the flow of regulations and decrees put in place during the first year of occupation. Their initial disarray is undoubtedly due to organizational problems and an extremely chaotic set of circumstances: the devastation of the invasion, the policies of population displacement and exclusion of Jews, and a sampling that was immediately predatory. After a year of restructuring under the rubric of administrative simplification, the backbone of the General Government remained macroeconomic, and although one-third of civil servants worked at the local level, the Zamość district was considered to have fewer than about a hundred civil servants,[25] most probably concentrated in the conurbations and relying on the Polish village administrations to control and regulate the implantation of habitats. One specific feature of the canton was that the head of its administration remained in post from its foundation to the liberation of the district of Lublin by the Soviets, while the other two cantons of the Zamojszczyzna saw no fewer than three holders each in under four years.

The initial principle of any orders given and measures taken by the German institutions was simple: 'When a representative of the German authority has taken a measure against a non-German, it must in principle be considered as valid', recalled a circular proposing the simplification of administrative relations in the General Government in July 1941.[26] Partiality and arbitrariness were thus set up as principles for the simplification of governance and administration, since they were directed towards the racial inferior: this was the first of the characteristics of an institutional landscape whose actors also had a large range of repressive measures at their disposal.

From death pure and simple to confinement on mere administrative request: from the effective practice of hostage-taking, which made each prisoner a potential target for reprisal shootings, to confiscation of property and eviction: a whole range of measures was left to the discretion of local civil officials who were the main actors in this hell of blind brutality and arbitrariness that constituted the German occupation in Zamość for the whole population from 1939 to the beginning of 1942.

In addition to this exorbitant power, local administrations in Zamość acted as conduits between the governor's office of the district and the small Polish administrative communities maintained in the villages, and held all power when it came to economic policy, predation, supply, and the allocation of capital labour in the programmes of forced labour. This may have seemed an anodyne question, but in 1942 it decided, inter alia, who would live and who would die among the Jews in the district. This civil administration, though relatively dense (especially compared with that which was later installed in the *Reichskommissariat* of Ukraine and Ostland), was thus called upon to implement very specific policies.

Throughout the district there was a very peculiar atmosphere of arbitrariness and omnipotence carefully constructed by the heads of the local areas, who made an insistent case in their reports so that this latitude would be as little as possible called into question by the traditional circuits of the regulation of power, ex gratia decrees and judicial appeals.[27] This atmosphere was all the more burdensome and pervasive in that the upper echelons did not merely endorse the local and daily arbitrariness of the village administrations, but rather encouraged and even provoked it.[28] The Lublin area and the Zamość district bristled with many SS institutions, which made it one of the most remarkably concentrated places in the Nazi Empire, structured into an extremely dense network of cells that can be differentiated in accordance with their four purposes: (1) institutions of control, domestication and repression; (2) institutions of government and planning; (3) institutions of forced labour, building and economic administration; and (4) an extermination organization. This typology, however brief, leads us to the heart of the radical specificity of the district of Lublin.

It should be remembered that it was not uncommon for a district awaiting Germanization to be given an SS research unit. As we have seen, Wilhelm Koppe in Poznań had set up a resettlement headquarters in the autumn of 1939. At the same time, in Poznań and Łódź, local settlement and expulsion agencies had been created, though they were quickly taken over by the Berlin HQs in collaboration with the local offices of the Gestapo and the SD. But in Lublin, the institution seems to have been more densely populated and far more active: it was on Globocnik's initiative that a 'Team House' (*'Mannschaftshaus'*) was set up on the model of those founded by the RuSHA in the Reich from 1934 onwards. These were collective houses occupied by students dedicated to the basic forms of SS militancy in that they had satisfied its racial and physical demands and participated in both the ideological training and the physical exercises required by the hierarchy, while continuing their studies.[29] This was the latest step in the collaboration between the SS and the NSDStB, whose importance in *Osteinsatz* militancy has been emphasized. These institutions had developed remarkably well before the war, and seven or so of them shared the territory of the Reich before the creation of that of Lublin. This one was officially founded in October 1940, after an interview between Globocnik and Himmler on 26 October.[30] It appears that it was initially conceived on the basis of a proposal by the head of the RuSHA office in Lublin, and was organized with a No. 1 Department in charge of race and lineage, a No. 2 Department responsible for settlement issues, a No. 3 Service for 'Points of settlement and support', and a No. 4 Department in charge of administrative matters.[31] The proposal expressed a need for 11 officers, 12 non-commissioned officers and 13 auxiliaries, divided into 26 offices. Transformed into the *Forschungsstelle für Ostunterkünfte* (Habitat Research Centre in the East), a code name used to hide its SS membership, the *Mannschaftshaus* never developed in the way the RuSHA had hoped: at the height of its activity, it employed, all in all, just under fifteen staff, including officers, non-commissioned officers and reservists. Its organizational chart at the end of 1942 shows that most of the scientific departments were dormant and that the real mission of the *Forschungsstelle* was to plan Germanization operations: the only departments functioning, out of a planned fourteen, were the general departments, department 1 (planning and statistical research), department 2 (architecture and works) and department 3 (legal affairs), while departments 4 to 14, which covered the entire academic spectrum, from *Ostforschung* to biology through medicine and literature, were not staffed. In 1942, two of its departments were located in Zamość, one in charge of town planning, the other of drainage works and foundations and subterranean buildings.[32] The *Forschungsstelle*, however, had a purely speculative activity, and relied, for all the measures it conceived, on a whole set of institutions under orders from the SSPF. In October 1941, an order from Globocnik revealed the density of the SS institutions, which to a large extent contributed to the Germanization plans of the planning authority set up by the SSPF:[33] there were no fewer than fifteen separate SS institutions, not to mention the already established SS 'Points of settlement and support' and labour camps such as Stary Dzików, though the garrisons of this were provided by the Dirlewanger battalion named in the list.[34]

Immediately associated with the local institutions responsible for the design and planning of the Germanization policies chosen by Globocnik, the local offices of economic administration and manpower constituted the second most important characteristic of the SS microcosm in Lublin and Zamość. Formed after Himmler's visit on 20 July 1941, the delegation for the building of 'Points of settlement and support' for the police and SS initially had a nebulous structure. Historians have been able to reconstruct its main lines by counting six departments, of which (with the exception of the first two, which traditionally administered administrative and personnel matters) one was devoted to the planning and management of building sites, another to the economy, and the last two to the transportation fleet and the acquisition of materials.[35] The existence of three branches outside the General Government, in Riga, Kiev and Mahiliow, reveals what was once again one of the main features of the Lublin SS microcosm: it took over the planning and building of the support points well beyond the district, and assumed, at least fleetingly, a fraction of the European ambition of the Nazi Utopia in the process of being realized.

It should be noted that this delegation of building was largely in the hands of the ORPO, the uniformed police, which, while practically absent in other areas of the conception of Germanization policies, provided the bulk of the police battalions which took over the expulsion and resettlement operations but also the shootings of Jewish populations undertaken in the summer of 1942. It must not be forgotten that the 101st battalion made famous by the magnificent study of Christopher Browning operated for the first time in Józefów, a conurbation of the district of Zamość, prior to the Germanization operations.[36] The ORPO was well represented in the spectrum of the repressive units with a police regiment, the 101st Battalion and a KdO (local command). These forces of repression also included an SS cavalry squadron in Cholm, on the outskirts of the Zamość district, as well as the Trawniki police auxiliary training camp, also located a few tens of kilometres from Zamość. At the interface between repression and camp surveillance, the Trawniki guards shared this characteristic with the Special Commando Dirlewanger, a famous commando composed of poachers from the concentration camps selected to form a unit for surveillance and control of partisans (thereby reduced to the rank of game). I will not be discussing this commando any further, since it left the region in January 1942 without having been engaged in Germanization.[37]

It is difficult to count the total number of SS personnel in the Lublin district, and more specifically in Zamość. The fact remains, however, that the density of SS institutions here was remarkable and shows the attention paid to this territory even before it was designated for Germanization.

This part of the non-native world, i.e. the Lublin district in 1939–40, became one of the hearts of the emerging empire in June 1941. The institutions which had been installed there were now the spearhead of the most successful experiment in the Germanization of a territory and populations. Until then, the district of Lublin and Zamojszczyzna had been nothing more than a Far East in which staff transfers were often authoritarian, and where the Nazi authorities had the greatest difficulty in attracting talents. Here, prisoners made up the staff of institutions, and the poachers of the Dirlewanger special unit had changed status from being concentration camp detainees to guards.[38] The district of Lublin, for example, was a country in which arbitrary rule prevailed, a country of inversion in which the population was abandoned to a strange mixture of people: outlaws and social outcasts promulgated and enforced rules which were only very rarely applied – local institutions had the greatest difficulty in applying the regulatory fever of the lawyers of Governor General Hans Frank, by exercising an arbitrariness that was itself set up as a rule in the name of racial determinism.

We cannot speak of anomie in this case but of the subversion and perversion – in the psychoanalytic sense of the term[39] – of the legal order: laws and rules were systematically emptied of their content and their symbolic importance and subordinated to the omnipotent will of the German actors who twisted them as they pleased and used them against the local populations. Is this what the German-Polish historian Bogdan Musial wishes to emphasize by evoking – without really analysing it – the sense of being drunk on power that the district chiefs must have experienced? Disturbingly, another specialist in that region, Klaus-Michael Mallmann, observed the same experience of being drunk on power in the neighbouring regions of Galicia in 1941–2, even though other categories of personnel were involved.[40] The two regions had two massive social phenomena in common. The Nazis drew from the same memories of the Austro-Hungarian Empire – was it really a coincidence that Globocnik, a former *Gauleiter* from Vienna, brought with him a hard core of Austrian Nazis,[41] or if the members of the commando of Felix Landau sent to Galicia by the BdS Kraków also came mainly from Vienna?[42] They also shared the same deeply rooted Viennese anti-Semitism, nourished by the mental caricatures of Galician *Ostjuden* from the shtetls – an anti-Semitism that generated a peculiarly intense hatred.[43] On the other hand, the Jewish communities of these two regions were the object, as I have shown elsewhere, of a process of symbolic domestication pushed to its paroxysm. Confined to urban ghettoes, marked by the Star of David, and put to work in one of the earliest policies of forced mobilization, the Jewish communities of the Lublin district, Zamojszczyzna and Galicia thus shared the debatable privilege of being reduced to the state of human cattle by the Nazis, as few ethnic groups were outside the concentration camps.[44] Nowhere else, no doubt, was the Nazi effort of social and racial domination extended over such a long time and with such clear success. This is, no doubt, part of what made it the land of all Nazi radicalisms.

The land of all Nazi radicalisms

To complete this survey of Zamojszczyzna, we need to describe the hurricanes of violence that swept over it.

In Lublin, and in Zamojszczyzna, radicalism was embodied above all in Odilo Globocnik, the SSPF appointed by Himmler on 9 November 1939. It is very rare that a historian dares to argue that, without the action of a single man, nothing would have happened, but in Zamość, and in the district of Lublin, this statement indeed deserves to be seriously considered. Odilo Globocnik was in Lublin from November 1939 to 1 September 1943, and the last of the German initiatives known as Action Zamość dated from the fortnight before his departure. Before him, nothing had begun; after him, nothing was started. This shows how much he personally influenced the destiny of Zamojszczyna and its inhabitants.

Odilo Lothar Ludwig Globocnik was born in Trieste on 21 April 1904, to a middle-class family of German and Croatian descent.[45] He was sent to a cadet school in Lower Austria in 1915, but the collapse of the Danube monarchy put an end to his prospects and he joined his family in Klagenfurt, where he trained professionally and joined the municipal power station before becoming a foreman on various public works projects.

He soon joined self-defence militias defending the Klagenfurt basin, although his involvement was probably minimal in view of his age, and it was apparently only on his return to the city that his militant career took off, marked by an extremely intense activism. He was chief of the cell and a local propaganda officer from 1930 to 1933, when Chancellor Dollfuss banned the Nazi Party. It was at this moment that Globocnik used his experience and his family's social capital to organize a clandestine network gathering and distributing information and funds between Klagenfurt, Trieste and Munich, capital of the NSDAP. This was discovered by the Austrian police, who arrested him and several members of his family in December 1934.[46] Between September 1933 and October 1935, Globocnik was arrested twice, spending practically half of his time in prison but managing to extend the meshes of his network. This activism brought him to the attention of the highest members in the Nazi hierarchy, and he joined the ranks of the most important Austrian dignitaries, a little below Seyss-Inquart or Kaltenbrunner, the two dominant figures, but receiving orders from Hitler himself. After various vicissitudes that showed how Globocnik was a controversial person, difficult to find the right niche for, the new Austrian bosses decided to appoint him *Gauleiter* of Vienna in July 1938. As early as September, however, Franz Xaver Schwartz, the perpetual treasurer of the NSDAP, sounded the alarm on the 'uncontrolled financial policies' of the new *Gauleiter* and, threatening to cut off supplies to all Party bodies, demanded an explanation of the expenses incurred. Globocnik resigned on 30 January 1939. His rise had been meteoric, his fall was no less so.

So it was a disgraced man whom Himmler appointed ten months later to be SSPF of the district of Lublin. A disgraced man, yes, but a militant who had distinguished himself by his obstinacy, his activism, his total absence of inhibitions, and his unconditional loyalty to the Nazi cause.

Globocnik arrived in Lublin on 1 November and a fortnight later ordered the establishment of a self-defence militia composed of *Volksdeutsche*, in accordance with the circulars issued in October by Himmler and the efforts already put in place by his superior, the HSSPF Friedrich-Wilhelm Krüger. This militia served him as an instrument for meddling in anti-Jewish policies hitherto implemented by the civil administration, an instrument which he used in a particularly systematic and obstinate way. For the great feature of Globocnik, the one that made him so controversial, was his propensity to encroach on the areas of competence of neighbouring administrations, especially civil administrations. The conflict between the SS and the civil administrations is one of the leitmotifs in the administrative history of the General Government, but nowhere was it as acute and intense as in the Lublin district: and this was all down to Globocnik. It is difficult to disentangle the reasons for the absence of inhibition in the Lublin SSPF: the memories of actors are forever interwoven with their own practices, and memories of Globocnik, an imperial and Danubian personage, played a probably fundamental role in the radical nature of this institution. So, to a large extent, did the memories of the *Volksdeutsche* of Lublin, and their experiences of the exactions carried out against the German minority during the Great War. Is it indeed a coincidence that a study showed that 51 people out of a sample of 281 members of the Lublin *Selbstschutz* were born to deportees in Siberia or lost a relative there (18 per cent of the total)?[47]

Whatever the case, throughout 1940, Globocnik used this militia of self-defence as a Trojan horse which allowed him to interfere in the policies of forced labour for Jews and Poles and the confiscation of Jewish property. He also ordered the building under his personal supervision of the Bełżec labour camp south of Zamość, which acted as a prison camp first for Gypsies from Hamburg and Bremen and then for Jews from the district. The militia was also the first unit to carry out retaliatory massacres under Globocnik's leadership, until the *volksdeutsch* self-protection system was dissolved under pressure from the General Government and 'replaced' by a special department of *Volksdeutsche* and, especially, by Ukrainian militias. The continuity between the two apparatuses was evident to Globocnik: on the one hand, it was a question of instrumentalizing interethnic tensions in order to perfect Nazi domination by arming the *Volksdeutsche* first, and the Ukrainians – winners, as we shall see, in the great Nazi policy of divide and rule in Lublin and Zamość – second, as well as entrusting them with the exercise of violence against the Jewish and Polish populations. The 'Trawnikis', the indispensable aids to the policies of extermination and Germanization, were indeed one of the privileged instruments of the practices deployed by Globocnik in Lublin.[48]

Zamość was therefore the site of all the violently radical movements infused by the 'strange and disturbing' activism of SSPF Globocnik.[49] But this vision would be incomplete if we did not add the other side of the coin: Globocnik was indeed the embodiment of Nazi violence at its worst, but he also had the reputation of being 'so rational, so organic' in his resettlement projects in Zamość.[50] Beyond the apparent incongruity of such a judgement, it illustrates the fact that Globocnik had secured a second level of legitimacy among his men, gained from his obstinacy in building. If Germanization projects never went as far as they did in Zamojszczyzna, this was also because Odilo Globocnik carried out the Nazi project in just as voluntarist a way as his exterminating practice, and that he allocated resources, energy and means to it as no other regional manager did. Finally, he assigned men who, like Franz Stanglica, imparted a very specific character to this project, infusing it with a particular utopian tonality.

Born in 1907, Franz Stanglica was a historian who pursued his studies in Vienna and completed them in 1931 before beginning work on German colonial migrations and settlements in the southern and eastern confines of the Austrian Empire in the eighteenth century. He was obviously already a Nazi sympathizer, which caused him some difficulties when he sought a fixed post, although he took care to donate to Austrian Nazi structures under a false identity. He then carried out his work in coordination with the DAI (Institute of Germans Abroad, based in Stuttgart), which gave him money to document the Austrian Curial Archives and then to help draw up maps inventorying the localities of German settlements in Bačka and Banat, as well as the evolution of the ethno-national balances in these regions. The Anschluss led him to emerge from his clandestine militancy. He joined the SS and was a guard in the concentration camps in Oranienburg and Auschwitz. At the beginning of 1941, he was recruited by Globocnik and Gustav Hanelt to become head of the conception of Germanization policies in the *Mannschaftshaus* in Lublin. He was at the interface of the networks of the 'combatant ethnosciences' that we have already met and the Viennese militant networks at the centre of which Globocnik moved, which explains his recruitment.[51] Stanglica combined, as perhaps no other ethnocrat had, scientific capabilities, Nazi commitment and an experience of violence. This was something he probably gained first during his short stay as a guard in the camps, and again during his stay in Lublin, as he described in a letter: 'I work in ethno-politics, often holding a weapon.'[52] Beyond this pose, doubtless a little exaggerated, his work remains essentially a work of conception, coordination and scientific foundation.

It is he who gave a systematic character to the Germanization of Zamość. In particular, he drafted a long memorandum of about thirty pages for Globocnik dealing with the principles of spatial planning for Zamojszczyzna.[53] And in his private correspondence, he described its action in these terms:

> My activities include: shifting Jew and Poles from one place to another; the recuperation of Polonized persons with German blood, who have remained racially pure; the establishment of a *volksdeutsch* library in Lublin, the management of the *Volksdeutsche* in the district, the search for a German blood scattered across the Polish villages and its return to German nationhood. These are gratifying but trying missions in this atrocious and disgusting Poland [*scheußliche Polen*].[54]

More concretely, the documentation at our disposal shows him dealing pell-mell with spatial planning, population censuses, agronomic definitions and architecture. Stanglica was the Jack of all trades, it was he who gave the project its *total* dimensions, i.e. the combination of socio-racial engineering and a project uniting ideology and aesthetics, bringing together cultural policy, the style of buildings and the appearance of the countryside. The approximately three thousand pages in the six main files in the Lublin SSPF archives detailing Action Zamość demonstrate the omnipresence of Odilo Globocnik (as leader) and of Franz Stanglica, a sort of discreet demiurge of this form of specific *Volksgemeinschaft* that was to become the pioneer society of Zamojszczyzna.[55] It was the combination of the two forms of radicality (the violent and the utopian) incarnated by the two men – radicalities which they represented but were far from exhausting in their own persons – which explains the specificity of the Zamość project that we will need to study in depth in order to complete our investigation.

But before that, let us sketch out the course of the project and its chronological stages. The development of the plan needs to be narrated in four phases.

During the first of these, between November 1939 when the institutions stabilized and Globocnik was named SSPF, and the summer of 1940, the Lublin district and Zamojszczyzna were considered to be dumping grounds in which the administrations of incorporated territories could discharge undesirable Polish and Jewish populations. There was no question of Germanization, even though the district under Globocnik had undergone a certain number of developments turning it into a kind of laboratory for Nazi occupation policies, in particular those which aimed at the enslavement of Jewish populations, confined, marked and put to work in large programmes of forced labour building fortifications on the River Bug. However, these were policies that had no direct bearing on the question of the advent of Utopia.

In the summer of 1940 a second phase began: with the emergence of an insular scenario for the Jewish question, a transformation occurred that progressively led the local and then central Nazi leaders to consider this territory as ripe for incorporation into German nationhood. An alternative solution to what was seen as the problematic concentration of Jews in the General Government was formulated in the Madagascar project, and then its rapid replacement, the 'Polar Circle' project, born of the potential invasion of the Soviet Union. This invasion, moreover, upset the mental spatial representations of the Nazi dignitaries: Zamojszczyzna was no longer a Far East, but was now likely, in the case of victory, to become one of the hearts of the Thousand-Year Reich. Of course, the former image of the district of Lublin as an ethnic dump left its traces. This was evidenced by the 'migration' of the *Volksdeutsche* from Cholm to the incorporated territories of the Reich beginning in September 1940. But it went against the current: even though Globocnik had presented a first project of 'armed villages' (*Wehrdörfer*) a month earlier to Himmler, and mentioned the need for Germanic forces, they were actually removed from this sector![56] This first project showed that the representation of Zamojszczyzna was gradually changing. At the same time, in the autumn of 1940, Globocnik launched the 'Search for German Blood' action, a vast operation for the search for and coopting of the descendants of families of German settlers who had emigrated to the region in the eighteenth century; they had been culturally Polonized, and were to be re-Germanized.[57] Characterized by local initiatives that were not really noticed or approved by the central SS hierarchies, this period ended in the summer of 1941. The invasion of the USSR radically changed the apprehension of the central authorities and thus the missions they assigned to the civil administration and even more to the SS agencies installed in the district.

The third phase in the development of the Lublin and Zamojszczyzna districts thus began with a sudden shift which occurred during Himmler's visit to the city and the district on 20 July 1941, at the moment of the euphoria engendered by the invasion of the USSR.[58] Himmler approved, systematized and generalized the initiatives taken by Globocnik. He strengthened them by radicalizing them, broadening their territories of exercise and assigning them immensely more ambitious objectives than hitherto. The time was now coming for the accomplishment of Utopia, in Zamojszczyzna, in the district and then in the General Government. In the autumn of 1941, with the slowing down of the progress of the Wehrmacht, a second development began, equally characteristic of the period: in a series of sudden moves, the extermination of all the Jews of the General Government was decided, entrusted to Globocnik in a programme involving the arrival there of the specialists of Operation T4, the organization of a network of killing plants operating with carbon monoxide gas chambers, and the murder of the Jews of the district of Lublin.[59] Globocnik conceived of their extermination as a preliminary to the operational phase of the plan for the Germanization of Zamojszczyzna that was being laid at the same time.

The fourth and final phase of the sequence began on 1 November 1942. While the extermination of the Jews of Zamość and the region had been tragically completed, mainly in Bełżec and Sobibór, the SS administrations launched the operational phase of Action Zamość that day. Three weeks later, on 27 November, a vast expulsion of Poles and settling of *Volksdeutsche* took place, lasting ten months, with a pause in May 1943. We have to conclude that the German colonization action came to an end on 1 September 1943: Globocnik and a large part of his team were transferred to the Adriatic coast, and the German initiatives ended. This, as we shall see, did not mean that the region was now stable or pacified.

That, then, is a summary account of the fate of Zamojszczyzna, a region whose situation, structures and evolution we have described at some length. In order to complete this inquiry, we still need to try and give an account of what became of the Nazi promise of the East and its accomplishment. Conceived as the laboratory for the Nazi Utopia, Zamojszczyzna was subjected to policies which we must now study.

Chapter 8

The politics of the laboratory

It is not easy to attempt to describe or explain the Germanization policies that were pursued by the SS in Zamojszczyzna. The studies are numerous, the documentation rich and diverse, but it is precisely this abundance that makes the exercise difficult. We must do justice to the different stories, to the variety of documentation, to the specificity of the region; we need to remain attentive to changes in the chronology, while respecting our objective: to describe these policies of Utopia-building and to study their lineaments. Finally, it is sometimes difficult to disentangle, among these practices, what stemmed from predatory, brutal and murderous occupation policies, and what was solely meant to prepare the Nazi future.

More deeply, however, we must decide whether Zamojszczyzna was truly a 'special laboratory of the SS'. What status did it gain from the Germanization policies that were applied to it? It is also this question that we must answer, as we reach the end of our survey of the Nazi practices of Germanization.

From the arrival of Globocnik in Lublin in November 1939 to April 1940, Zamojszczyzna does not seem to have been the target for any special projects. In this period, the horizon of the Germanizers was dominated by the *Fernplan* and the *Nahpläne*, which dealt only with incorporated territories and thus indirectly made the General Government a mere dumping ground for expelled populations. And even in March 1940, the project of transforming the Lublin district into a 'Jewish reserve' automatically made Zamojszczyzna a 'racial dump', but it did not remain so over time, since the Madagascar project in the summer disrupted plans for expulsion. It was precisely at that moment that Globocnik seemed to present Himmler for the first time with a settlement plan based on armed villages, populated exclusively by SS veterans.[1] Himmler refused it in its entirety, but this plan is the first trace of the perception of Zamojszczyzna as a specific territory, the object of policies that were then to be extended to the whole empire. From the summer of 1940, Zamojszczyzna gradually became the laboratory for Germanization policies. During this period from the summer of 1940 to that of 1944, policies for the building of new communities took three distinct forms: in the eyes of the Nazis, it was first necessary to shape the peoples involved and then to do the same with the territory; after this, communities could be founded.

Classifying, expelling, deporting: the social engineering at the basis of Utopia

From November 1939 to September 1940, Zamojszczyzna was a dumping ground. It received the Poles and Jews from Wartheland, West Prussia and Silesia, expelled as part of the Germanization of the incorporated territories. In the autumn of 1940, however, the conjunction of two events contributed to the gradual modification of this state of affairs: on the one hand, the 'migration' of the *Volksdeutsche* of the Cholm region, northeast of Zamojszczyzna; and on the other hand, the practitioners of the Germanization of Lublin 'discovered', in two different ways, the existence of German communities that had emigrated to the region in the eighteenth century.[2] It was this twofold fact that signalled the arrival in the region of the material and ideological devices of Nazi social engineering. In October, discussions between Himmler and Globocnik resulted in the creation of the *SS-Mannschaftshaus*, and the arrangements were thus completed by an institution responsible for theoretical work and the detailed planning of projects concerning the region.[3] Beginning in January 1941, the first measures of social engineering were put in place to reshape the ethnic makeup of the region, favouring groups identified as Nordic in character. And on 5 April of that same year, Globocnik announced at a Party ceremony his intention to transform the entire district of Lublin into a racially pure northern settlement area.[4] From then on, several types of population filtering procedures were set up in Zamojszczyzna, and were the focus of most of the policies of Germanization.

One first procedure thus stemmed from the discovery of the existence of these *volksdeutsche* settlers in the Viennese archives of the Hofkammer. It is very likely that Franz Stanglica, the archivist from this institution who was transferred in January 1941 to the *Mannschaftshaus* in Lublin, was the author of this discovery. Globocnik was immediately alerted and took this as a pretext to plan an operation entitled 'In Search of German Blood' (*Fahndung nach deutschem Blut*) that Édouard Conte and Cornelia Essner compare to a kind of racial vampirism.

It was Wilhelm Gradmann, a historical member of the DAI incorporated since 1939 into the EWZ, who in a report of 19 March 1942 retrospectively described the procedure used in Zamość to 're-Germanize' the populations. But these procedures were in fact only the result of the discovery of this German blood concealed by centuries of 'Polonization'. It was still necessary to go in search of this blood, to track down every drop of it. To this end, the ethno-social filtering procedures developed by the EWZ in the incorporated territories constituted an essential example and precedent, imported into the General Government from March 1941.[5]

At that time, practitioners from Flying Commission G, succeeded by the Herold Commission (named after its leader), put in place an ambitious, indeed exhaustive selection procedure for the *Volksdeutsche* of the Lublin district. These flying commissions consisted of about eighty people and had an assessment capacity of about 140 people per day. In the occupied territories they travelled from one migrant camp to another, but in the General Government they travelled on a special train that went from one village to another and the *Volksdeutsche* they encountered were 'evaluated' or filtered. The potential colonial candidates, deloused, washed and freshly clothed, had to make their way through a kind of path leading through 'turnstiles' on the train wagons and were subject to at least four types of criteria.

Individuals grouped by family first had to establish their identity in a registration office (*Meldestelle*), attached to a photographic workshop. Once this was established, it was necessary to pass purely physical raciological examinations, with evaluation of the phenotype by different measurements of the body, the skull and the face. In addition, a clinical examination and an interview on their personal history were carried out to establish nationality, linguistic level, genealogy, and elements of hereditary biology, making it possible for Nazi doctors and raciologists from the EWZ and the RuSHA to specify the racial and health profile of the individuals and families assessed. This was followed by an 'ethno-political evaluation', in which the experts from EWZ and VOMI had to make a judgement on the social makeup, ethnic consciousness and political attitude of the migrants, alone and as part of their families. The question of religious belonging and practice constituted a key criterion in this rather impressionistic appraisal.

A first procedure was thus put in place from March 1941, but it seems that it did not meet with the hoped-for success: the EWZ was obliged to launch a second operation, as soon as the first one was completed, from May 1942. It would have been surprising if this had not been the case: first, the *Volksdeutsche* had been subjected to repatriation operations in 1939 and 1940, for example in the Cholm area, and second, many of them from the territories of Galicia, Volhynia and Podolia occupied by the USSR in September 1939 had been subjected to trade-offs before June 1941. Many of the *Volksdeutsche* had already been repatriated to the territories incorporated into the Reich even before the Germanization of Zamojszczyzna had been dreamt of. In total, apart from the descendants of the 151 families and 782 individuals identified in the Hofkammer archives, some 4,000 *Volksdeutsche* from the Lublin district and 9,000 from different European countries were found by the EWZ to be suitable for resettlement in the district of Zamość.[6]

The Germanization of Zamojszczyzna, however, involved a second selection procedure, carried out by the UWZ in the expellee camps where those who had not managed to escape the expulsion operations of the SS ended up. These operations did not happen concurrently with the EWZ's census operations. Indeed, a first test phase of the expulsion of undesirable populations was launched by Globocnik's department in November 1941. From 6 to 25 November, no fewer than 2,098 people were expelled from six villages in the environs of Zamość. Interned in barracks in the conurbation, they were then directed to the township of Hrubieszów.[7] This first expulsion was regarded as a success, opening the way to the systematization of this policy throughout Zamojszczyzna a year later, starting on 27 November 1942, and marking the beginning of the general offensive against the Polish populations of the region. In total, until August 1943, when the expulsions were finally halted, no fewer than 100,000 Poles were displaced for the benefit of the *volksdeutsche* settlers.[8]

As regards this filtering procedure, we have fewer documents that describe it. At best, it is known that this was an operation meant to establish identity, a matter of racial and socio-ethnic assessment in which individuals were assessed without great regard for the integrity of the family. This fundamental lack of consideration, which went so far as to separate parents from their children, or even to kidnapping the children with a view to their adoption, is chilling but hardly surprising.[9]

Moreover, as well as these first two procedures we should mention other operations which involved a number impossible to determine of Ukrainian families whose expulsion was carried out in a manner quite different from that of the 100,000 Poles mentioned here in that it was subordinated to non-filtering resettlement practices, such as the radically different procedure to which the approximately 50,000 Jews were subjected prior to their confinement, racial marking and forced labour, and then extermination in the Bełżec camp.

A total of more than 170,000 people, approximately one-third of the population of Zamojszczyzna, had to go through the narrow straits of Nazi social engineering and were subjected to policies of fashioning, identification, ethnic, racial and cultural evaluation, classification and hierarchical procedures that led to contrasting destinies, most of which were appallingly cruel.

These operations categorized individuals and families according to categorizations on which we must linger a bit, in order to understand their essence, nature and logic, but also because they determined the fate of individuals and families. The Act of 4 March 1941, which extended to all incorporated territories the arrangements for the Germanization of the populations of Warthegau and West Prussia, provided for the assessment of the population, its inclusion in a German Ethnic List (*Deutsche Volksliste*, henceforth DVL) and its distribution into four classes.[10] On 12 September 1940, a directive from Himmler and the RKFdV had defined the four classes into which the Poles of the incorporated territories were to be divided.

In Group 1 were to be incorporated the ethnic Germans who had distinguished themselves by their belonging to German nationhood (the so-called 'confession', *Bekenntnis*) and who had been extracted (*ausgesiedelt*) from the Soviet Union, the Baltic and Southern Europe – in other words, the pan-Germanist activists of the *volksdeutsche* minorities. In Group 2, the German-speaking Polish citizens who had not committed themselves would be included. In Group 3, Polish citizens of German origin and assimilable – but not German-speaking – were to be incorporated, while Group 4 was to be made up of all those who, although of German origin, could not be immediately integrated, since they were seen as 'renegades' for having demonstrated political opposition to the NSDAP or loyalty to the Republic of Poland.[11] Again, this classification was a sort of synthesis: on the practical level, there were a multitude of criteria which, taken up and developed during filtering, were no longer mentioned and only appeared as guidelines in this scale of assessments. Thus the raciologist experts of the RuSHA had their own scale, composed of craniological and physical measurements, which constituted a racial assessment whose ambitions (in terms of comprehensiveness and objectivity) were beyond doubt in the eyes of the ethnocrats.[12] This was a kind of citizenship whose conditions were racial, ethnic and cultural, but whose 'fine classification' – the term used by practitioners of Germanization[13] – also emerged from considerations identified as 'moral' by the practitioners of the EWZ or RKFdV, that is, loyalty to the regime.

Moreover, with this first classification there came a number of rights and duties which assigned to individuals a place in the *Volksgemeinschaft* under construction. If Groups 1 and 2 had undeniable rights to full and complete participation in the community, including being able to immediately participate in militant life, enter the NSDAP and all organizations whose requirements the candidates would satisfy, Group 3 provided less of a way into the *Volksgemeinschaft*, expressed by the prohibition on leadership positions, civil servant status, entry into the Party, and submission to compulsory military service, though this status did mean they were eligible for certain tax exemptions, benefits in kind, and non-confiscation of property under Germanization. Group 4, on the other hand, lost the right to any leave, and the children of couples from this group were destined for a rudimentary education, without any possibility of secondary education.[14]

Clearly, destinies were decided by whether individuals or family groups were classified in Category 1, 2, 3 or 4 of the DVL – and even this ranking only concerned those who, at the end of the filtering process, had been considered to be Germanizable.

It was quite different for the Poles who, forced out of their villages and expelled to make room for the *Volksdeutsche*, fell into the hands of the UWZ evictors and the armed formations supporting them, then ended up in the regroupment camps in Zamość, where the RuSHA experts awaited them. These experts then evaluated them on another scale of value.

If the raciological scale used by the RuSHA experts who were part both of the EWZ flying commissions and of the evaluation commissions present at the Zamość regroupment camp was identical in terms of racial criteria – for this was where racial determinism was embodied in practice – the hierarchization into which it was inserted differed radically from the DVL used for the *Volksdeutsche*. Here, there appeared a new scale of four levels. Levels 1 and 2 of the grid developed by the UWZ practitioners (the only one used was actually Level 2: in the view of the RuSHA, there was no longer anybody belonging to Level 1 in the Zamość district) included individuals whose genealogy and phenotype made them individuals of Germanic ancestry, and thus likely to be integrated *eventually* into Level 4 of the DVL. Levels 3 and 4 of the UWZ grid were profiles unacceptable to raciologists. And it was at the end of this assessment that the fate of the individuals and families expelled was determined. Thus, with the exception of those in Level 2, who were seen to be capable of re-Germanization and who were meant, by the UWZ, to stay in migrant camps in Łódź for purposes of re-education, or even to be kept on Polish farms confiscated and reassembled (*Z-Höfe*) in the event of a shortage of *volksdeustch* migrants,[15] Levels 3 and 4 were of significant value only in terms of labour power in the eyes of the UWZ ethnocrats. Level 3 members were graded with a stamp on their identity papers. The stamp 'AA' (*Arbeitseinsatz Altreich*, Labour Service in the former Reich) destined them for work in Germany; a second and a third stamp, 'RD' and 'Ki' (*Rentendörfer* = retirement villages, *Kinder* = children), designated elderly people and children under 14 years old who would be left to die in abandoned villages; the 'AG' stamp (*Arbeitseinsatz im Generalgouvernement*) designated them for labour service in the General Government.[16] That left the individuals in Level 4, who were destined for the Auschwitz labour camp as long as their age was between 14 and 60 years.[17]

In total, in May 1943, when the resettlement and deportation operations were stopped, probably more than 100,000 people had been expelled from their homes. The vast majority of them seem to have managed to flee the power of the UWZ and the practitioners of ethnic cleansing. According to Hermann Krumey, the head of the UWZ in Zamość, a total of 47,902 people went through the filtering process at Zamość camp between November 1942 and December 1943. Of this 47,902 people, 697 were declared Germanizable, nearly 35,000 were destined for forced labour, almost 10,000 evacuated, presumably to the 'retirement villages' which served as places where children and the elderly would die – without this being specified in the report for 1943 – and 1,594 were sent to the Auschwitz labour camp. In addition, 814 persons had died or escaped from the camp.[18]

The great Germanizing selection process thus functioned in Zamość as an immense predatory machine, controlling people's existences after subjecting them to the yardstick of racial determinism. It formed a hierarchy whose foundation was obviously racial, but whose fine contours also traced out a political and racial order. Indeed, if we attempt to merge the DVL with the UWZ classifications, a large proportion of the destinies imagined by the practitioners of the RKFdV is represented. At the top of the hierarchy, with full access to the *Volksgemeinschaft* in the process of building and purification, Category 1 of the DVL demarcated the racially conscious elite of the *Volksgemeinschaft*, an elite which had demonstrated its excellence and purity, and had a monopoly on militant activity; only a minority, also rigorously selected, would have access to the SS. This was a racial, social, but also political and militant elite. Differentiated from this Category 1 by the absence of a militant past, Category 2 had the same civil rights as the first, without access to the higher militant bodies or civil service.

Category 3 was composed of people of excellent racial ancestry, but not German-speaking. This was the precious northern blood that needed to be tapped and brought back to German nationhood; this the category that legitimized Nazi ethno-cultural vampirism. It was guaranteed civil rights and social benefits which were those of the *Volksgemeinschaft*. However, it was debarred from all management and decision-making functions, from militant activities and any rapid prospects of social upgrading by the school system. Category 4, that of political renegades, was subject to the chicaneries of a repressive apparatus sensitive to the question of loyalty. It was in these Categories 3 or 4 that the 697 individuals declared Germanizable who had been extracted by UWZ filtering could hope to be classified. The best they could hope for was a revamped farm in the district or, more often, a transit camp in the Łódź region, and cultural Germanization by RKFdV, the VOMI and the students of the NSDStB and the *Frauenschaft*, who inculcated hygiene and the fairy tales of the brothers Grimm in children constantly faced with the threat, at the slightest breach of Nazi order, that like hundreds of orphans they would be taken from their families and handed over to fully German families. In Zamojszczyzna, this was the situation of 4,500 children, mainly orphans, but also children of persons who refused to be included in Category 4 of the DVL.[19]

Although this hierarchy immediately consigned those at the bottom of the heap to a future that was, to say the least, difficult, the four groups were still part of the *Volksgemeinschaft*, an ethnic community with rights and duties as well as civil guarantees which differentiated it very definitely from the following categories, which were fully subject to the socio-racial domination of the SS. In the UWZ classifications, from Level 3 onwards, individuals and families had no rights and were subject to fundamental arbitrariness. Their sole raison d'être, in the eyes of the Nazis, was their labour power. Level 3, composed of Polish 'mestizos' with no Nordic ancestors, was offered only the status of helots, deported to the great factories working for the total war effort of the Reich, or to the agricultural estates (the men and a considerable proportion of the women), while the youngest women experienced domestic servitude in the service of Germans of the Reich of a privileged racial and social or

militant status. Again, these were adults of sufficiently satisfactory health
to be deported to the Reich. The others, old people and children under
the age of fourteen, were destined to die in retirement villages or transit
camps. In this respect, two considerations emerge: on the one hand, the
great difference between this group and the previous ones was marked
by the fundamental attack which the Nazis carried out on the *family ties* of
these 'non-natives'. As much as RuSHA raciologists and ethnic cleansers
were attentive to the northern *Sippen*, they denied all existence to non-
native families, disrupted by the deportation of adults in the Reich, while
the children and the aged were destined to die in the abandoned villages,
the *Rentendörfer*. A second reflection: the fate reserved for these elderly
people and children basically involved sending them to an indirect death
by malnourishment and short-term or long-term illness. In this, the practice conformed to the implicit paradigms of the latest RSHA and RKFdV
plans. Hermann Krumey, the signatory of the activity reports for the
UWZ selection process in Zamość, attended in person the presentation by
Justus Beyer and Hans Ehlich in Bernau on 1–2 February 1943. As we have
said, he took the notes which are the only trace left to historians of the key
numerical figures of those who could not be assimilated and were thus
doomed to die – more than 17 million Slavs in the Germanization operations.[20] And among these, old people and children expelled from their
farms, torn from their adult kinsfolk, and left to starve in what amounted
to prisons without barbed wire. In the case of persons classified in Level 4,
in which the raciologists detected 'hereditary defects' or a minority Jewish
ancestry and who were destined for a 'natural death' in Auschwitz or
Majdanek,[21] the elderly and the children of Level 3 constituted the proof
of the deadly coherence of the Nazi project, of which Krumey was both
the spokesman and the operator, only a few weeks apart.

There remained, however, a category of persons that had not been
mentioned, and were no longer mentioned, in the letters of the Zamość
UWZ; one last category that lay outside classification: the Jews. But there
was a good reason for this in the eyes of the ethnocrats: the last convoy
to Bełżec of Jews from Zamojszczyzna had left Szczebrzeszyn for direct
and immediate extermination on 22 October 1942, and the last one in the
direction of Sobibór had departed from Hrubieszów on 28 October, one
day less than a month before the Germanization action.[22] As far as they
were concerned, filtering had been carried out well upstream, and the
selection led to a direct and inevitable death. This was the fundamental
and tragic specificity of their racial categorization, at least from December
1941.

Building: the Nazi attempt to shape the territory

It is undoubtedly when it comes to contruction, equipment and building that the policies of Utopia are at least initially the most difficult to

distinguish from a fierce policy of predation of the labour force as pursued by the Nazi occupation and its institutions throughout the conflict. In this respect the General Government and the Lublin district were indeed laboratories, but at least until July 1941 it is very difficult to say whether they were utopian laboratories or laboratories of economic mobilization.

From November 1939 to the end of the occupation, the Germans transformed the district of Lublin and, more generally, the southeast of the General Government into a huge open-pit site. The day after the founding of the Governorate, forced labour was imposed for the Jewish population. Again, Odilo Globocnik's 'strange and disturbing activism' played a fundamental role. On the basis of the self-defence militia he had founded upon his arrival in Lublin, the SSPF set up, in the first half of 1940, camps stretching along the demarcation line between the General Government and the Soviet zone. Their objective was to build, along the River Bug, a set of fortifications designed to prevent a possible invasion. Globocnik's idea was based on two models: on the one hand, the Wehrmacht had demanded the building of an 'Eastern Wall', and on the other, the paradigm that had dominated the 'solution of the Jewish question' was that of a 'reserve for Jews' in 'his' own district.[23]

The invasion of the USSR fundamentally changed the situation: first, Zamojszczyzna was no longer at the end of the world and the frontier space of the Nazi Empire but now lay at its heart; second, the question of manpower took on a whole new dimension with the enormous encirclement battles of the Wehrmacht; finally, symbolically, what was gained there was not one of those wars of revenge that the Reich had been leading since September 1939, but rather the Great Racial War from which the *Tausendjähriges Reich* was to emerge. It was in this context and with this state of mind that the encounter between Himmler, Pohl and Globocnik took place in Lublin on 20 July 1941. It is useful to quote here the note summarizing the main results of this meeting.

The *Reichsführer*, on the occasion of his visit [*Besichtigung*, in the sense of a museum visit] of 30 July 1941, ordered the following:

(1) The RFSS delegate constructs a KL [concentration camp] of 25–30,000 prisoners for employment in SS and police workshops and work sites. From the KL, additional camps are built on each locality. Should the camp be built by the KL inspector?

(2) *Deutsche Ausrüstungswerke* [SS equipment company]. The pre-existing camp must be preserved as a car repair shop and as a carpentry shop. A new labour camp, equipped with necessary workshops in clothing and iron-work, with tanners, cobblers and wheelwrights, must be reinstalled further east of Lublin.

(3) The garment factory of the *Waffen-SS* in Lublin must cover its needs from the activities of the Lublin workshops. The Berlin textile factory is opening an office in Lublin to handle the demands.

(4) The new local buildings for the SS and police shall be constructed, in accordance with the proposed plans, on the grounds of the former Lublin airfield. The former German city must be taken into account and incorporated into the general plan of building of the SS and police district. Implementation [. . .] must begin immediately with the renovation of old buildings.

(5) The SSFHA shall make the necessary spare parts available to the central car repair shop and must therefore set up a spare parts plant in Lublin. [. . .]

(8) Original equipment manufacturers [including the SS equipment firm] must take over the training of masons, carpenters, etc. (skilled building workers) for employment in the East. It will also be necessary to open large sewing workshops with Jewish female [workers].

[. . .]

(10) The market place in Zamość must be retained but fundamentally re-equipped [*überholt* = updated], including with modern central heating installations. As the apartments are currently confiscated by the Eastern Trust Company [*Treuhandstelle Ost*], the RFSS will contact the mayor for the provision of apartments for the SS. In Zamość, it will also be necessary to create an SS House for the *Reichsführer* and his guests.

(11) The 'Search for German blood' action is extended to the whole of the General Government and a Germanic colonial settlement area is to be created in the region of Zamość. The layout of the farms, fields, etc., has to be decided rapidly to give it as quickly as possible a German 'feel' or brand as soon as possible. Hedge planting should be given special care.

(12) A school must be created immediately for the thirty children of Zamość and Hrubieszów.

(13) The RFSS delegate has until the autumn of this year to apply the measures already ordered for the erection of 'Points of support' for the police and the SS. Particular attention should be paid to the creation of family residences for the police and SS forces and their families. Particular emphasis should be placed on the arrangements for the social life of single persons.

[. . .]

Himmler[24]

Himmler's visit, as this notice showed, radically changed the outlook for all the protagonists of the policies carried out until then. The first was the overlap of labour and equipment policies with strategic considerations and local policies of occupation. Globocnik's labour initiatives, well received by the Wehrmacht but often viewed with disfavour by the local civil administrations, here led to the prospect of a real SS city in the city, with its own built structure but also its own reservoir of concentration labour, thanks to the planning of a gigantic concentration camp at Majdanek. It also saw the reorientation of these policies towards such aims as garrison settlement and the stabilization of the SS presence in view of the organization of a territory entirely dedicated to it. Lastly, connected to these first two transformations, a settlement project for the colonization of Zamojszczyzna emerged, the result of the systematization to the whole General Government of operations for the tapping of Germanic blood and the decision to combine this Germanization with a project to Germanize spaces, terroirs and urban appearance which involved immense efforts of building and equipment.

Five days before the visit, Himmler had received from the hands of Meyer-Heitling the second version of the *Generalplan Ost*, and no doubt realized that now Zamojszczyzna was in a specific position, both as a land to be Germanized immediately as it was destined to become one of the hearts of the *Tausendjähriges Reich*, and also as a gateway to the great East which was 'Germany's future'. As a sign of the times, the labour camps that Globocnik had set up, and that had exhausted in every sense of the term the labour force of thousands of Jews available by making them construct this Defensive Wall of the East, could now be replaced further south by this 'Transverse Route No. 4', which Lemberg's SSPF, Katzmann, was to start on in February 1942, partly on the orders of Globocnik.[25] This route constituted both a basic supply route for the troops from the East rushing towards Kiev and then the Caucasus, and one of the radials along which the SS dreamed of setting up their colonial forts. It was a road for invasion and a thoroughfare for settlement.[26]

Himmler's visit had not only given impetus to the equipping of the region, to the organization of the companies responsible for the equipment and the productions themselves: Himmler had also endorsed the initiative of social engineering by capturing Germanic blood that Globocnik and his team had been working on since January 1941. Even better: he had generalized it to the whole of the General Government, and had assigned to it a new horizon of expectation, namely the total Germanization, by colonization and restocking, of Zamojszczyzna. Zamość, a town with a fundamental architectural identity – it should be remembered that its centre was built by Baroque Venetian architects invited by Jan Sariusz Zamojski – became the residence town of the RFSS, who wanted to find a holiday resort for himself and his guests. Zamość was the paradigm city of the SS, the capital of a settlement, meant largely to appeal to the settlement of SS veterans; after Himmler's visit to Lublin, Zamość started to look like a laboratory/residence, the Germanization of which involved, as we have seen, the shaping of populations, but also that of the town, the villages and the other small rural areas.

This was the work of the team of the Research Centre for the East, established by Globocnik and headed by Gustav Hanelt, with Franz Stanglica as its backbone. Since November 1940, they had recruited architects and reflected on the forms that a German habitat should take on this Germanized soil.[27]

The work of the research centre lay at the interface between planning and implementation. Of course, considering that the implementation was limited to a period of six months between November 1942 and May 1943, as the latent insurrection prevented not only the continued displacements of population but any practical Germanization of these areas and their landscapes, any practical activity of settlement was reduced to an inadequate level, which speaks volumes about the failure of Action Zamość. Nevertheless, in March 1943, Stanglica made a proposal for the simplification and modification of districts and town quarters, the main lines of which were adopted in a directive issued by Frank.[28] He also worked from the *Autobahn* master plan for the General Government and the guidelines for the redevelopment of the villages of Zamojszczyzna.[29] Other documents show him thinking about village plans, studying and correcting in minute detail small rural areas and the plans of houses, taking a close interest in the exterior aspect of these, and in particular their façades.[30]

This was an operational plan to prepare for the reshaping of the countryside. However, by establishing lists of names, identifying the populations to be expelled and the lists of *Volksdeutsche* to be settled, lists that were probably transmitted to the EWZ and the UWZ respectively, the work of the Research Centre was resolutely aiming to contribute both to the prescription and to the implementation and the realization of Utopia.[31]

This is where the connection between planning and building was strongest. At the end of 1942 and at the beginning of 1943, *SS-Hauptsturmführer* Thomalla, close to Globocnik, combined the dual function of heading the building department responsible for work in the villages to be Germanized and designing the 'Points of settlement and support' in Ukraine. Lublin and Zamojszczyzna were clearly conceived as the laboratory for the new Reich that was being created.[32]

As the preparations for Action Zamość were being made, the continental ambitions of Globocnik and his departments had already been transferred to the WVHA; but the fact remains that the prescriptions were still being formulated by the collaborators of Thomalla, who was at the same time a liegeman of Globocnik and an engineer who perfectly fulfilled the standards issued by the WVHA.

On 22 November 1942, in the order of intervention that structured the first phase of Action Zamość, Thomalla was confirmed as responsible for the building of an organization which had twenty site chiefs and 150 artisans at its disposal for the action of colonization.[33] These 'Points of settlement and support', which Thomalla was supposed to build, bore witness to the scale of the settlement project of which Zamość was the forerunner, and also showed the European stature which the *Bauleitung* (works management) of Lublin aimed to assume until the revival of the WVHA in 1944.[34]

As early as November 1941, the question of 'Points of settlement and support' had been the object of the first reflections of the departments run by Globocnik, who then acted as delegate for the organization of these points. True, the SS developers in Lublin knew what their plans were for the General Government: Zamość, Hrubieszów and Lublin were the main points in the south and east of the proconsulate: but the list of 'Points of support' determined by Thomalla and the engineers did not mention a complete hierarchy of the nascent settlement network. Of the fifty-one 'Points of support' selected, only thirty-eight were given a ranking of importance. The documents of the Directorate of Building give a clear idea of what these 'Points of support' were to be: as major vectors of occupation and colonization, they had very important functions of control and repression, and the majority of their staff were assigned to these activities. However, the actors of economic predation and building, along with the SS officers of the RuSHA, were present in the first-class 'Points of settlement and support', which meant that the functions of economic exploitation, colonization and Germanization were also important at the regional level.[35] The over-representation of repressive functions is clear from the building specifications, including prison facilities for 300 prisoners in first-class 'Points of support'. The premises, however, were a sign of the will to colonize and provided for the housing and residence of the families of the officials transferred to the *Osteinsatz*.

The projects produced by the WVHA offices also outlined areas of sociability and conviviality that give a somewhat more precise picture of the society that was to arise in these conquered Eastern spaces. It was a world of strongholds, encampments and fortified farms that conditioned the *Osteinsatz* of the actors. What constituted the reality of the citizens of the Reich in Zamojszczyzna, an experience oscillating between the experience of socio-racial domination, violence and a feeling of shared German nationhood, took place in a material framework that the actors were establishing on several scales.

On the other hand, the Building Department of Zamość and Lublin testified to the regional activity of the WVHA, but also to the very high level of autonomy of the regional body. Lublin and Zamość, in 1941, claimed to set the tone for all Germanization and colonial building in the Nazi Empire; in 1942–4, the situation had admittedly been taken over by Kammler's departments, but the activity of Richard Thomalla's offices, beyond their theoretical subordination to the WVHA, testified to their specificity. When, on 6 January 1943, Odilo Globocnik issued the orders for organizing the Directorate of Building for the planning work in the framework of Action Zamość, he designated teams in the main villages with a site manager, a project manager and state-run teams whose aim was to restore a German appearance to the exteriors of colonized villages.[36] The plans were supposed to become reality, the teams were already on the job. By the summer, however, the failure of this policy of erecting Nazi buildings on colonial land was looking obvious. The settlements were stopped on 31 May 1943 on the orders of the HSSPF Krüger because of the insecurity prevailing in Zamojszczyzna.[37]

From the autumn of 1941 to the summer of 1944, however, the Lublin

Bauleitung, headed by Richard Thomalla, assumed responsibility for the building of the urban and rural developments in the district taken over by the building companies in Lublin and Galicia, even if this had been done in an atmosphere of incompetence and marked dilettantism.[38] The *Bauleitung* had designed and built the fortifications that the developers wanted for the rural settlements in the district, but had also built the extermination camps of Bełżec, Sobibór and Treblinka, and controlled the building sites at Majdanek and the former Lublin airfield. The inextricability of all these facets of the building of the Nazi future was all too clear.

Building, installing, settling: at the heart of a new world

From 22 November 1942, Action Zamość was in full swing. The villages – close to 300 of them – were to be emptied and the chaotic hordes of Poles driven out from them would almost cross the columns of *Volksdeutsche* that the EWZ was leading to the farms that were still full of the oppressors' victims. At the beginning of January 1943, a *Warschauer Zeitung* journalist witnessed the arrival of the migrants in one of these villages:

> From the most remote villages in the East there came, three years ago, German peasants and craftsmen, responding to the Führer's call. A convoy full of tribulations and privations, a convoy of wagons in the ice and snow bringing German people to the demarcation line. One of them, indeed, grew scared at the journey, but was led along by the others who promised that the hill would soon be in sight from which the River Bug would be seen, and beyond that the refounded [*wiederentstandenen*] Reich. And one day the great convoy reached the top of this hill. People were laughing and crying because, down in the valley, they could see a snowy stream crossed by a long wooden bridge. Tears of emotion poured down the cheeks of the most hardened men, who threw their caps into the air in glee, in the coldness of this winter morning. [. . .]
>
> Time has passed since then. The frontier of the German zone of power is far away, and has been shifted well to the East thanks to the bravery of our German soldiers. The *Volksdeutsche*, who came in great convoys, have been through a process of spiritual recovery. Staying in a German-only environment has not only tied them more deeply to their People, who had lived a life surrounded by hatred and jealousy, but has also freed them from all the anguish they felt in a foreign country because of the constant danger.[39]

This familiar rhetoric is perfectly representative of the myth of the Great Trek, one of the landmarks of the Nazi fervour of the *Osteinsatz*; but this passage is merely a narrative introduction to an account of the settlement that shows what was happening in the Zamość project, the cutting edge of the realization of the Nazi Utopia. The journalist takes care to precede his description of the settlement with the great account of the invasion of the

USSR, and thus retraces the time from conquest to colonization, setting out the economic stakes of the operation:

When the leaders anticipated the plan to exterminate Europe as imagined by the Bolsheviks, and the conquering German soldiers had infiltrated far to the East, the territories of colonization of German space changed markedly. Thus the men of the Reich Commissariat for the Strengthening of German Nationhood found much German blood of value, and many descendants of Germans, in the district of Zamość. As the soil is also relatively favourable, the *Reichsführer* SS made this territory available for the settlement of many *Volksdeutsche*, for persons of German origin following internal migration, as well as for soldiers with war wounds. The settlers were assembled into new village communities so that one national group could complement the knowledge and abilities of another. With this settlement, the aim was first and foremost to eliminate the land fragmentation caused by the egalitarian practices of inheritance prevailing until then. The purification and reorganization of the village were conducted in such a way that four to five micro-farms were brought together into a settlement farm. [. . .] In each territory, part of the cultivated land and part of the village was left to the Poles. In these villages, Polish peasants, who supply their production quota and conduct themselves in a loyal manner, receive farms far larger than those they had hitherto owned. Here are some figures to illustrate the fragmentation of land: in the Lublin district, nearly 60,000 farms did not exceed 2 hectares, 150,000 were between 2 and 5 hectares, 90,000 were between 5 and 10 hectares, and only 80 exceeded 50 hectares. With such unsustainable holdings, it was not possible to carry out a modern agrarian policy. The future will show that these measures have proved beneficial to this country.[40]

The journalist, whose account had hitherto oscillated between the ideological and the strictly factual, and described a racial and modernizing Nazi practice entirely made up of re-parcelling and attention to merit, then becomes something of an ethnographer as he describes the settlement of this new village:

The winter wind whistles between the residence barracks of the migrants' camp. On the premises, however, this Sunday afternoon is pleasantly warm: the men sitting together talk about their future, the women take care of the young children, the biggest are gambolling about and have to be constantly watched by their parents. Suddenly, all the children rush out. In the courtyard, the *Propaganda-Kompanie* has just installed loudspeakers, and the first musical broadcast begins. The youngsters dance and jump around the mast on which the loudspeakers have been installed. They scream and sing aloud so much that the music cannot be heard. The older ones are also spellbound, and listen to the melodious rhythms. Their eyes, sparkling with joyful expectation, shine even more clearly, and they sway in rhythm to the bars of the haunting melody. The joy of the children has quietened down after a moment of exuberance, and the old people continue their conversation. They discuss life as it was before they left in their great convoy to the new homeland. In this hut live Germans from the Volga. Their destiny has been unpredictable and hard. [. . .]

From the loudspeakers now rings out the voice of the camp chief, calling the men to the common room, for a new convoy must assemble for the next day. In the great room, at a table, is seated the representative of the Commissariat of the Reich for the economic communities of colonization. One by one, the migrants are called up. They approach the table, receive their settlement papers and the coupon book for the Economic Colonization Community; with these coupons, in the first days before the farm can provide for their necessities, they can make their purchases in the shops of the Economic Colonization Community. Patiently, the men stand in line and await their turn.[41]

After the announcement and preparation of the settlement, with the distribution of documents, the next day finally arrives, the time for the settlement convoy.

The next morning. The sun has not yet risen, and a long line of carriages stretches out in the camp courtyard. Each migrant who has received his number brings his luggage and accompanies his family to the carriages. The children are still sleepy, they curl up in the straw against their mothers and soon fall back to sleep. The importance of the moment has not been impressed upon their minds. This strikes the elders even more. [. . .] Yet the loading of hundreds of people into the carriages does not go so fast. Finally, it's done. The sign is given, the convoy moves off.

The journalist then goes on to describe the village and the arrival of the migrants:

But let's look at the village in which migrants are arriving today for the first time. On both sides of the country road there are farms spread wide apart from one another. Everything is still quiet in the village, and houses, barns and stables seem to be dead out here in the countryside. Not a human being on the horizon, not a sound. And yet some men leave a house and go into the next one: it's the village chief, with many SS, and the women from the *Frauenschaft*, the NSV nurses, and the BDM girls, who have cleaned the houses and lit fires in the hearths, so that the new owners would be received in heated houses. Now they look at the completed work.

The sun has now risen and it surrounds the village with a soft light, illuminates the white walls of the houses, and a special atmosphere envelops the arrivals. The village chief stands on the road with his men, ready to welcome the new inhabitants of the village. And it is then that appears in the sunlight, far off down the road, the first car. The other cars follow in an impressive convoy arriving in the village [. . .].

The village chief stops the head of the convoy. We can now see the men, their eyes full of hope but also a little anxious as they gaze down the long village. What will my farm, our farm, look like? Calm, strangely calm are the people on the carriages, despite the presence of many children and elderly people. [. . .]

The village chief has a plan of the village to which figures have been added. Following his instructions, the different carriages are driven into the village. We climb into one of them to experience the great moment. The little draft horses give a tug, and the carriage starts moving up the bumpy road of the village towards the white houses. [. . .] We arrive at the first house, on which is inscribed a number. The village chief calls this number. The answer goes up from the wagon behind us. 'Here!' The column stops. The village chief shows the property to the peasant. [. . .] Finally comes the property at which our carriage stops. Above, a peasant, with six sons and a daughter. The mother is no longer alive, the girl has to look after the housekeeping. The carriage has entered a farmyard. Full of hope, everyone has jumped off the carriage and entered the house. The father is pensive, the children impetuous, all dashing through the rooms and uttering exclamations of joy. The peasant quickly looks at the house and strides out into the yard. His first journey leads him to the stable where he contemplates the building, tapping the throats of the animals and smiling to himself with satisfaction. With a few gestures, he picks up misplaced objects and then goes into the barn. There are several machines there and he checks their condition. He crosses the courtyard and looks at the garden. It is here that a special surprise awaits him: one hive after another and, next to them, beekeeping equipment which he examines with an experienced eye. Behind a well-tended vegetable garden begin the fields. Slowly and heavily, he walks over the frozen glebe of the fields, bends over, scrapes the ground, nods his head with satisfaction. [. . .] Everyone then immediately goes to work. The father divides the tasks up between each of his six sons. The most important thing is to take care of the animals. The boys go to their tasks with a will, the courtyard quickly fills with people jostling and men singing as they work. The girl does not sit idly by for a single moment: she has ardently embarked on a great cleaning and tidying, in the fireplace a fire sparkles and the kitchen gradually becomes comfortable. The luggage is unpacked, their few belongings arranged and ordered.

But let us return for a moment to the peasant: his eyes glow with joy, he cannot believe it. He wants to impose some order on the farm, he wants to make it a shining example. He will put all his joy into it and then go back to work immediately: the next day, the agricultural manager of the district will come to give him the livestock allocated to this farm. The village chief is accompanied by the nurse dressed in brown (from the NSV) to contribute to tidying up this motherless house. And when the spring returns, the agricultural manager of the district will come to distribute the seeds and the agricultural machinery, while the inspector will come to survey the fields with precision.

[. . .] The oppressive silence has been driven away, everywhere is a hustle and bustle, in the farms and in the fields. The children frolic around the farms and their cries of triumph are heard on the road. These children have many reasons to indulge in such joy, for a radiant future filled with work is opening up before them.[42]

This is how the story of this *Ansiedlung* (settlement/implantation) ends. It will be noted that the journalist has taken great care to underline the economic rationality at work behind the distribution of the land and the reparcelling of these open fields. He also stresses the highly supervised nature of these facilities: the villages are run by a village chief, surrounded by a group of *Waffen-SS*, students and activists from the BDM and the *Frauenschaft*, and agricultural institutions responsible for ensuring the conformity of the way the farms are run. It is an economic, social, hygienic and racial order that is being described here. In addition, land measures are designed to ensure that this order lasts in the long term: after a period of economic, social, political and racial probation, it is planned to allocate 30 hectares of land to each peasant who has settled with his family, and to make this property inalienable and indivisible.[43] A Nazi world is being set up.

Less than a week after this resettlement, Odilo Globocnik, as delegate of the RKFdV, issued the first of a series of complementary instructions designed to clarify how these utopian communities were to be structured and consolidated. If the first of these instructions specified the organization of the settlement, as well as the coordination of the services,[44] the following ones create an image of how the collective spirit of the new communities should be shaped. On 12 May 1943, in his service instruction no. 7, Globocnik details the measures to be taken.

In the first place, the instruction concerns the method to be used by the Nazi cadres in order to achieve their objectives: 'The work of education', says the text, 'must be based on strictly pragmatic foundations, encouraging people to do the best job of building their farms, increasing their profits, reorganizing the farms, and ensuring that, far from being profiteers, they are the guarantors that their successors in the lineage will be rooted in this soil.'[45] It is indeed, in the eyes of the Germanizers who drafted this text, important to strengthen the racial awareness of lineage. In order to do so, it is necessary to awaken the consciousness of the colonists to the glory of their past and the experience of their predecessors, made of misery and distress, but also of migration and work. It is only by this work, according to the writer of the order, that the strength of their blood is guaranteed, the maintenance of its purity and the preservation of the lineage ensured. The Germans are also encouraged to recall the crimes of their enemy peoples, the predation of property, the conditions under which Germans had lived, and 'the National Socialist Reich's determination to found a great German ethno-national state [*Großer deutscher*

Volkstaat] so that the Germans will never again have to pay the price of distress and annihilation'.[46]

For the writer of the text, therefore, the individual is not capable of living and acting for the German people unless he is made part of a community which has the same aims as himself, for the German people is the result of many lineages which mean nothing in themselves but are invincible in a community. There follows a series of syllogisms, and then the editor concludes: 'Thus the conception of Race, Blood and Lineage is erected into a basis for the Community and as the realization of National Socialist doctrine.'[47] The racial determinism underlying the Nazi faith and future could not be better expressed.

The following instructions for the cultural support given to migrants deals with the means of this support. The author of the document is particularly circumspect and advances his arguments only very slowly: it must be said that the objective he is pursuing is a surprising one, even if we are here at the cutting edge of Nazi belief and practice. He begins as follows:

[. . .] The cultures of the past have agreed to fashion the ancient Germanic uses to their own ends. The fact that they have been preserved proves that this use was relevant, and that they spoke and still speak to men. To bring them here, where they contain true concepts (albeit without falling into a Germanic cult which would have nothing to do with present times), is to recognize the true meaning of these uses by bringing them into harmony with current conceptions of National Socialism. That is why the organization of such Days as: birth, marriage, and death, has in its conception the idea of giving individuals the thought of the continuation of life in the eternity of one's people.

Rarely has the expression of Nazi belief as a system reinserting the individual into the chain of ancestors and reconfiguring the conception of the past, but also the future, been formulated in such an elaborate way, even though the prose of the author is almost unreadable. But one thing is certain: it is in Zamość, in these new colonies of the Nazi future, that the quasi-religious conception of National Socialism as a belief linking the living and the dead finds, in the words of SS officers in charge of these policies, its most complete formulation. It is here that, in their view, the communities will be so new that even the calendar will be turned topsy-turvy. The author gives the details:

Such festivals as the *Julfest*, the 1 May, and the harvest festival, have the meaning of expressing our gratitude to nature and omnipotence. They have given men and their lives such a rich flow of existence, which must be preserved. Other traditions, however, such as horse racing, sports days, the ring, etc. [have the meaning] of awakening human beings to their aptitudes, such as courage, boldness, dexterity, bodily robustness, energy, and so on. It is in the use of these functional concepts [*Zwecksbedingten Begriffe*] that one recognizes the meaning of a feast.[48]

In this way, the neo-pagan decor of *Gottgläubigkeit* (belief in God) is established. It is the foundation of the new society created in Zamojszczyzna, in the view of the Nordicists of the SS.[49] But this framework must be extended and the author sees numerous opportunities for the promotion of belief, such as the evocation of ancient customs, the inauguration of housing estates and common houses, the creation of peasant houses, the promotion of traditional customs and costumes, popular music, theatre and dance, and of course the different days of celebration: the *Julfest*, the feast of Advent, the jubilation of Carnival, the festivities of 1 May, which, it is noted, 'are to replace Easter and Whitsuntide', the feast of the solstice, the feast of the village community, the harvest festival, and entry into life, marriage and death. The course of the year and the ages of life will be perfectly framed by the new *gottgläubig* order of colonization. This is nothing new, the author tells us: the forms of all these festivals already exist and it is only necessary to generalize them. Each ceremony, however, is meant to assume a special function in the service of the community. For example, the birthday celebration does not have the 'vocation of formally welcoming the child into the state by inscribing him in the registers but that of expressing the fact that a new member of the lineage has been generated for the future. Every child must continue the work of its predecessors.' Parents' responsibility, we are told, is decisive, but no distinction should be made between children born in wedlock and children born out of wedlock, because in many parts of Germany couples have children before the wedding. Marriage, on the other hand, must have as its content the sense of community and its obligatory character for individuals, who bear not only the responsibility of the perpetuity of their lineage, but all the acts aimed at securing it. Death, on the other hand, is:

> [. . .] the execution of a vital constraint that transmits an accomplished and completed life to those who will follow on. This is why we must not differentiate between the rich and the poor, but between actions and works performed for the community that constitute the true measure of the merit of death.[50]

Again, one could not be more abstruse in the formulation or clearer in the dogmatic organization of the life of settler communities. At the foundation of the Nordic faith lies the fact that individuals are not just defined as individuals, but that they form the living part of physical-spiritual entities called lineages (*Sippen*) which constitute the structures of a people and the place where northern racial excellence can be preserved. The new social order must therefore, in the eyes of the writer of these instructions for the edification of settlers, inculcate racial consciousness by infusing it with consciousness of a lineage composed of living, dead and future members of a family, and whose life is celebrated in regular festivals and uses that supervisors must use to found and solidify the spirit of community. These festivals, these common cultural uses, must bring the community together at many points in life, whether they are marking the times of the year or shaping human existence, and these moments must structure the time of the community. It is also necessary, say the instructions, that places be dedicated to this collective life, perhaps by building a *Sippenhaus*, a House of Lineage, where all these festivities would be held, and where all the written records resulting therefrom would be retained. The author advocates:

> The external appearance remains modest. A pleasant hall decorated with Reich insignia, flowers and lights should illustrate the modesty of our consideration of the acts of life. Only the symbol of our action, that is to say, a child, an heir to his ancestors, must be given to show the future spouses at the ceremony that the time of their lives reminds them that they have a duty of fidelity, and also something of the dead to preserve, something which must serve as an admonition to those who succeed them.[51]

This is a good illustration of the coherence of the Nazi Utopia, as Odilo Globocnik and the SS planned to practise it in Zamojszczyzna: the *gottgläubig* project encompassed all of collective life, time, space and the sequences of existence, and even shaped the design of common facilities that the *Bauleitung* of Zamość under Richard Thomalla was to build. The elected officials who had passed through the selection of social engineering and thus demonstrated their racial excellence, succeeding in making their way into the great land redistribution led by the SS, based on the *Siedlungs-und Stützpunkte* of Zamojczczyzna, formed a special group in the eyes of the Nordicists in the entourage of Globocnik, a group from which the Nazi future would emerge, made of communities with strengthened faith, with racially sound and conscious lineages, living new rural lives, lives that would be modernized, abundant but modest, all fit for the thousand years of the 'promised reign'.[52]

It is now clear how specific were the policies of this laboratory of Zamojszczyzna in the terrible grip of Odilo Globocnik: no territory in the Nazi Empire was subjected to such elaborate policies of filtering and socio-racial shaping of its populations, with so many people being thrown out onto the streets and roads. And probably no other territory was so completely reshaped, in its built environment and the structuring of its land and demography. Finally, nowhere else was the Nazi attempt to revolutionize history, the building of a radically different future, so precisely formulated, or taken so far. In this sense, indeed, Action Zamość is highly revealing of what, in the eyes of the Nazis, *one could dare to dream*, and thus of the meanders of the Nazi belief and project.

Chapter 9

The nightmare: from the ethnic domino effect to the flames of despair

As we come to the end of our investigation, it is time to explore the other side of the Nazi promise. Of course, we have already had a dark presentiment of this; and some of the preceding chapters have already to some extent raised the veil laid over those who did not fit into the social and racial frameworks imposed by the SS, that pitiless process of selection that was to precede the advent of Utopia. But the impressionistic nature of what we have hitherto noted is not enough to allow us to gauge the considerable inertia which these sometimes anecdotal policies impressed upon the destinies of Europe.

Destinies of Europeans, destinies of Europe: this is what we now must seek, as we describe the fateful mechanism initiated by the ethnocrats of the SS, that ethnic domino effect of which Götz Aly spoke in 1995 where one domino falls over, knocking down a second, which then topples a third, with the cascading fall of each of the pieces eventually affecting the whole of Europe to the east of the Rhine, along the Danube, and even as far as the Veneto.[1] At the heart of this space lay the Zamojszczyzna, a laboratory for the politics of Utopia and the advent of the new Reich, with its high density of ethnic dominoes – a tragically intense field of observation for this upheaval, and an accelerator for the genocidal particles launched by the Nazis in Eastern Europe.

The first of the main characteristics of what came to pass in this region was the specific, early and almost complete extermination of its Jews, who formed the majority of the population of the urban centres, in an operation that was a visible prelude to the Germanization of Zamojszczyzna, combining the know-how of administrations juggling social, economic, logistical and food supply imperatives with the radical determination of the Nazis and the exhaustive logistical and murderous engineering of Operation Reinhard.

In full sight of all: the extermination of the Jews, prior to Germanization

As we have already suggested, the situation of the Jews in the Lublin area and Zamojszczyzna was very specific and we should start with this specificity if we are to describe the main characteristics of their destiny. From the autumn of 1939 onwards the sudden application of Nazi anti-Semitic legislation by occupying elites still filled with Austrian imperial memories and a tragic sense of radicality, coupled with the logistical and economic conditions prevailing in the district of Lublin, created a very particular situation. Let us recall that it was in January 1940 that the measures decided by Globocnik a few weeks earlier were confirmed by Himmler and that the Jewish communities in the Lublin district, Zamojszczyzna first and foremost, were destined to become reservoirs of manpower for the pharaonic projects of defensive building along the River Bug, the demarcation line between the General Government and the Soviet occupation zone. The district was remarkable in that Globocnik was the only one of the SSPFs to carry out this policy of putting to work – or reducing to slavery, to be more precise – Jewish communities on closed building sites: by the summer of 1940 between 50,000 and 70,000 Jews were already working in the seventy-six central working camps built in the district, of which nearly forty-three were placed in the service of the Inspectorate of the water supply, in charge of drainage works. Not all of them – far from it – were Jews from the district: many of them were Jews from the territories incorporated into the Reich who had been deported under the Germanization policies, or prisoners of war selected in the camps to which they had been confined.[2] At the local level, the implementation of a complex identification and filing system had accompanied this first set of measures,[3] and de facto the whole policy pursued tended to confine the native Jewish population in residential areas in the city and the Jewish deportees in labour camps in the countryside, to register these Jews in identification and assessment files for the labour force, and to compel them to a type of work that reduced them to the ranks of beasts of burden. This process, implemented in the first six months of the occupation, was unique to the destiny of the communities of the district for several reasons. First, the process, which was to be repeated in many parts of the Nazi Empire, was here notable for its precocity, but also for its duration: this regime lasted from autumn 1939 to summer 1944 (at least for the few who survived). Second, it was characterized by its very great completeness and coherence: the exhaustiveness of the identification of the Jews, their confinement and their putting to work was probably unmatched throughout the Nazi Empire, with the possible exception of Galicia. The Jews were then forced to identify themselves by a visible badge of shame: in the eyes of the Nazis, they conformed phenotypically to the stereotype of 'Jews from the East' and the shtetls, a stereotype that was very largely

Austrian (as were many of the SS forces of occupation mobilized in Lublin); and the Nazis very rapidly endeavoured to impose the wearing of the Star of David as an armband, a measure which came into effect as early as 23 November 1939 throughout the General Government.[4]

In total, in the summer of 1940, the entire Jewish population of Zamojszczyzna, including the 50,000 or more predominantly urban Jews residing in the district and the 70,000 forced labourers in the camps set up there along the River Bug, was the subject of a policy characterized by confinement, branding and putting to work, in a systematic, radical and avowedly exhaustive approach that had no equal elsewhere. This was one of the most successful efforts in the history of mankind to domesticate and reduce a human population to the status of a herd of livestock. The Jewish population of Zamojszczyzna was now reclassified as a herd, under the total control of the SS administration: the only thing that counted was its capacity for work and the control of its reproduction and nutrition, while it was exploited in every conceivable way. Since at least the spring of 1940 and the launching of the action 'In Search of German Blood', the SS had been pursuing a policy of Germanization, with specific population displacements in which Jews were not even a variable. At best, the fact that they provided a labour force legitimated their being *allowed* to feed themselves – though, as early as February 1940, Globocnik proposed to starve the Jewish people to death if they were unable to provide for themselves.[5] And at the very least their disappearance from the landscape, in any way whatsoever, constituted a precondition for the planning and execution of the refounding of German nationhood.

The evolution of the situation of the General Government and, more generally, of the Eastern Front which was opened in June 1941 involved a fundamental aggravation of the fate of the Jews. In the summer, Himmler's visit confirmed the plans for Germanization and imbued them with an even more intense and radical edge. In the autumn, the fear of the spread of epidemics born in what were in effect the immense death camps for Soviet POWs, and in the starving ghettoes, prompted the Lublin district officials to issue an order for the shooting and elimination of all Jews found outside the towns.[6] The Jews were the only herd that could be exploited at will; when they were 'free', they were, in the eyes of the Nazis, wild beasts who had to be eradicated because of the danger of spreading diseases, and because of their supposed malignity – harmful, like a pest;[7] hence, inexorably, began the practice of the *Judenjagd*, the 'hunt for the Jews', which began in the autumn of 1941 and lasted until the summer of 1944, becoming one of the main activities of the various armed formations in the district and Zamojszczyzna.[8] The more radical the policy became, the more the Jewish population was perceived by the SS as a herd assigned to a specific setting, to certain places and spaces (camps and ghettoes), subjected to strictly controlled circulation – the transhumance, as it were, of herds marked by a yellow star – and to an activity that was assessed strictly by the yardstick of the labour force.

Those who were not situated within this framework of animal domestication were treated as game to be freely hunted.[9]

November 1941 represented another major turning point: according to Bogdan Musial, this was when the order to exterminate the Jewish populations of the General Government was given. Since the summer, the fortifications of the Bug frontier had become useless: why fortify it when the border had been pushed back by nearly a thousand kilometres, and would soon be located in the Urals? Moreover, it was now assumed that new massive labour supplies would soon be available to the economy thanks to the great encirclement battles being carried out by the Wehrmacht. Finally, the food requisitions imposed on the General Government by the Reich took on astronomical proportions, whereas the Famine plan seemed on the verge of being realized.[10] Odilo Globocnik then brought to the Lublin district a team of technicians from Operation T4 in charge of the killing (the 'euthanasia') of mentally ill and incurable patients; they were to set up an extermination programme for the Jews of the General Government. The determinants of this policy are certainly difficult to specify. Nevertheless, at that time there was a massive consensus among those involved locally: a short-term direct killing programme should be initiated. Hans Frank described the Jews as 'extraordinarily harmful greedyguts', his administration thought no more highly of them than did Globocnik, and the SS and the RKFdV perceived them as a major obstacle to the realization of the millennial Utopia. The Jews of Zamojszczyzna were now destined for certain and relatively rapid death; a death not caused by famine and epidemics, but rather by a deliberate mechanism of murder.[11]

Since the autumn of 1940, Globocnik had formed a team which had acquired a decisive level of expertise. He had, as we know, founded a network of labour camps that ran along the Bug down the old line of demarcation, and with this aim in mind had formed two types of teams. The first, under the leadership of Richard Thomalla, was comprised of experts in building, in charge of the 'Points of settlement and support', but also of all the prison infrastructures of the district.[12] In the second place, Globocnik organized, on the model of self-defence militias (and as part of Heydrich's order of intervention no. 8, 17 July 1941, fixing the modalities for the selection of prisoners in prison camps), a selection of detainees sent to the Trawniki training camp to form a militia for the surveillance of confinement facilities from the autumn of 1940.[13] The following autumn, when the extermination of the Jews in the General Government was decided on, Globocnik added to these two groups of building and surveillance a third group, coming from the Reich and originating from the exterminator teams of the euthanasia programme: this was initially just five persons, who arrived in October 1941. This group opted for a locality along the Bug, on the former demarcation line, on the border between Galicia and Zamojszczyzna, where one of the many labour camps in the network built by Richard Thomalla already existed, and which thus already had an operational contingent of 'Trawnikis'.[14] Bełżec was where the first extermination facilities were built between the beginning of November and the Christmas of 1941 by a group of Polish craftsmen recruited through the municipal administration. It was this little group that put up the main buildings, including the gas chambers. In mid-October, the first units of supervisors arrived, some sixty former Soviet prisoners of war. The weeks between 1 January 1942 and mid-March were those of the first attempts at gassing, first with gas trucks, then with chambers equipped with a Soviet armoured car or truck engine, whose carburation had been modified to enrich itself with carbon monoxide. The first victims, political detainees from Zamość, disabled men and women from surrounding villages and Jews from the region, died in the trucks and, in late February and early March, in the gas chambers that were being tried out for the first time.[15]

Beginning in mid-March 1942, the first phase of the continuous arrival of convoys for immediate extermination began, a sign that the hierarchy had considered the tests satisfactory and wanted to get the extermination process going at full capacity. This first phase, however, caught the exterminators short. There were not enough of them, only fourteen at most; the facilities were imperfectly developed, and they had to work very fast. Christian Wirth, the camp commander and head of the T4 team, was overtaken by events and the pace of the arrivals. At the end of four weeks he was forced to demand a halt to the convoys. From 12 April to 22 May 1942, with the exception of one convoy on 8 May, Bełżec's killing facility did not function. At the end of this time, the convoys resumed, and then took a second break, from 18 June to 17 July. The technicians of the T4 took advantage of these two breaks to develop six new gas chambers. Following the second break, the litany of convoys began uninterruptedly until December of the same year. The network was now in place; having started in Bełżec, it was extended in April, to Sobibór first and then Treblinka. The time for exhaustive extermination had begun; Bełżec was, in this tragic project, more particularly responsible for Zamojszczyzna and Galicia.[16]

The first convoy from Zamojszczyzna set off from Chelm on 2 April 1942. Jews from the district had already died in Bełżec during the test phase, but this was where systematic extermination in the region began. Now, the long lines of convoys were unending: on 11 April, a convoy from Zamość led to their deaths between 2,500 and 3,000 people; on 8 May, a convoy came from Szczebrzeszyn, in the district of Biłgoraj, bringing 280 persons; from 22 to 27 May, 4,000 Jews transported from the whole district were gassed. On 12 April, the day after the killing of the Jews in Zamość, the camp closed, and Wirth was recalled to Germany. He did not return until several weeks later, and took charge of the building of new gas chambers which did not start operating at full speed until 22 May. It is worth noting that the first convoys exterminated in these new installations also came from Zamość. This proves the centrality of these contingents in the raison d'être of the camp's existence in the first half of 1942.

In all, however, from April to November, nine convoys from Zamojszczyzna reached Bełżec, 5,500 victims in April 1942, 4,000 in the last week of May, 3,400 in August, 4,000 in October, 9,000 in November. No Jew from Zamojszczyzna died in Bełżec after that date. The Sobibór camp made up for the six weeks in which Bełżec stopped operating between 12 April and 22 May, when a total of 25,000 victims were gassed.[17] 21,000 Jews from the districts of Chelm and Hrubieszów also died in Sobibór in October 1942.[18] The two genocidal pushes of summer and October 1942 were linked in part to the Germanization projects for the district. In October–November, time was running out: the action of population displacement was scheduled for 27 November. All in all, for the Chelm district, a total of 79,750 victims, including 43,800 from Zamojszczyzna, were transported to Bełżec and Sobibór for immediate gassing: more than 25,000 in Bełżec, more than 54,000 in Sobibór. At the same time, Globocnik's police battalions carried out massacres by shooting, which, like Sobibór, served to alleviate the selection in Bełżec's capacity for murder. The operations carried out by these police battalions, both the setting up of raids in the ghettoes and the massacres by shooting, conferred on the genocide in Zamojszczyzna a *demonstrative* dimension unique in Europe, if we except the case of the occupied USSR. It can be assumed that it was the colonial status of the region that also determined this special character.[19] In the eyes of Globocnik and his teams, it was a matter of making a lesson out of the exhaustive extirpation of the Jewish community in the region, making a show of it so as to fill Polish bystanders and – to a lesser extent – Ukrainians with an ever more intense terror and, thus, to firmly establish the domination of representatives of the Nordic race in the process of settlement.

Thus, it was in full sight of *all* that the Jews of Zamojszczyzna were exterminated, some gassed at Bełżec or Sobibór, the others shot. In full sight of all – but first and foremost in full sight of *themselves*. It is particularly tragic to note, with the historian David Silberklang, that the *Judenräte* (Jewish councils that the Germans put in charge of the daily management of the ghettoes and reservoirs of hostages) of Lublin and Zamość were very quickly aware of what happened to those people who were so violently forced to get into the trains.[20] As early as 17 March, a member of the *Judenrat* of Lublin telephoned the Jewish welfare office in Kraków to inform him that the mass deportation of the Jews from Lublin had begun. Two days later, the same man called again to inform the same office that the destination of people not indispensable to the war effort was not the USSR, but the locality of Bełżec.

A week later the head of the *Judenrat* of Zamość, Mieczysław Garfinkel, himself received a phone call from the *Judenrat* of Lublin asking him to inquire about the destination of the trains and the fate of the passengers, a phone call that he passed on to the *Judenrat* of the town of Hrubieszów Lubelski, very close to Bełżec. In any case, on 1 April, the delegates of the main *Judenräte* of Lublin, Zamość and Hrubieszów Lubelski knew that no one was coming out of Bełżec alive. At that time, the camp had been in operation for only four weeks.[21]

One is struck by the ease of communication between the communities and by the precocity of information about the fate of the deportees. However, this was not a specific feature of Jewish communities, more urban than others. There is another source that explains it – an exceptional source: the diary of Zygmunt Klukowski, a Polish doctor residing in Szczebrzeszyn, a small village 25 kilometres west of Zamość. This remarkably reflects the level of awareness of all the protagonists of the tragedy. On 8 April 1942, Klukowski wrote:

> The Jews are terrified. We know for sure that every day two trains, consisting of twenty cars each, come to Belzec [Bełżec], one from Lublin, the other from Lwow [Lvov]. After being unloaded on separate tracks, all Jews are forced behind the barbed-wire enclosure. Some are killed with electricity, some with poison gases, and the bodies are burned.
>
> On the way to Belzec the Jews experience many terrible things. They are aware of what will happen to them. Some try to fight back. At the railway station in Szczebrzeszyn a young woman gave away a gold ring in exchange for a glass of water for her dying child. In Lublin people witnessed small children being thrown through the windows of speeding trains. Many people are shot before reaching Belzec.[22]

The level of information available to local elites could not be clearer. But the issue is not only the capacity that bystanders and victims had to ask questions and seek information. Once the phase of total extermination of Jewish communities had been launched, the Germans did not in any way seek to mask or cover their practices with a veil of discretion. As well as detailing the horrors he witnessed,[23] Klukowski also tells of the horrors that occurred in Lublin which he knew of second hand, and his 'tone' describes things with a certain, strictly topographical distance – which vanishes when it is the turn of the Jews of Szczebrzeszyn to suffer the genocidal tornado. On 21 October 1942, the deportation of the Jews from his locality began. Here is what he says:

> *October 21.* Today I planned to try to go to Zamosc [Zamość] again. I woke up very early to be ready, but around 6 a.m. I heard noise and through the window saw unusual movement. This was the beginning of the so-called German displacement of Jews, in reality a liquidation of the entire Jewish population in Szczebrzeszyn.
>
> From early morning until late at night we witnessed indescribable events. Armed SS soldiers, gendarmes, and 'blue police' [Nazi-run Polish police

– Translator] ran through the city looking for Jews. Jews were assembled in the marketplace. The Jews were taken from their houses, barns, cellars, attics, and other hiding places. Pistol and gun shots were heard throughout the entire day. Sometimes hand grenades were thrown into the cellars. Jews were beaten and kicked; it made no difference whether they were men, women, or small children.

By 3 p.m. more than 900 Jews had been assembled. The Germans began moving them to the outskirts of the city. All had to walk except for members of the *Judenrat* and the Jewish police; they were allowed to use horse-drawn wagons. The action didn't stop even after they were taken out of town. The Germans still carried on the search for Jews. It was posted that the penalty for hiding Jews is death, but for showing their hiding places special rewards will be given.

All Jews will be shot. Between 400 and 500 have been killed. Poles were forced to begin digging graves in the Jewish cemetery. From information I received approximately 2,000 people are in hiding. The arrested Jews were loaded onto a train at the railroad station to be moved to an unknown location.[24]

The list of convoys established by the historian Sara Berger indicates that a convoy arrived on 22 October from Szczbrzeszyn to Bełżec with 2,000 persons.[25] The destination was, as we have seen, not unknown to Zygmunt Klukowski. In the following days the author describes with horror and alarm the continuation of the manhunt pursued in this immense trap patiently set up during the incarceration of the Jewish community; he insists on the help provided by the local population, the abject behaviour of certain protagonists, the unfathomable cruelty shown by the German police. He also describes the bewilderment, shame and impotence, and finally, with a certain bitterness, the fact that his sensibility is being blunted by it all.[26] It is as if, without becoming accustomed to horror, he were accustoming himself to some of its manifestations.

The numbers involved in the extermination speak for themselves. Of the 250,000 Jews from the district of Lublin, 90 per cent succumbed to this immense and murderous operation. On 22 November 1942, when the Germanization operations of Action Zamość began, more than 47,000 of the 50,000 Jews residing in Zamojszczyzna had been exterminated, including 44,000 in the gas chambers of Sobibór and Bełżec. And the operation was conducted with ostentation and violence such that the communities of bystanders were literally paralysed by the ongoing genocide. And they knew everything that was happening.

A society martyred

If we are to understand the ordeal that the society of Zamojszczyzna passed through, we must go back to the beginnings of the German occupation in the region. From the outset, of course, discriminatory practices had led to increased polarization in a society that was already undermined by significant social, denominational and ethnic divisions. They crystallized with the installation of a local branch of the KdS Lublin in Zamość, which confiscated for its own use a building known as the Rotunda, a fort built under the Tsarist Empire that served before the war as a munitions warehouse.

From the start of the occupation, Polish elites constituted, in Zamość as elsewhere, a privileged target for the SS. In the summer of 1940, when the BdS for the General Government, Bruno Streckenbach, launched *AB-Aktion*, an 'Extraordinary Action of Pacification' which targeted the elites, the Rotunda served as a gathering point for the prisoners who were too many to fit into the Gestapo prison in Zamość. Some 400 prisoners were brought there on 19 June. On 24 June, the vast majority of the prisoners were taken to the castle of Lublin, which housed a prison. Although a small number were freed, most of them were deported to Dachau and Sachsenhausen. The executions began in the Rotunda on 8 July 1940. Forty people, arrested in the city and in the district, were executed. From that moment, the Rotunda gained a sinister reputation. It served as an assembly camp and an execution station for political prisoners.[27]

Reading the diary of Zygmunt Klukowski, written with the obvious intention of providing material to be used in the history of the martyrdom of the region, we can see the *AB-Aktion* as the inaugural scene of an experience of violence that increased in intensity from the summer of 1940 onwards. He himself was arrested on 19 June and transferred to the Rotunda after a body search. He was there for two days and witnessed multiple scenes of humiliation. What was being played out in these walls Klukowski was aware of, even though he did not clearly formulate it: a ritual of national reduction, together with a procedure of social neutralization. Polish elites were targeted; some were sent to a concentration camp, while others were simply executed, and yet others were released, as he was. The logic of Gestapo officials was impossible to understand. The fact remains, however, that the effect was remarkable: he was relieved not to have been hit, or forced to run, but admits to being incapable of understanding the arbitrariness of the Nazi power. And he describes the terror he felt when, a few days later, his steps led him by chance to the Rotunda.[28] But that was not all. By attacking the elites in this way, the Germans caused very specific disruptions in the social fabric of the occupied society, and Klukowski's diary echoes these: the 'missing' persons in the camps, whose death notices took time to arrive; those who were freed but were more dead than alive on their return – they all unwittingly instilled a climate of terror that left a permanent mark, especially since arrests were happening practically daily. On 24 November 1940, for example, Jan Franszak, the former mayor of Szczebrzeszyn, returned from the Dachau camp. His journey had taken him since the summer from Zamość to Lublin, from Lublin to Oranienburg and from Oranienburg to Dachau before he was released. Klukowski describes his return:

> I was told by people who had visited him that he is completely sick, looks terrible, and his feet are so bady swollen that he cannot wear shoes. He is a complete wreck, both physically and mentally.
>
> [. . .] More news: in Dachau, a well-known civic leader, Stanislaw Kowerski, from Zamosc [Zamość] died.[29]

What is deployed here is the performative nature of the system of aggression exercised towards the elites by the occupiers. Klukowski *intuited* this, with almost mathematical fineness, but he escaped it, he was confined for only two days,[30] and he was all the more sensitive to the existence of the disappeared, these human beings suspended between the dead and the living in a teratology that made them akin to zombies or spectres. Some died, others returned, and those, 'complete wrecks, both physically and mentally', were perceived as genuine revenants. On 28 November, Klukowski spoke with Franszak, but the discussion left open the question of the treatment of the victims, and the ordeals they were forced to suffer. The two men talked of the extent of the losses for the Polish intelligentsia, but could only react to the experience of violence with a stunned silence. The extent and depth of the policies of 'disappearance' inaugurated by the Germans in Poland, and formalized by the circular *Nacht und Nebel* in December 1941, are clear in all their deeply traumatogenic dimension, their power of *dereliction*.[31]

This society in the throes of terror was also subjected to policies whose logics were incomprehensible. Zamość could not understand the meaning of the arrival of the 'evacuees' from Łódź, victims of the UWZ and the harbingers of the third *Nahplan*. First, there were a thousand evacuees, and a further 4,800 were announced. According to Klukowski, these evacuees 'are dying by the hundreds'.[32] The litany of announcements of deaths of the members of the elite sent to German concentration camps continues to punctuate the diary, accompanied by arrests and shootings. Klukowski, grief-stricken, mentions the death in Dachau of one of his friends for whom he had expressed his anxiety at the end of the first week of February 1941:

> *February 23.* Today Mrs Kamila Kopcinska called me from Zamosc [Zamość] with the news that notary Rosinski died in Dachau. I have never in my life been in such a state of grief over the death of a friend. I cannot control myself; I cannot cover up my tears.
>
> With his death I lost my best friend and co-worker in my seventeen-year-old study of the history of the Zamosc region. We did everything together. I always consulted him when I planned for the future. No one gave me more support. Now who will take his place? I cannot foresee any work about the

Zamosc region without Rosinski. People like him are hard to find. They come along only once in a while.

From our close group of friends, only I am still here, alone and very sad.[33]

Echoing these intimate centrifugal forces, the whole social body vibrates, crossed by tensions and fault lines, on which the Germans played without our really being able to tell if this was a formulated strategy. The attack on family ties, however, was systematic: if one particular suspect does not appear, it is his family who is arrested; if one mother-in-law denounces her son-in-law, the whole family is rounded up, not to mention the 30,000 children separated from their parents over this period, of whom 4,500 went to Germany to be brought up.[34]

In this way, with its 'head' being struck by the systematic repression of its elites, its anthropological foundations undermined by the attacks on social bonds (in particular the family), and its affective universe by the waves of multiple bereavements that the sombre increase in mortalities occasioned, Zamojszczyzna passed through an ordeal which, in the spring of 1941, was still representative of the one affecting the whole of Poland. Once again Zygmunt Klukowski summarizes it most effectively:

> *March 10.* I am very tired. This life – under constant fear of arrest, constant struggle to supply my hospital, and constant uncertainty of the future for already 1½ years – is shattering my nerves.
>
> I believe in British victory but I am not sure that I will see it because of my physical condition. My heart is slowing visibly and nothing is pointing to a quick end to the war; everything seems so complicated that the struggle may go on for years.
>
> In Poland we see complete devastation in all facets of life. Our best people are dying by the thousands. People can be replaced, but the worst is the destruction of our national character. How will Poland look after a few more years of devastation? [. . .]
>
> Every few hours someone comes to tell me that the gestapo are looking through some lists at city hall, that gendarmes are stopping everyone on this or that street, that so and so was arrested. And so it goes.[35]

The effect of Nazi policies could not be evoked more vividly. Klukowski's diary mentions his first contacts with the resistance of the secret army, the ZWZ, a few weeks after this emotional low point, but it must be noted that these first contacts were merely a factor of additional tension. The predatory dimension of the occupation did not escape anyone. As early as 1940, the issue of volunteering for the Labour Service, and the registration of Jewish men for forced labour, had not escaped the attention of a close observer such as Klukowski.

It was therefore a society whose very foundations were being undermined, one 'twisted by grief',[36] which underwent the policies of extermination and Germanization, in their most paroxystic and most selective form. Of course, the 'divide and rule' maxim of the Nazi strategy, formulated from the outset by Hans Frank,[37] was brought to bear on a grave dispute which in 1940 constituted a specific feature of the district of Lublin, in the German zone of occupation. It should be remembered that 71.8 per cent of the population of the district was made up of Polish-speaking Catholics, that 14 per cent were Catholic Greek or Ukrainian-speaking Orthodox Christians, living alongside 0.9 per cent Protestants who were at least partially German-speaking and 12.6 per cent Jews.[38] In Zamojszczyzna, 345,000 Poles co-existed with 127,000 Ukrainians and 50,000 Jews.

German policies were obviously discriminatory right from the start, and affected the Jews in an incomparably more rigorous way than they did other communities. Very soon, the Germans also put in place some occasionally vague practices expressing a certain level of Nazi support for the Ukrainian minority: for example, there were cases of Catholic churches being handed over to the Greek Catholics or to the Orthodox clergy.[39] This difference in policy was noted by Polish protagonists and Klukowski himself showed a growing irritation at these cultural practices of favourit- ism towards the Ukrainians. On 20 September 1943, he noted with some bitterness: 'Already the third month has passed since the Catholic church in Szczebrzezyn has been closed.' But 'the Orthodox Church [previously St Catherine's Catholic Church] is still open, and the Orthodox priest can celebrate Mass, even though the number of parishioners has declined'.[40] These were essentially symbolic measures which certainly expressed the hierarchy promoted by the occupiers and the different destinies of the occupied. Of much more consequence, however, was the opening up of Trawniki recruitment to Ukrainians, who would bear a fundamental responsibility in the multiple policies of repression and pacification, not to mention their fundamental participation in the genocide of the region's Jews. In terms of the balance between the various ethnic communities, this opening gave the Ukrainians a very specific status in the context of the occupation.[41]

So there were bitter memories of the tensions between the two com- munities, and while Zamojszczyzna was not Galicia, and the pre-war violence was less intense there, the policies of the occupiers were fanning embers that needed only the faintest breath to glow afresh. The extermi- nation of the Jews and Action Zamość constituted a decisive and pivotal paroxysm in the destabilization of whatever prospect remained for ethno- national concord in Zamojszczyzna – all the more so as their continuity struck all observers, *exactly* as Globocnik and his entourage had desired.

Without going back over the course of the murderous mechanics which presided over the extermination of the Jewish community of Zamojszczyzna, we still need to focus on a dimension that we have not as yet examined: the behaviour of the society within which it operated. This behaviour was, to say the least, extremely varied. Abjection rubbed shoulders with mutual aid, and economic scrambling took precedence over the desire to rescue others. Confronted with the prospect of their extermination, the Jews of Zamojszczyzna often tried to escape by fleeing to the forests. The small groups of this largely urban population who opted for this solution, lacking any knowledge of rural or forest life, predominantly fell victims to the *Judenjagde* and the murderous rapacity of the local peasants. The few survivors were either those who avoided having to register as Jews and lived under a false Polish or Ukrainian identity, or those – fewer still – who no longer had the energy for resistance but were still fit for work, handed themselves in at a labour camp, and managed to survive the liquidation of these camps in November 1943.[42] The relief measures enacted by the civil society of Zamojszczyzna were either non-existent or ineffective. There are many indications that the massive transfers of goods and the enormous pressure exerted by the Nazis, who ruthlessly executed all who were suspected of housing Jews, made the survival of Jewish refugees in rural areas almost completely impossible. Estimates for the General Government as a whole suggest that fewer than 3,000 Jews survived in the countryside. These figures are non-existent for Zamojszczyzna, but this is equivalent to less than 10 per cent of the territory of the General Government, which makes it realistic to assume that under 10 per cent of this total – 300 Jews, 0.6 per cent of the 50,000 living in Zamojszczyzna in 1939 – survived in the forests.[43] In this respect, there were no social or ethno-national differences: rural or urban, Catholic or Greek Orthodox, Poles or Ukrainians, it was the entire non-Jewish population of Zamojszczyzna who, willingly or not, failed to assist the Jewish community during the genocide which swept across the land. Whether these communities observed with indifference, even vindictive satisfaction, the mass extermination of the Jews, and whether, by informing on them, plundering their goods, even massacring them, they played a significant part in their end, the disappearance of the Jews had an overwhelming impact on their systems of representation. The Polish majority of Zamojszczyzna, frozen by the horror of the treatment inflicted on the Jews, internalized the belief that once the extermination of the latter had ended, it would be subjected to the same treatment until the last of its members was dead. On 25 January 1943, Friedrich-Wilhelm Krüger, the HSSPF for the General Government, spoke to Hans Frank with visible satisfaction about the rumours circulating within Polish communities that, 'after the extermination of the Jews, it would be the turn of the Poles'.[44] The date here needs to be borne in mind: the Jewish community of Zamojszczyzna had ceased to exist in November 1942, eight weeks earlier. Since the same date, Action Zamość had begun. The rumour spread an eschatological anguish that spoke volumes about the narcissistic attack suffered by the Polish community of Zamojszczyzna, and about the depth of the split that now ran through the society of Zamość, since the Ukrainians felt quite immune to this existential threat.

The reaction of the communities threatened to their very foundations by an expulsion experienced as a prerequisite for extermination was twofold.

Initially, a number of Poles tried to escape their ethno-racial categorization by registering as Ukrainians in the community registers. The latter were the object of a policy that was visibly more favourable, being less subject to expulsion and the confiscation of their lands. Polish clandestine newspapers were offended by such manoeuvres.[45] Zygmunt Klukowski, who also reported this type of parade, described the reaction of the Polish community of Szczebrzeszyn to the spectacle of Action Zamość and the the waves of deportation of whole villages:

> *December 5* [1942]. Today soldiers began evacuating the villages of Polski [Ploskie] and Zawada, and they finished Wielacz [Wielacza]. People here are in a panic. They move from place to place, sleep completely clothed, and wait for the gendarmes to come. In Szczebrzeszyn the only topic of conversation is future evacuation. [. . .] People are asking what the next day will bring.
>
> *December 6.* This is the most difficult time of the last three years. People talk only about the evacuation of Szczebrzeszyn. They base their opinions on discussions overheard between gendarmes, some remarks made by the mayor, or the statements of drunken policemen. Many households are packing and leaving the city. Besides evacuation, the fear of deportation for forced labor in Germany is hanging over us. [. . .] Throughout the city horse-drawn wagons carry people escaping the forced evacuation. This morning gendarmes have gathered a number of wagons at the marketplace, pending further instructions. The atmosphere is tiring and very depressing.
>
> *December 7.* People live in panic. Some are packing and sending families to so-called safe places. Horse-drawn wagons continue to roll through the city loaded with household goods belonging to people escaping mostly from Zamosc County. [. . .]
>
> *December 8.* We ask ourselves, Where are the Germans taking the fully loaded trains of evacuees [from Zamość]? We know that the general direction is west, so it is possible there is a special camp somewhere in Germany. If this is true, an uprising by the villagers will be difficult to contain.[46]

Klukowski, an admirable chronicler, narrates the way local society started to realize, day by day, the scale of Nazi colonization plans, but he also notes the eschatological anguish of extermination, the apocalyptic feeling that seized everyone. The narcissistic wound was a consequence of the shock caused by the extermination of the Jews, and it explains a whole society's decision to try and evade the immense social-racial mechanism imagined by the ethnocrats of the UWZ and the EWZ to filter out the population. It will be recalled that UWZ chief Hermann Krumey estimated at the end of 1943 that almost 50,000 Poles and Ukrainians had been seized during the expulsion operations, only 30 to 50 per cent of the total expelled from the villages.[47] The corollary of these figures and of the reaction to the imminent and collective mortal anguish felt by the Polish peasants and city dwellers was an escape en masse to the forests; in March and April 1943, these forests were probably increasingly filled with the rustle of leaves that were providing shelter for tens of thousands of souls.

Wars of the *entre-soi* ('inter-self wars') (1943–1945)

The policies pursued by the UWZ, the KdO and the *Mannschaftshaus* of Lublin were supposed to provide a foundation for the communities of the Nazi Utopia, but also threw out onto the roads a whole society which took refuge in the woods. However, as we have noted, Zygmunt Klukowski first met with members of the resistance in the summer of 1941.[48] These were supporters of the ZWZ, the Union of Armed Struggle, which originated from units of the Polish armed forces who had gone underground after their defeat in 1939, including the two main Polish resistance movements in the region, the *Arma Krayowa* (AK) or Army of the Interior, and the *Bataliony Chlopsie* (BCh), the Peasant Battalions.[49] The two Polish formations took advantage of the influx of populations into the forest massifs and were more structured. In mid-December 1942, one of the former leaders of the pre-war secular peasant movement and leader of the great peasant strike of 1937, Franciszek Kamiński, returned to Zamość and, as the head of the Peasant Battalions, reorganized the troops and prepared the response to the operations of Germanization.[50] This was quickly noticed by the SS security officials of the district. On 16 February 1943, the head of the police battalion based in Zamość reported a Polish uprising effective since the beginning of the month. He estimated that 700–800 insurgents were operating in the south and west of the area. He concluded that the Polish police were unreliable, and was also perfectly aware that the Poles of Zamojszczyzna were convinced of the German plans for extermination. He was well informed, and quickly pointed out that the German forces present were insufficient to put an end to the uprising.[51] The level of incidents and attacks by partisans had increased since January, and the police forces were not in a position to regain control of the situation. On 28 May 1943, the civilian administrations reported a grave situation: in March and April the number of attacks rose to almost 2,000 per month and the number of partisans was estimated at 6,000 armed individuals. For Globocnik and Krüger, it had to be admitted that German colonization had come up against local resistance and that the processes of colonization and expulsion of peasant populations must be stopped.[52] We should not, however, imagine that this was a whole society united and rising as one man against the policies of the occupiers. If the Germans seemed to have lost control of the situation, we must also recognize that the insurgent forces reproduced the profound social, political, religious and ethnic splits which the Nazi ethnocrats had exploited during the whole period of the occupation. Thus, from the start of Nazi colonization in the winter of 1942–3, a multifaceted dynamic was triggered, combining enforced flows of populations, directed but ubiquitous

violence and ethno-national calculation, which made the situation intoler-
able and disruptive for all the protagonists, but remains almost illegible
for analysts. In spite of the difficulties, let us try in conclusion to restore
the logics of the process: was this not the ultimate nightmare generated
by the Nazi promise?

Confronted with a large-scale rejection of the Germanization operations,
a rejection characterized by a massive flight on the part of the Polish peasants evading the UWZ marshalling camps and the growing strength of a
resistance that was now well established in remote rural areas, notably
in Puszcza Solska, the vast forest mass south of the Zamojszczyzna,
Globocnik and the SS security forces in the region reacted brutally. At
the same time as Globocnik and Krüger were halting the settlement of
Volksdeutsche for safety reasons, the Lublin SSPF launched a major operation called *Wehrwolf* ('Werewolf') planned in two stages (*Wehrwolf* 1 and
2). *Wehrwolf* operations were in many respects a breach of previous policies. First, they combined social engineering, apparently analogous to that
pursued in previous Germanization operations, with an unprecedented
level of struggle against partisans of a kind now practised throughout Eastern Europe by the SS under the leadership of Erich von dem
Bach-Zelewski, HSSPF in charge of anti-partisan activities throughout
Europe.[53] Second, the *Wehrwolf* operations were no longer aimed at the
Germanization of the cantons of the Zamojszczyzna. The objective had in
fact fundamentally changed – and this demonstrates the disappearance
of Nazi hopes, a clear echo of the general situation: it is now necessary to
empty the districts of the South, in particular that of Biłgoraj where the
Puszcza Solska lay, of their Polish population, which comprised the main
supporters of the underground Army of the Interior and of the Peasant
Battalions, so as to settle Ukrainian peasants, including those who had
been expelled at the time of the great operation begun in November
1942.[54] The intention was now openly to set communities against one
another: the resettled Ukrainians were supposed to fight the partisans
for land, once the latter had been deprived of their supply base in the
Polish villages. The figures provided by the UWZ, which took part in
the operation by preparing to filter and 'welcome' the deported, speak
for themselves: the Poles numbered 125,833, of which only 24,584 fell
into the hands of the social engineers of expulsion, while 101,249 'could
not be captured'.[55] The huge extent of the operation was intimidating.
A police report taking stock of the security situation in the Biłgoraj area
shows the extent of the operation and provides us with a first glimpse of
its consequences:

In June–July 1943 there took place Operation *Wehrwolf* 1 and 2 in the
Biłgoraj district. On this occasion the villages occupied mainly by Poles
were besieged and the population, when they had not escaped from the
operation by fleeing into the woods, were totally expelled and taken to

Zwierzyniec, Zamość and Lublin transit camps. It can be estimated that only 50 per cent of the population at most were captured. These were essentially old men, women and children, as the younger men had taken to the woods. [. . .]

The following days can be described as disastrous in their consequences, in that the localities remained completely empty and the flocks of animals were left to themselves. The consequences were that the cattle roamed freely, which caused damage in the fields, and some were caught and slaughtered by the Poles who had taken refuge in the woods. Moreover, the refugees in the woods returned to the empty villages and took whatever they could. The houses were literally pillaged, as I was able to see for myself after a few days in Aleksandrów and Łukowa.[56]

For an operation aimed primarily at stopping supplies reaching partisan units in the Puszcza Solska, this was a bitter failure that the platoon leader did not try to hide. But this was only one of *Wehrwolf*'s goals. More fundamentally, the aim involved the relatively original strategy of regaining control of the territory by settling armed men in the villages to fight the insurgents. But as far as this second objective was concerned, the author of the report was equally negative in his analysis:

What we can see from the start is that the Ukrainian population settled there did not see what they would gain by staying – and this was made clear by a local exodus caused by harassment from bandits and the Polish population and by a lack of enthusiasm for work.

As of mid-July, attacks and robberies in (Ukrainian) settler villages began, leading to frequent exchanges of gunfire between bandits and police. The fact that these attacks and thefts were committed by the populations who had evaded the expulsion is illustrated by the Bukowina attack on 26 July 1943, during which thirty properties, including the SS 'Point of settlement and support', extending across the eight kilometres of the village, were set on fire. What can be seen retrospectively is that it was the former Polish owners who lit the fires and then fled to the forests, which made it impossible to catch them.

This attack was carried out by a gang of approximately 100 men, armed with machine guns, rifles and hand grenades. There were also attacks on the other villages, Różaniec, Łukowa and Aleksandrów, where, despite the small fort occupied by 15–20 Ukrainian police, the settlers could not prevent [the fires].[57]

The process triggered by the November 1942 expulsions, far from being blocked by the new strategy, was reinforced: the Polish resistance units were strengthened by the martyrdom that the SS formations were imposing on the rural Polish population. The situation was serious enough for elements of the Polish resistance to attack the Biłgoraj prison on 24 September 1943; and with part of the town under their control, they freed sixty-seven prisoners. The day before, the same report indicated the appearance of three small groups of insurgents and a formation of 120 people on the territory of the town.[58] Did this mean that the tactic of divide and rule had not worked, and that the AK and the BCh had taken control of the region without encountering too many obstacles? This conclusion would be misguided. First, the operations of the Polish movements remained isolated and they had no means of recapturing urban centres more than temporarily. True, they managed to create an atmosphere of insecurity in the countryside, harassing police troops and Ukrainian communities, burning villages and farming facilities, robbing and pillaging farms, but they could not sustain a frontal combat against SS formations. In the second place, as the police reports note, the operations were costly for the BCh in terms of human life: on just one day, 25 September 1943, the Germans killed thirteen resistance fighters and one Jew, shot one suspect and imprisoned three others. They had also seized two weapons, two hand grenades and a quantity of ammunition. Only two were wounded on the German side, in seventeen attacks over two days.[59]

The context of chaos and violence is indisputable. A Germanized Zamojszczyzna had no longer been a possibility since at least the spring of the same year. By launching *Wehrwolf* and renouncing the establishment of *Volksdeutsche* in the district of Zamość, had Globocnik not de facto renounced the dream? In September 1943, he was removed from Lublin at the insistence of von dem Bach-Zelewski and the new governor of the Lublin district (and Himmler's brother-in-law), Richard Wendler.[60] Our investigation could end here.

But German tactics, which consisted in setting communities against one another, had borne fruit, and in the autumn of 1943, which saw the end of the Nazi dream, the nightmare of Zamojszczyzna grew even worse.

In December 1943 the editor of the *Wehrwolf* report looked back and stated, not without malice:

The national hatred between Poles and Ukrainians was increasingly perceptible and was further aggravated by the intervention of Ukrainian police during the arrests of bandits and members of their families. After the successful arrest of two bandits by the Ukrainian police station in Łukowa, which also had two German policemen, there were several attacks. After a further attack on the post on 24 October when, after an exchange of gunfire lasting several hours, the bandits had not succeeded in storming the fort, they set the post on fire using mines and explosives and eleven Ukrainian policemen and the two German police were burned alive. In the same night, the police station in Ksieszpol was also attacked, the bandits being in both cases some hundred in number and armed with numerous heavy machine-guns.

After the terrorist acts in Łukowa there was a real panic amongst the Ukrainian population in the district, which was further increased by threatening letters in which Ukrainians were required to leave the sacred Polish soil on pain of murder and the triggering of a second Łukowa.[61]

A few days earlier, Zygmunt Klukowski had given another, perhaps somewhat broader view of what was happening: he mentioned the arrival in Szczebrzeszyn of columns of Polish refugees from nearby Volhynia where the Ukrainian insurgents of the UPA fascist organization were practising an intensely violent policy of scorched earth and ethnic cleansing. Terrible things are happening in Volhynia, wrote the old Polish doctor, and he noted that this 'terror' was drawing closer and now affected the Hrubieszów district, east of Zamojszczyzna.[62] Indeed, the practices established by the UPA on the other side of the Bug, which involved undifferentiated massacre, mass rape and the burning of property and people, plunged the whole border region into an indescribable chaos, in direct line with the Nazi practices of planned destruction. And Zamojszczyzna was not to be left out.

On 6 June, Klukowski had mentioned the refugees from Galicia and Volhynia and their 'horror stories'.[63] These stories had a profound impact, redoubled in the autumn by the involvement of the Ukrainian police and the SS 'Galicia' division, exclusively composed of Ukrainians, in the *Wehrwolf* operations. Again, the ethnocrats of the SS had fanned the embers of ethnic hatred, a hatred that now glowed all the stronger as it was enacted in the neighbouring regions. And it is one of the few published testimonies written by Polish partisans from the region that best evokes the interethnic confrontation that occurred at the end of the German occupation in Zamojszczyzna. Waldemar Lotnik had been raised in Galicia but his family lived in the canton of Hrubieszów. He was a member of a Peasant Battalion. He was due to visit his family and his uncles on Christmas Eve 1943. He described the events thus:

It was 22 December 1943, the fresh snow crunched underfoot and I discovered that I could see a mile or two away thanks to the full moon light reflected on the snow. As I approached the farm across the fields, I saw four sledges drawn by horses slipping into the yard. I was still 400 yards away when I saw two groups of men, half a dozen each, getting down from the sleds and surrounding the farmhouse. I hid in a haystack and looked and listened as the beauty of the night disappeared in the noise of a shootout. I assumed that they had come for Kasimir [his uncle] and were expecting resistance. A few bursts of gunfire continued to ring out in the fields and were followed by isolated shots. No other sound penetrated the cold night, and after what seemed to me to be several hours, the men left the house and set off on their sledges. I did not have time to count them and no means to know if all had left or if some had stayed behind. That's why I stayed in the haystack and waited for sunrise before crawling towards the building, unable to distinguish anything through the windows. I heard someone weeping and saw the door swinging on its hinges. [. . .] When I came inside, I could not believe the amount of thick, damp blood spilled on the sanded floors. It was then that I saw grandmother and Aunt Sophie.[64]

Waldemar Lotnik had just witnessed one of those very numerous murderous expeditions which fuelled a spiral of retaliation. His uncle Kasimir was one of the Polish rural notables who had joined the resistance right from the start[65] and was one of the targets of the Ukrainian militias who were trying to decimate the Polish resistance in order to eliminate its capacity to respond to the planned ethnic cleansing. Waldemar Lotnik continues:

Bit by bit, they told me what had happened. After breaking down the door, the undesirable visitors from the local Ukrainian militia had dragged Kasimir into the living room where they had beaten him with a rifle butt, threatening to break his teeth. [. . .] Kasimir was the biggest catch and so he was the one subjected to the worst punishment. They had no intention of really questioning him, as the repeated ferocity of their blows meant that he was quickly unable to speak. 'Death to the *Lacki*', they shouted, raining down blows upon him. I was practically unable to recognize his body when I saw him. His face had ceased to be a face: all his teeth were missing, each bone was broken, his jaw had been wrenched back, his nose and mouth had been torn off and the bones of his legs, arms and hands had been broken into fragments emerging from the blood-stained skin that hung from his body.[66]

We are here in the theatre of cruelty that Véronique Nahoum-Grappe and Denis Crouzet have each closely studied: the former, an anthropologist, has insisted on the necessity, for the murderer, of cruelty, of his excessive use of a violence going beyond murder to accomplish his project,[67] while the latter, a historian of the St Bartholomew's Day Massacre, encourages the observer to analyse the gestures of violence as a language allowing us to gain access to the murderer's system of representations.[68] In this case, it is important to note that, on the one hand, violence is dramatized, that it takes place only in the presence of spectators whom it is meant to terrorize, and on the other hand, that it aims, by carrying out acts of aggression on the face and the limbs, to deny any human character to the victim, who is thus reduced to being a *cruor*, a shapeless mash of flesh which, in the eyes of the killers, comprises the Polish resistance fighter they are eliminating. The testimony continues:

My grandmother had stayed in another room, where the others, Anthony, his wife Helena, Aunt Sophie and Anthony's three daughters were cowering. She was praying before an image of the Virgin and begging that her son be spared. 'Go ahead! Pray to your old whore and see if that can save him!' the intruders yelled. Once they had finished beating Kasimir, they pushed him into the room, finished him off with bayonets, and shot half a dozen bullets into his body. Then they came after Anthony, who would have had plenty of time to flee. But as he knew that the killers would have avenged his flight on his wife and children, he had waited his turn. They did not use torture. [. . .] He was taken out of the room and killed by several bullets.[69]

The rest of the family was spared, but Waldemar Lotnik, filled with hatred for the Ukrainians, swore, on the day of the funeral, to avenge his uncles. Violence is often a local affair: when he went with his aunt Sophie to his landlady, a beautiful crippled Polish woman whose lover was a Ukrainian captain, Sophie whispered to him that the captain in question was none other than the man who had uttered the tirade against the 'old whore' to his grandmother. So he was the ringleader of the killers.[70] He was a captain in the police, a collaborator by day, an infernal leader of columns at night, and he clearly embodied the practices of violence deployed by the UPA in Galicia and Volhynia, practices that were now being imported into Zamojszczyzna, and the central role assumed by the Germans in the promotion of men in the service of a project of total ethnic war against the Poles. Lotnik continues his narrative thus:

I set off to join my unit. It was a fifteen-mile walk and I arrived in the early evening. The sergeant of my section told me he was sorry to hear what had happened to my uncles and regretted that he had not been there to help. I nodded and went to drink vodka with the others. Everyone knew that something was going to happen. Towards 9 o'clock we set out for Modryn, where the officer assembled the sections to give them orders.

'Do not burn, do not loot. Shoot only young men of an age to bear arms. If someone resists, be sure to shoot before you are shot. We have to teach them that they cannot select and take away Poles to torture and kill them. We have to teach them that they can't get away with it.'

They had killed seven men two nights before, and we killed sixteen of their number, including an eight-year-old schoolboy. He died accidentally when shots were fired through a door. He got caught in the line of fire, it was a mistake. There were three hundred of us and we did not encounter any resistance or suffer any loss. Most of us knew people in Modryn. We knew who was pro-Nazi, and who was a Ukrainian nationalist militant. We took them prisoner.

A week later, the Ukrainians replied by completely destroying a Polish colony, burning the houses, killing the inhabitants who were unable to flee, and raping the women who fell into their hands, whether they were young or old. This was the behaviour they had adopted on the other side of the Bug River, where tens of thousands of Poles had been expelled or killed. We replied by attacking an even larger village, and this time two or three of our men killed women and children. Some of them were so full of hatred after losing entire generations of their families in the Ukrainian attacks they had sworn to take an eye for an eye and a tooth for a tooth. For my part, I felt no remorse in what happened: it was war and revenge. The Ukrainians took their revenge by destroying a village of 500 Poles. [. . .] We responded with the destruction of two of their biggest villages. They then assembled their forces for a simultaneous attack on five Polish villages and this time they were joined by a regiment trained by Germans east of the Bug. [. . .] So the fighting escalated. [. . .] On both sides, adolescents were the worst perpetrators of atrocities. [. . .] Special treatment was always reserved for women. Rape is an instinctive privilege of the conqueror, his way of defiling and possessing his victim, and murder and sex are intrinsically linked.[71]

The account that the young resistance fighter gives then describes unflinchingly the atrocities inflicted by Ukrainians and Poles in this civil war with ethnic underpinnings. Victims were impaled or raped; women who had compromised themselves with men from the other side had their heads shaved, and then were executed; attacks on the female genital organs were extremely frequent: everything, in this war, was aimed at undermining the social bond. It was the community of the Other that was the target of the mutilating fury of the combatants. To attack women and children is to destroy the foundation of communities; it is to undermine transmission and filiation, it is to destroy the other, but it is *also* a way of reconfiguring one's own community.

Anthropologist Pierre Clastres has brilliantly shown that war is a structural tool used by non-state societies to keep their forms of social organization unchanged, by counteracting the centripetal dynamics of matrimonial alliances enlarging human societies to the point where they are obliged to resort to state organization:[72] war marks the boundary between those with whom a group makes an alliance, exchanging women, information and goods, and those with whom war is waged and with whom exchange does not exist, but gives way to predation: rape instead of wedding or alliance; torture instead of exchange of information; looting instead of goods-trading. War thus keeps unbreached the boundaries of the home group. By this measure, in the devastated Zamojszczyzna of 1943–4, it was the *volksdeutsche*, Nazi, Communist, Nationalist, Polish and Ukrainian communities that were reconfiguring themselves in a process of tearing apart and mutilation.[73] If the Nazi 'community' no longer even appears in the narrative of the young resistance fighter, it is indeed two antagonistic forms of national community which, through the mutilation of their wives, the murder of their respective children and the decimation of their men, exclude alliances – this is the meaning of these rituals of shaving the heads of women who have slept with outsiders – and are rearranged in a foundational confrontation and violence founders.

An 'inter-self war'? 'Inter-self wars', more exactly. The story of Waldemar Lotnik did not stop in the first half of 1944 when the BCh and the Ukrainian militia, soon backed up by the UPA formations from Volhynia and Galicia, clashed in a great ethnic war. He does not mention two variables in the equation. The first variable is this: the Germans have practically disappeared from his narrative while they continue to play a fundamental role of support for the Ukrainians, hoping always their bet would pay off, hoping that only exhausted fighters would be left at the end. And the second variable: during the first half of 1944, movements of Communist partisans from Ukraine and Belarus infiltrated the General Government and Zamojszczyzna, joining up with the few groups of Red Army fighters who had escaped from the camps and forming an entity of increasing importance.[74]

In the summer of 1944, a great number of wars of community were waged by all against all, arising from the ethnic game of dominoes played by the SS since 1941: the war of the Polish 'bourgeois' formations of the AK and the BCh against Ukrainian nationalist formations; the war of the left-wing Polish formations against the Ukrainians, the AK and the BCh; the war of the UPA Ukrainians against the Poles, civilians and resistant fighters, and against the Soviet partisans; the struggle of all to impose, through blood and the dramatic division of bodies and social and ethnic groups, their own vision of the future of the communities that were to possess Zamojszczyzna. Wars of all against all, these intercommunity wars were indeed the paroxysmal and teratological offspring of the advent of the Nazi Utopia. Nazi racial determinism had dreamed of a Nordic, agrarian and colonial Zamojszczyzna. Instead, it had triggered the fires of hatred, which only the 'migrations of people (*remues d'hommes*)',[75] the exchange of populations, stabilized between September 1944, when the border was fixed, and August 1947, the date of the end of Operation Vistula that completed the flow of forced migration. An extension of the Nazi dream by the persistence of the methods introduced by the SS officers of the RKFdV and the EWZ, this exchange of populations – but this is another story[76] – constituted the only strategy envisaged by the governments to stabilize an area that the ogre Globocnik had plunged into an immense ethnic blaze. The Nazi dream had become the nightmare of the borderlands.

Conclusion

Our investigation ends here, in a blaze of despair and hatred, with wagons jolting along the roads of wandering that lead to the displacement camps. Sometimes stumbling, always a little hesitant, it will have led us from the mists of foundation to those fires that the observer of this tormented beginning of the twenty-first century knows have never really gone out. At the end of these 1,399 days, several massive facts seem to emerge.

The first could be the intensity of the Nazi investment in its imperial hope, its own plans for a sociobiological refoundation of German nationhood. Between September and November 1939, and then at the beginning of 1942, in two main phases, the essential institutions for creating the new Reich and the *Volksgemeinschaft* were created. While some of them pre-existed, such as security institutions and the RuSHA, all were subject to complex reorganizations designed to adapt them to the changing horizons of Nazi expectations and to the new European scope of action of the Third Reich. The RSHA, RKFdV, WVHA, EWZ and UWZ formed a constellation of institutions that federated utopian energies, police know-how, and racial and logistical practices, and mobilized them for a policy that would bring about the *Volksgemeinschaft* in a Nazi Europe that now stretched out to the East. They endorsed SS control over Nazi policies in this area and conditioned their characteristics: the future would be Nordic, elitist, warlike and – this was less easy to see – *gottgläubig*.

This institutional nebula constituted a world in itself, the world of Nazi hope. It was a world of women as well as men: of the thirty thousand people who invested in it, often but not always in a voluntary and militant way, about half were women or girls who were anxious to come and help the migrants of the *Heim ins Reich*, and thus to incarnate this *Volksgemeinschaft* full of kindness and solicitude which they hoped to help bring about. Nazi care was an inevitable reality in the experience of these young people of both sexes who took part in the *Osteinsatz*, as students or as young activists. One must be careful not to see this as the only aspect of

Nazi hope. Their profile is marked by a very high degree of generational coherence, representative of the great achievements of recent historiography. The Nazi revolution was inevitably a matter of young people, and fifty-year-olds already seemed somewhat elderly in this world, faced with forty-year-olds who held immense responsibilities, and those young people who had just emerged from adolescence who comprised the foot soldiers of the army of Nordic hopes. A well-trained army, many of whom were university graduates and, in all the great institutions of the SS, could boast diplomas, which reinforced its claim to excellence and which gave its ideological radicality a specific hue.

Finally, this study will have allowed us to take a slightly less impressionistic look at the emotional universe of this world in itself, to conceive at least here and there the intensity of the fervour that seized many of these actors when, in a camp of migrants, a return trek, a *Siedlung* of peasant-soldiers, or simply a research office, they had the feeling of bringing about the empire, of *keeping* the promise of reign. In short, it seems that we have been able to advance a little in this social anthropology of Nazi emotions without which, we are convinced, it is hardly possible to account for the coherence of the behaviour of those who, one day, internalized this belief made up of racial determinism, eschatological anxiety and imperial expectation.

The Nazi dream, as this cohort of some thirty thousand people tried to make it happen, was first and foremost a 'migration of people', which became more and more immense as the conquest progressed. Initiated in the form of the Germanization of two provinces incorporated into the Reich in November 1939, the history of the advent of Utopia was first of all its spread on an unprecedented scale, from the Arctic Circle to the Black Sea, from the great plains of Central Asia to the Seine, from the Alps to the marshes of St Petersburg and the Urals. At the end of the revolution of history which was comprised by this process of racial regeneration, 600 million Nordic Germans were to occupy this immense territory with all the happy frugality of the *Volksgemeinschaft*. This was the vision of the Nazi promise, which could not, however, have happened without gigantic displacements of non-native and inferior populations, without the untrammelled selection of a racial heritage as excellent as it was fragile, and without practices of ethnomorphosis and depopulation which were the paroxystic and murderous reverse side of the Nazi refoundation project: at the height of Nazi ambition, the advent of the *Tausendjähriges Reich* involved the expulsion of 31 million people and the more or less rapid death of 25 million sacrificed in its name.

The great specificity of the Nazi Utopia was that the militants believed themselves in a position to make it happen during the 1,399 days that form the framework of our inquiry, and a non-negligible part of it consisted in writing the history of the successive failures of all attempts at the realization of Utopia. There was the failure of the short-term plans between 1939 and January 1941, the failure of the Madagascar Plan in the summer of 1940, the failure of the building projects of Odilo Globocnik and those of Hans Kammler and the WVHA; the failure, finally, of the huge famine policies hatched by the *Wehrmacht*, the SS and the Nazi political leaders. The only almost completed plan was, tragically, that of the exhaustive extermination of European Judaism, which became a prerequisite for the imperial and utopian Nazi dream to be realized, and which, as regards its Polish part, was implemented until what the Nazis believed was its end with Operation Reinhard. These incessant and bloody failures were always transcended by the establishment of a broader, more ambitious, more murderous plan, a true illustration of what the late Hans Mommsen called cumulative radicalization.

The fact remains that, at a certain moment in the first half of 1943, Nazi hope seems to have gradually vanished. The horizon of expectation and the temporal regime in which the actors of these policies moved underwent a decisive change: the main time frame was no longer the future, the present of struggle arose again, and the imperious necessity to invest in total and immediate mobilization in a war that was being fought *here and now* took over from the advent of tomorrow. Hope did not disappear, but it was subordinated to the demands of the moment.

From the large-scale views of the research offices of the RKFdV and Konrad Meyer-Heitling, the Master of Plans, to the local detail of the barracks put up for the so-called homecoming of the *Volksdeutsche*, we have needed to vary the scales and perspectives. This was the only method by which we could hope to grasp the whole set of the elements constituting the object of our study. Only at the large scale can we assess the extent and scale of the Nazi project, the complexity of the rivalry between institutions and their radicalizing impulses; only at the local level can one grasp the complexities of the mechanisms involved, the profusion of the determinants that come into play, the indescribable richness of the actors' experiences. This variety shows us that the historian's inquiry is imprisoned by a mechanism that could be compared to Heisenberg's uncertainty principle. The German physicist had formalized the non-commutability of the operators of a wave function in quantum physics, indicating that the theory itself definitively ruled out obtaining, within the same measurement of a system, precise results giving the position and momentum of a particle simultaneously. In a quantum system, therefore, if one obtains precise information about the position at a moment t of a particle, one can only very imperfectly acquire an idea of its momentum, while the converse is also true: if the momentum p of a particle is measured with great precision, we can obtain only vague information about its position x. The precision of one is inversely proportional to that of the other. Thus, during our investigation, we willingly or unwillingly had to get used to the mediocre quality of the information delivered by sets of documents dealing with the big picture when it came to the local interactions caused by their actions. Similarly, it would have been unwise to ask sets of documents constituted by local actors to give us information on the circumlocutions of the plans being laid by the RKFdV. This is at least partly the meaning of our attempt to grasp the most complete attempts to realize the Nazi dream through the study of the most advanced of the SS laboratories, namely Zamojszczyzna.

This territory on the Polish–Ukrainian borders, an archetype of the interweaving of the religious, national and social communities of the imperial territories before the Great War, initially struck us as the locus of the hypothetical encounter between the dynamics from above and those from below: the observer can discern the radical impulses coming from the top of the Nazi hierarchy, notably through Himmler's visit on 16 July 1941 to Lublin, where the Majdanek camp was being built, where the plans for the Germanization of the district by large movements of population were being settled, where the building programmes and activism of Globocnik and his men were being granted approval. But the encounter is also an opportunity to take stock of the equally radical initiatives taken from below by the SSPF and approved by the *Reichsführer*: in this sense, the event, the encounter, is in itself a kind of interaction between the two levels.

Zamojszczyzna was thus the object of a set of practices which made it specific, right from a very early stage in the history of the occupation. The Jews of the region were first subjected to a treatment that can be analysed as a ritual procedure of symbolic domestication, which, in the eyes of the Nazis, amounted to treating them as a mass of individuals akin to a herd: only their capacity for work and reproduction counted. Confinement, branding and forced labour constituted an animalistic treatment which, for the Nazis, made the sending of these communities to gassing facilities at Bełżec and Sobibór from March 1942 onwards tantamount to a practice of slaughtering cattle. The genocide in the region was as early, brutal and comprehensive as it was highly demonstrative: Globocnik and his men had made the extermination of Jewish communities the visible prerequisite for the start of large-scale displacement operations in Polish communities which constituted the first step in a policy of resettling the *Volksdeutsche*, through the mechanism of the EWZ racial assessment, in villages with reassembled lands. The concatenation of the two major social engineering operations, one against the Jews, involving total extermination, and the other against the Poles, with a view to purification, provoked a mortal dread of their own imminent deaths in the Polish population, reflected in a massive and absolute refusal to allow themselves to be captured after their expulsion. It was therefore a large number of Zamojszczyzna inhabitants who took the roads to the forest and its refuge to escape from Action Zamość. The SS, unintentionally, thus gave a fundamental impulse to the resistance of the AK and the BCh. What they did do deliberately and continuously, however, was stir up the endemic ethno-national dispute between the Polish majority and the Ukrainian minority, relying on the latter for all oppressive operations against the Poles. The last stage of this Faustian calculation, given the failure of the settlement of the *Volksdeutsche* of the Nordic revival in Zamojszczyzna, consisted in relocating Ukrainians to Polish villages during Operation *Wehrwolf* and driving them to stoke the flames of ethnic hatred.

The summer of 1944 struck us as what we could call, inspired by Pierre Clastres and Françoise Héritier, the 'guerres de l'*entre-soi*' or 'inter-self wars', i.e. the wars of those with specific shared values and the same ethnic identity waged by all against all: the war of the Poles loyal to London against the Germans, the Ukrainians of the UPA, the formations infiltrated by the NKVD (the Soviet Union's Interior Ministry) and the Red Army; the war of the UPA against the Poles and the 'Reds', whether these were Polish or Soviet; the pending Soviet war against the Polish and nationalist Ukrainian formations; the war of the Germans against all; and the war, finally, of all or almost all against the few Jews surviving in the forests; atrocious wars where representations of the future of antagonistic communities vied with one another, where the redefinition of communities and their environments – who should one form an alliance with, who should one wage war on so as not to make an alliance with them and thus preserve one's integrity? – involved an attack on social ties, filiation and alliance; wars against the anthropological foundations of societies prompt to sexually assault the enemy's women, the locus of the transformation of the alliance into filiation, the place of reproduction of the community, now become a battlefield by the systematic use of rape. These 'inter-self wars' produced an extremely graphic violence, resorting massively to practices of the most spectacular cruelty, in which children also constituted a target of choice in that the attack on their bodies was an attack on the future and the integrity of the enemy.

The Nazis, in the last instance, were hoping to win at the end of this struggle that would leave their racial enemies exhausted; Ukrainians and Poles hoped to emerge as sole victors and possessors of Zamojszczyzna at the end of this ubiquitous conflict; and the 'liberators' of the Red Army and the Polish Communist elements wanted to subjugate this whole world to the Soviet victors of the war. All, however, whether actors or observers of this paroxysm of violence, agreed basically on one thing and one thing alone: the only outcome of such a confrontation would come through the use of a single instrument: population displacements. SS officers, Ukrainian fascists, NKVD agents, Soviet and English statesmen and Polish insurgents imagined that only the wagons of the 'migration of people' would achieve their ends, in a great homogenizing tide. In the summer of 1944, the Nazi policy of Germanization had finally imposed on all Eastern Europe a national homogenization. It had begun as the utopian dream of the refounding of German nationhood; it sought to set itself up as an immense operation of socio-racial engineering aiming at the extermination of the Jews and, probably, nearly 17 million Slavs; and it stumbled from failure to failure. In the last instance, it succeeded solely in bringing fire and bloodshed to Eastern Europe, subjecting it to a martyrdom of violence, and throwing almost an entire continent out onto the roads of wandering and despair.

The Nazi Utopia plunged Europe into a darkness from which the continent found the strength to emerge and build a future. It is undoubtedly this that we need to remember, in our own 'times of damned algebra',[1] made up of the wars of the Middle Eastern homelands, the despairing refugees on our borders, the spread of policies of renunciation or abandonment, and existential darkness.

Paris, 22 February 2016

Notes

Introduction

1 'Mort d'un nazi', lexpress.fr, 7 April 2010: http://www.lexpress.fr/actualite/societe/mort-d-un-nazi_882739.html.

2 Michael Wildt, *Generation des Unbedingten: Das Führungskorps des Reichssicherheitshauptamtes* (Hamburg: Hamburger Edition, 2002).

3 Christian Ingrao, *Believe and Destroy: Intellectuals in the SS War Machine*, trans. Andrew Brown (Cambridge: Polity, 2013).

4 Markus Leniger, *Nationalsozialistische 'Volkstumsarbeit' und Umsiedlungspolitik 1933–1945: Von der Minderheitenbetreuung zur Siedlerauslese* (Berlin: Frank & Timme, 2006), pp. 148–54.

5 See for example: Götz Aly, *Final Solution: Nazi Population Policy and the Murder of the European Jews*, trans. Belinda Cooper and Allison Brown (London: Arnold, 1999); Édouard Conte and Cornelia Essner, *La Quête de la race: Une anthropologie du nazisme* (Paris: Hachette, 1998); Jan Erik Schulte, *Zwangsarbeit und Vernichtung. Das Wirtschaftsimperium der SS: Oswald Pohl und das SS-Wirtschafts-Verwaltungshauptamt* (Paderborn: Ferdinand Schöningh, 2001); Bogdan Musial, *Deutsche Zivilverwaltung und Judenverfolgung im General-Gouvernement: Eine Fallstudie zum Distrikt Lublin* (Wiesbaden: Harrassowitz, 1999); Elizabeth Harvey, *Women and the Nazi East: Agents and Witnesses of Germanization* (New Haven, CT: Yale University Press, 2003); Elizabeth Harvey, *'Der Osten braucht dich!' Frauen und nationalsozialistische Germanisierungspolitik* (Hamburg: Hamburger Edition, 2010); and Czesław Madajczyk, *Die Okkupationspolitik Nazideutschlands in Polen 1939–1945* (East Berlin: Akademie Verlag, 1987). See also, more recently: Johann Chapoutot, *La Loi du sang: Penser et agir en nazi* (Paris: Gallimard, 2014); Isabel Heinemann, *'Rasse, Siedlung, deutsches Blut': Der Rasse- und Siedlungshauptamt der SS und die rassenpolitische Neuordnung Europas* (Göttingen: Wallstein, 2003); Leniger, *Nationalsozialistische 'Volkstumsarbeit'*; and Elissa Mailänder, '"Going East": Colonial Experiences and Practices of Violence among Female and Male Majdanek Camp Guards (1941–44)', *Journal of Genocide Research*, 10 (2008), pp. 563–82.

6 The following works have been of fundamental significance: Czesław

Madajczyk (ed.), *Vom Generalplan Ost zum Generalsiedlungsplan* (Munich: Saur Verlag, Einzelveröffentlichungen der Historischen Kommission zu Berlin), vol. 80, 1994; Czesław Madajczyk (ed.), *Zamojszczyzna – Sonderlaboratorium SS: Zbior dokumentow polskich i niemieckich z okresu okupacji hitlerowskiej* (Warsaw: Ludowa Spoldzielnia Widawnicza, 1979), 2 vols (my thanks to Maciej Hamela for obtaining a copy of this rare work for me).

7 Aly, *Final Solution.*

8 Christopher Browning, *Ordinary Men: Reserve Police Battalion 101 and the Final Solution in Poland* (London: Penguin, 2001); Daniel Goldhagen, *Hitler's Willing Executioners: Ordinary Germans and the Holocaust* (London: Little, Brown, 1996); and for a (somewhat dated) overview of *Täterforschung*, Gerhard Paul (ed.), *Die Täter der Shoah: Fanatische Nationalsozialisten oder ganz normale Deutsche?* (Göttingen: Wallstein, 2003).

9 Götz Aly, *Hitler's Beneficiaries: Plunder, Racial War, and the Nazi Welfare State*, trans. Jefferson Chase (London: Verso, 2007).

10 Frank Bajohr and Michael Wildt, *Volksgemeinschaft: Neue Forschungen zur Gesellschaft des Nationalsozialismus* (Frankfurt: Fischer, 2009), especially the introduction.

11 Heinemann, *'Rasse, Siedlung, deutsches Blut'.*

12 Quentin Deluermoz and Pierre Singaravélou, *Pour une histoire des possibles: Analyses contrefactuelles et futurs non advenus* (Paris: Seuil, 2016).

13 Christopher Menaul, *Fatherland*, 1994, starring Rütger Hauer among others.

Prologue

1 Princess Irulan, in Frank Herbert, *Dune* (London: Gollancz, 1966).

2 Information taken from the entry on 'moment' in the *Grand Larousse universel en 15 volumes* (Paris: Larousse, 1984), vol. 10, p. 7031.

3 The others comprise a general chronology of the Second World War, the essential framework for the development of the Nazi hope.

4 See the pioneering study by G. Aly, *Aktion T4 – 1939–1945: Die 'Euthanasie'-Zentrale in der Tiergartenstraße 4* (Berlin: Edition Hentrich, 1989).

5 Among the many studies on this topic, see Ulrich Herbert, *Best: Biographische Studien über Radikalismus, Weltanschauung und Vernunft* (Bonn: Dietz, 1996), and Michael Wildt, *Generation des Unbedingten: Das Führungskorps des Reichssicherheitshauptamtes* (Hamburg: Hamburger Edition, 2002).

6 For SA, SS and other abbreviations and acronyms, please see appendix 1; for an organizational chart of SS institutions, please see appendix 2. (Translator's note.)

7 On all these questions, see Robert Lewis Koehl, *The Black Corps: The Structure and Power Struggles of the Nazi SS* (Madison: University of Wisconsin Press, 1983). On the SS takeover of behind-the-scenes diplomacy, see Hans-Adolf Jacobsen, *National-sozialistische Außenpolitik. 1933–38* (Frankfurt: Alfred Metzner, 1968).

8 George C. Browder, *Hitler's Enforcers: The Gestapo and the SS Security Service in*

the Nazi Revolution (Oxford and New York: Oxford University Press, 1996); and Wildt, *Generation des Unbedingten*; see also M. Wildt, *Die Judenpolitik des SD, 1935–1938: Eine Dokumentation* (Munich: Oldenbourg, 1995).

9 Markus Leniger, *Nationalsozialistische 'Volkstumsarbeit' und Umsiedlungspolitik 1933–1945: Von der Minderheitenbetreuung zur Siedlerauslese* (Berlin: Frank & Timme, 2006).

10 See Götz Aly, *Final Solution: Nazi Population Policy and the Murder of the European Jews*, trans. Belinda Cooper and Allison Brown (London: Arnold, 1999).

11 These debates are discussed in Herbert, *Best*, Wildt, *Generation des Unbedingten*, and Christian Ingrao, *Believe and Destroy: Intellectuals in the SS War Machine*, trans. Andrew Brown (Cambridge: Polity, 2013).

12 Wildt, *Generation des Unbedingten*, pp. 259–82.

13 This is documented in the report written jointly by the *Sonderreferat* IV R (future *Referat* IV D-4, later IV B-4 under Eichmann) and the *Sondergruppe* ES (future *Gruppe* III B under Hans Ehlich) on the meeting held on 30 January 1940, Bundesarchiv Berlin-Lichterfelde, (BABL), R-58/1032.

14 The two quotations are taken from the orders issued on 7 October 1939 and quoted in Isabel Heinemann, *'Rasse, Siedlung, deutsches Blut': Der Rasse- und Siedlungshauptamt der SS und die rassenpolitische Neuordnung Europas* (Göttingen: Wallstein, 2003), pp. 190–1.

15 Heinemann, *'Rasse, Siedlung, deutsches Blut'*, pp. 190–1.

16 Memorandum issued by Ehlich, 1 November 1939, BABL, R-69/493, fos. 6ff.

17 Martin Broszat, *The Hitler State: The Foundation and Development of the Internal Structure of the Third Reich*, trans. John W. Hiden (London: Longman, 1981).

18 On the HSSPF, see Ruth Bettina Birn, *Die höheren SS- und Polizeiführer: Himmlers Vertreter im Reich und in den besetzten Gebieten* (Düsseldorf: Droste, 1986).

19 See the details in Aly, *Final Solution*.

20 BABL, R-43 II/1412, fo. 53; Aly, *Final Solution*, p. 63; see also n. 20.

21 BABL, film no. 14906 (documents EWZ Poznań and Gotenhafen, Settlement of the *Volksdeutsche* of Volhynia and the Baltic countries). These films can be consulted on demand at the Bundesarchiv but the documents held there on microfilm are also available in the R-69 collection. I hope the reader will forgive me for not supplying the links between the films and the documents on paper.

22 See the organizational chart showing the 'SS institutions of Utopia' in appendix 2.

23 Aly, *Final Solution*.

24 Memorandum from Ehlich, 1 November 1939, BABL, R-69/493.

25 On the RSHA's planning, see Karl Heinz Roth, '"Generalplan Ost" – "Gesamtplan Ost": Forschungsstand, Quellenproblem, neue Ergebnisse', in Mechtild Rössler and Sabine Schleiermacher (eds.), *Der 'Generalplan Ost': Hauptlinien der nationalsozialistischen Planungs- und Vernichtungspolitik* (Berlin: Akademie Verlag, 1993).

26 Circular from Koppe, 12 November 1939.

27 Circular from Heydrich, quoted by Karl Heinz Roth, Introduction, in '"Generalplan Ost" und der Mord an den Juden: Der "Fernplan um der

Umsiedlung in den Ostprovinzen" aus dem Reichssicherheitshauptamt vom November 1939', *1999: Zeitschrift für Sozialgeschichte des 20. und 21. Jahrhunderts*, 12 (1997), pp. 50–70.

28 BABL, R-69/1146: Fernplan Ost; Karl Heinz Roth, the 'discoverer' of this document, published it *in extenso* in his Introduction (see n. 26).

29 Order no. I/II, RKFdV, 30 October 1939, quoted in Heinemann, *'Rasse, Siedlung, deutsches Blut'*, p. 192, and in Roth, '"Generalplan Ost" und der Mord an den Juden', p. 56.

30 I am here closely following Aly, *Final Solution*.

31 United States Holocaust Memorial Museum (USHMM), RG-15.015 M (collection AGKBZH 68), roll no. 2, call no. 68/97, fos. 1–7.

32 Aly, *Final Solution*.

33 Order issued by Koppe, 14 January 1940, USHMM, RG-15.015 M (collection AGKBZH 68), roll no. 2: UWZ Poznań, box 97. See also Aly, *Final Solution*.

34 Report on the Ehlich/Eichmann discussion, signed by Ehlich, 17 January 1940, Bundesarchiv Dahlwitz-Hoppegarten (BADH), ZR/890, A. 2: Document EWZ, RSHA: Sammlung zum Krumeys Prozeß, fos. 218–20.

35 USHMM, RG-15.015 M (collection AGKBZH 68), roll no. 1, call no. 68/94, fos. 8–10. The documents give details of the daily routine for the transports over the twenty-two days of the plan.

36 See Aly, *Final Solution*.

37 BABL, R-49/157, reproduced in Czesław Madajczyk (ed.), *Vom Generalplan Ost zum Generalsiedlungsplan* (Munich: Saur Verlag, Einzelveröffentlichungen der Historischen Kommission zu Berlin), vol. 80, 1994, pp. 3–14, where he dates it, without much evidence, to May 1940. I am here following the date given in Aly, *Final Solution*, p. 81.

38 BABL, R-49/157, fo. 2; Madajczyk, *Vom Generalplan Ost*, p. 3.

39 It was this action that would soon become the second *Nahplan*.

40 Joint memorandum issued by Ehlich and Eichmann reporting the meeting, in BABL, R-58/1032.

41 Aly, *Final Solution*.

42 Himmler gave the total number as 1 million and Meyer-Heitling's plan put the long-term figure at 3.4 million Poles and 560,000 Jews.

43 Aly, *Final Solution*.

44 Dieter Pohl, *Von der 'Judenpolitik' zum Judenmord: Der Distrikt Lublin des Generalgouvernement. 1939–1944* (Frankfurt: Peter Lang, 1993), p. 81; Thomas Sandkühler, *'Endlösung' in Galizien: Der Judenmord in Ostpolen und die Rettungsintiativen von Berthold Beitz 1941–1944* (Bonn: Dietz, 1996).

45 Minutes of the session of 12 February 1940, Document 305 EC, in *Trial of the Major War Criminals* (TMWC), vol. 36, pp. 299–307.

46 Order issued by Heydrich on 19 February 1940, quoted in a letter written by Goering on 4 March 1940. See Aly, *Final Solution*.

47 Aly, *Final Solution*. On 8 April, a letter from the head of the bureau for population movements of the civil administration of Warsaw mentions the fact that there was no longer any question of assembling the Jews in the Lublin region. Details in Aly, *Final Solution*.

48 USHMM, RG-15.015 M (collection AGKBZH 68), roll no. 2, call no. 68/97 for the second *Nahplan*.

49 Concluding report on the third *Nahplan*; summary report on the second *Nahplan*, in USHMM, RG-15.015 M (collection AGKBZH 68), roll no. 3, call no. 68/227.

50 *Sondergruppe* ES had become the RSHA *Amt* III B on 21 March 1940 and Ehlich had written a long memorandum on the organization and the missions of a potential UWZ on 2 February 1940: BADH, ZR/890, A.2, here fos. 210–17, and Aly, *Final Solution*.

51 See the analysis in Aly, *Final Solution*.

52 On the Madagascar Plan, see Magnus Brechtken, *'Madagaskar für die Juden': Antisemitische Idee und politische Praxis 1885–1945* (Munich: Oldenbourg, 1997).

53 Aly, *Final Solution*; Leniger, *Nationalsozialistische 'Volkstumsarbeit'*; see also Heinemann, *'Rasse, Siedlung, deutsches Blut'*, pp. 232–301.

54 See Aly, *Final Solution*, and Leniger, *Nationalsozialistische 'Volkstumsarbeit'*.

55 See Brechtken, *'Madagaskar für die Juden'*, p. 142.

56 There is a very detailed account of the meeting and a presentation of the minutes in Michael Alberti, *Die Verfolgung und Vernichtung der Juden im Reichsgau Wartheland 1939–1945* (Wiesbaden: Harrassowitz, 2006), pp. 241–2.

57 Aly, *Final Solution*; Alberti, *Die Verfolgung und Vernichtung der Juden*, p. 240.

58 So long, of course, as we ignore all the concrete considerations that come into play, including the reactions of local populations.

59 This is brilliantly demonstrated by Brechtken, *'Madagaskar für die Juden'*, pp. 251–2.

60 I take this expression from Karl A. Schleunes, *The Twisted Road to Auschwitz: Nazi Policy Toward German Jews, 1933–1939* (Champaign: University of Illinois Press, 1990).

61 Aly, *Final Solution*; Ralf Meindl, *Ostpreußens Gauleiter: Erich Koch – eine politische Biographie* (Osnabrück: Fibre, 2007), pp. 289–90.

62 Note by Eichmann, BABL, NS-19/3979, no fo. no., mentioned in Aly, *Final Solution*.

63 Document reproduced in Hans-Adolf Jacobsen, 'Kommissarbefehl und Massenexekution sowjetischer Kriegsgefangener', in Hans Buchheim et al. (eds.), *Anatomy of the SS State*, trans. Dorothy Long and Marian Jackson (London and New York: Granada, 1970).

64 Himmler's desk diary, BABL, NS-19/3954; quoted in Aly, *Final Solution*.

65 The question of the key figures of the third *Nahplan* is complex and a complete set of figures is provided in Aly, *Final Solution*. See also the report on the meeting of 8 January 1941, in USHMM, RG-15.015 M (collection AGKBZH 68), roll no. 1, call no. 68/97, and roll no. 2, call no. 68/227.

66 Aly, *Final Solution*.

67 See the monumental work by Christian Gerlach, *Kalkulierte Morde: Die deutsche Wirtschafts- und Vernichtungspolitik in Weißrußland* (Hamburg: Hamburger Edition, 1999).

68 Dieter Pohl stated this most clearly in a short introductory article, 'Die Einsatzgruppe C', in Peter Klein (ed.), *Die Einsatzgruppen in der besetzten*

Sowjetunion 1941/42: Die Tätigkeits- und Lageberichte des Chefs der Sicherheitspolizei und des SD (Berlin: Edition Hentrich, 1997), pp. 71–87 (p. 73).

69 Aly, *Final Solution*.
70 For further details, see the huge work by Roth, '"Generalplan Ost" – "Gesamtplan Ost"', pp. 25–118.
71 Letter from Meyer-Heitling to Himmler, 15 July 1941, BABL, NS-19/1739, published in Madajczyk, *Vom Generalplan Ost*, pp. 14–15. This document is sometimes called the 'second' *Generalplan Ost* in reference to the first general planning document, the 'General Planning Principles for the Occupied Territories in the East', delivered by Meyer-Heitling at the beginning of 1940. This *Generalplan Ost*, however, is mentioned only by Roth, and while we do have the letter accompanying the delivery of this plan by Meyer-Heitling and Greifelt to Himmler, the actual plan has left no archival trace (Roth, '"Generalplan Ost" – "Gesamtplan Ost"', p. 91, note 231). Isabel Heinemann forgets this or (more probably) chooses tacitly not to mention it (Heinemann, *'Rasse, Siedlung, deutsches Blut'*, p. 359).
72 Aly, *Final Solution*.
73 Aly, *Final Solution*.
74 Bogdan Musial, *Deutsche Zivilverwaltung und Judenverfolgung im General-Gouvernement: Eine Fallstudie zum Distrikt Lublin* (Wiesbaden: Harrassowitz, 1999); Heinemann, *'Rasse, Siedlung, deutsches Blut'*, pp. 382–3.
75 In Serbia, it was 'only' the men who were shot in a policy of hostage-taking. Women and children were killed in gas vans in the autumn of 1941. Walter Manoschek, *'Serbien ist Judenfrei': Militärische Besatzungspolitik und Judenvernichtung in Serbien 1941–1942* (Munich: Oldenbourg, 1993).
76 See, respectively, Pohl, 'Die Einsatzgruppe C'; Manoschek, *'Serbien ist Judenfrei'*; Alberti, *Die Verfolgung und Vernichtung der Juden*; and Musial, *Deutsche Zivilverwaltung*.
77 This whole story is now well known, even if there are still debates over certain points. See Florent Brayard, *La 'Solution finale de la question juive': La technique, le temps et les catégories de la decision* (Paris: Fayard, 2004); and Christian Gerlach, 'Die Wannsee-Konferenz, das Schicksal der Deutschen Juden und Hitlers politische Grundsatzentscheidung, alle Juden Europas zu ermorden', *WerkstattGeschichte*, 18 (1998), pp. 7–44. For another point of view, less relevant in my own opinion, highlighting the decision to exterminate the Jews taken in summer 1941, see Christopher Browning, *The Origins of the Final Solution: The Evolution of Nazi Jewish Policy September 1939–March 1942* (London: William Heinemann, 2004).
78 See Roth, '"Generalplan Ost" – "Gesamtplan Ost" ', pp. 39–43.
79 BABL, NS-19/2065. On Kammler, see Roth, '"Generalplan Ost" – "Gesamtplan Ost"', pp. 73ff and p. 94; Jan Erik Schulte, *Zwangsarbeit und Vernichtung: Das Wirtschaftsimperium der SS. Oswald Pohl und das SS-Wirtschafts-Verwaltungshauptamt* (Paderborn: Ferdinand Schöningh, 2001), p. 253 and p. 347; Adam Tooze, *The Wages of Destruction: The Making and Breaking of the Nazi Economy* (London: Penguin, 2007).
80 Roth, '"Generalplan Ost" – "Gesamtplan Ost" ', p. 61 and n. 242.

81 Letter from Himmler to Pohl, 31 January 1942, in Madajczyk, *Vom Generalplan Ost*, pp. 466–7.
82 Report by Erhard Wetzel, 7 February 1942, Nur. Dok. NO-285, in Madajczyk, *Vom Generalplan Ost*, pp. 38–41.
83 BABL, R-49/157a: Generalplan Ost. RKFdV *Amt* VI (planning), published several times, e.g. in Madajczyk, *Vom Generalplan Ost*, pp. 91–129.
84 Czesław Madajczyk (ed.), *Zamojszczyzna – Sonderlaboratorium SS: Zbior dokumentow polskich i niemieckich z okresu okupacji hitlerowskiej* (Warsaw: Ludowa Spoldzielnia Widawnicza, 1979), 2 vols.
85 I am here using the term in its quantum mechanical sense, where entanglement is a phenomenon of correlation between two systems that are spatially separated but whose states are not independent, so that in spite of the spatial or temporal distance between them they need to be considered *as one and the same system*. See Jean-Louis Basdevant, Jean Dalibard and Manuel Joffre, *Mécanique quantique* (Palaiseau: Éditions de l'École polytechnique, 2002), pp. 291ff.
86 This is my deliberately somewhat free translation of the German word *Volkstum*, which fits the context here better than the more literal, if rather colourless, term 'ethnicity'.
87 Himmler's note, 22 September 1942, BABL, film 4141; published in Madajczyk, *Vom Generalplan Ost*, p. 173. 'Globus' was Odilo Globocnik's nickname. For an exhaustive account which brings together multiple archival sources, see Peter Witte, Michael Wildt, Martina Voigt, Dieter Pohl, Peter Klein, Christian Gerlach, Christoph Dieckmann and Andrej Angrick (eds.), *Der Dienstkalender Heinrich Himmlers 1941/42* (Hamburg: Hamburger Edition, 1999), p. 566.
88 Christopher Browning, *Ordinary Men: Reserve Police Battalion 101 and the Final Solution in Poland* (London: Penguin, 2001), p. xxi, where he cites Raul Hilberg. Browning mentions the dates March 1942 and February 1943. But the month of May in both years seems more correct to me.
89 'Stellungsnahme und Gedanken zum Generalplan Ost des Reichsführer SS', 27 April 1942, Nur. Dok., NG-2325, quoted in Madajczyk, *Vom Generalplan Ost*, pp. 50–81 (pp. 51–2).
90 Covering letter from Meyer-Heitling to Himmler, 23 December 1942, BABL, NS-19/1739; Roth, '"Generalplan Ost" – "Gesamtplan Ost"', p. 72.
91 Hans Ehlich, 'Die Behandlung des fremden Volkstums', lecture given in Salzburg on 11 December 1942, to the NSDStB. Volkstpolitiches Referat (ed.), *Vertrauliche Berichte*, BABL, R-4901 (Alt R-21)/764, fos. 3–9.
92 I will be returning to these questions, especially the 'paradigmatic' questions of *Umvolkung* and *Entvolkung*, and the issue of overlapping documentation, in ch. 4.
93 Broszat, *Hitler State*, Introduction.

Chapter 1 A nebula of institutions

1 See the organizational chart in Robert Lewis Koehl, *RKFDV: German Resettlement and Population Policy, 1939–1945. A History of the Reich Commission for Strengthening of Germandom* (Cambridge, MA: Harvard University Press, 1957).

2 See Isabel Heinemann, *'Rasse, Siedlung, deutsches Blut': Der Rasse- und Siedlungshauptamt der SS und die rassenpolitische Neuordnung Europas* (Göttingen: Wallstein, 2003), pp. 191–2; she correctly notes that we need a new study of the RKFdV to replace the classic but now dated study by Robert Lewis Koehl.

3 Valdis O. Lumans, *Himmler's Auxiliaries: The Volksdeutsche Mittelstelle and the German National Minorities of Europe 1933–1945* (Chapel Hill: University of North Carolina Press, 1993); see also Markus Leniger, *Nationalsozialistische 'Volkstumsarbeit' und Umsiedlungspolitik 1933–1945: Von der Minderheitenbetreuung zur Siedlerauslese* (Berlin: Frank & Timme, 2006), pp. 53–66.

4 Heinemann, *'Rasse, Siedlung, deutsches Blut'*, pp. 49–126.

5 See Michael Wildt, *Generation des Unbedingten: Das Führungskorps des Reichssicherheitshauptamtes* (Hamburg: Hamburger Edition, 2002); Ulrich Herbert, *Best: Biographische Studien über Radikalismus, Weltanschauung und Vernunft* (Bonn: Dietz, 1996); and Christian Ingrao, *Believe and Destroy: Intellectuals in the SS War Machine*, trans. Andrew Brown (Cambridge: Polity, 2013).

6 Hans Safrian, *Eichmann und seine Gehilfen* (Frankfurt: Fischer, 1995). There is a subtle discussion of this point in Götz Aly, *Final Solution: Nazi Population Policy and the Murder of the European Jews*, trans. Belinda Cooper and Allison Brown (London: Arnold, 1999). There is a large range of studies on Eichmann and his men, but they mainly treat the later period.

7 Karl Heinz Roth, '"Generalplan Ost" – "Gesamtplan Ost": Forschungsstand, Quellenproblem, neue Ergebnisse', in Mechtild Rössler and Sabine Schleiermacher (eds.), *Der 'Generalplan Ost': Hauptlinien der nationalsozialistischen Planungs- und Vernichtungspolitik* (Berlin: Akademie Verlag, 1993), is practically the only author to consider this planning activity as such.

8 Letter from Heydrich/Eichmann, 23 December 1939, USHMM, RG-15.015 M (collection AGKBZH 68), roll no. 2, call no. 68/97, fos. 1–7.

9 See Aly, *Final Solution*, for an illustration of the overlap between the expulsions implemented by Eichmann and the question of the transports.

10 IPN in Warsaw: AGKBZH, 362/228; for Moscow: USHMM, RG-11.001 M.01 (Osobyi collection no. 500), roll no. 14, collection 500/4/70; for the collections of the VOMI, the EWZ and the UWZ, in archives spread across the whole of formerly occupied East Europe: USHMM, RG-18.002 M (ZStA Lithuania, Riga, various collections), roll no. 17: KdO Ostland and others; USHMM, RG-15.040 M (collection AGKBZH 358), roll no. 2: UWZ Poznań, Außenstelle Łódź; USHMM, RG-15.015 M (collection AGKBZH 68), roll no. 1: UWZ Poznań; USHMM, RG-15.021 M (collection AGKBZH 167), roll no. 6: EWZ Außenstelle Litzmannstadt; USHMM, RG-18.002 M (ZstA Lithuania, Riga, various collections), roll no. 16: Civil administration in Ostland; USHMM, RG-15.015

M (collection AGKBZH 68), roll no. 1: UWZ Poznań; and in Berlin: BABL, R-58/13, 37, 238 and 1032; BABL, R-59/46 and 53; BABL, R-69/42 and 1063 in particular.

11 Wildt, *Generation des Unbedingten*, pp. 663–70, devotes some seven pages to this – useful enough, but derisory in quantity given the space his fine work gives to other matters. See also Karl Heinz Roth, 'Heydrichs Professor: Historiographie des "Volkstums" und der Massenvernichtungen. Der Fall Hans Joachim Beyer', in Peter Schöttler (ed.), *Geschichtsschreibung als Legitimationswissenschaft, 1918–1945* (Frankfurt: Suhrkamp, 1997), pp. 262–342; and, also by Karl Heinz Roth, 'Ärzte als Vernichtungspläner: Hans Ehlich, die Amtsgruppe IIIB des Reichssicherheitshauptamts und der nationalsozialistische Genozid 1939–1945', in Michael Hubensdorf et al. (eds.), *Medizingeschichte und Gesellschaftskritik: Festschrift für Gerhard Baader* (Frankfurt: Matthiesen, 1997), pp. 398–419.

12 For the end of the war, see report II B-2 in BABL, R-58/1002: RSHA III B2 Works, BdS Krakau: Lageberichte.

13 On this, see Jan Erik Schulte, *Zwangsarbeit und Vernichtung: Das Wirtschaftsimperium der SS. Oswald Pohl und das SS-Wirtschafts-Verwaltungshauptamt* (Paderborn: Ferdinand Schöningh, 2001); Michael Thad Allen, 'Engineers and Modern Managers in the SS: The Business Administration Main Office (*SS Wirtschafts- und Verwaltungshauptamt*)', PhD thesis, University of Pennsylvania, 1995.

14 See the remarkable study focusing on Majdanek and thus also on Lublin by Barbara Schwindt, *Das Konzentrations- und Vernichtungslager Majdanek: Funktionswandel im Kontext der 'Endlösung'* (Würzburg: Königshausen & Neumann, 2005), pp. 74–6. See also appendix 2.

15 On the HSSPFs in general, see Ruth Bettina Birn, *Die höheren SS- und Polizeiführer: Himmlers Vertreter im Reich und in den besetzten Gebieten* (Düsseldorf: Droste, 1986).

16 In the context of the expulsions in Silesia around Auschwitz, the *SS-Ansiedlungsstab Süd* selected a contingent of 2,000 forced labourers to work in the Buna industrial complex (Stefan Hörner, *Profit Oder Moral* (BoD – Books on Demand, 2012), pp. 235–6.

17 See Heinemann, *'Rasse, Siedlung, deutsches Blut'*, p. 382; Michael G. Esch, 'Das SSMannschaftshaus in Lublin und die Forschungsstelle für deutsche Osterkünfte', in Götz Aly (ed.), *Modelle für ein deutsches Europa: Ökonomie und Herrschaft in Großwirtschaftsraum* (Berlin: Rotbuch, 2002). There is also a fine discussion in Schulte, *Zwangsarbeit und Vernichtung*, pp. 265–6.

18 Leniger, *Nationalsozialistische 'Volkstumsarbeit'*.

19 Michael Alberti, *Die Verfolgung und Vernichtung der Juden im Reichsgau Wartheland 1939–1945* (Wiesbaden: Harrassowitz, 2006).

20 Monthly UZW report for July 1942, 5 August 1942, BABL, R-75/4.

21 For our purposes, these were basically the occupied and incorporated Polish territories, even if we need to add Ukraine, the Baltic states, and scattered parts of the westernmost fringes of Russia after the summer of 1941.

22 For the Warthegau, see Alberti, *Die Verfolgung und Vernichtung der Juden*; for the General Government, see Bogdan Musial, *Deutsche Zivilverwaltung und Judenverfolgung im General-Gouvernement: Eine Fallstudie zum Distrikt Lublin*

(Wiesbaden: Harrassowitz, 1999); for East Prussia and Ukraine, see Ralf Meindl, *Ostpreußens Gauleiter: Erich Koch – eine politische Biographie* (Osnabrück: Fibre, 2007).

23 Alberti, *Die Verfolgung und Vernichtung der Juden*, pp. 49–58.

24 Musial relates that the General Government (here abbreviated to GG) was even called the GG (i.e. *Gangsters' Gau*)!

25 See Musial, *Deutsche Zivilverwaltung*, pp. 85–7.

26 Telegram from Heydrich to the HSSPF Warthegau and the General Government, 28 November 1939; quoted in Roth, '"Generalplan Ost" und der Mord an den Juden', p. 57; see also Robert Gerwarth, *Hitler's Hangman: The Life of Heydrich* (New Haven, CT: Yale University Press, 2011).

27 Gerwarth, *Hitler's Hangman*, p. 63.

28 There is a classic analysis in Robert Lewis Koehl, *The Black Corps: The Structure and Power Struggles of the Nazi SS* (Madison: University of Wisconsin Press, 1983).

29 For the *Zwischenplan*, see Aly, *Final Solution*; for the Meyer-Heitling plan, see BABL, R-49/157, fo. 3, reproduced in Czesław Madajczyk (ed.), *Vom Generalplan Ost zum Generalsiedlungsplan* (Munich: Saur Verlag, Einzelveröffentlichungen der Historischen Kommission zu Berlin), vol. 80, 1994, pp. 3–14 (p. 3); for the *Fernplan Ost*, see Roth, '"Generalplan Ost" und der Mord an den Juden', p. 63.

30 Aly, *Final Solution*.

31 Götz Aly, in Wolfgang Schneider (ed.), *'Vernichtungspolitik': Eine Debatte über den Zusammenhang zwischen Sozialpolitik und Genozid im national-sozialistischen Deutschland* (Hamburg: Hamburger Edition, 1991), p. 125.

32 Roth, '"Generalplan Ost" und der Mord an den Juden', pp. 68–9.

33 I am using this term to refer to the fact that they were actively 'seen' as different.

34 Max Domarus, *Hitler: Reden und Proklamationen, 1932–1945* (Leonberg: Pamminger & Partner, 2 vols.; vol. 1: *Triumph (1932–1938)* (1962); vol. 2: *Untergang (1939–1945)* (1963). The reference here is to vol. 2, pp. 1377–93.

35 Götz Aly and Suzanne Heim, *Vordenker der Vernichtung: Auschwitz und die deutschen Pläne für eine neue europäiche Ordnung* (Frankfurt: Fischer, 1991), p. 397. However, the date is unclear: Roth dates this to two days later and he is better supported by the archival evidence than are Aly and Heim in this short paragraph: Roth, '"Generalplan Ost" – "Gesamtplan Ost"', p. 59.

36 Christian Gerlach, *Krieg, Ernährung, Völkermord: Forschungen zur deutschen Vernichtungspolitik im Zweiten Weltkrieg* (Hamburg: Hamburger Edition, 1998), p. 177, insists that Hitler repeatedly made this promise throughout 1941.

37 See the Protocol of the Wannsee Conference, 20 January 1942: http://www.jewishvirtuallibrary.org/the-wannsee-protocol. See also Christian Gerlach, 'Die Wannsee-Konferenz, das Schicksal der Deutschen Juden und Hitlers politische Grundsatzentscheidung, alle Juden Europas zu ermorden', *WerkstattGeschichte*, 18 (1998), pp. 7–44.

38 Roth, '"Generalplan Ost" – "Gesamtplan Ost"', p. 61.

39 BABL, NS-19/4009, fo. 177. See Heinemann, *'Rasse, Siedlung, deutsches Blut'*, p. 371.

40 See the synoptic table at the beginning of this volume.
41 J. Adam Tooze, *Statistics and the German State, 1900–1945: The Making of Modern Economic Knowledge* (Cambridge: Cambridge University Press, 2001); Gerald Fleming, *Hitler and the Final Solution* (Oakland: University of California Press, 1987), p. 135, for the passing of messages between Eichmann and Korherr, albeit on slender archival evidence: here, Fleming quotes only the interrogations of Eichmann in Jerusalem and the Korherr report.
42 Twice over, Wetzel noted in the first half of 1942 that in his view the RSHA was the dominant institution in the field of Nazi policy: on 17 February 1942, in a report on the meeting to discuss Germanization in the ministry where he met Heinz Hummitzsch, Ehlich's deputy in RSHA *Amt* III B, and the second time on 27 April of the same year, in his memorandum on the position to be taken on the RFSS's *Generalplan Ost*, both reproduced in Madajczyk, *Vom Generalplan Ost*, pp. 38–41 and pp. 50–80 respectively.
43 In 1939, Wetzel wrote a memorandum on the treatment of non-natives in the *Gau* of Poznań quoted in Alberti, *Die Verfolgung und Vernichtung der Juden*, p. 88, with an error in the first name corrected in a footnote.
44 Wolf Gruner even dates this change in Eichmann's interests to March 1941; see Wolf Gruner, 'Von der Kollektivausweisung zur Deportation der Juden aus Deutschland: Neue Perspektiven und Dokumenten', in Birthe Kundrus and Beate Meyer (eds.), *Die Deportation der Juden aus Deutschland: Pläne – Praxis – Reaktionen 1938–1945* (Göttingen: Wallstein, 2012), pp. 21–60 (p. 45).
45 Gerlach, 'Die Wannsee-Konferenz'.
46 Schulte, *Zwangsarbeit und Vernichtung*, pp. 308ff.
47 NO-5711, Roth, '"Generalplan Ost" – "Gesamtplan Ost"', p. 61.
48 Roth, '"Generalplan Ost" – "Gesamtplan Ost"'. For a critique of Roth, see Karsten Schulz, 'Nationalsozialistische Nachkriegskonzeptionen für die eroberten Gebiete Osteuropas vom Januar 1940 bis Januar 1943', unpublished thesis, 1996, kamen-jahr.livejournal.com/124032.html.
49 Reproduced in Rössler and Schleiermacher, *Der 'Generalplan Ost'*, pp. 48ff.
50 Reproduced in Madajczyk, *Vom Generalplan Ost*, pp. 261ff. On all of this, see Ingrao, *Believe and Destroy*, ch. 7, 'Thinking the east, between utopia and anxety'.
51 Politische Archive des Auswärtigen Amts, R-100857, fos. 197–214. Reproduced in *Die Verfolgung und Ermordung der europäischen Juden durch das nationalsozialistische Deutschland 1933–1945*, vol. 3: *Deutsches Reich und Protektorat September 1939–September 1941* (Berlin: De Gruyter, 2012), pp. 266–74.
52 Nur. Dok. NG-2586, fos. 1–15.
53 BABL, NS-19/2065. Roth, '"Generalplan Ost" – "Gesamtplan Ost"', pp. 73ff. Thanks to Nicolas Patin for procuring a scan of this item.
54 Roth, '"Generalplan Ost" – "Gesamtplan Ost"'.
55 Roth, '"Generalplan Ost" – "Gesamtplan Ost"'.
56 BABL, R-49/157: Reorganization of the territories in the East: reports of RKFdV *Amt* VI (planning).
57 Roth, '"Generalplan Ost" – "Gesamtplan Ost"', p. 60.
58 BABL, R-49/157a: RKFdV *Amt* VI (planning).

59 Reproduced in Madajczyk, *Vom Generalplan Ost*, pp. 215–18, pp. 208–9 and pp. 235–6 respectively.
60 Collections R-49, R-59 and R-69 in the Bundesarchiv, Berlin-Lichterfelde, respectively.

Chapter 2 Networks and trajectories of the men of the East

1 On the question of female involvement, see Wendy Lower, *Hitler's Furies: German Women in the Nazi Killing Fields* (Boston, MA: Houghton Mifflin Harcourt, 2013), which is perhaps a little sketchy. For a more detailed if more 'local' analysis, see Elissa Mailänder, *Gewalt im Dienstalltag: Die SS-Aufseherinnen des Konzentrations- und Vernichtungslagers Majdanek* (Hamburg: Hamburger Edition, 2009).
2 Karl Stuhlpfarrer, *Umsiedlung Südtirol, 1939–1940* (Vienna: Löcker, 1985), p. 251, quoted in Gerhard Wolf, *Ideologie und Herrschaftsrationalität: Nationalsozialistische Germanisierungspolitik in Polen* (Hamburg: Hamburger Edition, 2012), p. 130.
3 Organizational chart RKFdV-Stabshauptamt, 1 August 1942, BABL, R-49/1.
4 Isabel Heinemann, '"Ethnic Resettlement" and Inter-Agency Cooperation in the Occupied Eastern Territories', in Gerald D. Feldman and Wolfgang Seibel, *Networks of Nazi Persecution: Bureaucracy, Business, and the Organization of the Holocaust* (New York: Berghahn Books, 2004), pp. 213–35 (p. 228).
5 I have not included the SS officers from the VOMI. Valdis Lumans mentions an increase in numbers but does not give any exact figures. Valdis O. Lumans, *Himmler's Auxiliaries: The Volksdeutsche Mittelstelle and the German National Minorities of Europe 1933–1945* (Chapel Hill: University of North Carolina Press, 1993), pp. 137ff.
6 Many organizational charts in BABL, R-58/3528: Plan of the organization of RSHA activities.
7 Numbers given on the website Hotel Silber, the historical institute in BadenWürtemberg: 'Europa – Das Netz der Gestapo': http://www.geschicht-sort-hotel-silber.de/das-netz-der-gestapo/europa.
8 Wolf, *Ideologie und Herrschaftsrationalität*.
9 Jan Erik Schulte, *Zwangsarbeit und Vernichtung: Das Wirtschaftsimperium der SS. Oswald Pohl und das SS-Wirtschafts-Verwaltungshauptamt* (Paderborn: Ferdinand Schöningh, 2001), p. 159.
10 That is, 500 racial experts + 100 logisticians and city planners/agronomists + 120 personnel from the RSHA and BdS/KdS + 56 + 210 men from the WVHA = 986 men. This figure is merely a minimal extrapolation.
11 This is one of the main lines of argument in Isabel Heinemann, *'Rasse, Siedlung, deutsches Blut': Der Rasse- und Siedlungshauptamt der SS und die rassenpolitische Neuordnung Europas* (Göttingen: Wallstein, 2003).
12 On all these issues, see Elizabeth Harvey, *'Der Osten braucht dich!' Frauen und nationalsozialistische Germanisierungspolitik* (Hamburg: Hamburger Edition, 2010), pp. 120–33.

13 Sabine Arend, 'Studien zur historischen "Ostforschung" im Nationalsozialismus: Die kunsthistorischen Institute an den (Reichs-) Universitäten Breslau und Posen und ihre Protagonisten im Spannungfeld von Wissenschaft und Politik', PhD thesis, Humboldt University, Berlin, 2009, p. 292: http://edoc.hu-berlin. de/dissertationen/arend-sabine-2009–07–15/PDF/arend.pdf.

14 That is, 1,228 SS officers and officials + (3,500 + 1,027 + 2,683) girls and women from the BDM + 13,000 from the *NSFrauenschaft* and the *Arbeitsdienst* + (e.g. 2,000 + 1,200 + 2,500 = c. 6,000) students in the *Studentenführung* = 27,438 persons. This figure is in fact only a minimum, as I have not included, for example, the officials involved in the fideicommissary and accountancy activities of the DUT and the DAG (German Settlement Society), though these employed some 500 persons in the financial year 1941. See Schulte, *Zwangsarbeit und Vernichtung*, p. 245.

15 Jürgen Weber and Peter Steinbach, *Vergangenheitsbewältigung durch Strafverfahren? NS-Prozesse in der Bundesrepublik Deutschland* (Munich: Olzog, 1984), p. 58.

16 Ulrich Herbert, *Best: Biographische Studien über Radikalismus, Weltanschauung und Vernunft* (Bonn: Dietz, 1996); Michael Wildt, *Generation des Unbedingten: Das Führungskorps des Reichssicherheitshauptamtes* (Hamburg: Hamburger Edition, 2002); Heinemann, '*Rasse, Siedlung, deutsches Blut*'.

17 Herbert F. Ziegler, *Nazi Germany's New Aristocracy: The SS Leadership 1925–1939* (Princeton, NJ: Princeton University Press, 1989).

18 The Nazi expression could even serve as a defence strategy for those whom certain historians now call 'ethnocrats' when they appeared before the Nuremberg Tribunal and the prosecutors of Ludwigsburg (Heinemann, '"Ethnic Resettlement"', p. 228).

19 Herbert, *Best*; Wildt, *Generation des Unbedingten*; Christian Ingrao, *Believe and Destroy: Intellectuals in the SS War Machine*, trans. Andrew Brown (Cambridge: Polity, 2013).

20 See for example the *Litzmannstädter Zeitung*, 2 August 1942, which mentions Scheel's arrival in Łódź for the students' *Osteinsatz* and a speech given with the *Gauleiter*, Greiser.

21 The existence of this network is well known; witness the previously cited publications as well as the remarkable article by Karl Heinz Roth, 'Heydrichs Professor: Historiographie des "Volkstums" und der Massenvernichtungen. Der Fall Hans Joachim Beyer', in Peter Schöttler (ed.), *Geschichtsschreibung als Legitimationswissenschaft, 1918–1945* (Frankfurt: Suhrkamp, 1997), pp. 262–342; see also Horst Junginger, 'Tübinger Exekutoren der Endlösung: Effiziente Massenmörder an vorderster Front der SS-Einsatzgruppen und des Sicherheitsdienstes': https://homepages.uni-tuebingen.de//gerd.simon/ exekutoren.pdf.

22 Wildt, *Generation des Unbedingten*, pp. 89–103. See also Uwe Dietrich Adam, *Hochschule und Nationalsozialismus: Die Universität Tübingen im Dritten Reich* (Stuttgart: Franz Steiner, 1977), pp. 49ff.

23 Together they raised a flag with a swastika on the mast of the university's main building on 8 March 1933. See Wildt, *Generation des Unbedingten*, p. 100.

24 Karl Heinz Roth, 'Ärzte als Vernichtungspläner: Hans Ehlich, die Amtsgruppe IIIB des Reichssicherheitshauptamts und der nationalsozialistische Genozid 1939–1945', in Michael Hubensdorf et al. (eds.), *Medizingeschichte und Gesellschaftskritik: Festschrift für Gerhard Baader* (Frankfurt: Matthiesen, 1997), pp. 398–419 (p. 401).

25 Interrogation of Rolf-Heinz Höppner, 1 August 1946, *Trial of the Major War Criminals*, vol. XX, pp. 184–5.

26 The Zeppelin operations involved recruiting and 'turning' Soviet prisoners of war, who were trained in sabotage and sent in civilian costumes behind the Soviet lines for guerrilla warfare and acts of destruction. See Michael Wildt (ed.), *Nachrichtendienst, politische Elite und Mordeinheit: Der Sicherheitsdienst des Reichführers SS* (Hamburg: Hamburger Edition, 2003).

27 On the 'Black Hand' and, more generally, the processes of socialization at the University of Leipzig, see Wildt, *Generation des Unbedingten*, pp. 104–37.

28 Matthias Schröder, *Deutschbaltische SS-Führer und Andrej Vlasov 1942–1945: Erhard Kroeger, Friedrich Buchardt und die 'Russische Befreiungsarmee'* (Paderborn: Ferdinand Schöningh, 2001), p. 167.

29 On Königsberg, see Lutz Hachmeister, *Der Gegnerforscher: Zur Karriere des SS-Führers Franz Alfred Six* (Munich: Beck, 1998); Ingo Haar, '"Revisionistische" Historiker und Jugendbewegung: Das Königsberger Beispiel', in Schöttler, *Geschichtsschreibung als Legitimationswissenschaft*, pp. 52–103; in the same volume, Roth, 'Heydrichs Professor'.

30 Roth, 'Heydrichs Professor', pp. 262–342; see Karl Heinz Roth, '"Generalplan Ost" – "Gesamtplan Ost": Forschungsstand, Quellenproblem, neue Ergebnisse', in Mechtild Rössler and Sabine Schleiermacher (eds.), *Der 'Generalplan Ost': Hauptlinien der nationalsozialistischen Planungs- und Vernichtungspolitik* (Berlin: Akademie Verlag, 1993) on the correlations between the SDOA Südwest and the *Studentenführung*; see also Wildt, *Generation des Unbedingten*, pp. 89–103, for Nazi militancy before 1938.

31 Robert Lewis Koehl, *RKFDV: German Resettlement and Population Policy, 1939–1945. A History of the Reich Commission for Strengthening of Germandom* (Cambridge, MA: Harvard University Press, 1957), and Markus Leniger, *Nationalsozialistische 'Volkstumsarbeit' und Umsiedlungspolitik 1933–1945: Von der Minderheitenbetreuung zur Siedlerauslese* (Berlin: Frank & Timme, 2006).

32 These biographical data are taken from Hachmeister, *Der Gegnerforscher*, for Oebsger-Röder, and more generally for the other officers, from Wildt, *Generation des Unbedingten*, and Ingrao, *Believe and Destroy*, all of which provide more detailed accounts.

33 Michael Thad Allen, *The Business of Genocide* (Chapel Hill: University of North Carolina Press, 2002), pp. 140–8.

34 See Allen, *Business of Genocide*, and Schulte, *Zwangsarbeit und Vernichtung*, pp. 252–3.

35 Harvey, 'Der Osten braucht dich!', pp. 122–31.

36 On the doctors of the EWZ and their activities, see Leniger, *Nationalsozialistische 'Volkstumsarbeit'*, pp. 184–90.

37 This term covered a variety of scientific research institutions in Berlin and

other places, established in 1911. Originally independent of the state, the work done here came under Nazi influence. (Translator's note.)

38 On Meixner and his career, see Maria Fiebrandt, *Auslese für die Siedlergesellschaft: Die Einbeziehung Volksdeutscher in die NS-Erbgesundheitspolitik im Kontext der Umsiedlungen 1939–1945* (Göttingen: Vandenhoeck & Ruprecht, 2014), pp. 502–9. Her analysis concludes that he was representative of a panel of fifty EWZ doctors (pp. 509–13).

39 On these questions, until the work of Fabien Théofilakis is published, see Ernst Ritter, *Das Deutsche Ausland-Institut in Stuttgart 1917–1945: Ein Beispiel deutscher Volkstumsarbeit zwischen den Weltkriegen* (Wiesbaden: Franz Steiner, 1976); Katja Gesche, *Kultur als Instrument der Aussenpolitik totalitärer Staaten: Das Deutsche Ausland-Institut 1933–1945* (Cologne and Weimar: Böhlau, 2006); Tammo Luther, *Volkstumspolitik des Deutschen Reiches 1933–1938: Die Auslanddeutschen im Spannungsfeld zwischen Traditionalisten und Nationalsozialisten* (Stuttgart: Franz Steiner, 2004), pp. 52–63, for a brief overview of the way the question developed up until 1933.

40 Harvey, *'Der Osten braucht dich!'*, pp. 45–94.

41 On the Nazification of pre-existing cadres, see Luther, *Volkstumspolitik des Deutschen Reiches*, pp. 62ff.

42 See Roth, *'"Generalplan Ost" – "Gesamtplan Ost"'*, and Roth, *'Heydrichs Professor'*.

43 On the harshly predatory policies pursued by Gottberg in Prague, see Heinemann, *'Rasse, Siedlung, deutsches Blut'*, pp. 131–43.

44 Peter Klein, 'Curt von Gottberg', in Klaus-Michael Mallmann and Gerhard Paul (eds.), *Karrieren der Gewalt: Nationalsozialistische Täterbiographien* (Darmstadt: Primus, 2013).

45 Until her book is published, see the fine thesis by Masha Cerovic, 'Les Enfants de Joseph. Les partisans soviétiques: Guerre civile, révolution et résistance armée à l'occupation allemande (1941–1944)', PhD thesis, University of Paris 1 Panthéon-Sorbonne, 2012.

46 Order for and reports on Operation Nuremberg, StA Hamburg, 147 Js 11/71U (Documents from the archives of the StAs [StA Munich, 118 Js 6/71, StA Coburg, Js 296/65]), Beiaktenordner 2.

47 Interrogation of Georg Heuser, head of the Gestapo in Minsk, ZStL, 202 AR-Z 282/59 (Slusk case, against Reinhard Breder, Georg Heuser and KdS Minsk), vol. 1, p. 135.

48 See Christian Gerlach, *Kalkulierte Morde: Die deutsche Wirtschafts- und Vernichtungspolitik in Weißrußland* (Hamburg: Hamburger Edition, 1999), pp. 1036–54; the interrogation of Johannes Feder, IVA head of the KdS Minsk, on 29 October 1960, reports a paper he gave on this problem. The KdS Minsk and the general staff of the HSSPF were in charge of this operation. See StA Hamburg, 147 Js 11/71U (Kamfgruppenstab interrogations A-J), vol. S, part 1, fos. 39–43.

49 Gerlach, *Kalkulierte Morde*, pp. 1050–1.

50 On the place, see Gerlach, *Kalkulierte Morde*, pp. 115–16; 'Stellungnahme und Gedanken Erhard Wetzels', NG 2325, published in Czesław Madajczyk

(ed.), *Vom Generalplan Ost zum Generalsiedlungsplan* (Munich: Saur Verlag, Einzelveröffentlichungen der Historischen Kommission zu Berlin), vol. 80, 1994, pp. 50–81 (pp. 66–8).

51 Heinemann, *'Rasse, Siedlung, deutsches Blut'*, pp. 149ff.

52 There is now an abundant literature on these questions. On the *Partisanenbekämpfung*, see Gerlach, *Kalkulierte Morde*, pp. 980–1054; on the way the fight against the *Partisanenbekämpfung* was like a bestial hunt, see Christian Ingrao, *The SS Dirlewanger Brigade: The History of the Black Hunters*, trans. Phoebe Green (New York: Skyhorse, 2011).

53 Sandberger's career has been studied in many works, including Wildt, *Generation des Unbedingten*, and Ingrao, *Believe and Destroy*. For a more detailed account, see Andreas Stripper, '..."Zum Allein zu gebrauchen": Die Karriere des Dr. Martin Sandberger': http://www.fzbg.ut.ee/9–2014/2014%20 Mitteilungen/274_pdfsam_FzbG-9–2014.pdf.

54 BADH, ZR-544, A.3 [file on the war and post-war period for Martin Sandberger]: fo. 3.

55 *Referendar* file, in DZAP Reichsjustizprüfungsamt, p. 6, 706/36 (noted in the central Stasi file for the BADH). PhD thesis: Martin Sandberger, 'Die Sozialversicherung im nationalsozialistischen Staat. Grundsätzliches zur Streitfrage: Versicherung oder Versorgung?', Bühler, Unrach im Württemberg, 1934, VII.

56 BADH, ZA-V/230, A.4: (List of nominations for the medal of 1 October 1938).

57 He even became the representative in absentia of the head of the SDOA, BABL [ex-DZAP], film no. 16982.

58 Staatskommissar Baltendeutsche, BABL [ex-DZAP], DAI-Film no. 3887/N, fos. 414880, 414924, 414941, 414951, 414957, 414959.

59 See Prologue.

60 There is now a rich literature on the *Einsatzgruppen*. I will here mention only the major thesis by Hans-Heinrich Wilhelm, *Die Einsatzgruppe A der Sicherheitspolizei und des SD 1941/42* (Frankfurt: Peter Lang, 1996); Wolfgang Scheffler's fine introduction to *Einsatzgruppe* A in Peter Klein (ed.), *Die Einsatzgruppen in der besetzten Sowjetunion 1941/42: Die Tätigkeits- und Lageberichte des Chefs der Sicherheitspolizei und des SD* (Berlin: Edition Hentrich, 1997); and Anton Weiss-Wendt, *Murder Without Hatred: Estonians and the Holocaust* (Syracuse, NY: Syracuse University Press, 2009).

61 Sandberger was KdS in Verona in 1943: BABL [ex-DZAP SS Versch. Prov.], film 2935, fos. 9/342 045, 9/342 047ff. and 9/341 985.

62 Head of RSHA Group VIA, BABL, film [SS Versch. prov.] no. 2705, fos. 1138, 1148, 1187, 1194, 1199, 1220, 1223, 1323, 1341.

63 Letter from RSHA III B to RSHA I A-1, 22 November 1941, signed Ehlich, in BABL, R-58/7103, fo. 63; quoted in Stripper, '"'Zum Allein zu gebrauchen"', p. 279; BADH, ZR-890, A.2: [Document EWZ, RSHA: Sammlung zum Krumeys Prozeß], fo. 14.

64 Christian Gerlach, 'Die Einsatzgruppe B', in Klein, *Die Einsatzgruppen in der besetzten Sowjetunion*.

65 See for example EM no. 24, 16 July 1941, whose list of addresses indicates

that one of the bodies to which it was sent was Group III B of the RSHA, BABL, R-58/214. Published in *Sowjetunion mit annektierten Gebieten I: Besetzte sowjetische Gebiete unter deutscher Militärverwaltung, Baltikum und Transnistrien* (Berlin: De Gruyter, 2011), pp. 174–83 (p. 174, n. 2 for the address list).

66 I have attempted to explain this paradox in Ingrao, *Believe and Destroy*, part 3.

67 Interrogation of Erich R., 26 March 1968, ZStL, 207 AR-Z 246/59 (affair Sk 1a), vol. 7, fos. 1303–6 (fo. 1304). Also published in Hans-Heinrich Wilhelm, *Rassenpolitik und Kriegsführung: Sicherheitspolizei und Wehrmacht in Polen und der Sowjetunion* (Passau: Richard Rothe, 1991), pp. 202–4.

68 Interrogation of Erich R., 26 March 1968, ZStL, 207 AR-Z 246/59 (affair Sk 1a), vol. 7, fos. 1303–6 (fo. 1305).

69 Remarks that emphasized Sandberger's intelligence were also made by other witnesses such as Karl Tschierschky, 15 February 1968, ZStL, 207 AR-Z 246/59 (affaire Sk 1a), vol. 7, fos. 1288–98 (fo. 1288).

70 Schröder, *Deutschbaltische SS-Führer*, p. 167.

71 Roth, 'Heydrichs Professor', and Schröder, *Deutschbaltische SS-Führer*.

72 Valjaveca specialized in the history of the Danubian monarchy and was an advisor on 'cultural matters' for Pesterer. Traces of his move to Group D can be found in ZStL, 213 AR-1899/66 (case of Pesterer et al. [investigations]), vols. 4, 5, 8.

73 Andrej Angrick, 'Einsatzgruppe D', in Klein, *Die Einsatzgruppen in der besetzten Sowjetunion*.

74 Rolf-Dieter Müller, *Hitlers Ostkrieg und die deutsche Siedlungspolitik* (Frankfurt: Fischer, 1991), p. 220.

75 On these two HSSPFs, see Ruth Bettina Birn, *Die höheren SS- und Polizeiführer: Himmlers Vertreter im Reich und in den besetzten Gebieten* (Düsseldorf: Droste, 1986); on Behrends, see Lumans, *Himmler's Auxiliaries*; and on von dem Bach-Zelewski, see Gerlach, *Kalkulierte Morde*.

Chapter 3 *Osteinsatz:* the journey to the East, a form of Nazi fervour

1 Quentin Deluermoz, Emmanuel Fureix, Hervé Mazurel and M'hamed Oualdi, 'Écrire l'histoire des émotions: De l'objet à la catégorie d'analyse', *Revue d'histoire du XIXe siècle: Société d'histoire de la révolution de 1848 et des révolutions du XIXe siècle*, 47 (2013), pp. 155–89. This article gives a comprehensive overview of the epistemological challenges posed by the history of emotions, even though it focuses mainly on the French nineteenth century. See also Jan Plamper, 'Wie schreibt man die Geschichte der Gefühle? William Reddy, Barbara Rosenwein und Peter Stearns im Gespräch mit Jan Plamper', *WerkstattGeschichte*, 54 (2010), pp. 39–69.

2 A new survey of the main tendencies in the historiography of Nazism and genocide is a pressing need for international research. The fact remains that no convincing, unifying paradigm has yet emerged to replace the one set out

in 'Conquérir, aménager, exterminer: Nouvelles recherches sur la Shoah', *Annales: Histoire, sciences sociales* (2003).

3 On this issue, see Tammo Luther, *Volkstumspolitik des Deutschen Reiches 1933–1938: Die Auslanddeutschen im Spannungsfeld zwischen Traditionalisten und Nationalsozialisten* (Stuttgart: Franz Steiner, 2004), pp. 25–56.

4 Figures in Luther, *Volkstumspolitik des Deutschen Reiches*, pp. 45ff.

5 On all this, see Luther, *Volkstumspolitik des Deutschen Reiches*, pp. 150–3 and 175. See also Valdis O. Lumans, *Himmler's Auxiliaries: The Volksdeutsche Mittelstelle and the German National Minorities of Europe 1933–1945* (Chapel Hill: University of North Carolina Press, 1993), p. 63 on the two expulsions.

6 The expression 'Kämpfende Wissenschaften' was used by the historian Kleo Pleyer at a *Volkswissenschaftlicher Arbeitskreis* conference in the presence of at least three historians from the RSHA, BABL, R-8043/62731, fo. 122.

7 Ingo Haar, *Historiker im Nationalsozialismus: Die deutsche Geschichtswissenschaft und der 'Volkstumskampf' im Osten* (Göttingen: Vandenhoeck & Ruprecht, 2000), pp. 255ff.

8 Attendance list and conference programmes in BABL, R-8043/62731: correspondence between the *Deutsche Stiftung* and the VDA, especially fos. 122, 195, 239. See also report and attendance list for the conference of 5 and 6 January 1939 in BABL, R-153/96: *Volksbund für das Deutschtum im Ausland*.

9 Notes and correspondence in BABL, R-153/95.

10 Erich Windt and Wilhelm Hansen, *Was weißt du vom deutschen Osten? Geschichte und Kultur des deutschen Ostraums* (Berlin and Ulm: Verlag Ebner und Peter, 1942).

11 G. A. Walz, 'Die Entwicklung der deutschen Volksgruppen in Polen und in Ungarn', conference given at the session of 7 May 1938 of the Akademie für deutsche Recht. BABL, R-8043/1333, here fos. 128–9. Also quoted in Christian Ingrao, *Believe and Destroy: Intellectuals in the SS War Machine*, trans. Andrew Brown (Cambridge: Polity, 2013).

12 Götz Aly and Suzanne Heim, *Vordenker der Vernichtung: Auschwitz und die deutschen Pläne für eine neue europäiche Ordnung* (Frankfurt: Fischer, 1991).

13 On Breslau and Gustav Adolf Walz, see Sabine Arend, 'Studien zur historischen "Ostforschung" im Nationalsozialismus: Die kunsthistorischen Institute an den (Reichs-)Universitäten Breslau und Posen und ihre Protagonisten im Spannungfeld von Wissenschaft und Politik', PhD thesis, Humboldt University, Berlin, 2009, p. 292: http://edoc.hu-berlin.de/dissertationen/ arend-sabine-2009–07–15/PDF/arend.pdf.

14 Hans Baumann, 'Im Osten', in Reichsfrauenführung (ed.), *Gemeinschaftslieder: Lieder für Frauengruppen*, 1940; quoted in Norbert Frei, *National Socialist Rule in Germany: The Führer State 1933–1945*, trans. Simon B. Steyne (Oxford: Blackwell, 1993).

15 Mathias Eidenbenz, *'Blut und Boden': Zur Funktion und Genesis der Metaphern des Agrarismus und Biologismus in der nationalsozialistischen Bauernpropaganda R. W. Darré* (Berne: Peter Lang, 1993); see also the remarkable analysis in Édouard Conte and Cornelia Essner, *La Quête de la race: Une anthropologie du nazisme* (Paris: Hachette, 1998).

16 BABL, R-49/3044: [Action for population displacement and scientific actions carried out in liaison with the *NS-Studentenführung* in the East, various reports, poems, etc.], fos. 99–101 (fo. 101).

17 Correspondence Sandberger/Scheel, 20 and 27 October 1939, BABL, R49/3044, fo. 1.

18 Circular on the application of the action for colonization and the specialized action of summer 1941, 19 June 1941, BABL, R-49/3044, fos. 12–14 (fo. 12).

19 Circular no. 1 of the general staff of the action in the East, in BABL, R-49/3044, fos. 23–30, with a detailed account, by district and institution, of posts available for volunteers. Maria Fiebrandt gives an assessment of 1,500 students for 1941: see Maria Fiebrandt, *Auslese für die Siedlergesellschaft: Die Einbeziehung Volksdeutscher in die NS-Erbgesundheitspolitik im Kontext der Umsiedlungen 1939–1945* (Göttingen: Vandenhoeck & Ruprecht, 2014).

20 Arend, 'Studien zur historischen "Ostforschung"', p. 292.

21 'Der *Osteinsatz* der Deutschen Studentenschaft und seine Bedeutung für die Gesundheitsführung', *Deutsches Ärztesblatt*, 72 (1942), 10, pp. 120ff. (p. 121), quoted in Fiebrandt, *Auslese für die Siedlergesellschaft*, p. 526.

22 This does not belong to the present work. I tackled it in Ingrao, *Believe and Destroy*, part 3.

23 Report in BABL, R-59/409: Reports of *Sonderkommando* R on German nationhood in the Leningrad Region, fos. 48–52. This report has already been used by Valdis Lumans in his thesis on the VOMI. See following note.

24 On *Sonderkommando* R and its action in the Leningrad region, see Lumans, *Himmler's Auxiliaries*, pp. 182–3.

25 BABL, 59/409, fos. 48–52.

26 All this has been illuminatingly brought out in Götz Aly, *Final Solution: Nazi Population Policy and the Murder of the European Jews*, trans. Belinda Cooper and Allison Brown (London: Arnold, 1999). On the Germans in the Baltic states, see Matthias Schröder, *Deutschbaltische SS-Führer und Andrej Vlasov 1942–1945: Erhard Kroeger, Friedrich Buchardt und die 'Russische Befreiungsarmee'* (Paderborn: Ferdinand Schöningh, 2001).

27 BABL, R- 59/409, fo. 49.

28 On the idea of the fighting community, see (even though it concentrates on the case of the German SA) Sven Reichardt, *Faschistische Kampfbünde: Gewalt und Gemeinschaft im italienischen Squadrismus und in der deutschen SA* (Cologne and Weimar: Böhlau, 2009).

29 See previous chapter.

30 BABL, R-59/409, fo. 49.

31 BABL, R-59/409, fo. 50.

32 On all this, see Ingrao, *Believe and Destroy*, and Klaus Latzel, *Deutsche Soldaten: Nationalsozialistischer Krieg? Kriegserlebnis – Kriegserfahrung 1939–1945* (Paderborn: Ferdinand Schöningh, 1998).

33 The Hermannfeste is a medieval fortress on the river at Narva.

34 BABL, R-59/409, fo. 52.

35 BABL, R-59/409, fo. 50.

36 BABL, R-59/409, fo. 50.

37 BABL, R-59/409, fos. 51–2.

38 BABL, R-59/409, fo. 49 (my italics).

39 BABL, R-59/409, fo. 52.

40 See Ingrao, *Believe and Destroy*.

41 Exhibition catalogue in BABL, R-69/42, fos. 23–30.

42 Christoph Zuschlag, *'Entartete Kunst': Ausstellungsstrategien im Nazi-Deutschland* (Worms: Wernersche Verlagsgesellschaft, 1995), p. 133. Consulted on Googlebooks.

43 'Introduction', exhibition catalogue for *Der Große Trek*, fos. 32–64.

44 Exhibition catalogue for *Rückführung der Deutschen aus Galizien*, in BABL, 69/42, fos. 23–30 (fo. 26).

45 Exhibition catalogue for*Rückführung der Deutschen aus Galizien*, in BABL, 69/42, fos. 26–7.

46 Exhibition catalogue for *Rückführung der Deutschen aus Galizien*, in BABL, 69/42, fos. 25 and 41.

47 Karl Götz, *Die Große Heimkehr* (Stuttgart: J. Engelhorns Nachf. Adolf Spemann Verlag, 1943); see Katja Gesche, *Kultur als Instrument der Aussenpolitik totalitärer Staaten: Das Deutsche Ausland-Institut 1933–1945* (Cologne and Weimar: Böhlau, 2006), p. 276.

48 Alphonse Dupront, *Le Mythe de croisade* (Paris: Gallimard, 1997), 4 vols., vol. 1, pp. 1210–11.

49 This is not an easy question, since while bibliography has made great progress here, it has in some ways become bogged down in irrelevant questions. For example, setting up a contrast, as does Gerhard Wolf in *Ideologie und Herrschaftsrationalität: Nationalsozialistische Germanisierungspolitik in Polen* (Hamburg: Hamburger Edition, 2012), between an instrumental rationality of domination and an ideological slant in the determinants of Germanization policies in occupied Poland is probably not the best strategy for analysing the practices of application of racial criteria in the management of local populations. His meticulous method becomes superficial when he wages guerrilla warfare on Isabel Heinemann throughout his work, and when he reduces the practices of Nazi institutions to instrumental criteria. In short: a binary approach to these practices means that you cannot go into what Édouard Conte and Cornelia Essner called, a good twenty years ago, the 'labyrinth of racial logic', arguing as they did for an anthropology that took care to identify the inner coherence of Nazi discourse and practice. See Conte and Essner, *La Quête de la race*, 'Introduction'.

50 Fiebrandt, *Auslese für die Siedlergesellschaft*, especially the Introduction.

51 On all this, see Fiebrandt, *Auslese für die Siedlergesellschaft*, pp. 470–3.

52 Letter from the head of the RuSHA, SS-Gruf. Günther Pancke, to the *Ansiedlungsstab* Poznań, 14 December 1939, RGVA Moscow, f. 1386/o.1/d.1, fo. 38, quoting *Mein Kampf*, trans. James Murphy (London: Hurst and Blackett, 1939): http://gutenberg.net.au/ebooks02/0200601.txt; Fiebrandt, *Auslese für die Siedlergesellschaft*, p. 470.

53 As far as the combatant troops were concerned, Latzel, *Deutsche Soldaten*, has some useful chapters on the question of alterity, exoticism, the prejudices and

revulsions of the Germans in the East, in both the First and Second World Wars.

54 Zygmunt Bauman, *Modernity and the Holocaust* (Hoboken: John Wiley & Sons, 2013); see especially pp. 91–3.

55 Herta Miedzinski, 'Deutsche Antlitz an der Weichsel', *Die Bewegung*, 8: 41 (1940), p. 8; quoted in Elizabeth Harvey, *'Der Osten braucht dich!' Frauen und nationalsozialistische Germanisierungspolitik* (Hamburg: Hamburger Edition, 2010), p. 192.

56 Renate Kalb, 'Fahrt in den Osten', *Die Bewegung*, 8: 41 (1940), p. 8; quoted in Harvey, *'Der Osten braucht dich!'*, p. 194.

57 Anna G., (Dresden), 'Our action of assistance', BABL, R-49/3052; quoted in Harvey, *'Der Osten braucht dich!'*, p. 220.

58 Resettlement activity in the Leslau (Vistula) district, 1941, IfZ, Fb115; quoted in Harvey, *'Der Osten braucht dich!'*, p. 212.

59 One need think only of the succession of controversies over the questions of consent and constraint in the Great War; for an overview, see François Buton, André Loez, Nicolas Mariot and Philippe Olivera, '1914–1918: Retrouver la controverse', *La Vie des idées*, 10 December 2008; and Stéphane Audoin-Rouzeau, 'Controverse ou polémique?', *La Vie des idées*, 5 February 2009.

60 Report of a young woman student on the *Osteinsatz*, n.d., BABL, R-49/3044, fos. 96–7.

61 Other historians studying women or soldiers have already fully emphasized this fact. See Harvey, *'Der Osten braucht dich!'*, and Latzel, *Deutsche Soldaten*.

62 Melita Maschmann and Helga Grebing, *Fazit: Mein Weg in der Hitler-Jugend* (Munich: dtv, 1983 (1963)), pp. 35ff.; quoted in Frank Bajohr and Michael Wildt, *Volksgemeinschaft: Neue Forschungen zur Gesellschaft des Nationalsozialismus* (Frankfurt: Fischer, 2009), p. 7.

Conclusion (Part I)

1 I feel that this is a capital dimension that is neglected by Ian Kershaw in *Hitler, 1936–45: Nemesis* (London: Allen Lane, 2000).

Chapter 4 General planning for the East

1 On the invasion of Poland, see Alexander B. Rossino, *Blitzkrieg, Ideology and Atrocity: Hitler Strikes Poland* (Lawrence: University Press of Kansas, 2003); Jochen Böhler, *Auftakt zum Vernichtungskrieg: Die Wehrmacht in Polen 1939* (Frankfurt: Fischer, 2006).

2 Minutes of Reichstag session, third legislature, Friday 1 September 1939; Legislature 1939–42, 1, p. 45: http://www.reichstagsprotokolle.de/Blatt2_n4_bsb00000613_00046.html.

3 Lecture 15, 'The Thirty Years War, a German catastrophe', conclusion BABL,

R-58/844; quoted in Christian Ingrao, *Believe and Destroy: Intellectuals in the SS War Machine*, trans. Andrew Brown (Cambridge: Polity, 2013).

4 I have already discussed this theme in *Believe and Destroy* – I am here going into the main factors in rather more depth.

5 The expression '*Eine Welt von Feinden*' (a world of enemies) is drawn from the address given by Marshal Hindenburg to German soldiers just after the armistice on the Western Front. Hindenburg described the German army as fighting 'a world of enemies', and still unvanquished in military terms.

6 AGKBZH, 362/209: *Sonderbericht* (special report): *Die Politik Polens im Baltikum*, pp. 33–8 (fos. 38–43); fo. 58 for the Jews.

7 *Kurzbericht* no. 8 (3 June1942): 'Die Wiederverpolung des Netzgaues unter preussischer Herrschaft mit 7 Karten', BABL, R-49/3040: fos. 37–56 (fo. 37).

8 This linguistic stranglehold was evident, to German eyes, in the fact that Poles seemed to 'Polonize' local dialects such as Silesian, and attempted to prove that the Silesian dialect stemmed from Polish. A German 'press agency' in Allenstein monitored this type of activity and produced reports on it: BABL, R-153/1655: Volkstumskampf in Polen.

9 See the conference organized by the working panel on *Auslandsdeutsche Volksforschung* devoted to the processes of Polonization and the question of dissimilation (*Umvolkung*): programme of conference held 11–13 August 1937, published on 2 August 1937, BABL, R-153/108, no fo. no.

10 Reinhard Höhn, former head of the SD Inland, was a professor in Berlin. He left the SD after the polemic with Carl Schmitt, but remained an SS *Standartenführer*. In 1943, he published the *Festschriften* of Himmler and contributed to the debate on the Nazi imperial administration, BAAZ, SSO Reinhard Höhn; AGKBZH, 362/241. On Höhn, see the exemplary investigation by Johann Chapoutot, *La Loi du sang: Penser et agir en nazi* (Paris: Gallimard, 2014), who mentions him on several occasions.

11 BABL, R-53/1178a, fos. 1–11, archive report no. 6 on the activity of the Bishop of Poznań between 1887 and 1907.

12 AGKBZH, 362/766, fo. 30, for the Poles' aptitude for *Volkstumskampf*, and fo. 123 for accusations of dispossession of the soil.

13 BABL, R-49/157: Reorganization of the territories of the East, reports of RKFdV *Amt* VI (planning), fos. 1–21, published in facsimile in Czesław Madajczyk (ed.), *Vom Generalplan Ost zum Generalsiedlungsplan* (Munich: Saur Verlag, Einzelveröffentlichungen der Historischen Kommission zu Berlin), vol. 80, 1994, pp. 3–14. Madajczyk dates, without evidence, the document to April–May 1940, while Götz Aly dates it to the start of 1940: see Götz Aly, *Final Solution: Nazi Population Policy and the Murder of the European Jews*, trans. Belinda Cooper and Allison Brown (London: Arnold, 1999). From my point of view, the precise date matters little, since what interests me here is the mental structure which the document reveals in its narrative and discursive structures.

14 Aly, *Final Solution*, p. 3.

15 BABL, R-49/157, fos. 1–21 (fo. 6); also quoted in Madajczyk, *Vom Generalplan Ost*, pp. 5–6. See map 1.

16 See Karl Heinz Roth, '"Generalplan Ost" – "Gesamtplan Ost": Forschungsstand, Quellenproblem, neue Ergebnisse', in Mechtild Rössler and Sabine Schleiermacher (eds.), *Der 'Generalplan Ost': Hauptlinien der nationalso-zialistischen Planungs- und Vernichtungspolitik* (Berlin: Akademie Verlag, 1993), maps pp. 64–5 and details on the plan pp. 59–60.

17 The terms 'army of revenge' and 'army of Crusade' were used by the late Pierre Ayçoberry in his fine book *La Société allemande sous le Troisième Reich* (Paris: Seuil, 1998), and I investigated this distinction between a war of memory and a racial memory in *Believe and Destroy*, part 3, which provides elements of the most relevant bibliography.

18 The plan is dated to June 1942, as it was sent by Meyer-Heitling to Greifelt on 28 May and the latter forwarded it to the *Reichsführer* only on 3 June. See letter from Greifelt to Himmler, 3 June 1942, BABL, NS-19/1739, fo. 3, reproduced in Madajczyk, *Vom Generalplan Ost*, p. 90.

19 *Generalplan Ost*, June 1942, BABL, R-49/157a, reproduced in Madajczyk, *Vom Generalplan Ost*, pp. 91–130 (p. 123).

20 AGKBZH, NTN, vol. 253, fos. 93–139; reproduced in Madajczyk, *Vom Generalplan Ost*, pp. 172 and 173.

21 Cornelia SchmitzBerning, *Vokabular des Nationalsozialismus* (Berlin: De Gruyter, 2000), pp. 617–18.

22 I am here following closely Alexander Pinwinkler, '"Assimilation" und "Dissimilation" in der Bevölkerungsgeschichte ca 1918 bis 1960', in Rainer Mackensen (ed.), *Bevölkerungsforschung und Politik in Deutschland im 20. Jahrhundert* (Berlin: Springer, 2008), pp. 23–45. As the reader will note, the neologism 'dissimilation' is also used by Pinwinkler, who is, I think, the only specialist in the social sciences to do so.

23 Pinwinkler, '"Assimilation" und "Dissimilation"', p. 29.

24 The term exists in biology and linguistics, though of course it has radically different meanings in those domains. I decided on this term in the late 1990s, in my thesis and then in *Believe and Destroy*, though it was systematically changed by the publishers to 'dissemination'. . .

25 Pinwinkler, '"Assimilation" und "Dissimilation"'.

26 Probably Alexander Dolezalek.

27 BABL, R-49/159: 'German nationhood in Lithuania', memorandum of the *Amt Raumplanung* of the RKFdV, 1940, fos. 31–2.

28 BABL, R-59/409: Report of the Petersburg *Sonderkommando* of the VOMI: 'German nationhood in the Leningrad region', fo. 10 for the example of Kiopen.

29 Ulrich Herbert, *Best: Biographische Studien über Radikalismus, Weltanschauung und Vernunft* (Bonn: Dietz, 1996), part 1; and Ingrao, *Believe and Destroy*.

30 Karl Heinz Roth, '"Generalplan Ost" und der Mord an den Juden: Der "Fernplan um der Umsiedlung in den Ostprovinzen" aus dem Reichssicherheitshauptamt vom November 1939', *1999: Zeitschrift für Sozialgeschichte des 20. und 21. Jahrhunderts*, 12 (1997), pp. 50–70 (pp. 68–9).

31 Speech by Heydrich on the Nazi principles behind the reorganization of

Europe, Prague, 2 October 1941, in Madajczyk, *Vom Generalplan Ost*, pp. 20–5 (p. 21).

32 Erhard Wetzel, 'Stellungnahme und Gedanken Erhard Wetzels', NG 2325, published in Madajczyk (ed.), *Vom Generalplan Ost zum Generalsiedlungsplan* (Munich: Saur Verlag, Einzelveröffentlichungen der Historischen Kommission zu Berlin), vol. 80, 1994, reproduced in Madajczyk, *Vom Generalplan Ost*, pp. 50–81 (p. 66).

33 Wetzel, 'Stellungnahme', p. 54.

34 On this whole question, see Ayçoberry, *La Société allemande*; and Norbert Frei, *National Socialist Rule in Germany: The Führer State 1933–1945*, trans. Simon B. Steyne (Oxford: Blackwell, 1993).

35 Édouard Conte and Cornelia Essner, *La Quête de la race: Une anthropologie du nazisme* (Paris: Hachette, 1998), chapter entitled 'Noces macabres au seuil du néant'.

36 Wetzel, 'Stellungnahme', p. 55.

37 Jochen August, '*Sonderaktion Krakau': Die Verhaftung der Krakauer Wissenschaftler am 6. November 1939* (Hamburg: Hamburger Edition, 1997).

38 Michael Wildt, *Generation des Unbedingten: Das Führungskorps des Reichssicherheitshauptamtes* (Hamburg: Hamburger Edition, 2002), pp. 482 and 939.

39 Christian Gerlach, *Kalkulierte Morde: Die deutsche Wirtschafts- und Vernichtungspolitik in Weißrußland* (Hamburg: Hamburger Edition, 1999); Dieter Pohl, 'Die Einsatzgruppe C', in Peter Klein (ed.), *Die Einsatzgruppen in der besetzten Sowjetunion 1941/42: Die Tätigkeits- und Lageberichte des Chefs der Sicherheitspolizei und des SD* (Berlin: Edition Hentrich, 1997), pp. 71–87 (p. 73).

40 See the meeting of 7 February 1942 with representatives of RSHA *Amt* III B-2. Report in Madajczyk, *Vom Generalplan Ost*, pp. 38–41; see also meetings of 29 January and 6 March 1942 there, p. 60, quoting NG 2586.

41 Wetzel, 'Stellungnahme', p. 54.

42 See Christian Gerlach, *Krieg, Ernährung, Völkermord: Forschungen zur deutschen Vernichtungspolitik im Zweiten Weltkrieg* (Hamburg: Hamburger Edition, 1998), and the more recent work by Christoph Dieckmann and Babette Quinkert (eds.), *Kriegführung und Hunger 1939–1945: Zum Verhältnis von militärischen, wirtschaftlichen und politischen Interessen* (Göttingen: Wallstein, 2015).

43 Gerlach, *Kalkulierte Morde*.

44 I am here drawing on the apt title of the work by Götz Aly and Suzanne Heim, *Vordenker der Vernichtung: Auschwitz und die deutschen Pläne für eine neue europäiche Ordnung* (Frankfurt: Fischer, 1991).

45 Wetzel, 'Stellungnahme', p. 69.

46 Wetzel, 'Stellungnahme', p. 74.

47 BABL, R-49/984.

48 On *Vernichtung durch Arbeit*, see Miroslav Karny, 'Vernichtung durch Arbeit: Die Sterblichkeit in den NS-Konzentrationslagern', *Beiträge zur National-sozialistischen Gesundheits- und Sozialpolitik*, 5 (1987), pp. 133–58; Hermann Kaienburg, '*Vernichtung durch Arbeit': Der Fall Neuengamme* (Bonn: Dietz, 1991); Ulrich Herbert, 'Arbeit und Vernichtung: Ökonomisches Interesse und

Primat der "Weltanschauung" im Nationalsozialismus', in Ulrich Herbert (ed.), *Europa und der Reichseinsatz: Auslandische Zivilarbeiter, Kriegsgefangene und KZ-Häftlinge in Deutschland 1933–1945* (Essen: Klartext, 1991); and finally, Jan Erik Schulte, *Zwangsarbeit und Vernichtung: Das Wirtschaftsimperium der SS. Oswald Pohl und das SS-Wirtschafts-Verwaltungshauptamt* (Paderborn: Ferdinand Schöningh, 2001).

49 Roth, '"Generalplan Ost" und der Mord an den Juden', pp. 72–3.
50 Roth, '"Generalplan Ost" – "Gesamtplan Ost"', p. 53; Aly and Heim, *Vordenker der Vernichtung*, pp. 365–76; Gerlach, *Kalkulierte Morde*, pp. 44–94.
51 Letter from Backe to Himmler, 6 June 1942, BABL, NS-19/3418, published in Madajczyk, *Vom Generalplan Ost*, p. 133.
52 RSHA Liaison officer with Hitler's Chancellery.
53 Notes taken by Hermann Krumey, head of the UWZ, on Beyer's lecture, AGKBZH, 358/82. Document discovered and published in Madajczyk, *Vom Generalplan Ost*, pp. 261–6 (p. 265).
54 *SS-Standartenführer* Hans Ehlich, 'Die Behandlung des fremden Volkstums', lecture delivered in Salzburg, 11 December 1942, Der Reichsstudentenführer. Volkspolitiches Referat (ed.), *Vertrauliche Berichte*, BABL, R-4901 (Alt R-21)/764, fos. 3–9.
55 Instructions signed by Ohlendorf, 28 December 1942, AGKBZH, 358/82. Document discovered and published by Madajczyk, *Vom Generalplan Ost*, pp. 261–6.
56 Notes taken by Hermann Krumey, head of the UWZ, on Beyer's lecture, AGKBZH, 358/82, in Madajczyk, *Vom Generalplan Ost*, pp. 261–6 (p. 265).
57 And not 35, as I mistakenly wrote in *Believe and Destroy*. The figure of 31 million people to be expelled, which had been mentioned by Wetzel, is repeated in Krumey's notes; see Madajczyk, *Vom Generalplan Ost*.
58 The calculation for Jewish populations was based on statistics established by RSHA *Ämter* IV B-4 and III B and used by Heydrich and Eichmann at the Wannsee Conference in January 1942. The protocol of the conference and statistical data have been published in German and with an English translation in Reinhard Rürup (ed.), *Topography of Terror: Gestapo, SS and Reichssicherheitshauptamt on the 'Prinz-Albrecht-Terrain'. A Documentation*, trans. Werner T. Angress (Berlin: W. Arenhövel, 1993); see also the report of *SS-Oberführer* Richard Korherr, March and April 1943, BABL, NS-19/1570.
59 16,925,000 'undesirables' + 8,391,200 Jews, even though we could also add the 2,900,300 Jews or so who came from spaces not concerned by Germanization, also condemned to death, giving a total of 28,216,500 planned deaths.

Chapter 5 At the School of Fine Arts

1 Peter Witte, Michael Wildt, Martina Voigt, Dieter Pohl, Peter Klein, Christian Gerlach, Christoph Dieckmann and Andrej Angrick (eds.), *Der Dienstkalender Heinrich Himmlers 1941/42* (Hamburg: Hamburger Edition, 1999), p. 135 and p. 140.

2 Konrad Meyer-Heitling, 'Introduction', in the *Planung und Aufbau im Osten* catalogue, p. 4, BABL, R-49/157, fo. 47.

3 Meyer-Heitling, 'Introduction', p. 4, fo. 47.

4 Meyer-Heitling, 'Introduction', p. 4, fo. 47.

5 Meyer-Heitling, 'Introduction', p. 4, fo. 48.

6 Meyer-Heitling, 'Introduction', p. 4, fo. 48.

7 Mechtild Rössler, *'Wissenschaft und Lebensraum'. Geographische Ostforschung im Nationalsozialismus: Ein Beitrag zur Disziplingeschichte der Geographie* (Berlin: Dietrich Reimer, 1990), pp. 172–4.

8 See the Wikipedia entry on the district of Kutno: https://en.wikipedia.org/wiki/Kutno_County, which quotes the official statistics and the 2006 census.

9 Meyer-Heitling, 'Introduction', p. 10, fo. 50.

10 See Martin Broszat, *Nationalsozialistische Polenpolitik 1939–1945* (Berlin: De Gruyter, 1961), p. 35. The city was one of the places where the Polish Army, perhaps under fire from the German self-protection militias, responded by killing civilians, which led to their being suppressed by SS commandos from the *Einsatzgruppen*, but also by special ops groups: some 5,000 people were shot up until November 1939. See Kai Struve, *Deutsche Herrschaft, ukrainischer Nationalismus, antijüdische Gewalt: Der Sommer 1941 in der Westukraine* (Berlin: De Gruyter, 2015), pp. 58–9.

11 'Planungsgrundlagen für den Aufbau der Ostgebieten', in BABL, R-49/157, fos. 1–21 (fo. 6); cited by, among others, Czesław Madajczyk (ed.), *Vom Generalplan Ost zum Generalsiedlungsplan* (Munich: Saur Verlag, Einzelveröffentlichungen der Historischen Kommission zu Berlin), vol. 80, 1994, pp. 5–6.

12 'Planungsgrundlagen für den Aufbau der Ostgebieten', fo. 10.

13 Maps accessible on the website for the Bundesamt für Kartographie und Geodäsie: http://www.posselt-landkarten.de/grossblatt_056.htm.

14 Friedrich Gollert, *Warschau unter deutscher Herrschaft: Deutsche Aufbauarbeit im Distrikt Warschau im Auftrage des Gouverneurs des Distrikts Ludwig Fischer unter Benutzung ämtlicher Unterlagen* (Kraków: Burgverlag Krakau, 1942), p. 59: http://www.wintersonnenwende.com/scriptorium/deutsch/archiv/warschau/wdh05.html. An almost identical map is reproduced in Barbara Klein, 'Warschau 1939–1945: Vernichtung durch Planung', in Mechtild Rössler and Sabine Schleiermacher (eds.), *Der 'Generalplan Ost': Hauptlinien der nationalsozialistischen Planungs- und Vernichtungspolitik* (Berlin: Akademie Verlag, 1993), pp. 294–327 (p. 319).

15 Clearly illustrated in Klein, 'Warschau 1939–1945', especially p. 305.

16 Włodzimierz Borodziej, *The Warsaw Uprising of 1944*, trans. Barbara Harshav (Madison: Wisconsin Press, 2005); Christian Ingrao, *The SS Dirlewanger Brigade: The History of the Black Hunters*, trans. Phoebe Green (New York: Skyhorse, 2011).

17 *Planung und Aufbau im Osten* catalogue, p. 4, BABL, R-49/157, fo. 51. Even so, the author does this in order to deny the specificity of the two, saying that urban habitats can also have rural characteristics and alluding to 'garden-city' projects, though he does not actually use that word.

18 Map and model in Niels Gutschow, 'Stadtplanung im Warthegau 1939–1944',

in Rössler and Schleiermacher, *Der 'Generalplan Ost'*, pp. 232–70 (pp. 236 and 237).

19 Comparisons made with a city plan from 1911: http://www.mapywig. org/m/City_plans/Central_Europe/PHARUS-PLAN_POSEN_1911.jpg.

20 Gutschow, 'Stadtplanung im Warthegau', pp. 234–5.

21 Letter to the mayor from Wilhelm Hallbauer, 17 August 1940, Archiwum Państwowe Łódź, municipal administration archives, Building department, 111, fo. 91, quoted by Gutschow, 'Stadtplanung im Warthegau', p. 241.

22 Peter Klein and Gedenkstätte Haus der Wannsee-Konferenz (Berlin), *Spuren aus dem Getto Łódź 1940–1944. Dokumente der Sammlung Wolfgang Haney, Berlin: Eine Ausstellung in der Gedenk- und Bildungsstätte Haus der Wannsee-Konferenz vom 28. März 1999 bis zum 30. Dezember 2000*, Haus der Wannsee-Konferenz, 1999, p. 6. Gutschow quotes figures that are considerably higher. But the latter are not found in any manual or inventory.

23 Gutschow, 'Stadtplanung im Warthegau', pp. 239–49, and especially pp. 247–8.

24 General order no. 13/II, RFSS, RKFdV, 30 January 1942, Reichsarbeitsblatt 1942, 10/11, 1st part, pp. 1–8, reproduced in Rössler and Schleiermacher, *Der 'Generalplan Ost'*, pp. 259–70.

25 Same diagnosis in Niels Gutschow, *Ordnungswahn: Architekten planen im 'eingedeutschten Osten' 1939–1945* (Basel: Birkhäuser, 2001); for Poznań, see p. 166.

26 Anna Bitner-Nowak, 'Wohnungspolitik und Wohnverhältnisse in Posen 1890–1939', in Alena Janatková and Hanna Kozińska-Witt, *Wohnen in der Grossstadt, 1900–1939: Wohnsituation und Modernisierung im europäischen Vergleich* (Stuttgart: Franz Steiner, 2006), pp. 151–79 (p. 166).

27 See Jerzy Jan Lerski, *Historical Dictionary of Poland, 966–1945* (Westport, CT: Greenwood, 1996), p. 324.

28 'Étude urbanistique sur la question des implantations industrielles et commerciales de la capitale provinciale Posen' by municipal engineer Reichow, extracts in Rössler and Schleiermacher, *Der 'Generalplan Ost'*, pp. 154–74 (p. 161).

29 Rössler and Schleiermacher, *Der 'Generalplan Ost'*, pp. 164–5, and p. 163 for the chart showing the occupation of land and the plan. Thanks to Christoph Dieckmann, Alexandra Rybinczka and Claudia Lebovic for helping me to decipher the almost illegible caption.

30 Rössler and Schleiermacher, *Der 'Generalplan Ost'*, p. 165.

31 Rössler and Schleiermacher, *Der 'Generalplan Ost'*, p. 166.

32 Gutschow, 'Stadtplanung im Warthegau', p. 239.

33 Gutschow, 'Stadtplanung im Warthegau', p. 239.

34 The 'Ring' is the circular railway that typically goes round a German city.

35 *Planung und Aufbau im Osten* catalogue, p. 4, BABL, R-9/157. The following discussion is entirely based on this catalogue.

36 On the geography of these three forms, and the references to the work of German geographers, it is still worth remembering the celebrated work by René Lebeau, *Les Grands Types de structures agraires dans le monde* (Paris: Masson, 1969), which was carefully studied by entire generations of students, including the present author.

37 BABL, R-49/157, fo. 56, p. 18 of the catalogue.
38 BABL, R-49/157, fo. 57, p. 20 of the catalogue.
39 Hartmut Harnisch, 'August Meitzen und seine Bedeutung für die Agrar- und Siedlungsgeschichte', *Jahrbuch für Wirtschaftsgeschichte*, 1975/1, Berlin, Akademie Verlag, pp. 97–119 (pp. 110ff); http://www.digitalis.uni-koeln.de/JWG/jwg_index.html.
40 Adolf Helbok, *Deutsche Siedlung: Wesen, Ausbreitung und Sinn* (Halle (Saale): Max Niemeyer, 1938) (*Volk*, vol. 5), a work which unfortunately I have not been able to consult. On Helbok, see Ingo Haar, *Historiker im Nationalsozialismus: Die deutsche Geschichtswissenschaft und der 'Volkstumskampf' im Osten* (Göttingen: Vandenhoeck & Ruprecht, 2000), especially pp. 282–3.
41 BABL, R-49/157, fo. 57, p. 21 of the catalogue.
42 BABL, R-49/157, fo. 55, p. 16.
43 BABL, R-49/157, fo. 59, pp. 26 and 27.
44 At present, nothing has replaced the essentially descriptive but useful work by the archivist Herwart Vorländer, *Die NSV: Darstellung und Dokumentation einer nationalsozialistischen Organisation* (Munich: Oldenbourg, 1988).
45 We should also add the presence of a dairy, fo. 73, p. 52 of the catalogue.
46 The term is repeated on six comments on plans out of nine presented, with two of them having no comment. So six out of seven comments mention the separation.
47 BABL, R-49 9/157, fos. 63–70.
48 However, the plans show a significant contribution in cereals for animal foods (especially birds and pigs).
49 BABL, R-49/157, fo. 63, p. 33 of the catalogue.
50 BABL, R-49/157, fo. 67, pp. 40 and 41.
51 BABL, R-49/157, fos. 71–2.
52 BABL, R-49/157, fos. 76–8, pp. 60–2 of the catalogue.
53 BABL, R-49/157, fo. 77, pp. 60 and 61.
54 BABL, R-49/157, fo. 78, p. 62.
55 For a magnificent and detailed description of this ritual, see Édouard Conte and Cornelia Essner, *La Quête de la race: Une anthropologie du nazisme* (Paris: Hachette, 1998), pp. 143–9. It corresponds with the codification drawn up by a registrar, Stadtamtmann Rieve, 'Eine Hochzeitsfeier im Standesamt der Gauhauptstadt', *Zeitschrift für Standesamtswesen*, 1942, pp. 189–91.

Chapter 6 From one plan to the next? The Kammler sequence

1 This was established by Martin Broszat, in *The Hitler State: The Foundation and Development of the Internal Structure of the Third Reich*, trans. John W. Hiden (London: Longman, 1981) and confirmed when several major new overviews of Nazism were published in France in the late 1990s, including Norbert Frei, *National Socialist Rule in Germany: The Führer State 1933–1945*, trans. Simon B. Steyne (Oxford: Blackwell, 1993) and Pierre Ayçoberry, *La Société allemande sous le Troisième Reich* (Paris: Seuil, 1998) and has not been questioned since.

2 See Isabel Heinemann, '*Rasse, Siedlung, deutsches Blut*': *Der Rasse- und Siedlungshauptamt der SS und die rassenpolitische Neuordnung Europas* (Göttingen: Wallstein, 2003), pp. 127–43.

3 See Jan Erik Schulte, *Zwangsarbeit und Vernichtung: Das Wirtschaftsimperium der SS. Oswald Pohl und das SS-Wirtschafts-Verwaltungshauptamt* (Paderborn: Ferdinand Schöningh, 2001), pp. 168–73.

4 'Planungsgrundlagen', in Czesław Madajczyk (ed.), *Vom Generalplan Ost zum Generalsiedlungsplan* (Munich: Saur Verlag, Einzelveröffentlichungen der Historischen Kommission zu Berlin), vol. 80, 1994, document no. 1, pp. 3–14 (p. 13).

5 Schulte, *Zwangsarbeit und Vernichtung*, pp. 250–7.

6 Peter Witte, Michael Wildt, Martina Voigt, Dieter Pohl, Peter Klein, Christian Gerlach, Christoph Dieckmann and Andrej Angrick (eds.), *Der Dienstkalender Heinrich Himmlers 1941/42* (Hamburg: Hamburger Edition, 1999).

7 Six meetings in the first half of the year, seventeen in the second.

8 Witte et al., *Der Dienstkalender Heinrich Himmlers*, p. 104.

9 Witte et al., *Der Dienstkalender Heinrich Himmlers*, p. 206.

10 Witte et al., *Der Dienstkalender Heinrich Himmlers*, p. 287.

11 Witte et al., *Der Dienstkalender Heinrich Himmlers*, pp. 316–17.

12 See Karl Heinz Roth, '"Generalplan Ost" – "Gesamtplan Ost": Forschungsstand, Quellenproblem, neue Ergebnisse', in Mechtild Rössler and Sabine Schleiermacher (eds.), *Der 'Generalplan Ost': Hauptlinien der nationalsozialistischen Planungs- und Vernichtungspolitik* (Berlin: Akademie Verlag, 1993), quoting Czesław Madajczyk, *Die Okkupationspolitik Nazideutschlands in Polen 1939–1945* (East Berlin: Akademie Verlag, 1987), p. 89. However, Madajczyk's point is more that Meyer-Heitling needed to bear in mind the juridical, economic and political foundations of planning.

13 Letter from Himmler to Pohl, 31 January 1942, BABL, NS-19/2065, fos. 13–14. Thanks to Nicolas Patin for the digitization of this file.

14 Michael Thad Allen, 'Engineers and Modern Managers in the SS: The Business Administration Main Office (*SS Wirtschafts- und Verwaltungshauptamt*)', PhD thesis, University of Pennsylvania, 1995; Schulte, *Zwangsarbeit und Vernichtung*.

15 Letter from Pohl to Himmler, 4 December 1941, BABL, NS-19/2065, fos. 2 and 3.

16 Letter from Himmler to Pohl, 31 January 1942, BABL, NS-19/2065, fos. 13 and 14.

17 BABL, R-49/986, in Madajczyk, *Vom Generalplan Ost*, pp. 47–8.

18 These figures have been calculated from the list of contents reproduced in Madajczyk, *Vom Generalplan Ost*, pp. 91–2.

19 The figure of 67 billion RM mentioned by Meyer-Heitling in his letter to Kammler of 18 April does not appear as such in the Plan, but can be found (66.6 billion RM) in the résumé of this plan of 28 May 1942, in *Trial of the Major War Criminals*, NO-2055, reproduced in Madajczyk, *Vom Generalplan Ost*, pp. 86–90 (p. 90).

20 Order given by Oswald Pohl, 17 November 1941, quoted in Schulte, *Zwangsarbeit und Vernichtung*, p. 254.

21 As noted by Schulte, *Zwangsarbeit und Vernichtung*, pp. 260–2.

22 Its creation can be dated from at least 9 August 1941, thanks to notes taken by one of Globocnik's collaborators, in AGK, CA MSW 891/6, fo. 11, quoted in Schulte, *Zwangsarbeit und Vernichtung*, p. 265.

23 Witte et al., *Der Dienstkalender Heinrich Himmlers*, p. 186.

24 Letter from Himmler to Globocnik, 17 July 1941, BAAZ, SSO Globocnik, quoted by Schulte, *Zwangsarbeit und Vernichtung*, p. 262. Memorandum sent by Himmler to Globocnik, 21 July 1941, published in Czesław Madajczyk (ed.), *Zamojszczyzna – Sonderlaboratorium SS: Zbior dokumentow polskich i niemieckich z okresu okupacji hitlerowskiej* (Warsaw: Ludowa Spoldzielnia Widawnicza, 1979), 2 vols., vol. 1, pp. 26–7. See Witte et al., *Der Dienstkalender Heinrich Himmlers*, p. 186.

25 *'Befehlsmaßnahmen durchzuführen'* (!!!) are the exact words in the document: the literal sense is 'to apply, implement, execute the orders' measures'.

26 Barbara Schwindt, *Das Konzentrations- und Vernichtungslager Majdanek: Funktionswandel im Kontext der 'Endlösung'* (Würzburg: Königshausen & Neumann, 2005), p. 68; Schulte, *Zwangsarbeit und Vernichtung* p. 263.

27 On this euphoria, see Christopher Browning, *The Path to Genocide: Essays on Launching the Final Solution* (Cambridge: Cambridge University Press, 1995).

28 One of the witnesses of that time remembers that 'the head of the Department of Planning and Building' [Lenzer] worked more with the Central Department for Budget and Building than with the offices in Lublin', in Interrogatation E. Sch., 15 February 1960, ZStL, 208 AR-Z 268/59, vol. 3, fo. 553 verso, quoted by Schulte, *Zwangsarbeit und Vernichtung*, p. 274.

29 Circular from Pohl, 25 February 1942, quoted in Schulte, *Zwangsarbeit und Vernichtung*, p. 278.

30 Himmler's order, 15 May 1942, *Wirtschafts- und Verwaltungsverordnungen* 1 Jg 1942, p. 13, NS D 41/16. The text of Himmler's order creating the Department of Building in the general staff of the RKFdV has not been preserved. See Schulte, *Zwangsarbeit und Vernichtung*, pp. 308–9.

31 Memorandum of Kammler, 10 February 1942, BABL, NS-19/2065, fos. 20–32 (fos. 27–8).

32 Memorandum of Kammler, 10 February 1942, BABL, NS-19/2065, fo. 29.

33 Memorandum of Kammler, 10 February 1942, BABL, NS-19/2065, fo. 29; here I am closely following Schulte, *Zwangsarbeit und Vernichtung*, pp. 346–7.

34 On the question of prisoners of war, see the pioneering work by Christian Streit, *Keine Kameraden: Die Wehrmacht und die sowjetischen Kriegsgefangenen 1941–1945* (Bonn: Dietz, 1997); see also Schulte, *Zwangsarbeit und Vernichtung*, pp. 334ff.

35 Florent Brayard, *La 'Solution finale de la question juive': La technique, le temps et les catégories de la decision* (Paris: Fayard, 2004).

36 There is a similar analysis in Adam Tooze, *The Wages of Destruction: The Making and Breaking of the Nazi Economy* (London: Penguin, 2007).

37 Summarized in Schulte, *Zwangsarbeit und Vernichtung*, p. 326.

38 Felix Kersten, *The Kersten Memoirs 1940–1945* (Mountain View: Ishi Press, 2011),

pp. 132–40, quoted in Tooze, *Wages of Destruction*, p. 526. The *Dienstkalender* does not mention any meeting between Hitler and Himmler in the previous week, but confirms Kersten's presence in Himmler's entourage on 17 July 1942 – and not 16 July – without mentioning the massage. So while the factual background – especially Tooze's description of the final version of the *Generalplan Ost* – appears to be relatively fragile, Kersten's remarks have no strategic importance that would legitimize a lie. In any case, the question of the date is a minor issue. And thus, like Adam Tooze, I have decided to trust his account. See Witte et al., *Der Dienstkalender Heinrich Himmlers*, p. 491.

39 Ulrich Herbert, *Hitler's Foreign Workers: Enforced Foreign Labor in Germany under the Third Reich*, trans. William Templer (Cambridge: Cambridge University Press, 1997).

40 Tooze, *Wages of Destruction*.

41 Witte et al., *Der Dienstkalender Heinrich Himmlers*, p. 443 and p. 464.

42 Christian Gerlach, *Krieg, Ernährung, Völkermord: Forschungen zur deutschen Vernichtungspolitik im Zweiten Weltkrieg* (Hamburg: Hamburger Edition, 1998); Christoph Dieckmann and Babette Quinkert (eds.), *Kriegführung und Hunger 1939–1945: Zum Verhältnis von militärischen, wirtschaftlichen und politischen Interessen* (Göttingen: Wallstein, 2015); Tooze, *Wages of Destruction*.

43 Letter from Kammler to the SS-Wirtschafter, Group C, 13 May 1943, ZStL, UdSSR 406, fos. 439–470, 502–505, quoted in Schulte, *Zwangsarbeit und Vernichtung*, p. 323.

44 Schulte, *Zwangsarbeit und Vernichtung*, p. 327.

45 Schulte, *Zwangsarbeit und Vernichtung*, p. 328.

46 Rainer Fröbe, 'Die Arbeitseinsatz von KZ-Häftlinge und die Perspecktive der Industrie', in Ulrich Herbert (ed.), *Europa und der Reichseinsatz: Auslandische Zivilarbeiter, Kriegsgefangene und KZ-Häftlinge in Deutschland 1933–1945* (Essen: Klartext, 1991), pp. 351–83 (p. 353).

47 Schulte, *Zwangsarbeit und Vernichtung*, p. 220.

48 Schulte, *Zwangsarbeit und Vernichtung*, p. 329.

49 Letter from Greifelt to Himmler, 23 December 1942, in Madajczyk, *Vom Generalplan Ost*, p. 234; pp. 235–55 for the statistical annexes of the *Generalsiedlungsplan*; p, 208 for its detailed table of contents.

50 Nur. Dok. NO-2255, in Madajczyk, *Vom Generalplan Ost*, pp. 266–7.

51 BABL, NS-19/1739, fo. 22, in Madajczyk, *Vom Generalplan Ost*, p. 267.

52 BABL, NS-19/2743, in Madajczyk, *Vom Generalplan Ost*, p. 273.

53 Note for Brandt, NS-19/1739, fo. 30, in Madajczyk, *Vom Generalplan Ost*, p. 274.

54 NS-19/1739, fo. 32, in Madajczyk, *Vom Generalplan Ost*, p. 282.

Introduction (Part III)

1 Here I will cite merely Dieter Pohl, *Von der 'Judenpolitik' zum Judenmord: Der Distrikt Lublin des Generalgouvernement. 1939–1944* (Frankfurt: Peter Lang, 1993); Bogdan Musial, *Deutsche Zivilverwaltung und Judenverfolgung im Generalgouvernement: Eine Fallstudie zum Distrikt Lublin* (Wiesbaden:

Harrassowitz, 1999); Bruno Wasser, *Himmlers Raumplanung im Osten: Der Generalplan Ost in Polen 1940–1944* (Basel: Birkhäuser, 1994).
2 Czesław Madajczyk (ed.), *Zamojszczyzna – Sonderlaboratorium SS: Zbior dokumentow polskich i niemieckich z okresu okupacji hitlerowskiej* (Warsaw: Ludowa Spoldzielnia Widawnicza, 1979), 2 vols.; see also the documents published in Czesław Madajczyk (ed.), *Vom Generalplan Ost zum Generalsiedlungsplan* (Munich: Saur Verlag, Einzelveröffentlichungen der Historischen Kommission zu Berlin), vol. 80, 1994,, which I will be drawing on intensively, combined with the holdings of archives from Lublin consulted in Washington. See also the same author's *Die Okkupationspolitik Nazideutschland in Polen 1939–1945* (East Berlin: Akademie Verlag, 1987).
3 See Zygmunt Klukowski, *Diary from the Years of Occupation, 1939–44*, trans. George Klukowski, edited by Andrew Klukowski and Helen Klukowski May (Urbana: University of Illinois Press, 1993), and Zygmunt Klukowski, *Red Shadow: A Physician's Memoir of the Soviet Occupation of Eastern Poland, 1944–1956*, trans. George Klukowski and Andrew Klukowski, edited by Andrew Klukowski (Jefferson and London: McFarland, 1997).

Chapter 7 The microcosms of radical policy: Zamojszczyzna

1 Édouard Conte and Cornelia Essner, *La Quête de la race: Une anthropologie du nazisme* (Paris: Hachette, 1998).
2 We have the text of the prayer in which he offers the Polish crown to Henri III: Jan Sariusz Zamoyski, *L'Oraison du Seigneur Iean de Zamoscie . . . l'vn des Ambassadeurs enuoyez en France par les Estats du Royaume de Poloigne . . . Au Serenissime Roy eleu de Poloigne, Henry . . . Traduitte de Latin en François par Loys Regius . . .* (by Michel de Vascosan, 1574), consulted on Google Books.
3 Wacław Wierzbieniec, 'Zamość', in *The YIVO Encyclopedia of Jews in Eastern Europe*, 2010: http://www.yivoencyclopedia.org/article.aspx/Zamosc. The following paragraphs rely entirely on this minutely detailed work.
4 Wierzbieniec, 'Zamość'.
5 Prit Buttar, *Collision of Empires: The War on the Eastern Front in 1914* (Oxford: Osprey, 2014), pp. 203–26.
6 Halik Kochanski, *The Eagle Unbowed: Poland and the Poles in the Second World War* (Cambridge, MA: Harvard University Press, 2012), 'Introduction', especially pp. 19ff.
7 On this question, especially the question of violence against local populations, particularly the Jews, see the excellent thesis by Thomas Chopard, 'La Guerre aux civils. Les violences contre les populations juives d'Ukraine (1917–1924): Guerre totale, occupations, insurrections, pogroms', PhD thesis, EHESS, Paris, 2015.
8 See David Krupka, *Histoire économique de la Pologne 1919–1989* (Lulu.com: 2014), pp. 49–50.
9 I am drawing in what follows on the agronomic and land studies produced by the Austrian Institute for Regional Studies and Spatial Planning, in the

framework of project TERESA financed by the sixth programme-cadre of the European Union: http://www.oir.at/files2/download/projekte/Forschung/ TERESA/TERESA_D_2_3_Case_study_report.pdf; also available in abbreviated form in TERESA Studies.

10 I am also here following the admirable article by Édouard Conte, 'Terre et "pureté ethnique" aux confins polono-ukrainiens', *Études Rurales*, 138 (1995), pp. 53–85 (pp. 68–71): http://dx.doi.org/10.3406/rural.1995.3527.

11 TERESA Studies, p. 359.

12 Raymond L. Buell, *Poland: Key to Europe* (New York: Knopf, 1939), p. 206, quoted in Conte, 'Terre et "pureté ethnique"', p. 68.

13 Czesław Madajczyk stipulates that the population of the district was 517,000, from which are subtracted 20 per cent of the population living in a few towns including Zamość. Czesław Madajczyk, *Die Okkupationspolitik Nazideutschlands in Polen 1939–1945* (East Berlin: Akademie Verlag, 1987), p. 422, note 45; see also Conte andEssner, *La Quête de la race*, p. 266.

14 TERESA Studies, p. 363.

15 The many villages around Zamość can be viewed on Google Earth: Przeorsk, for instance, is a good example of a street-village.

16 TERESA Studies, p. 370.

17 This is the conclusion reached by Édouard Conte in 'Terre et "pureté ethnique"', after a minute description of the policies set in place by Polish governments to confront the problem of the hunger for land (see pp. 70–1).

18 All these figures are quoted by JewishGen.

19 Christopher Browning, *Ordinary Men: Reserve Police Battalion 101 and the Final Solution in Poland* (London: Penguin, 2001), ch. 1, pp. 1–3.

20 See Conte, 'Terre et "pureté ethnique"', pp. 67–71, especially p. 71. The following pages are indebted to this remarkable study.

21 I am here drawing intensively on Conte, 'Terre et "pureté ethnique"'.

22 Conte, 'Terre et "pureté ethnique"', p. 73, and, on all ethnic questions, Timothy Snyder, *The Rebuilding of Nations: Poland, Ukraine, Lithuania, Belarus, 1569–1999* (New Haven, CT: Yale University Press, 2003), pp. 123–53, though the vision of policies in Poland is somewhat irenic. See also, of couurse, the work of Nicolas Werth on the question of the famine in Ukraine and a well-argued summary in Andrea Graziosi, Lubomyr A. Hajda and Halyna Hryn (eds.), *After the Holodomor: The Enduring Impact of the Great Famine on Ukraine* (Cambridge, MA: Harvard University Press, 2014).

23 Jan T. Gross, *Revolution from Abroad: The Soviet Conquest of Poland's Western Ukraine and Western Belorussia* (Princeton, NJ: Princeton University Press, 2002).

24 This is the argument put forward by Timothy Snyder in *Bloodlands: Europe between Hitler and Stalin* (London: Bodley Head, 2010), and it is completely valid for those regions even though, as I have said, before, it is regrettable that Snyder's narrative did not go back to 1905, which would have revealed other logics; see Christian Ingrao, 'L'ingénieur, l'abatteur et l'historien: Remarques sur les *Terres de sang* de Timothy Snyder', *Le Débat*, 172 (2012), pp. 152–92.

25 Bogdan Musial, *Deutsche Zivilverwaltung und Judenverfolgung im*

General-Gouvernement: Eine Fallstudie zum Distrikt Lublin (Wiesbaden: Harrassowitz, 1999), p. 72 for the overall numbers of civil servants, which I have deducted for the three *Kreise* in the district of Zamość.

26 AGKBZH, Akta Buhlera, 260, fo. 27; quoted in Musial, *Deutsche Zivilverwaltung*, p. 60.

27 AGKBZH, Akta Buhlera, 260, fo. 27; quoted in Musial, *Deutsche Zivilverwaltung*, p. 60.

28 Markus Roth, *Herrenmenschen. Die deutschen Kreishauptleute im besetzten Polen: Karrierewege, Herrschaftspraxis und Nachgeschichte* (Göttingen: Wallstein, 2009). Markus Roth, in his remarkable study of the administrators in small towns, makes a point of emphasizing this situation by describing, on the basis of letters sent by civil servants to their wives, what he calls the lifestyle of these civil servants, with their experiences of social domination via racial criteria, a description prior to a study of the practices of domination that brings out the fundamental role played by these civil servants in the implementation of ever more repressive policies.

29 Isabel Heinemann, *'Rasse, Siedlung, deutsches Blut': Der Rasse- und Siedlungshauptamt der SS und die rassenpolitische Neuordnung Europas* (Göttingen: Wallstein, 2003), pp. 92ff.

30 Report of a meeting, dated in the ms 30 October 1941, and on the typewritten account 5 November 1942, point 6, USHMM, RG-15.027 M (archive AGKBZH 891/6), roll no. 1: SSPF Lublin, fos. 16 and 17 (fo. 16).

31 Undated document proposing an organization, signed by the head of the RuSHA to the SSPF Lublin, USHMM, RG-15.027 M (archive AGKBZH 891/1), roll no. 1: SSPF Lublin. Various business, repression, Germanization, fos. 9 and 10. As the bundle dates to 1940, it can be supposed that this was a suggestion made on the basis of the interview between Globocnik and Himmler mentioned by Isabel Heinemann and Michael Esch.

32 Czesław Madajczyk (ed.), *Zamojszczyzna – Sonderlaboratorium SS: Zbior dokumentow polskich i niemieckich z okresu okupacji hitlerowskiej* (Warsaw: Ludowa Spoldzielnia Widawnicza, 1979), 2 vols., vol. 1, pp. 289–91; quoted in Jan Erik Schulte, *Zwangsarbeit und Vernichtung: Das Wirtschaftsimperium der SS. Oswald Pohl und das SS-Wirtschafts-Verwaltungshauptamt* (Paderborn: Ferdinand Schöningh, 2001), p. 268.

33 USHMM, RG-15.027 M (archive AGKBZH 891/1), roll no. 1, fos. 20–21.

34 Christian Ingrao, *The SS Dirlewanger Brigade: The History of the Black Hunters*, trans. Phoebe Green (New York: Skyhorse, 2011).

35 Schulte, *Zwangsarbeit und Vernichtung*, p. 270.

36 Browning, *Ordinary Men*.

37 USHMM, RG-15.027 M (archive AGKBZH 891/1), roll no. 1, fos. 20–1, for the details of the units.

38 Musial, *Deutsche Zivilverwaltung*, especially p. 82.

39 For a good definition of perversion based on the splitting of the ego, see Sigmund Freud, 'Die Ichspaltung im Abwehrvorgang' (1938), *Gesammelte Werke*, vol. 17 (Berlin: S. Fischer, 1951), pp. 59–63; see also Lucien Israël, *La Jouissance de l'hystérique: Séminaire 1974* (Paris: Seuil, 1999).

40 Klaus-Michael Mallmann, '"Mensch Ich feiere heut den tausendsten Genickschuß": Die Sicherheitspolizei und die Shoah in Westukraine', in Gerhard Paul (ed.), *Die Täter der Shoah: Fanatische Nationalsozialisten oder ganz normale Deutsche?* (Göttingen: Wallstein, 2003), pp. 109–36.

41 This had already been noted by Tuviah Friedman in *Himmlers Teufelsgeneral* (Haifa: Institute of Documentation in Israel for the Investigation of Nazi War Crimes, 1998), p. 136; figures reproduced in Joseph Poprzeczny, *Odilo Globocnik: Hitler's Man in the East* (Jefferson, NC: McFarland, 2003), p. 136.

42 See the excerpts from Landau's diary in Ernst Klee, Willi Dreßen and Volker Rieß, *'Schöne Zeiten': Judenmord aus der Sicht der Täter und Gaffer* (Frankfurt: Fischer, 1997).

43 This is well noted by Dieter Pohl, *Nationalsozialistische Judenverfolgung in Ostgalizien 1941–1944: Organisation und Durchführung eines staatlichen Massenverbrechens* (Berlin: De Gruyter, 1997), pp. 34–6.

44 Ingrao, *SS Dirlewanger Brigade*; see also, for the region just to the west of the one we are discussing, Christopher R. Browning, *Remembering Survival: Inside a Nazi Slave-Labour Camp* (New York and London: W. W. Norton, 2010); and, for the camp in Majdanek, the remarkable article by Elissa Mailänder, '"Going East": Colonial Experiences and Practices of Violence among Female and Male Majdanek Camp Guards (1941–44)', *Journal of Genocide Research*, 10 (2008), pp. 563–82. Thanks to Elissa Mailänder for providing me with a copy of her article.

45 There are several studies of Globocnik. I will merely note the most important: Poprzeczny, *Odilo Globocnik*; Peter R. Black, 'Odilo Globocnik: Himmlers Vorposten im Osten', in Ronald Smelser, Enrico Syring and Rainer Zitelmann (eds.), *Die Braune Elite 2: 21 weitere biographische Skizzen* (Darmstadt: Wissenschaftliche Buchgesellschaft, 1993), pp. 103–15; Peter R. Black, 'Odilo Globocnik, Nazi Eastern Policy and the Implementation of the Final Solution', in Dokumentationsarchiv des österreichischen Widerstandes (ed.), *Forschungen zum Nationalsozialismus und dessen Nachwirkungen in Österreich: Festschrift für Brigitte Bailer* (Vienna, 2012): http://www.doew.at/cms/download/70s5n/bb_black.pdf; Siegfried Pucher, *'. . . in der Bewegung führend tätig'. Odilo Globocnik: Kämpfer für den Anschluß, Vollstrecker des Holocaust* (Klagenfurt: Drava, 1997); and, more recently, Johannes Sachslehner, *Zwei Millionen ham'ma erledigt. Odilo Globocnik: Hitlers Manager des Todes* (Vienna: Styria Premium, 2014).

46 Black, 'Odilo Globocnik, Nazi Eastern Policy', p. 93.

47 This is magnificently demonstrated in Peter R. Black, 'Rehearsal for "Reinhard"? Odilo Globocnik and the Lublin Selbstschutz', *Central European History*, 25: 2 (1992), pp. 204–26 (p. 209): http://www.jstor.org/stable/4546260.

48 Black, 'Rehearsal for "Reinhard"?', pp. 221–6.

49 I am using the words of Dieter Pohl, *Von der 'Judenpolitik' zum Judenmord: Der Distrikt Lublin des Generalgouvernement. 1939–1944* (Frankfurt: Peter Lang, 1993), quoted in Schulte, *Zwangsarbeit und Vernichtung*, p. 246.

50 Report of *SS-Hstuf.* Müller to the heads of the RuSHA *SS-Gruf.* Hofmann, 15 November 1941, AGKBZH, Akta Sporrenberga, published in Madajczyk, *Zamojszczyzna – Sonderlaboratorium SS*, vol. 1, pp. 29–31 (p. 30).

51 For Stanglica's biography, I am closely following Herbert Hutterer and Thomas Just, 'Zur Geschichte des Reichsarchivs Wien 1938–1945', *Tagungsdokumentationen zum Deutschen Archivtag* 10, pp. 313–25: http://www.oesta.gv.at/site/4973/default.aspx#a9.

52 Letter from Stanglica to Fritz Braun, 15 January 1942, quoted in Hutterer and Just, 'Zur Geschichte des Reichsarchivs Wien', p. 321.

53 USHMM, RG-15.027 M (archive AGKBZH 891/6), roll no. 2, fos. 267–95, also in Michael G. Esch, 'Die "Forschungsstelle für Ostunterkünfte" in Lublin', *1999: Zeitschrift für Sozialgeschichte des 20. und 21. Jahrhunderts*, 11: 2 (1996), pp. 62–96 (pp. 75–95).

54 Letter from Stanglica to the *Mittelstelle*, 12 March 1941, quoted in Hutterer and Just, 'Zur Geschichte des Reichsarchivs Wien', p. 321.

55 USHMM, RG-15.027 M (archive AGKBZH 891/1 to 6), rolls nos. 1 and 2.

56 Bogdan Musial, 'The Origins of "Operation Reinhard": The DecisionMaking Process for the Mass Murder of the Jews in the *Generalgouvernement*', *Yad Vashem Studies*, XXVII (2000), pp. 113–53 (p. 121).

57 Musial, *Deutsche Zivilverwaltung*, pp. 202–3; Heinemann, '*Rasse, Siedlung, deutsches Blut*', pp. 381ff.; Conte and Essner, *La Quête de la race*, pp. 270–5.

58 Report on the meeting, incorrectly dated 30 July 1941, document no. 3, in Madajczyk, *Zamojszczyzna – Sonderlaboratorium SS*, vol. 1, pp. 26–7; Peter Witte, Michael Wildt, Martina Voigt, Dieter Pohl, Peter Klein, Christian Gerlach, Christoph Dieckmann and Andrej Angrick (eds.), *Der Dienstkalender Heinrich Himmlers 1941/42* (Hamburg: Hamburger Edition, 1999), p. 186.

59 On the extermination operations, see Yitzhak Arad, *Belzec, Sobibór, Treblinka: The Operation Reinhard Death Camps* (Bloomington: Indiana University Press, 1987); Musial, *Deutsche Zivilverwaltung*, p. 201, for the connection between Germanization and genocide, and pp. 215–306 for the genocide itself; and more recently, Sara Berger, *Experten der Vernichtung: Das T4-Reinhardt-Netzwerk in den Lagern Belzec, Sobibór und Treblinka* (Hamburg: Hamburger Edition, 2013).

Chapter 8 The politics of the laboratory

1 See Jan Erik Schulte, *Zwangsarbeit und Vernichtung: Das Wirtschaftsimperium der SS. Oswald Pohl und das SS-Wirtschafts-Verwaltungshauptamt* (Paderborn: Ferdinand Schöningh, 2001), pp. 248–9, where he discusses these early projects in detail, and contradicts some of the points in Bogdan Musial, *Deutsche Zivilverwaltung und Judenverfolgung im General-Gouvernement: Eine Fallstudie zum Distrikt Lublin* (Wiesbaden: Harrassowitz, 1999), pp. 201–4, and Dieter Pohl, *Von der 'Judenpolitik' zum Judenmord: Der Distrikt Lublin des Generalgouvernement. 1939–1944* (Frankfurt: Peter Lang, 1993). Pohl saw these initiatives as evidence of the existence of a policy of Germanization that Globocnik wanted to introduce autonomously.

2 Report by Wilhelm Gradmann on German nationhood in the Zamość region, 19 March 1942, reproduced in Czesław Madajczyk (ed.), *Zamojszczyzna – Sonderlaboratorium SS: Zbior dokumentow polskich i niemieckich z okresu okupacji*

hitlerowskiej (Warsaw: Ludowa Spoldzielnia Widawnicza, 1979), 2 vols., vol. 1, pp. 53–66 (pp. 53–4).

3 Note of 5 November 1940 on the account of the discussion between Globocnik and Himmler on 26 October 1940, USHMM, RG-15.027 M (archive AGKBZH 891/6), roll no. 1, fos. 16–23; also quoted in Isabel Heinemann, *'Rasse, Siedlung, deutsches Blut': Der Rasse- und Siedlungshauptamt der SS und die rassenpolitische Neuordnung Europas* (Göttingen: Wallstein, 2003), p. 381.

4 Czesław Madajczyk, *Die Okkupationspolitik Nazideutschlands in Polen 1939–1945* (East Berlin: Akademie Verlag, 1987), p. 422; Édouard Conte and Cornelia Essner, *La Quête de la race: Une anthropologie du nazisme* (Paris: Hachette, 1998), p. 270.

5 The following discussion is essentially based on Markus Leniger, *Nationalsozialistische 'Volkstumsarbeit' und Umsiedlungspolitik 1933–1945: Von der Minderheitenbetreuung zur Siedlerauslese* (Berlin: Frank & Timme, 2006), pp. 148–222 for the system of filtering, p. 213 for the commissions and the General Government, and pp. 161–74 for the criteria and procedures of selection.

6 Figures quoted in Wilhelm Gradmann's report on Germandom in the Zamość region, 19 March 1942, reproduced in Madajczyk, *Zamojszczyzna – Sonderlaboratorium SS*, vol. 1, pp. 53–66 (pp. 53–4), for the families which emigrated in the eighteenth century. For the filtering of migrant populations, see Leniger, *Nationalsozialistische 'Volkstumsarbeit'*, pp. 213–14; Madajczyk, *Die Okkupationspolitik Nazideutschlands*, p. 422 for the overall figures.

7 Report of the district head (*Kreishauptmann*) for Zamość, 25 November 1941, in Madajczyk, *Zamojszczyzna – Sonderlaboratorium SS*, vol. 1, p. 35; Conte and Essner, *La Quête de la race*, p. 276.

8 Madajczyk, *Die Okkupationspolitik Nazideutschlands*, p. 422; Isabel Heinemann, drawing on the sources of the RuSHA official and the filtering commissions, questions Madajczyk's overall figure and reduces it to 48,534, with over 32,000 in summer 1943 corroborating the UWZ figures, i.e. the evacuees who had actually reached the transit camps (approx. 50,000), effectively corresponding to those of the RuSHA (Heinemann, *'Rasse, Siedlung, deutsches Blut'*, p. 410). The figure given by Madajczyk is indeed imprecise, but it may be including runaways who managed to evade German institutions and swelled the ranks of the underground fighters who were gradually moving into the rural areas of the south of the region; all the UWZ reports estimate at 30 per cent the men who were effectively counted in the statistics that lie behind Heinemann's argument. She thinks it plausible that 50,000 people fled. For this reason, I have decided to stick to her estimate.

9 Conte and Essner, *La Quête de la race*, pp. 296ff., drawing on Polish testimony that I have not been able to consult.

10 RGBI, Jg. 1941, Teil 1, pp. 18–120: http://alex.onb.ac.at/cgi-content/alex?aid=dra&datum=1941&page=146&size=45.

11 Hans-Jürgen Bömelburg, 'Deutsche Besatzungspolitik in Polen 1939–1945', in Bernhard Chiari (ed.), *Die polnische Heimatarmee: Geschichte und Mythos der Armia Krajowa seit dem Zweiten Weltkrieg* (Munich: Oldenbourg, 2003), pp. 51–86 (pp. 78–9).

12 Maria Fiebrandt, *Auslese für die Siedlergesellschaft: Die Einbeziehung Volksdeutscher in die NS-Erbgesundheitspolitik im Kontext der Umsiedlungen 1939–1945* (Göttingen: Vandenhoeck & Ruprecht, 2014), pp. 470–99, for the filtering, and especially for the role played by the RuSHA in health matters (as *Gesundheitsstelle*); see p. 496 for the raciological scale.

13 This is noted by Conte and Essner in *La Quête de la race*, p. 298.

14 Bömelburg, 'Deutsche Besatzungspolitik in Polen', p. 79.

15 This is mentioned in communication from RSHA IV B to RFSS Himmler, signed *SSGruf*. Müller, 31 October 1942, quoted in Madajczyk, *Zamojszczyzna – Sonderlaboratorium SS*, vol. 1, pp. 152–3.

16 Hermann Krumey, Report on the activities of the 'Zamość' office of the UWZ, 27 November to 31 December 1942, in Madajczyk, *Zamojszczyzna – Sonderlaboratorium SS*, vol. 1, pp. 256–7.

17 Krumey, Report, in Madajczyk, *Zamojszczyzna – Sonderlaboratorium SS*, vol. 1, pp. 256–7, and communication from RSHA IV to RFSS Himmler, signed *SS-Gruf*. Müller, 31 October 1942, quoted in Madajczyk, *Zamojszczyzna – Sonderlaboratorium SS*, vol. 1, pp. 152–3. See also Conte and Essner, *La Quête de la race*, pp. 300–1.

18 Figures taken from the report on activities for 1942 and the report on 1943 of the 'Zamość' office of the UWZ, signed by Krumey, in Madajczyk, *Zamojszczyzna – Sonderlaboratorium SS*, vol. 1, pp. 256–9 for 1942; vol. 2, pp. 286–87 for 1943. Krumey states a figure of 40,837 people for 1943, and 9,771 arrested and 7,065 taken to the camp in Zamość for 1942.

19 Madajczyk, *Zamojszczyzna – Sonderlaboratorium SS*, vol. 1, 'Introduction', p. 14; this is also quoted by Isabel Heinemann, who devotes a chapter of her thesis to the question of racially Nordic children taken from their parents, in *'Rasse, Siedlung, deutsches Blut'*, pp. 495–535. Christian Gerlach gives a figure of between 11,000 and 14,500 children (Christian Gerlach, *Kalkulierte Morde: Die deutsche Wirtschafts- und Vernichtungspolitik in Weißrußland* (Hamburg: Hamburger Edition, 1999), pp. 1090–1; quoted in Heinemann, *'Rasse, Siedlung, deutsches Blut'*, p. 513).

20 See Madajczyk, *Vom Generalplan Ost*, document no. 74, pp. 261–6, reproducing Krumey's notes. See also chapter 4.

21 The term is used by the author of the report on the transport of 644 Poles to the Auschwitz labour camp on 10 December 1942, quoted in Madajczyk, *Zamojszczyzna – Sonderlaboratorium SS*, vol. 1, pp. 220–1 (p. 221), also quoted in Conte and Essner, *La Quête de la race*, p. 299.

22 This is noted in Conte and Essner, *La Quête de la race*, p. 293; list of convoys in Sara Berger, *Experten der Vernichtung: Das T4-Reinhardt-Netzwerk in den Lagern Belzec, Sobibór und Treblinka* (Hamburg: Hamburger Edition, 2013), pp. 416–31 (p. 420 and p. 424).

23 I am here following Dieter Pohl, 'Die großen Zwangsarbeitslager der SS- und Polizeiführer für Juden im Generalgouvernement 1942–1945', in Christoph Dieckmann, Ulrich Herbert and Karin Orth (eds.), *Die nationalsozialistischen Konzentrationslager. Entwicklung und Struktur* (Göttingen: Wallstein, 1998), 2 vols., vol. 1, pp. 415–38 (pp. 416–17).

24 Memorandum from Himmler to Globocnik, 21 July 1941, published in Madajczyk, *Zamojszczyzna – Sonderlaboratorium SS*, vol. 1, pp. 26–7. See also, for the rectification of the erroneous date of the memorandum in Madajczyk, Peter Witte, Michael Wildt, Martina Voigt, Dieter Pohl, Peter Klein, Christian Gerlach, Christoph Dieckmann and Andrej Angrick (eds.), *Der Dienstkalender Heinrich Himmlers 1941/42* (Hamburg: Hamburger Edition, 1999), p. 186.

25 Pohl, 'Die großen Zwangsarbeitslager der SS- und Polizeiführer', pp. 416–18; Hermann Kaienburg, 'Jüdische Arbeitslager ans der "Straße der SS"', *1999: Zeitschrift für Sozialgeschichte des 20. und 21. Jahrhunderts*, 1 (1996), pp. 13–39.

26 See the maps.

27 Correspondence between *SS-Hstuf.* Padel, a subordinate of Hanelt, and the 'Cultural Politics' department of the *Reichsjugendführung*, from November 1940, in USHMM, RG-15.027 M (archive AGKBZH 891/1), roll no. 1.

28 USHMM, RG-15.027 M (archive AGKBZH 891/6), roll no. 1, fos. 93ff. It is impossible to know whether Frank's directive was based on Stanglica's suggestions or whether the connection was fortuitous.

29 USHMM, RG-15.027 M (archive AGKBZH 891/5), roll no. 1, fos. 100ff.

30 USHMM, RG-15. 056 M (archive WAP Lublin), roll no. 2, archive 'Forschungsstelle für deutsche Osterkunft', dossiers 7 to 11.

31 See USHMM, RG-15.027 M (archive AGKBZH 891/4), roll no. 1.

32 Organization chart for the *Forschungsstelle*, in Madajczyk, *Zamojszczyzna – Sonderlaboratorium SS*, vol. 2, pp. 289–91; also quoted in Schulte, *Zwangsarbeit und Vernichtung*, p. 268 and p. 270.

33 Madajczyk, *Zamojszczyzna – Sonderlaboratorium SS*, vol. 2, pp. 312–13.

34 Madajczyk, *Zamojszczyzna – Sonderlaboratorium SS*, vol. 2, p. 313.

35 Schulte, *Zwangsarbeit und Vernichtung*, p. 303. A 'Point of support' on the first level was designed to have 1,690 SS and police, with SSPF and BdO (regional command of uniformed police) general staffs, a police company of 73 people, 17 WVHA officers, and 8 others from the RuSHA. Provision was also made for 1,000 police from the *Schutzpolizei*, as well as a BdS of 473 functionaries of the Gestapo, the KRIPO (criminal police) and the SD, commanded by an SS colonel and a senior government advisor. For a 'Point of support' on the first level that was the seat of an SSPF, provision was made only for a KdS with 147 SIPO functionaries, headed by an SS commander with a post as government advisor. A 'Point of support' on the second level had only some hundred or so functionaries from the SIPO or the SD, and 15 men of the future WVHA, out of a total of 453 personnel. The 'Points of support' of the third order were hierarchized in three sizes: small posts of which the biggest had 63 police, the medium-sized 31, and the smallest 21. All in all, 39,630 personnel were to staff these forts of Germanization.

36 Directive no. 3, 6 January 1943, signed by Globocnik, BABL, R-49/3533, fos. 21–4.

37 Conte and Essner, *La Quête de la race*, p. 328.

38 The implications are hinted at by Schulte, *Zwangsarbeit und Vernichtung*, p. 249 and pp. 276–7.

39 'Ein Dorf erwacht zu neuem Leben' ('A village awakens to a new life'), article published in the *Warschauer Zeitung*, 3 January 1943, reproduced in Madajczyk, *Zamojszczyzna – Sonderlaboratorium SS*, vol. 1, pp. 278–86; also quoted in Conte and Essner, *La Quête de la race*, pp. 303ff.

40 'Ein Dorf erwacht zu neuem Leben', in Madajczyk, *Zamojszczyzna – Sonderlaboratorium SS*, vol. 1, p. 279.

41 'Ein Dorf erwacht zu neuem Leben', in Madajczyk, *Zamojszczyzna – Sonderlaboratorium SS*, vol. 1, p. 280. I am here cutting an interesting passage on the way that the peasants did not feel at ease on big farms, and preferred to 'live off their own', as was said of peasants in the *Ancien Régime*. The text is particularly long and filled with literary pretentiousness. I have thus cut several passages, selecting only the most useful for demonstration.

42 'Ein Dorf erwacht zu neuem Leben', in Madajczyk, *Zamojszczyzna – Sonderlaboratorium SS*, vol. 1, pp. 281–2.

43 Conte and Essner, *La Quête de la race*, p. 306.

44 Directives nos. 3–5, BABL, R-49/3533: Action Zamość, fos. 21–9.

45 Directive no. 7, BABL, R-49/3533: Action Zamość, fos. 30 and 31.

46 Directive no. 7, BABL, R-49/3533: Action Zamość, fo. 31 verso.

47 Directive no. 7, BABL, R-49/3533: Action Zamość, fos. 30–4 (fol. 31).

48 Directive no. 7, BABL, R-49/3533: Action Zamość, fo. 32.

49 This, in my view, is what intuitively explains the interest for several historians of the questions of colonization and the advent of the new Reich. These historians include Édouard Conte and Cornelia Essner, as anthropologists of Nordic racial dogma, in *La Quête de la race*, and Johann Chapoutot, a historian of Nazi beliefs and the way they were expressed as so many categorical imperatives dictating action. See Johann Chapoutot, *La Loi du sang: Penser et agir en nazi* (Paris: Gallimard, 2014). This question was the ideological heart of the most novel aspects of Nazism.

50 Directive no. 7, BABL, R-49/3533: Action Zamość, fos. 30–4 (fo. 32).

51 Directive no. 7, BABL, R-49/3533: Action Zamość, fo. 33.

52 I am taking this phrase from Alphonse Dupront, *Le Mythe de croisade* (Paris: Gallimard, 1997), 4 vols., vol. 2, pp. 1210–11.

Chapter 9 The nightmare: from the ethnic domino effect to the flames of despair

1 This is the main leitmotif of Götz Aly, *Final Solution: Nazi Population Policy and the Murder of the European Jews*, trans. Belinda Cooper and Allison Brown (London: Arnold, 1999).

2 Dieter Pohl, 'Die großen Zwangsarbeitslager der SS- und Polizeiführer für Juden im Generalgouvernement 1942–1945', in Christoph Dieckmann, Ulrich Herbert and Karin Orth (eds.), *Die nationalsozialistischen Konzentrationslager: Entwicklung und Struktur* (Göttingen: Wallstein, 1998), vol. 1, pp. 415–38 (p. 417).

3 Bogdan Musial, *Deutsche Zivilverwaltung und Judenverfolgung im*

General-Gouvernement: Eine Fallstudie zum Distrikt Lublin (Wiesbaden: Harrassowitz, 1999), pp. 112ff.

4 Musial, *Deutsche Zivilverwaltung*, p. 124.

5 A proposal made by Globocnik at a meeting of the economic authorities of the General Government on 14 February 1940, quoted in Musial, *Deutsche Zivilverwaltung*, p. 206.

6 Dieter Pohl, 'Die Ermordung der Juden im Generalgouvernement', in Ulrich Herbert (ed.), *Nationalsozialistische Vernichtungspolitik 1939–1945: Neue Forschungen und Kontroversen* (Frankfurt: Fischer, 1998), pp. 98–121 (p. 103).

7 On harmful elements and these questions of the *imaginaire* of the hunt, the Savage and pastoralism, see Bertrand Hell, *Le Sang noir: Chasse et mythe du sauvage en Europe* (Paris: Flammarion, 1994).

8 See the very fine study by Christopher Browning, *Ordinary Men: Reserve Police Battalion 101 and the Final Solution in Poland* (London: Penguin, 2001), and – though I have many reservations about the overall argument – the impressive array of sources on the *Judenjagd* in Daniel Goldhagen, *Hitler's Willing Executioners: Ordinary Germans and the Holocaust* (London: Little, Brown, 1996).

9 This was the interpretive approach I adopted in my earlier work: see Christian Ingrao, *Believe and Destroy: Intellectuals in the SS War Machine*, trans. Andrew Brown (Cambridge: Polity, 2013), and, more systematically but applied to a single unit, present in Lublin only until January 1942, in Christian Ingrao, *The SS Dirlewanger Brigade: The History of the Black Hunters*, trans. Phoebe Green (New York: Skyhorse, 2011).

10 See Christoph Dieckmann and Babette Quinkert (eds.), *Kriegführung und Hunger 1939–1945: Zum Verhältnis von militärischen, wirtschaftlichen und politischen Interessen* (Göttingen: Wallstein, 2015).

11 Musial, *Deutsche Zivilverwaltung*, pp. 193–214. The expression 'Außergewöhnliche schädliche Fresser' is used by Hans Frank.

12 See previous chapter, and Jan Erik Schulte, *Zwangsarbeit und Vernichtung: Das Wirtschaftsimperium der SS. Oswald Pohl und das SS-Wirtschafts-Erwaltungshauptamt* (Paderborn: Ferdinand Schöningh, 2001) pp. 312–13.

13 Dieter Pohl, *Nationalsozialistische Judenverfolgung in Ostgalizien 1941–1944: Organisation und Durchführung eines staatlichen Massenverbrechens* (Munich: Oldenbourg, 1996), p. 113.

14 Sara Berger, *Experten der Vernichtung: Das T4-Reinhardt-Netzwerk in den Lagern Belzec, Sobibór und Treblinka* (Hamburg: Hamburger Edition, 2013), pp. 38–40.

15 Berger, *Experten der Vernichtung*, pp. 47–51.

16 Berger, *Experten der Vernichtung*, p. 417 for the convoys, pp. 93–5 for the analysis.

17 Indeed, this seems to have been practically Sobibór's sole function; its only really significant activity in 1942 lasted two months (from April to the end of May) and declined as Bełżec gradually became more active after the rebuilding of the camp's extermination facilities, which became effective at the end of June 1942 (Berger, *Experten der Vernichtung*, p. 177). It should be noted that the periodizations of Sara Berger and Florent Brayard do not coincide: according to the former, the trains were running again from 1 June, while

the French historian says that they did not resume until the end of June. See Florent Brayard, 'Comment écrire l'histoire sans archives? Un regard sur l'historiographie du camps d'extermination de Bełżec', in Florent Brayard (ed.), *Le Génocide des Juifs entre procès et histoire 1943–2000* (Brussels: Éditions Complexe, IHTP, 2001), pp. 135–88 (p. 163). The sources on which Sara Berger draws have been more systematically explored, so I am here following her chronology.

18 A table of the convoys arriving at Bełżec and Sobibór can be found in Berger, *Experten der Vernichtung*, pp. 416–426.

19 This is carefully noted in Édouard Conte and Cornelia Essner, *La Quête de la race: Une anthropologie du nazisme* (Paris: Hachette, 1998), p. 285.

20 David Silberklang, 'What Did They Know? The Jews of the Lublin District and the Deportations', in Roni Stauber, Aviva Halamish and Esther Webman (eds.), *Holocaust and Antisemitism: Research and Public Discourse. Essays Presented in Honor of Dina Porat* (Jerusalem: Tel Aviv University and Yad Vashem, 2015), pp. 25–52. I must give my warmest thanks to David Silberklang for allowing me to see the proofs of his text.

21 Silberklang, 'What Did They Know?', pp. 38–9.

22 Zygmunt Klukowski, *Diary from the Years of Occupation, 1939–44*, trans. George Klukowski, edited by Andrew Klukowski and Helen Klukowski May (Urbana: University of Illinois Press, 1993), p. 191. (I am very grateful to Jean-Yves Potel for sending me a copy of the French translation of Klukowski's magnificent work.) Klukowski's testimony was partly published in Czesław Madajczyk (ed.), *Zamojszczyzna – Sonderlaboratorium SS: Zbior dokumentow polskich i niemieckich z okresu okupacji hitlerowskiej* (Warsaw: Ludowa Spoldzielnia Widawnicza, 1979), 2 vols., and it is quoted extensively in Conte and Essner, *La Quête de la race*, pp. 278–93.

23 Klukowski, *Diary*, entry for 8 April 1942, p. 191.

24 Klukowski, *Diary*, p. 219.

25 Berger, *Experten der Vernichtung*, p. 420.

26 Klukowski, *Diary*, entry for 28 October (p. 222) for the blunted sensibilities.

27 Yasmine Shooman, 'Die Rotunde von Zamość', in Wolfgang Benz and Barbara Distel (eds.), *Der Ort des Terrors: Geschichte der nationalsozialistischen Konzentrationslager* (Munich: C. H. Beck, 2009), vol. 9, pp. 497–509 (p. 498).

28 Klukowski, *Diary*, p. 99.

29 Klukowski, *Diary*, p. 126.

30 He was most likely freed because, as director of the hospital, he was in contact with typhus patients and was indispensable for their treatment. See Shooman, 'Die Rotunde von Zamość', p. 508, note 14.

31 On the Wehrmacht and orders to bypass the usual legal channels, see Jürgen Förster, *Die Wehrmacht im NS-Staat: Eine strukturgeschichtliche Analyse* (Munich: Oldenbourg, 2009), p. 66.

32 Klukowski, *Diary*, entries for 14, 15, 18 January 1941, pp. 132–3 (p. 133).

33 Klukowski, *Diary*, pp. 137–8. The entry for the following day again mentions the depth of his grief.

34 Klukowski, *Diary*, entries for 15–18 November 1940, for the first example, p. 125,

and, for the second, entry for 14 February 1941, pp. 135–6. For children being taken from their parents, see Madajczyk, *Zamojszczyzna – Sonderlaboratorium SS*, 'Introduction', and Shooman, 'Die Rotunde von Zamość', p. 501.

35 Klukowski, *Diary*, pp. 140–1.
36 I have taken this expression of the pain felt by a bereaved person from *Feuillets d'Hypnos*, fragment no. 157, in René Char, *Œuvres complètes* (Paris: Gallimard, Bibliothèque de la Pléiade, 1983), p. 213.
37 Conte and Essner, *La Quête de la race*, p. 311.
38 Musial, *Deutsche Zivilverwaltung*, p. 22.
39 Klukowski, *Diary*, entry for 4 April 1942, p. 190.
40 Klukowski, *Diary*, p. 281.
41 Pohl, *Nationalsozialistische Judenverfolgung in Ostgalizien*, p. 113; on the whole question of the Trawnikis, see also Peter R. Black, 'Odilo Globocnik, Nazi Eastern Policy and the Implementation of the Final Solution', in Dokumentationsarchiv des österreichischen Widerstandes (ed.), *Forschungen zum Nationalsozialismus und dessen Nachwirkungen in Österreich: Festschrift für Brigitte Bailer* (Vienna, 2012): http://www.doew.at/cms/download/70s5n/bb_black.pdf, pp. 109–23.
42 Silberklang, 'What Did They Know?', pp. 25–54 (pp. 53–4 for reflections on the factors that helped some from the Lublin district to survive).
43 The figure is given in Conte and Essner, *La Quête de la race*; they tackle head-on (pp. 289–93) the question of the survival of Jews in the forests and give an estimate of the numbers (p. 292).
44 Werner Präg and Wolfgang Jacobmeyer (eds.), *Das Diensttagebuch des deutschen Generalgouverneurs in Polen 1939–1945* (Stuttgart: Deutsche Verlags-Anstalt, 1984), p. 603, quoted in Shooman, 'Die Rotunde von Zamość', p. 508, note 22.
45 *Biuletyn Informacijny*, 7: 162 (18 February 1943), reproduced in Madajczyk, *Zamojszczyzna – Sonderlaboratorium SS*, vol. 1, p. 482; quoted in Conte and Essner, *La Quête de la race*, pp. 312–13.
46 Klukowski, *Diary*, p. 230.
47 See previous chapter. The figures are taken from the report on activities for 1942 and for the 1943 report of the 'Zamość' office of the UWZ, signed by Krumey, in Madajczyk, *Zamojszczyzna – Sonderlaboratorium SS*, vol. 1, pp. 256–9 for 1942; vol. 2, pp. 286–7 for 1943.
48 Klukowski, *Diary*, p. 155.
49 For a general historical overview, see Bernhard Chiari (ed.), *Die polnische Heimatarmee: Geschichte und Mythos der Armia Krajowa seit dem Zweiten Weltkrieg* (Munich: Oldenbourg, 2003); for the creation of the ZWZ, see the chronology there, p. 865.
50 Klukowski mentions Kamiński in his *Diary*, p. 329.
51 Report of the Head of the Police First Motorized Batallion, 16 February 1943, USHMM, RG-15.011 M (archive AGKBZH 156/76), roll no. 5, fos. 15–19.
52 Präg and Jacobmeyer, *Das Diensttagebuch des deutschen General-gouverneurs*, pp. 672–7; quoted in Conte and Essner, *La Quête de la race*, p. 328.
53 He was actually in Kraków in June and July 1943 to discuss questions of security (and insecurity) with Hans Frank, at the very same time that *Wehrwolf* was

happening. See Conte and Essner, *La Quête de la race*, p. 327. BABL, R-20/45b, fo. 76, for the meeting in Kraków of 20 May 1943; fo. 77 for the meeting with Globocnik and Krüger on 1 and 2 June 1943.

54 Martin Winstone, *The Dark Heart of Hitler's Europe: Nazi Rule in Poland under the General Government* (London and New York: I. B. Tauris, 2014), pp. 206–7; Conte and Essner, *La Quête de la race*, pp. 329ff.

55 Figures for the UWZ, October 1943, published in Madajczyk, *Zamojszczyzna – Sonderlaboratorium SS*, vol. 2, pp. 231–2.

56 Report of police detachment, Biłgoraj, 8 December 1943, USHMM, RG-15.011 M (archive AGKBZH 156/68), roll no. 5, fos. 30–1.

57 USHMM, RG-15.011 M (archive AGKBZH 156/68), roll no. 5, fo. 30 verso.

58 Daily report of KdO Lublin to the BdO, 25 September 1943, USHMM, RG-15.011 M (archive AGKBZH 156/107), roll no. 5, fos. 8–10. The details are reported in Klukowski, *Diary*, entry for 28 September 1943, p. 282.

59 USHMM, RG-15.011 M (archive AGKBZH 156/107), roll no. 5, fo. 8.

60 Black, 'Odilo Globocnik, Nazi Eastern Policy'.

61 Report of police detachment, Biłgoraj, 8 December 1943, USHMM, RG-15.011 M (archive AGKBZH 156/68), roll no. 5, fos. 30–1 (fo. 30 verso).

62 Klukowski, *Diary*, entry for 20 October 1943, p. 286.

63 Klukowski, *Diary*, entry for 6 June 1943, p. 259.

64 Waldemar Lotnik and Julian Preece, *Nine Lives: Ethnic Conflict in the Polish–Ukrainian Borderlands* (London: Serif Books, 2013), non-paginated Kindle format: the locations are 27 per cent, location 930 out of 3516.

65 Lotnik and Preece, *Nine Lives*, location 262/3516.

66 Lotnik and Preece, *Nine Lives*, location 939/3516.

67 Véronique Nahoum-Grappe, 'L'usage politique de la cruauté: L'épuration ethnique (ex-Yougoslavie, 1991–1995)', in Françoise Héritier (ed.), *De la violence* (Paris: Odile Jacob, 1996), pp. 273–323.

68 Denis Crouzet, *Les Guerriers de Dieu: La violence au temps des troubles de religion* (Paris: Champ Vallon, 1990), 2 vols.; see the introduction for the question of violence as a language.

69 Lotnik and Preece, *Nine Lives*, location 946.

70 Lotnik and Preece, *Nine Lives*, location 956–60.

71 Lotnik and Preece, *Nine Lives*, location 972–91.

72 Pierre Clastres, 'Archéologie de la violence: La guerre dans les sociétés primitives', in Pierre Clastres, *Libres 1* (Paris: Payot, 1977), pp. 137–73.

73 The notion of *entre-soi* is a basic concept in second-generation structuralist anthropology. There is a definition of it in Françoise Héritier, 'Les matrices de la violence et de l'intolérance', in Françoise Héritier (ed.), *De la violence* II (Paris: Odile Jacob, 1999), pp. 321–48 (pp. 325–6).

74 Lotnik mentions the presence of these groups in Lotnik and Preece, *Nine Lives*.

75 I am here using the felicitous expression of Abel Poitrineau; see Jean-Pierre Poussou, 'Abel Poitrineau, *Remues d'hommes: Les migrations montagnardes en France, XVIIe–XVIIIe siècles* [review]', *Annales: Économies, Sociétés, Civilisations*, 41 (1986), pp. 1086–8.

76 Another story admirably related by Catherine Gousseff, *Échanger les peuples:*

Le déplacement des minorités aux confins polono-soviétiques (1944–1947) (Paris: Fayard, 2015); this has useful information on subsequent exchanges of population, especially Operation Vistula, which I do not have time to discuss in detail.

Conclusion

1 René Char, *Feuillets d'Hypnos*, fragment no. 20, in René Char, *Œuvres complètes* (Paris: Gallimard, Bibliothèque de la Pléiade, 1983), p. 213.

Appendix 1:
Main acronyms used in the text

AGKBZH   (*Archivum Glownie Badania Zbrodnie Hitlerowskie*): Archives of the Commission of Inquiry into Nazi Crimes in Poland, deposited at the Institute of National Memory in Warsaw

AK   (*Arma Krayowa*): Army of the Interior, the main non-Communist Polish resistance movement

BABL   (*Bundesarchiv Berlin-Lichterfelde*): German Federal Archives, Berlin-Lichterfelde Centre

BADH   (*Bundesarchiv Berlin Dahlwitz-Hoppegarten*): German Federal Archives, Dahlwitz-Hoppegarten Centre

BCh   (*Bataliony Chlopsie*): Peasant Battalions, agrarian non-Communist Polish resistance movement

BDM   (*Bund Deutscher Mädel*): League of German Girls

BdO   (*Befehlshaber der Ordnungspolizei*): Regional command or commander of the uniformed police

BdS   (*Befehlshaber der Sicherheitspolizei und des SD*): Regional command or commander of the security police in the occupied territories

DAI   (*Deutsches Auslandsinstitut*): Institute of Germans Abroad.

DUT   (*Deutsche Umsiedlungs- und Treuhand GmbH*): German Resettlement Trust Ltd.

DVL   (*Deutsche Volksliste*): German Ethnic List

EWZ   (*Einwandererzentralstelle*): Central Immigration Office

Gestapo   (*Geheime Staatspolizei*): State Secret Police

HSSPF   (*Höhere SS- und Polizeiführer*): Supreme Head of the Police and SS for a particular country

HTO   (*Haupttreuhandstelle Ost*): Principal Trustee's Office East

IdS   (*Inspektion der Sicherheitspolizei*): Inspection of the Security Police, equivalent of the BdS for the Reich

KDO   (*Kommandeur der Ordnungspolizei*): Commander of the ORPO

KdS   (*Kommandeur der Sicherheitspolizei und des SD*): Local commander of the Security Police in the occupied territories

KL or KZ   (*Konzentrationslager*): Concentration camp

NSDAP	(*Nationalsozialistische Deutsche Arbeiterpartei*): National Socialist German Workers' Party, i.e. the Nazi Party
NSDStB	(*National-Sozialistischer Deutscher Studentenbund*): National Socialist German Students' League
NSV	(*Nationalsozialistische Volkswohlfahrt*): National Socialist Welfare Organization
ORPO	(*Ordnungspolizei*): Order Police (the uniformed police force in Nazi Germany)
RFSS	(*Reichsführer SS*): Reich Leader of the SS
RKFdV	(*Reichskommissariat für die Festigung deutschen Volkstums*): Reich Commission for the Consolidation of German Nationhood
RSHA	(*Reichssicherheitshauptamt*): Reich Main Security Office
RuSHA	(*Rasse- und Siedlungshauptamt*): Main Office for Race and Colorization
SA	(*Sturmabteilung*): Storm Detachment (Nazi paramilitary wing)
SD	(*Sicherheitsdienst der SS*): SS Intelligence Service
SS	(*Schutzstaffel*): The SS (literally 'Protection Squadron')
SS-HA	(*SS-Hauptamt*): Main Office of the SS
SSPF	(*SS- und Polizeiführer*): Chief of Police and SS for a region
UPA	(Українська Повстанська Армія, УПА, Ukrayins'ka Povstans'ka Armiya): Ukrainian Insurrectionary Army, a Ukrainian ultra-nationalist, fascistic, anti-Communist resistance movement
USHMM	United States Holocaust Memorial Museum (in Washington)
UWZ	(*Umwandererzentralstelle*): Central Emigration Office
VDA	(*Verein für das Deutschtum im Ausland*): Association of Overseas Germans
VOMI	(*Volksdeutsche Mittelstelle*): Coordination Centre for Ethnic Germans
WVHA	(*Wirtschafts- und Verwaltungshauptamt*): Main Office for the Economy and Administration
ZWZ	(*Związek Walki Zbrojnej*): Union of Armed Struggle, Polish non-Communist resistance movement uniting the AK and the BCh's

Appendix 2: Organizational chart of the SS institutions of Utopia

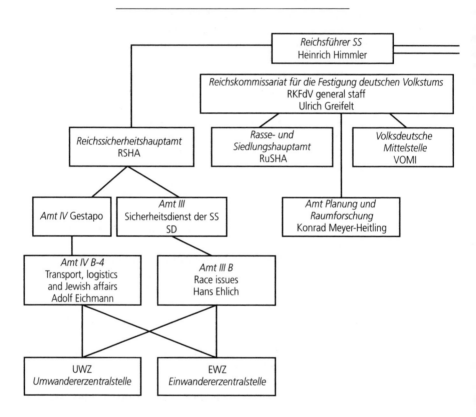

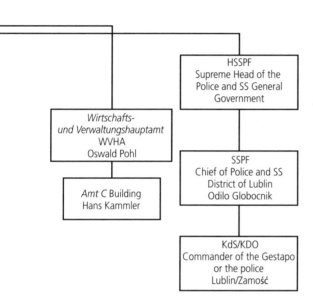

HSSPF
Supreme Head of the
Police and SS General
Government

*Wirtschafts-
und Verwaltungshauptamt*
WVHA
Oswald Pohl

Amt C Building
Hans Kammler

SSPF
Chief of Police and SS
District of Lublin
Odilo Globocnik

KdS/KDO
Commander of the Gestapo
or the police
Lublin/Zamość

Timeline

[This timeline details matters of general context; where information is relevant to specific contexts, it is labeled as follows:]
GO = *Generalplan Ost* RKFdV
GS = *Generalsiedlungsplan* RSHA
WV = WVHA
ZL = Zamość, laboratory of Germanization in Poland

1 September 1939

Invasion of Poland
Retroactive permission given to doctors to administer euthanasia to
  incurable patients

21 September 1939

Heydrich's directive to the *Einsatzgruppen*

28 September 1939

Signing of the confidential German–Soviet protocols on the repatriation
  of *Volksdeutsche*

1 October 1939

Official establishment of the RSHA
GS Reorganization and sharing of tasks between SD and Gestapo

6 October 1939

Order from Hitler formulating the project to reorganize interethnic relations in Europe

7 October 1939

Creation of the RKFdV
GO Appointment of Himmler as *Reichskommissar* FdV

12 October 1939

Hitler's order transferring powers in occupied Poland to a civil administration

15 October 1939

Signing of a treaty between the Reich and Estonia on the repatriation of the German minority

18–21 October 1939

GS/ZL Deportation of Jews to Nisko (district of Lublin): Eichmann/ Stahlecker experiment

26 October 1939

ZL Creation of the General Government. End of the provisional military administration

1 November 1939

GO Appointment of Greifelt, Chief of Staff of RKFdV. The HSSPF for Eastern territories appointed as regional delegates of the RKFdV, in charge of the logistics of repatriations. Probable transfer of Meyer-Heitling from RuSHA to RKFdV
GS First discussions between Greifelt, Ohlendorf, Ehlich and Sandberger

8 November 1939

GO Meeting of HSSPFs Koppe and Krüger (Poznań and Kraków) to coordinate expulsions

9 November 1939

ZL Appointment of Odilo Globocnik as SSPF Lublin

11 November 1939

GO Creation by Koppe of two special general staffs, one in charge of expulsions, the other in charge of resettlements. Prefigurations of the EWZ and UWZ

12 November 1939

GO Koppe's secret circular: 200,000 Poles and 100,000 Jews must be expelled by February 1940

16 November 1939

Signing of a new secret USSR/Reich agreement on the repatriation of *Volksdeutsche* from eastern Soviet-occupied Poland

23 November 1939

Jews in the General Government forced to wear identifying signs

28 November 1939

Fern- und Nahplan of the RSHA
GS Heydrich splits the programme of population displacement into a short-term plan and a long-term plan. 1st *Nahplan*: 80,000 expulsions scheduled, from 1 December to 17 December

30 November 1939

GS *Fernplan* of the RSHA *Amt* III B

4 December 1939

GO Koppe, HSSPF Poznań, recognized by the *Gauleiter* as sole competent authority for population displacements in the Warthegau

13 December 1939

GS Posen: EWZ and UWZ fix the beginning of the 2nd *Nahplan* for 21 December. 220,000 Jews and Poles must be expelled. Local consensus between RSHA and RKFdV under the personal umbrella of HSSPF Koppe. Deadline January–February 1940

19 December 1939

GS Meeting of the *Amtschef* RSHA. Question of the Jewish reserve and accommodation in the General Government. Eichmann appointed special representative for police business in population displacements

21 December 1939

GS Second version of 2nd *Nahplan*: 600,000 Jews to be expelled instead of 220,000

8 January 1940

GS Discussion between RSHA *Amt* III (Ohlendorf) and Labour Ministry on sending expelled Poles to the Reich for *Arbeitseinsatz*

17 January 1940

GS Discussions between Ehlich (*Sondergruppe* III ES) and Eichmann (*Sonderreferat* IV R, *Amt* IV D-4 and then IV B-4) on an intermediate solution to the 2nd *Nahplan*

20 January 1940

GO HSSPF Posen Koppe broadcasts the objectives of the 2nd *Nahplan* to local staffs

23 January 1940

First General Plan for the East
GO Konrad Meyer-Heitling, Chief of Planning Department of RKFdV, submits to Himmler a general population plan for the incorporated Eastern territories (R-49/157). The numbers advanced are the same as in the *Fernplan* of the RSHA. He bases his plan on the principle that the 560,000 Jews in these territories have already been evacuated or will be over the winter. 1st *Generalplan Ost*

30 January 1940

GS RSHA meeting on expulsions from General Government. Heydrich announces that 800,000 to 1 million Poles must now be sent to the Reich for *Arbeitseinsatz*

10 February 1940

GS Implementation of the 'intermediate plan': up until 15 March, 40,128 Poles and Jews from the towns and cities of western Poland are expelled to the General Government. Any other expulsion is strictly prohibited. Realization that the 2nd *Nahplan* has failed; it is postponed

14 February 1940

ZL Globocnik proposes starving the Jews of the district if they cannot be fed by their 'fellows'

29 February 1940

Himmler sets out the difficulties of the 2nd *Nahplan* to the *Gauleiter*, without mentioning its postponement

7 March 1940

The head of the office for expulsions in Łódź, Barth, proposes the creation of a KL for Polish and Jewish criminals, whose homes could be made available for the mass of *Volksdeutsche* now arriving. The proposal of 25 February is pursued on a larger scale on the date indicated

8 March 1940

ZL Plan to transform the district of Lublin into a place of concentration for all Jews in the General Government, especially those who have been expelled

21 March 1940

GS *Sondergruppe* ES becomes RSHA *Amt* III B, under Hans Ehlich

24 March 1940

Goering forbids any evacuation to the General Government

1 April 1940

GS Effective start of 2nd *Nahplan*. It does not provide any 'solution to the Jewish question' but arranges for the acquisition of space for peasants migrating from Volynia and Galicia. It is no longer 600,000 people but over 100,000 who are to be evacuated

8 April 1940

ZL Plan to concentrate the Jews of the General Government in the district of Lublin is abandoned

9 April 1940

German attack on Norway and Denmark

23 April 1940

Herbert Backe increases volume of supplies to be delivered by the General Government to Germany

24 April 1940

GS Eichmann's visit to Poznań: reappointment of UWZ Poznań, who now comes under the direct administration of RSHA *Amt* III B and IV B-4, draws on the resources of the local KdS and is financed from the assets administered by the RKFdV

30 April 1940

Closing of the Łódź ghetto

9 May 1940

GO Ordinance of RKFdV on selection of Germanizable Poles, signed by Himmler

10 May 1940

Attack on France, Belgium, Luxembourg and the Netherlands

17 May 1940

GO First transports of Germanizable Poles to Germany, as part of the 2nd *Nahplan*

19 May 1940

Second order putting the Jewish population in Warsaw into the ghetto

20 May 1940

Himmler's memorandum and letter to HSSPFs on the principles of Germanization of the incorporated territories. Mention of a plan to deport European Jews to an African colony

24 May 1940

Philipp Bouhler, Head of the T4, visits the General Government and leads discussions on the 'final solution to the Jewish question'

3 June 1940

Rademacher, *Judenreferat* from the Ministry of Foreign Affairs, first mentions Madagascar as a place of deportation for European Jews

15–17 June 1940

Occupation of the Baltic states by the USSR. Beginning of preparations for the SS to evacuate German minorities

18 June 1940

Ribbentrop mentions the Madagascar Plan to Ciano

21 June 1940

The leaders of *Aktion T4*, Bouhler, candidate for a post as Governor General in Western Africa, and Brack propose to place at the disposal of the Madagscar Plan the logistical arrangements they have developed for the euthanasia action

25 June 1940

GS Hans Frank refuses to assume responsibility in the General Government for the additional deportations not planned in the 2nd *Nahplan* because of the economic situation in the territory

28 June 1940

Annexation by the USSR of Bessarabia and the north of Bukovina

2 July 1940

'Madagascar Plan' of the Ministry of Foreign Affairs

8 July 1940

Meeting between Hitler and Frank. Transport of Jews to the General Government halted, dissemination of the Madagascar Plan
GS Decision to halt deportations to the General Government under pressure from Hans Frank and in the context of the Madagascar Plan

10 July 1940

GO Greifelt Memorandum on the resettlement of Germans from the South Tyrol to a certain area. The area under consideration: Burgundy

13 July 1940

GO RKFdV discussion of the four-year plan and Transport Ministry discussion of evacuation of the Saxons of Romania (BABL, R-5/817)

16 July 1940

France: expulsion of 3,000 Alsatian Jews to the future Free Zone. In two months, 24,200 French people are expelled from Alsace and Lorraine

21 July 1940

Official Sovietization of the three Baltic states. Acceleration of the evacuation preparations for the *Volksdeutsche*
31 July 1940 Meeting between Greiser, Frank, Koppe, Krüger and Streckenbach on the expulsion programmes. They are sceptical about the Madagascar Plan. Streckenbach announces that he has been given the mission by Heydrich to assess the number of Jews under German adminstration. First reference to a possible campaign against the USSR

1 August 1940

WV Hans Kammler is appointed *Standartenführer* and appointed to SS-HA *Verwaltung*
ZL Globocnik presents a *Wehrdörfer* plan to Himmler, who refuses. However, he accepts a policy for SS camps – the ancestors of the *SS- und Polizeistützpunkte*

5 August 1940

First plans for an attack on USSR

15 August 1940

Eichmann delivers the Madagascar Plan to Heydrich
GS Eichmann delivers the Madagscar plan, which provides for the deportation of nearly 4 million Jews (743,000 from the Reich, 2.3 million from the General Government, 77,000 from the Protectorate, 80,000 from Belgium, 160,000 from Holland, 270,000 from France, 95,000 from Slovakia, 2,500 from Luxembourg, 7,000 from Denmark, 1,500 from Norway)

2 September 1940

ZL Start of the displacement of *Volksdeutsche* from the General Government, from the region of Cholm and Lublin. They are to be settled in the district of Łódź and replaced by Poles expelled from there

12 September 1940

GO/GS Himmler's directives concerning the examination and selection for re-Germanization of the population of the incorporated territories. Of the 8 million Poles, only 1 million are re-Germanizable. The UWZ is given the mission of carrying out this selection and classifying the population on a *'Deutsche Volksliste'* with four degrees of assessment

17 September 1940

Adjournment of the landings in England. Abandonment of the Madagascar Plan

24 September 1940

Beginning of building by the VOMI of barracks to welcome the *Volksdeutsche* returning from Lithuania and Bukovina to the incorporated territories. In reality, the VOMI tries to lodge the *Volksdeutsche* in permanent buildings, and especially in sanatoria and care centres – which are emptied of their occupants beforehand by *Aktion T4*. There are increasing links between specialists in population displacement and experts in the logistics of murder

30 September 1940

Decision to establish the Warsaw ghetto. The ghetto is sealed off on 15 November

2 October 1940

Meeting between Hitler, Frank, von Schirach (*Gauleiter* for Vienna) and Koch (*Gauleiter* for East Prussia). All exert pressure on Frank to take in the expelled Jews and Poles. Frank refuses. For Hitler, the General Government is a labour reservoir for the lowliest tasks

5 October 1940

Resumption of deportations of Jews to the General Government from East Prussia

22 October 1940

France: expulsion of Jews from Baden to Free Zone

26 October 1940

ZL Discussion between Hitler and Globocnik in Kraków. Globocnik is given official permission to found an *SS-Mannschaftshaus* in Lublin; this brings together young scientists from the RKFdV, the RuSHA and the VOMI

27–30 October 1940

290 Jews, sick or aged, are shot in Kalisch

15 November 1940

Definitive sealing of the Warsaw ghetto
GO The RKFdV delegate for Upper Silesia states the case for the enlargement of the KL in Auschwitz and addresses to the general staff in Berlin the plans being prepared for this. The order is not given by Himmler until the following 1 March

26 November 1940

GO Himmler's directive for rural organization in the new territories of the East. 60% of family farms are to be between 20 and 115 hectares. A significant degree of mechanization and the extra use of the most modern techniques are to increase the productivity of these families

29 November 1940

First simulations of the plan for the invasion of the USSR signed at the OKH

4 December 1940

GS Eichmann, composing a basic set of terms for Himmler, now puts at 5.8 million the number of Jews to be expelled from the European economic zone of the German people to a territory still to be determined

10 December 1940

Himmer's lecture to the *Gauleiter* on the question of population displacements

17 December 1940

GS Meeting between Eichmann, Höppner, Krumey, etc., on the implementation of the 3rd *Nahplan*: settlement of *Volksdeutsche* of Bessarabia, Bukovina, Dobrudcha and Lithuania

18 December 1940

Hitler signs directive no. 21: establishment of preparations for Barbarossa; date set for the invasion: 15 May 1941

19 December 1940

Berlin: private conversations successively between Himmler and Heydrich, Greifelt, Lorenz and Goering on population displacements
GO The RKFdV begins preparations for resettlement of *Volksdeutsche* of Bukovina
GS The office of the EWZ of Łódź is informed of the beginnings of preparations for the resettlement of *Volksdeutsche* from Bukovina

21 December 1940

GO RKFdV ordinance on improving economic conditions of populations formerly occupying the Eastern territories, to counter their sense of being penalized in relation to newcomers. Implementation of the practice of *Verdrängung*: expellees are expropriated but allowed to seek accommodation with relatives on the territory in question

5 January 1941 (to February 1941)

GS Meeting between Hitler and Frank. Hitler imposes the demands made by Himmler and Heydrich as part of the 3rd *Nahplan*
ZL Sending of BDM and *volksdeutsche* activists to the villages of *Volksdeutsche* in the region of Zamość. Start of the first actions of educative Germanization. The *SS-Mannschaftshaus* prepares plans for the Germanization of Zamość

6 January 1941

GS Meeting between Koppe and Krumey (UWZ). They make plans for the expulsion of 330,000 Poles from the Warthegau in the course of 1941 (partly within the framework of the 3rd *Nahplan*)

7 January 1941

GO Meeting between Fähndrich (labour force bureau) of the RKFdV and the different directors of local RKFdV offices: distribution of arrivals from Buchenland, Dobrudcha and Bessarabia

8 January 1941

GS Meeting at the RSHA, chaired by Heydrich, to implement the 3rd *Nahplan*, bringing together representatives of the General Government, the officials of the RKFdV and the RSHA: plans made to evacuate 771,000 Poles from the incorporated territories. In the first phase of the 3rd *Nahplan*, up until 1 May, on a daily basis, two trains each with 1,000 Poles to be met in the General Government

20 January 1941

GO/GS Official start of the 3rd *Nahplan*

23 January 1941

GS Creation of an UWZ in Danzig by Eichmann: preparations for settlement of *Volksdeutsche* from Lithuania

28 January 1941

GO The director of the RKFdV 'Labour and Employment' department, Fähndrich, publishes the 'key figures' for deportation: for 1 arriving, 2 expelled to Danzig, 2 to 3 expelled to the Warthegau, in rural areas, 4 to 5 expelled to Upper Silesia, 3 for urban and manual milieux

5 February 1941

GS Start of deportations of Jews and Poles from the Warthegau in the framework of the 3rd *Nahplan*

15 February 1941

GS The Vienna evacuation centre for the General Government triggers the beginning of the deportation of Jews from the city. Transport is in fact stopped on 12 March

18 February 1941

GS The Ministry of Transport warns Eichmann that the forecasts of the first phase of the 3rd *Nahplan* cannot be kept to because of the military context (preparations for Barbarossa)

20 February 1941

Himmler writes to Frank to tell him that the deportations are going to have to be cancelled

28 February 1941

Himmler appointed by Hitler as solely responsible for ethnic issues inside the Party

1 March 1941

Himmler inspects Auschwitz. Orders given to expand the camp, now planned to hold 130,000 prisoners
ZL Early spring: flying commissions begin to work in the Zamość region, as part of the *Fahndung nach deutschem Blut* action

3 March 1941

First discussions between Hitler, Himmler and Heydrich on the special missions of the SIPO in the USSR

15 March 1941

GS Last transport in the framework of the 3rd *Nahplan*. Of the 250,000 meant to be expelled, only 25,000 have been so

20 March 1941

GO/GS Opening of the *Planung und Aufbau im Osten* exhibition. Planning of the *Die Große Heimkehr* (EWZ–VOMI–RuSHA) exhibition, which will eventually have to be abandoned

25 March 1941

ZL Hans Frank announces that the General Government is now set aside for Germanization. It is no longer the destination for those deported from the annexed territories

5 April 1941

Beginning of Action 14f13: technicians of T4 kill detainees in the concentration camps who are unfit for work

6 April 1941

The Reich invades Yugoslavia
GO/GS The RKFdV and RSHA create a general staff for the settlement of the Germans of Slovenia

2 May 1941

In the context of reduced rations announced for Germany, discussions between the economic authorities of the Wehrmacht and the state lead to the conclusion that 'dozens of millions of people will die of hunger, if we help ourselves to food from the country'. This is the formulation of the Famine plan

15 May 1941

GO The RKFdV head of staff, Greifelt, refuses to accept 1,500 *Volksdeutsche* from Bulgaria as they can be accomodated only in transit camps

20 May 1941

GS The RSHA forbids Jews to emigrate from France and Belgium

6 June 1941

Kommissarbefehl
GO Himmler's visit to Łódź. He announces the reshaping of the urban fabric and mentions urban planning

17 June 1941

GS Heydrich in Pretzsch

19 June 1941

Meeting between Hitler and Frank. Hitler promises that the Jews will be rapidly removed from the General Government

21 June 1941

GO Himmler tells Meyer-Heitling to produce a *Generalplan Ost*. This means, inter alia, that the General Government is now seen as Germanizable land

22 June 1941

Invasion of USSR

15 July 1941

GO Delivery of *Generalplan Ost* no. 2 by the RKFdV
ZL The *Krakauer Zeitung* announces that, since the spring, work has begun
    with the flying commissions of the *Fahndung nach deutschem Blut* action
    in Zamość district

16 July 1941

GS Höppner, head of the UWZ in Poznań, writes to Eichmann saying that
    the functionaries in charge of the Jewish question in the Warthegau are
    thinking of eliminating Jews who are unfit for work 'by some rapid
    means, in view of the approaching winter and the lack of supplies that
    is being forecast'

20 July 1941

ZL Himmler visits Lublin. The district is declared fit to be Germanized
    straight away. Orders given to construct the camp at Majdanek. Orders
    to extend the *Fahndung nach deutschem Blut* to the entire General
    Government. The Zamojszczyzna is now destined to become a major
    zone for Germanization and colonization, in Himmler's view

31 July 1941

Letter from Goering to Heydrich ordering him to prepare a final solution
    to the Jewish question, by migration or evacuation

1 August 1941

ZL Appointment of a head of the RuSHA in Lublin. Globocnik is tasked
    with constructing *Siedlungs- und Stutzpunkte* throughout the General
    Government and the USSR

15–16 August 1941

GS Himmler tours the front, stays in Minsk

16 August 1941 (to June 1942)

GS The four USSR *Einsatzgruppen* start to include women and children in
    their massacres

29–30 August 1941

HSSPF, Pol Reg 320 and EK5 kill 23,600 Jews in Kamenets-Podolski

1 September 1941

German Jews forced to wear identity markers. Soviet decision to deport 400,000 ethnic Germans from the Volga, announced 11 September in the *Völkischer Beobachter*

3 September 1941

GS Memorandum from Höppner (UWZ Poznań), discussed with Krumey (UWZ Łódź), sent to Eichmann and Ehlich, who proposes that after the victory the population displacements be speeded up, and focuses one of the points of the debate on the fate to be reserved for those undesirables who happen to be living in the destinations of those deported

3/5 September 1941 (to February 1942)

Tests of Zyklon B on Soviet prisoners of war in Auschwitz

13 September 1941

GS Memorandum by Rademacher (AA) on the impossibility of deporting the Jews from Serbia to the General Government and the USSR. Eichmann suggests that they be shot

16 September 1941

900 Soviet prisoners gassed in Auschwitz

29 September 1941

Building of camp in Mahiliow

29–30 September 1941

33,371 Jews slaughtered at Babi Yar

1 October 1941

ZL Letter from Globocnik to Himmer in which he notes that his preparations are complete and the phase of implementation of the plans for Germanization can begin immediately

2 October 1941

GS Heydrich announces the Germanization/deportation plan for the Protectorate

3 October 1941 (to February 1942)

GS Start of the systematic destruction of ghettoes behind the Centre Front by *Einstazgruppe B*. Operation Typhoon: start of the German offensive against Moscow

4 October 1941

ZL Establishment of a RuSHA bureau in Lublin. Mention of the participation of the SSHA *Verwaltungsamt*

10 October 1941

GS Himmler decides on the deportation of the German Jews to Riga and Minsk

13 October 1941

ZL Meeting between Himmler, Krüger and Globocnik: order to erect camp at Bełżec. Possible order to exterminate the Jews of the General Government

14 October 1941

GS Start of deportation of German Jews to Kaunas

15 October 1941

ZL Report by Müller to RuSHA on the conditions of Germanization in Lublin

17 October 1941

ZL Hans Frank visits Lublin, government meeting. Musial sees in Frank's speech the traces of Hitler's decision to exterminate the Jews in the General Government

21 October 1941

ZL It is forbidden to erect new ghettoes in the General Government

23 October 1941

GS Ban on German Jews emigrating

25 October 1941

GS Himmler visits Mahiliow. Plans to erect extermination camps in Minsk, Riga and Mahiliow

6 November 1941 (to June 1942)

ZL Test phase of Operation Zamość: expulsions of residents of six villages; their farms are handed over to *Volksdeutsche* from Bessarabia. The expelled Poles are sent to the Hrubieszów district

20 November 1941

GO Himmler's intervention (in a letter to Greifelt) to fulfil the directives of *Generalplan Ost*. Settlers will gain full ownership only after their sixth child, of which a minimum of two must be boys

27 November 1941

GS Sending of invitations to an interministerial conference on the Jewish question. Scheduled for 9 December, but postponed

30 November 1941

GS/ZL A hundred or so technicians of programme T4 sent to the district of Lublin and incorporated territories

4 December 1941

WV Memorandum by Hans Kammler on the 'Provisional Peacetime Building Programme'

5 December 1941

First convoy to Chelmno. Gas vans included in equipment of *Einsatzgruppen* in USSR

7 December 1941

Attack on Pearl Harbor. The United States enters the war

8 December 1941

First killings using gas vans in Chelmno

11 December 1941

Germany declares war on the United States

12 December 1941

Hitler informs the *Gauleiter* of the decision to exterminate European Jews

16 December 1941

ZL Hans Frank spreads the news of Hitler's decision throughout the General Government

18 December 1941

GS Meeting between Himmler and Hitler. Hitler tells Himmler of his decision to exterminate the European Jews

15 January 1942

Gassing of 5,000 Gypsies in gas vans in Chelmno

20 January 1942

GO/GS/ZL Wannsee Conference

27 January 1942

GO Discussion between Himmler, Greifelt and Meyer-Heitling; the last is ordered to present an estimate for the cost of the plan as regards western Poland and also for the plan as a whole

29 January 1942

GS Letter from RSHA to Ministry for Occupied Territories (Wetzel) on the Jewish question

31 January 1942

WV Letter from Himmler to Oswald Pohl on an estimate of SS costs for post-war building

1 February 1942

WV Foundation of WVHA through the fusion of HA *Haushalt und Bau* and the HA *Verwaltung*. Kammler head of *Amt* C Building

2 February 1942

GO Written order from Himmler telling Meyer-Heitling of the modes of general planning for the closed territories of Poland, including in those territories the new marches of settlement known as *Ingermanland* and *Gottengau*

ZL Circular from F.-W. Krüger appointing the RuS *Führer* of Lublin as RuS *Führer* for the whole General Government

4 February 1942

GS Meeting of *Ostministerium* (Wetzel) and RSHA *Amt* III B (Hummitzsch) on population displacements. Wetzel mentions the dominant role played by the RSHA in the Plan for the East

10 February 1942

WV 2nd memorandum by Kammler: 'Proposal for Organization of Building Brigades for Building Missions in Times of War and Peace'. He extends it to a period of ten years. Proposal to structure companies and building brigades (*Baubrigaden*)

15 February 1942

GS First RSHA *Amt* IV B-4 transport to Auschwitz from Upper Silesia

19 February 1942

GO Head of Wirtschaftsstab Ost presents his plan to Himmler in the presence of Meyer-Heitling, who is told of the '*Neue Agrarordnungen*' of the Ministry for Occupied Territories (policy of support points for long-term Germanization) and agreement between Speer and HSSPF Prutzmann on building motorways

20 February 1942

GO Memorandum of von Schauroth on estimates of cost and living standards in colonized territories. Preparation for the third version of the *Generalplan Ost*. Period: three months, with, however, a first accompanying letter ready at the beginning of April 1942

1 March 1942

WV The WVHA joins the Inspection of the KZ

3 March 1942

WV Richard Glücks inspector of camps at WVHA

5 March 1942

WV Transmission by Oswald Pohl of 2nd memorandum of Kammler, completed on 10 February 1942

10 March 1942

WV Letter from Kammler to the Inspection of camps, on the use of a workforce from the camps in the Reich and the General Government (NO-1292). Mention of Operation Heydrich in the document, mention of the decision to create *Baubrigaden*

17 March 1942

ZL Start of gassings in Bełżec

23 March 1942

WV Hitler replies to Pohl and Kammler: this letter provides the foundation for *Vernichtung durch Arbeit*

26 March 1942

Operation Bamberg in Belorussia: start of strategy of *Grossunternehmen*; first convoy from France to Auschwitz with immediate selection and gassings

18 April 1942

GO/WV Correspondence between Meyer-Heitling and Kammler on estimates of expenses linked to *Generalplan Ost*

20 April 1942

GO Conclusive conference preparing the 3rd *Generalpan Ost*

27 April 1942

GS Memorandum of Erhard Wetzel on the RFSS *Generalplan Ost* assigned to the RSHA with Ehlich designated by Wetzel

30 April 1942

WV Circular from Pohl to commandants of concentration camps on making the detainees do forced labour, which should be 'exhausting in the strongest sense of the word', an expression of the strategy of *Vernichtung durch Arbeit*

12 May 1942

Killing of 1,500 Jews in gas chambers in Auschwitz

27 May 1942

Attack on Heydrich in Prague

28 May 1942

GO *Generalplan Ost* no. 3 of RKFdV R-49/157a
ZL Start of selection of *Volksdeutsche* by the EWZ Herold Commission no. 15

30 May 1942 (to January 1943)

ZL Start of killings in Sobibor, building of Treblinka

1 June 1942

Appointment of Paul Blobel as head of special operation for exhumation and processing of bodies. Origin of Operation 1005. First experiments in Chelmno with incendiary bombs (?)

4 June 1942

Death of Reinhard Heydrich. Himmler orders a genocide to be completed within one year

12 June 1942

GO Deadline for *Generalplan Ost* brought forward from thirty to twenty years by Himmler

16 June 1942

GO/WV Organization of a 'building' department within the general staff of the RKFdV. Division of responsibilities between Kammler and Meyer-Heitling

18 June 1942

WV/ZL Himmler visits Lublin (Krüger and Pohl are also present), 18–20 June 1942. Order from Himmler creating the *SS-Wirtschafter* in the HSSPF

19 June 1942

ZL End of the first phase of gassings in Bełżec. Transformation and extension of gassing capacities. Building of six extra gas chambers. Order from Himmler to Krüger: a genocide must be completed by 31 December 1942 (NS-19/1757)

3 July 1942

The SIPO-SD assumes control of Westerbork. Start of the phase of murderous deportations to the Netherlands

7 July 1942

ZL Resumption of deportations to Bełżec

14 July 1942

GO Meyer-Heitling appointed delegate for Agrarian Planning and Reform at the Ministry of Supplies

15–16 July 1942

The so-called Vel' d'Hiv round-up: Jews in the Paris area are arrested, taken to Drancy and then sent to Auschwitz

22 July 1942

ZL Start of systematic deportations of Jews from Warsaw ghetto to Treblinka

19 August 1942

ZL Gerstein visits Bełżec

6 September 1942

ZL Major new round-up for deportation and murder in the Warsaw ghetto. Ghetto reduced to minimum before being destroyed

16 September 1942

GO Speech given by Himmler in Hegewald: confirmation of zones of colonization, 120 million Germans in 20 years, 600 million in 409 ... Officialization of the change in paradigm: an extended level of *Stützpunkte* created

31 October 1942

ZL Hitler's approval (by telegram) of Action Zamość

9 November 1942

Allied landings in North Africa

20 November 1942

Letter from Himmler to Müller on the rumours going round in many countries (Wise Report to the World Jewish Congress). Himmler notes that the bodies of Jews are to be buried or burned

22 November 1942

ZL General order no. 17 C: Zamość is now the 'First territory for German colonization in the General Government'

23 November 1942

The 6th Army is encircled in Stalingrad

27 November 1942

ZL Start of mass expulsions in Zamość and the district

30 November 1942 (to January 1943)

ZL Start of Operation 1005 in Bełżec and Sobibor

1 December 1942

ZL Start of process of closing the Bełżec camp

11 December 1942

GS Hans Ehlich's speech to the NSDStB: he starts from the assumption that 70 million natives are under German rule

23 December 1942

GO Himmler is presented with documents, figures and maps for a *Generalsiedlungsplan*

28 December 1942

GS Invitations sent out to the RSHA *Amt* III B conference to be held in February, in Bernau
ZL Attack of Polish resistance (Peasant Battalions and AK) on three villages colonized by Germans between Zamość and the forest of Zwierzyniec

31 December 1942

ZL End of first wave of expulsions in the district of Zamość. Only 28.9% of the people there are handed over to the UWZ

12 January 1943

GO Himmler's order for the complete Germanization of Belorussia and Crimea, which are to be totally Germanized and colonized

20 January 1943

WV Circular from Glücks ordering camp commandants to preserve their detainees' ability to work

31 January 1943

Capitulation of the 6th Army in Stalingrad

1–2 February 1943 (to January 1944)

Start of deportation of the Jews of Thessaloniki to Auschwitz
GS Conference of officials of RSHA *Amt* III B in Bernau. Krumey takes notes on a speech by Justus Beyer: key details for Germanization

15 February 1943

GO Letter from Meyer-Heitling to Himmler stating that his departments have started to work over the documents of the *Generalsiedlungsplan* and asking if they should continue to do so and to check the documentation. He will not receive any answer and the rest of the documentation available until August 1944 consists in a bureaucratic search for missing documents in the files. These documents are found on 6 January 1944. Himmler never replied to Meyer-Heitling's letter
ZL Opening the Ostlager SS Erlenhof in Jastkow, near Lublin. These camps visibly mix agronomy, control of populations and *Partisanenbekämpfung*

1 March 1943

ZL End of the process of closing Bełżec. Liquidation of the last detainees employed since December on the elimination of dead bodies. Destruction of the camp. Beginning of the process of destruction of the Sobibor camp

7 April 1943

End of the first phase of the extermination in Chelmno. Destruction of extermination facilities

19 April 1943

Warsaw ghetto uprising

9 May 1943

Capitulation of the last German troops in North Africa

31 May 1943

ZL Krüger halts settlements for security reasons

1 June 1943

Final liquidation of the Lemberg ghetto

23 June 1943

ZL Unleashing of *Wehrwolf* 1. It lasts until the end of July

1 July 1943

WV Letter from Kammler to EM von Unruh. Mention of WVHA *Nachkriegs-Bauprogramm* in the context of mobilization of resources. Probable point at which WVHA changes paradigm to concentrate its efforts on war production

5 July 1943

Start of Kursk offensive. Last major offensive on Eastern Front

2 August 1943

Rising of Treblinka *Sonderkommando* at the prospect of the camp being closed

15 August 1943

ZL End of Operation *Wehrwolf* 2. De facto end of Action Zamość

1 September 1943

WV Kammler appointed Himmler's delegate for programme A4 (V1). It is clear that priorities have changed
ZL Globocnik moved to post of HSSPF Kustenland (Slovenia). Presumed end of *Fahndung nach deutschem Blut* action

4 September 1943

German retreat in Crimea and Kuban

6 October 1943

Poznań speech. Completion of the Final Solution for Germany announced for end of the year

14 October 1943

Sobibor uprising. Auschwitz, the last gassing facility to be created, is still operating

3 November 1943

ZL Action Erntefest. Liquidation of the last survivors of the General Government

6 November 1943

Liberation of Kiev

24 December 1943

Liberation of Zhytomyr. Start of the work of the CGK in the city

16 January 1944

Soviet offensive on Leningrad and Ukraine

12 March 1944

Hitler gives order to invade Hungary

11 May 1944

Great Allied offensive in Italy

15 May 1944

Beginning of the mass deportation of Hungarian Jews. Extermination of the 'camp of Gypsy families'

1 June 1944

ZL Anti-partisan operations *Sturmwind* 1 and 2

6 June 1944

Operation Overlord

22 June 1944

Operation Bagration

23 June 1944

Liquidation of 7,000 Jews from the Łódź ghetto in the second version of the extermination camp of Chelmno

28 June 1944

Liquidation of Maly Trostenets

3 July 1944

Liberation of Minsk

20 July 1944

Assassination attempt on Hitler

22 July 1944

Evacuation of Majdanek

28 July 1944

Start of the 'death marches' from the General Government (Warsaw) to the Reich

1 August 1944

Warsaw uprising

7 August 1944

Beginning of liquidation by deportation of the Łódź ghetto, which still contains 70,000 people

6 October 1944

Rising of the Auschwitz *Sonderkommando*

20 October 1944

Liberation of Belgrade

25 November 1944

Start of the destruction of extermination facilities in Auschwitz

Index

academics' backgrounds 51, 52–5
agriculture 11, 58, 118, 134–5
  history and land reform,
    Zamojszczyzna 164–8
Aly, Götz xviii–xix, 14–15, 17, 39, 43,
    200
architecture and planning *see* School of
    Fine Arts

Baltics 60, 68, 73–4, 95, 104
Bangert, Walther 124, 125, 127
Belarus 58, 59, 112
Bełżec 175, 204–5, 206, 207
Beyer, Hans Joachim 53, 63, 67, 114,
    115, 186
Biłgoraj 215–17
Boehm, Max Hilderbert 103
Bonn, University of 53
Brandt, Rudolf 154–5
Bromberg 119–20
Broszat, Martin 6, 26
Browning, Christopher xix, 146, 172
building programmes *see* Kammler
    sequence (WVHA); WVHA;
    Zamojszczyzna (Zamość,
    Lublin), politics of the
    laboratory

central institutions *see* RKFdV; RSHA;
    WVHA
children and elderly people 186
Christaller, Walter 119, 123
civilian administrations
  incorporated and occupied
    territories 36–7
  and SS institutions 168–73

collective facilities, rural 133
concentration camps 206–10
  building plans 140
  labour force 148–9, 152
  see also labour/prison camps
Czechoslovakia 24, 138–9
  Heydrich speech 107
  land registry department, Prague
    58–9, 139

Danzig 93–4, 95
Dirlewanger battalion 171, 172
doctors 55–6, 80–2, 113, 181
Dolezalek, Alexander 34, 67
Dolezalek, Luise 96

education/re-education 77, 83–6,
    196–9
Ehlich, Hans (RSHA *Amt* III B) 8,
    10, 11, 13, 25, 32, 53, 54, 61,
    63
  General Plan 106, 114–15
  RSHA plans 43–4, 186
Ehrlinger, Erich 52
Eichmann, Adolf (RSHA IV B-4) 9, 10,
    11, 13, 16, 17–18, 31–2, 39, 41
elderly people and children 186
Engelhardt-Kyffthäuser, Otto 78–9
ethnic domino effect 200
ethnomorphosis or dissimilation
    102–8
EWZ 35–6
  doctors 55–6, 80–2, 181
  ethno-social engineering 180–2, 184,
    190
  Sandberger at 60

failure of Nazi dream 223–8
Famine Plan 19, 114
forced labour
  building programme,
    Zamojszczyzna 186–92
  Jews 20, 169–70, 202
  see also concentration camps;
    labour/prison camps
Frank, Hans 6, 12–13, 15–17, 20, 40–1,
  172, 190, 203, 212
Franszak, Jan 208–9

Galicia 167–8, 173, 218
gender
  dimension of journey to the East
    79–80
  see also women
General Plan for the East (1941–3) 21–6
general planning 93–4
  curse of Germanic insularity lifted
    95–102
  mass murder and Utopia 108–15
  Umvolkung: dissimilation or
    ethnomorphosis 102–8
German blood 101
  and Polonization 176, 180–1
  'Search for German Blood' action
    177–8, 188, 189
Germanization policies 2–8
  dream and failure 223–8
  maps xiv–xvi
  population displacements and
    construction xii–xiii
  see also general planning;
    institutions; networks and
    trajectories; Zamojszczyzna
    (Zamosc, Lublin)
Globocnik, Odilo (SSPF) 6, 12–13, 34,
  196, 199
  Habitat Research Centre in the East
    170–1, 189–90
  and Himmler 22, 144–6, 147, 170–1,
    174, 178, 179, 180, 187–9, 201
  Lublin 174–5, 179, 187–9, 190–1
  failure of building programme
    144–7
  institutions 170–1
  Jewish extermination and forced
    labour 178, 202, 203
  removal from 217
  social engineering 180
  radicalism 173–5, 176–7

Goering, Hermann 13, 18, 21
Gollert, Friedrich 121, 123
Gottberg, Curt von 57–9, 139
Götz, Karl 79
Great *Trek*, myths of 72–80
Great War 50, 56, 58, 74, 78
  Zamość 163–4

Habitat Research Centre in the East
  170–1, 189–90
Harvey, Elizabeth 50, 56
Heydrich, Reinhardt 4–5, 7, 8, 9, 10,
  11–12, 13, 16, 18, 21, 31, 39, 40
Himmler, Heinrich 3, 7
  classification of Poles 182–4
  General Plan 23–4, 25, 99–101, 102,
    150
  and Globocnik 22, 144–6, 147, 170–1,
    174, 178, 179, 180, 187–9, 201
  and Gottberg 59
  Kammler plan 138–55
  Lublin visit 22, 187–9, 202, 226
  Madagascar Plan 14
  and Meyer-Heitling 40–1, 42–3,
    99–100, 101, 141, 143, 149, 189
  Nahpläne and *Fernpläne* (short- and
    long-term plans) 8, 10, 11, 12,
    13, 17–18, 19, 20, 21
  and Pohl 140–3, 144–7, 149, 187–8
  RKFdV 5–6, 29–30
  urban planning and arrangement for
    incorporated territories 127–8
  WVHA 45–6
Hitler, Adolf 3, 17, 20, 24, 40–1
  concentration camp labour force 152
  General Plan 150
  language 82
  Madagascar Plan 14
  Poland invasion: Danzig problem
    93–4
  RKFdV 5–6
  USSR 17–18
HSSPF 6, 7, 10, 33–4, 63

institutions 7–8, 47, 66–7, 88–9, 223–4
  diversity of 29–37
  how consensus was generated 37–43
  main general plans 43–7
  Zamojszczyzna (Zamość, Lublin)
    168–73
  inter-self wars 214–22, 227–8
Ipsen, Gunther 103

Jews
  expulsion 6–7, 8–12, 13, 17–18, 19,
      32, 35, 41, 106
    and Jewish Reserve 12–13, 14–15,
      179
  extermination
    and escapes 211–14
    prior to Germanization 201–7,
      211–14
    programmes 22–3, 24, 43, 114, 178,
      186
    in USSR 61, 111, 112–13
  'final solution to the Jewish
      question' 21, 32, 35, 43, 44–5
  forced labour 20, 169–70, 202
  Madagascar Plan 14–17, 19, 20–1, 32,
      44, 111–12
  population statistics 42
  Zamojszczyzna (Zamość, Lublin)
      163, 166, 173, 178, 179, 180, 186,
      201–7, 211–14
journey to the East (*Osteinsatz*) 65–6,
    88–9
  between Utopia and anxiety
      66–72
  myths of the Great *Trek* 72–80
  racial, hygienic and educational
      dimensions 80–7

Kammler, Hans (WVHA) 22, 23, 33, 45,
    46, 55
  Central Department for Budget and
      Building 49, 145–6
Kammler sequence (WVHA) 138
  financial estimates 141–4
  institutionalization and failure of
      building programmes 144–9
  planning style 138–44
  Utopia evaporates 150–5
Klukowski, Zigmunt 161, 206–7,
    208–10, 213, 214, 218–19
Königsberg, University of 53, 103
Koppe, Wilhelm 6, 7, 8–9, 10–11, 12, 34,
    39, 170
Kraków
  Engelhardt-Kyffthaüser: exhibition
      of paintings 78–9
  Special Action in 110–11
Krüger, Friedrich-Wilhelm 6, 12, 34,
    174, 212
Krumey, Hermann 44, 184, 186,
    213–14

labour/prison camps 187–8, 202
  Bełżec 175, 182, 204–5, 206, 207
  Dirlewanger battalion 171, 172
  filtering process 182, 184, 186
  see also Lublin; Zamojszczyzna
      (Zamość, Lublin)
Leipzig, University of 52–3, 54–5
Leningrad resettlement 73–8, 104–6
local and regional institutions
  SS extensions (HSSPF/SSPF) 6, 7, 10,
      33–4, 63
  see also civilian administrations;
      EWZ; UWZ
Łódź 12, 14, 170
  urban planning 125–7, 128, 130–1
Loesch, Karl von 103
Lotnik, Waldemar 218–22
Lublin
  Central Inspectorate of Building
      146
  Himmler visit 22, 187–9, 202, 226
  Jewish Reserve 12–13, 14–15, 179
  SS institutions 170–2
  see also Globocnik, Odilo (SSPF);
      Zamojszczyzna (Zamość,
      Lublin)

Madagascar Plan 14–17, 19, 20–1, 32,
    44, 111–12
Madajczyk, Czesław 161
Maschmann, Melita 87
mass murder 108–15
  see also Jews, extermination
Meixner, Hanns 55–6, 63
Meyer-Heitling, Konrad (RKFdV)
  agrarian tendencies 124, 131, 133
  appointment as Head of Planning at
      Ministry of Supplies 151
  General Plan ('Planning Principles')
      11, 21–2, 23, 25, 46, 97–100, 114,
      139
  General Settlement Plan 153–5
  and Himmler 40–1, 42–3, 99–100,
      101, 141, 143, 149, 189
  Nahpläne and *Fernpläne* (short- and
      long-term plans) 16, 19–21,
      38–9, 42–3
  'Planning and Building the East'
      exhibition 117–18, 123, 124, 131,
      133, 136, 137
Midzinski, Hertha 83
migrant camps 192–6

military and professional networks
52–7, 103
moment of Utopia (1939–43) 1
foundations (1939) 2–8
General Plan for the East (1941–3)
21–6
short- and long-term plans (*Nahpläne*
and *Fernpläne Ost*) 8–21, 38–9,
42–3
timeline 1–2, 278–308 *appendix*
Müller, Bruno 110–11
myths of the Great *Trek* 72–80

Nahpläne and *Fernpläne Ost* (short- and
long-term plans) 8–21, 38–9,
42–3
networks and trajectories
itineraries of experts 57–64
'men' of the East 48–52
professional and military networks
52–7
Nordic blood 15, 24, 113–15, 136,
157
NSDAP 119, 127, 174, 183
NSDStB 25, 52, 53, 56, 59–60, 83

ORPO 171–2
Osteinsatz see journey to the East

Pancke, Günther 81
Pohl, Oswald (WVHA) 23, 33, 139–43,
144–7, 149, 187–8
Poland 68, 69
General Plan 97–8, 106–7
invasion 2, 4, 7, 70, 96–7
Danzig problem 93–4, 95
see also specific cities and regions
Poles
Catholics 166–7
classification of 182–6
expulsion 8–9, 10–12, 13, 15, 18, 19,
20, 32, 35, 39, 106, 178, 182
Germanizable 15, 39, 106
intellectuals and elites 110–11,
208–10
registered as Ukrainians 212–13
and Ukrainians: inter-self wars
214–22, 227–8
women 82
see also labour camps/prison camps;
Zamojszczyzna (Zamość,
Lublin)

police and SS
HSSPF/SSPF 6, 7, 10, 33–4, 63
points of settlement and support
144–9, 151, 171–2, 190–1, 203
Polonization 95–6, 167–8, 176, 177–8,
180–1
Pomerania 12
Poznań 34, 81, 96, 170
rural planning 136
urban planning 124–5, 127, 128–9
prison camps *see* labour/prison camps
prisoners of war, Soviet 148, 149, 202,
204
professional and military networks
52–7, 103

race
assessments and examinations 80–1,
181, 183, 184
classifying, expelling and deporting
180–6
euthanasia 2–3, 7
hygienic and educational
dimensions 80–7
Nordic blood 15, 24, 113–15, 136,
157
scientific studies 67–70
see also German blood
Rapp, Albert 52, 63
re-education/education 77, 83–6,
196–9
RKFdV 29–31
creation 5–6, 7–8
'men' of the East 48–9
planning 21–2, 41–2, 46–7, 95, 96,
97–100, 101, 102, 105–6, 114,
225–6
professional networks 54–5
racial engineers 14, 16, 17
Warthegau 're-Polonization' 95–6
see also Meyer-Heitling, Konrad
(RKFdV)
RSHA 31–3
Amt III B 22, 23, 25, 32–3, 49,
114–15
see also Ehlich, Hans (RSHA *Amt*
III B)
Amt IV B-4 31–2, 32, 49
see also Eichmann, Adolf (RSHA
IV B-4)
creation 4–5, 7
'men' of the East 48–9

planning 10, 11–13, 22, 41, 42–5,
106–12
professional networks 54–6
racial engineers 14–15
Sandberger at 60
rural planning 131–7
RuSHA 30–1, 49, 54, 81–2, 184
Russia 68
see also USSR

Sandberger, Martin xvii–xviii, 6–7, 8,
52, 53, 64, 74
itinerary 59–63
Sauckel, Fritz 152, 153
Schauroth, Udo von 118, 119–21, 123
Scheel, Gustav Adolf 52, 54, 56, 59–60
Schmidz-Berning, Cornelia 102
School of Fine Arts 116
city planning 124–31, 136–7
rural planning 131–7
spatial planning and networks
117–23
Silesia 12
Slavs 114, 157, 186
social engineering *see* race
spatial planning and networks 117–23
Speer, Albert 125, 151, 152, 153
SS 11, 13–14, 16–17, 36
institutions, Lublin 170–2
reorganization 3, 4–5, 8, 33
see also networks and trajectories;
police and SS
SSPF 6, 7, 33–4
see also Globocnik, Odilo (SSPF)
Stalingrad siege 153–4
Stanglica, Franz 175–7, 189
statistical knowledge 42
Streckenbach, Bruno 111
students 50–1, 69–70, 71–2, 85–6
women 70, 71, 83–4
and young people 50–1, 82

Thomalla, Richard 190, 192, 199,
203–4
'Trawnikis' 172, 175, 203–4, 211
Tübingen, University of 52, 54

Ukrainians
armed struggle 167–8
expulsions 182
and Poles: inter-self wars 214–22,
227–8

Poles registered as 212–13
Trawniki recruitment 211
Umvolkung: dissimilation or
ethnomorphosis 102–8
urban planning 124–31, 136–7
USSR 4, 7, 17–18, 61, 72
invasion 18–20, 99, 111–12, 168,
177–8, 187–8, 192–3
Jews 61, 111, 112–13
Leningrad resettlement 73–8, 104–6
occupied territories: points of
settlement and support 146–9
Soviet prisoners of war 148, 149, 202,
204
Stalingrad siege 153–4
UWZ 35–6, 184, 185, 186, 190, 213, 214,
215

VDA 60, 66, 67
village planning 131–7
village settlement 192–6
Volksdeutsche repatriation 4, 32
see also journey to the East
(*Osteinsatz*); Zamojszczyzna
(Zamość, Lublin)
Volksgemeinschaft 116, 117, 124–37
VOMI 30, 32, 34, 35, 63, 104, 140
journey to the East (*Osteinsatz*) 67,
69, 73, 79

Wallrabe, Herbert 73–8
Walz, Gustav Adolf 69
Wannsee Conference 23, 24, 32, 41, 43,
44
Warsaw 20, 121–3, 124
Warthegau 12, 34, 36, 182
're-Polonization' 95–6
students 50
Wehrwolf operations 215–18
Wetzel, Erhard 24, 41, 42, 43, 44,
108–10, 111–14, 115
women 50, 55, 82, 84–5, 87
Polish–Ukranian inter-self wars
221
students 70, 71, 83–4
WVHA 33, 41, 42–3
extermination by work/labour 114,
149
founding 23
memoranda 45–6
'men' of the East 49
professional networks 55

WVHA (*cont.*)
  Zamojszczyzna 190–1
  see also Kammler, Hans (WVHA);
    Kammler sequence (WVHA);
    Pohl, Oswald (WVHA)

Zamojski, Jan Sarius 162–3
Zamojszczyzna (Zamość, Lublin) 161,
    226–8
  from ethnic domino effect to despair
    200
    extermination of Jews prior to
      Germanization 201–7, 211–14

  society martyred 207–14
  wars of *entre-soi* (inter-self wars)
    214–22, 227–8
  microcosms of radical policy
    institutional microcosms 168–73
    land of all Nazi radicalisms 173–8
    men, space and past 162–8
  politics of the laboratory 179–80
    building, installing and settling
      192–9
    building programme 186–92
    classifying, expelling and
      deporting 180–6